THE ASHES

THE
ASHES

AN ILLUSTRATED HISTORY
OF CRICKET'S GREATEST RIVALRY

Every Series to 2007

KEN PIESSE

FOREWORD BY ASHLEY GILES

SPORTS
BOOKS

Published in Europe by
SportsBooks Limited
PO Box 422
Cheltenham
GL50 2YN

Tel: 01242 256755
email: info@sportsbooks.ltd.uk
www.sportsbooks.ltd.uk

Text copyright © Ken Piesse 2007.
Published by SportsBooks Ltd, April 2009.
First published by Penguin Group (Australia), 2007.

Photographs and other pictorial material in the picture sections are from the Ken Piesse Collection, except where otherwise stated. Every effort has been made to locate the copyright holders, and the publisher welcomes hearing from anyone in this regard.

The right of Ken Piesse to be identified as author of this Work has been asserted by him in accordance with the United Kingdom Copyright Designs and Patents Act 1988.

Cover image and design by Pigs Might Fly © Penguin Group (Australia).
Text design by Adrian Saunders © Penguin Group (Australia).
Typeset in 11.5/15 pt Bembo by Sunset Digital Pty Ltd, Brisbane, Queensland.

Printed in the UK by Bell & Bain Ltd, Glasgow.

A catalogue record for this book is available from the British Library.

ISBN 978 1899807 77 2

ABOUT THE AUTHOR

Ken Piesse has had a love affair with cricket since first accompanying his dad to the Melbourne Cricket Ground and scoring the old Sheffield Shield games. He was truly hooked by the time Santa brought him a copy of the 1965 *Wisden* one Christmas.

A radio commentator and feature journalist for Fox Sports' popular *Inside Cricket*, Ken is also the author of nearly thirty books on the sport, including *Cricket's Colosseum: 125 Years of Test Cricket at the MCG*, *T.J. Over the Top* and *All Out for One*, a compendium of his best interviews and anecdotes from the past thirty years. He edited *Cricketer* and *Australian Cricket* magazines for twenty-five years, and has won many Cricket Victoria media awards for writing, radio and his TV work. He is the president of the Australian Cricket Society.

As a player, Ken once dismissed Bob Hawke in a match at the MCG, prompting the Prime Minister to respond that it was the first time he'd been caught out by a journalist in twenty-five years. He also had David Hookes caught on the fence at the MCG one day, but says Hookesy was hitting into a howling gale and there was no such thing as roped-off boundaries back then.

His most recent book was *The Greatest Game: Timeless tales from the greats of Aussie Rules*.

ABOUT THE AUTHOR

CONTENTS

FOREWORD

● ●

When exactly I decided that I wanted to play cricket for England I am not sure. But I do know that from the age of nine I was living out my own great Test matches against a wall in the back garden with a stump and tennis ball. I would spend hours a day playing whole Test series against the great West Indies team of the eighties and, of course, the Australians. We lost the 'odd' Test back in those days, but I am pretty sure we won every series! How Mum and Dad tolerated that monotonous banging on the back wall I just don't know.

Our summer holidays were spent on the village green in Ripley, Surrey. This is where the vast majority of my early cricketing education took place. The nets, the outfield, the changing rooms and the bar after the game were my classrooms. The players, the personalities, were my tutors. Those summers on the green are still my purest cricketing memories.

My Grandad tells the story of me standing up in the club as a youngster and announcing that one day 'I will play for England'.

I am sure a few young cricketers have made similar statements in the past. Some will have realised that dream, most would not. I felt incredibly proud and honoured when my dreams were realised for the first time back in 1997 when I was picked to play against Australia in a home one-day series.

It's a great feeling to receive your England cap for the first time. But with it comes great responsibility. A responsibility to your country, yourself and to everyone, from family and friends to coaches and counties that have helped you get there.

Playing one day cricket was a proud moment but ultimately I had always wanted to play Test cricket. I wanted to relive those moments from the back garden and once again bring the Aussies to their knees. Unfortunately beating Australia had become far more difficult.

During my first two attempts in series against Australia I lasted just one Test match. In 2001, after losing at Edgbaston, I was forced to have achilles repair surgery. In 2002, after losing in Brisbane, Steve Harmison broke my arm in the nets before the Adelaide Test. I really began to think I would never get a chance to totally realise those childhood dreams. Then came 2005... We had become a far stronger, more resilient team when the Australians arrived in England in that magical summer. It had become the most anticipated Ashes series in decades. After two years of great successes, including seven straight Test wins in England in 2004 and an away win in South Africa the following winter, some were even tipping us to win.

Neither side disappointed. Just when you thought a game was over someone would stand up, take the game by the scruff of the neck, and rewrite the script. At last the nation was gripped by cricket again. To get down to the last day of the last Test was just remarkable. That week at The Oval will stay with me forever. As, indeed, will the whole summer.

It was a tough series. Every day seemed like a whole Test match. It was exhausting physically and mentally but the spirit in which the series was played was also amazing. A mutual respect of two teams trying to tear each other apart. I could not have contrived such a series even in my own back garden. To play in such a series was an experience that made everything, every hour practising, every disappointment, worthwhile. The biggest thing that will stay with me is the bond that the England team had that summer. It was a team that played for its parts and for the man sitting next to you. Of course the personal achievements are great but the most successful sides play for each other. That is certainly what we did in 2005.

Winning the Ashes was magical... after all we hadn't held them since about the same time I was playing my own Test series in the back garden. To play for England and to wear the lions... well, what an honour. To beat the Aussies and win the Ashes... well, that's everything!

Ashley Giles
Edgbaston, February 2009

INTRODUCTION

• •

It was at cricket's Colosseum, the Melbourne Cricket Ground, on the eve of the 2006–07 summer that I truly appreciated the significance of the Ashes and the effort the champions take to prepare themselves for the greatest challenges of their career.

An early-season interstate game was scheduled and after fielding all day, Tasmania's captain Ricky Ponting changed into his full batting regalia and hurried out the back into the indoor nets. His teammates said he'd been doing it all week, for an hour every morning and every night. 'He's a driven man. You can see it in his eyes,' said young teammate Tim Paine. 'The Ashes are only just around the corner. Ricky intends to be ready.'

Just over a month later, Australia had won its third Test in a row to reclaim the Ashes, the celebrations from Ponting and co. joyous and all embracing.

Afterwards, Ponting told how personally he'd taken Australia's defeats in England in 2005. He'd lived with the disappointment each and every day and had determined to be absolutely ruthless in winning back the celebrated urn, the long-time symbol of Anglo-Australian Test contests.

His back-to-back centuries in the opening two Tests fuelled Australia's winning momentum. By the summer's end, Ponting had become the first Australian captain in eighty-six years to lead a 5–0 series victory.

Like every captain before him, Ashes competition was a high point for Ponting and the opportunity to hold the tiny little urn, albeit a replica, after the Perth Test a moment to be savoured. Long-time teammates Shane Warne and Glenn McGrath were just as thrilled, Warne saying he would have retired eighteen months earlier, but for Australia having lost the Ashes in 2005.

So what is it about the Ashes urn? After all, it's so tiny it can be all but concealed in one's hand. And it had originally been presented purely on a whim after a semi-serious match on a paddock one Christmas well over 100 years ago.

Just why is it so integral to the story of Anglo-Australian cricket?

Back in 1882–83, England's touring captain the Hon. Ivo Bligh and his fellow amateurs were spending Christmas week at Rupertswood, the Sunbury mansion owned by the well-to-do Sir William and Lady Janet Clarke. A game was organised with members of the staff, Sir William even employing those who weren't playing to ring the boundaries to guard against balls being lost in the undergrowth. Lady Clarke thought it would be fun to present a memento from the match. As a joke, she had a bail used in the match burnt and the ashes housed in a tiny clay urn that was handed to Bligh at the match end – along with an accompanying tongue-in-cheek message in which she referred to England's famous defeat at The Oval just months earlier and the follow-up mock obituaries in the London newspapers suggesting that the ashes of English cricket had been cremated and would be sent to Australia. Now, Mr Bligh, she said, you have those ashes back!

Lady Clarke's governess, music teacher Florence Morphy, was also among the presentation party, and by all reports a jolly good time was had by all. Florence was later to marry Bligh, the pair living in East Melbourne, where the urn took pride-of-place on Bligh's lounge-room mantle piece.

Upon his death in 1926, it was donated by his wife to Lord's, where it has stayed basically ever since.

The urn now has an iconic status and is integral in the game's ultimate rivalry.

At times, however, its ownership has been so wearing that even the most-acclaimed, attacking captains like Richie Benaud did an about-face, not wanting to be saddled with the burden of being an Ashes loser.

So serious was the Ashes rivalry treated that in the summer of reconciliation, 1979–80, the Marylebone Cricket Club refused to give the short, three-Test series full Ashes status.

Reputations have been made and lost in the first 130 years of Ashes confrontation.

Just as Benaud worked for hours honing his leg-spinners and was to lead one of Australia's greatest wins at Old Trafford in 1961, England's super-charged all-rounder Andrew Flintoff emerged from an exhausting winter fitter than ever before in 2005 to be rewarded with the inaugural Compton-Miller Medal, named after two legendary Ashes performers, Denis Compton and Keith Miller.

In 2006–07, Ponting was the deserved recipient, his performances being acclaimed as some of the best since Bradman.

In *The Ashes: An Illustrated History of Cricket's Greatest Rivalry*, the contributions of Ricky Ponting and all the major Ashes heroes, from Jack Hobbs, Ian Botham, Warnie and The Don and going right back to Test cricket's first centurion the English-born Charles Bannerman are recognised and celebrated.

They are among our Ashes Players of the Decade, choices enhanced by Ken Williams's masterly end-of-chapter statistics.

May your enjoyment of the book be as great as mine in its preparation. And may the next batch of Ashes heroes be just as dynamic and charismatic as those whose stories are already such a feature of Ashes folklore.

Ken Piesse
Mt Eliza, February 2007

H.H. Stephenson's All-England XI arrive at the Café de Paris in Bourke Street on Christmas Eve, 1861. A Grand Match followed several days later, the Victorians captained by British-born George Marshall.
Ken Piesse Collection

1860s

THE PIONEERS

'Witnessing so many colonial fans crammed onto the docks, all craning their necks to see the champions from Home was undeniable proof that the enthusiasm for cricket in the Antipodes was seriously strong ...'

The first sight of the mighty steamship *Great Britain* in Hobson's Bay on Christmas Eve, 1861, triggered an extraordinary reception from thousands of Melburnians lining the old docks at Sandridge Pier. Among almost 700 on board were H.H. Stephenson's trailblazing cricketers. The cheering and flag-waving made it a celebration to savour. Dozens of smaller boats formed a welcoming flotilla, their skippers sounding horns and waving. There were smiles and handshakes aplenty and lots of laughter, too, when on alighting Stephenson quipped that the colonials should prepare 'for a jolly good licking'.[1]

The tour promoters, Bourke Street caterers Felix Spiers and Christopher Pond, had originally sought the celebrated Charles Dickens for a lecture tour, but he didn't bother to even answer. A cricket venture had purely been an afterthought. An English team had toured North America two years previously and been mobbed at Elsyian Fields in New York, where 25,000 attended over four days.[2] If the reaction on Australian shores was just as enthusiastic, serious money was to be made.

Witnessing so many colonial fans crammed onto the docks, all craning their necks to see the champions from Home was undeniable proof that the enthusiasm for cricket in the Antipodes was seriously strong. The two young businessmen greeted Stephenson and his men warmly. They knew they were on a winner.

Cricket in the colonies was only in its infancy, but Melbourne, Sydney and Hobart town were vibrant strongholds for the game. Already 120,000 lived in Melbourne, the majority having been born in Britain. Some of the more influential had been involved in the formation of the Melbourne Cricket Club, in 1838, including the club's first president, pastoralist Frederick Powlett, a descendant of the founder of the Hambledon Club.[3]

Heathfield Harman Stephenson, a Surrey and all-England man for almost a decade, was a capital bat, particularly good on the drive and a briskish round-arm bowler noted for a rare ability to break the ball back from the off. When the mood took him, too, he was a fearless keeper of wickets, standing over the stumps to even the fastest. His Eleven was far from fully representative of the might of British cricketing talent, but some like Billy Caffyn and Charles Lawrence were champion players who in following years were to become torchbearers for colonial cricket as coaches and mentors. Caffyn not only opened the bowling, he was a frontline bat.

Down the gangplanks came Stephenson and his men, easily discernible by their deerstalkers, complete with blue ribbons. Having edged their way through the hubbub, they were taken into town by a luxury horse-drawn coach to a reception to remember, the first of more than a dozen during their triumphant tour. 'How the Eleven got through the crowd at Sandridge to the Terminus Hotel, amid the huzzas and handshakes, no-one hardly knew,' commented one newspaper.

'Seating themselves astride Bevan's monster coach, drawn by eight greys, they proceeded to the Café de Paris (owned by the promoters), escorted by a motley company of coaches, cars, buggies and vehicles undefinable. Their arrival in Melbourne created quite a sensation and as they proceeded up Swanston Street and by the way of Elizabeth Street and Great Bourke Street to the café, the whole way was lined by an excited crowd and the English champions were everywhere greeted with enthusiastic cheers and well-wishes. The café was decorated with flags and many buildings in the neighbourhood were similarly bedecked.'[4]

The interest in the new arrivals was so considerable that their first practice was conducted outside Melbourne, 'at a secret destination in the bush, in order they might have some peace from the attentions of their admirers'.[5]

Further sessions, at St Kilda Cricket Club's Junction Oval and at Richmond's Punt Road Oval attracted thousands, players like Caffyn and the left-handed G. 'Ben' Griffith, dubbed 'the Lion Hitter', enjoying an immediate celebrity status.

'The town reception,' said Lawrence years later, 'made us feel the great honour for we were suppose [sic] to represent England.'[6]

Twenty-five thousand were to attend the first day's play of the inaugural international, between Eighteen of Victoria and Stephenson's Eleven, a phenomenal number for such a young colony. Stalls and tents adorned the ground perimeters, while the MCC's impressive new grandstand stretching almost 700 feet from one side of the ground to the other offered welcome relief from the summer heat. Stephenson said a finer cricket ground simply did not exist.[7]

Those who couldn't afford the admission climbed trees or gathered in groups on the Richmond Hill overlooking the ground. A public holiday had been granted for Government office workers and bank officials. Hundreds of others took the day off anyway to join in the celebrations.[8]

The Englishmen entered the field to the familiar strains of the National Anthem. Each player wore a white hat with a different-coloured ribbon for easy identification. 'The weather was so hot,' said Caffyn, 'as to fetch the skin off some of our faces. I commenced the bowling, but was obliged to come off after a short time owing to my arm being so painful from mosquito bites.'[9]

Caffyn recovered sufficiently to top score with 79 and was such a commanding and popular figure on tour that he was to be invited back as the MCC's coach.

Among the competing locals was Sam Cosstick, one of five Surrey men in Victoria's team. The colonials were no match for the visitors and lost by an innings, no fewer than eighteen of the locals out without scoring.

The follow-up receptions in Sydney, Hobart and beyond were equally grand, 15,000 cheering 'in most hearty fashion' at Circular Quay when the team's launch *Kembla* made its way across Sydney Harbour. The tramway cars *Old England* and *Young Australia* conveyed Stephenson and his team to town, the route being lined by thousands of cheering spectators. With church bells ringing and a band in full swing, it was quite an occasion.

Business came to a standstill during the team's stay in Sydney. Parliament was adjourned so members could witness the first match, at the Domain, which amid protests was open only to those prepared to pay for the privilege. This time Stephenson's men opposed twenty-two from New South Wales.

The English were unbeaten in ten of their twelve games. A Castlemaine XXII recorded a narrow win 'on a pitch beyond redemption'[10] as did an Australian combine at Sydney's Domain ground. Among those included in the Sydney match were E.J. 'Ned' Gregory, who was to join his brother Dave in the first official Test match in Melbourne in 1877. Also in the local XXII was Nat Thomson, Charles Bannerman's opening partner in the inaugural Test.

An extra match, too, was contested between Surrey and 'The World', the World side winning by six wickets.

Thousands again turned out as the Eleven left Australia from Melbourne. Team members planted twelve elm trees in Yarra Park, bordering the Melbourne Cricket Ground.

Flushed by the success of their venture and £11,000 richer, Spiers and Pond offered Stephenson and his men a further £100 each to remain another month, but their English commitments awaited. Charles Lawrence, however, remained behind as coach of Sydney's Albert Club. At the end of the decade, he was to lead the Aboriginal team tour to England.

It had been a grand experiment and within two years another side was to return under the captaincy of Nottinghamshire's 'Lion of the North', George Parr. Unbeaten during its sixteen-week campaign, the team cleared £250 a man – almost double the monies made by Stephenson's 1861–62 pioneers. They spent time in New Zealand and on their way back, just two hours from Sydney, their steamer *Wonga Wonga* collided with the brigantine *Viceroy* in 'dark and hazy conditions'.[11] Parr was beside himself with fear as the *Viceroy* sunk almost immediately, and while the *Wonga Wonga* was relatively undamaged, fast bowler George 'Tear 'em' Tarrant tried to jump into the rescue boat intended to pick up the *Viceroy*'s skipper and crew! One of the touring party, Julius Caesar, did his best to settle emotions, behaving 'in a manner worthy of his name'[12] while another, John 'Foghorn' Jackson, slept through the whole commotion!

Billy Caffyn was again a leading light and he was to remain in Melbourne after the tour, having agreed to the MCC's coaching terms of £300 per year. Later he went to Sydney in a similar role. In between coaching and playing duties, he cut hair for a living.

There were to be two more early tours, too, including one led by the mighty Dr W.G. Grace in 1873–74, before Anglo-Australian cricket took its most significant step in 1877, with the first Grand Combination Match between Combined Australia and Jim Lillywhite's visiting professionals in Melbourne. In time, it became known as the first official Test match and resulted in victory by Combined Australia by 45 runs. It was a memorable occasion with much barracking, the crowd support then being evenly divided, the majority of Australia's inaugural XI having been born or bred in Britain. As more 'Currency Lads' made their inter-colonial and representative debuts and the British-born players faded out, it intensified a rivalry that culminates every second year with the now-celebrated battle for the Ashes.

English powerhouse **W.G. Grace**.
Ken Piesse Collection

1870s
A MIGHTY OCCASION

• •

'. . . as Lord Harris marched towards the pavilion asking Gregory to continue the game, Gregory demanded that Coulthard be stood down. Harris refused and as the two skippers argued, enraged spectators jumped the fence and invaded the wicket.'

Test match cricket was first fashioned in 1876–77 when an English team captained and managed by noted Sussex all-rounder James Lillywhite contested the first XI-a-side matches down-under. The twenty-three-match program included eight mid-tour games in New Zealand, a costly sojourn as the team's extrovert wicketkeeper Edward Pooley was arrested on a charge of assault and maliciously damaging property after an altercation with a punter. While the rest of Lillywhite's team sailed for Melbourne, arriving less than twenty-four hours before the first 'Great Match', Pooley was cooling his heels in Christchurch awaiting trial.

Jim Lillywhite hailed from one of England's most noted cricketing families and in addition to his cricket skills, he possessed considerable entrepreneurial flair and adventure, visiting Australia six times, four in business partnership with famed pair Alfred Shaw and Arthur Shrewsbury. He also toured America in 1868.

His team was stronger in bowling than batting and was defeated in several early matches by a Fifteen of New South Wales and Fifteen of Victoria. When the English professionals lost another match-against-odds to a NSW combine, which included champions-to-be Billy Murdoch, Fred Spofforth and Ted Evans (then at the peak of his career), Lillywhite agreed to an additional game, on even terms – his XI versus the best NSW XI. The game was of just two days' duration with the Englishmen due to sail for New Zealand and was drawn in the English XI's favour, George Ulyett with 94 and Shaw with nine wickets the standouts. Eight thousand attended, ensuring handsome returns, and with the prospect of even bigger crowds in Melbourne and the promise of a further share of the gate receipts, Lillywhite readily agreed to more games on even terms and his team contested the first two internationals, later accorded Test status, in Melbourne from mid-March.

The selecting of the first fully-representative Australian Combined team caused an immediate storm, especially as the sole selector was a Victorian, no-nonsense Jack Conway. A fast bowler and capital slip fielder, he'd played against Stephenson's XI in 1861–62 before taking on managerial and journalism roles, which further extended his influence. He triggered immediate angst among Sydney officials when he approached the leading NSW players direct, totally bypassing the authorities. Given the already-fierce inter-colonial rivalry between Victoria and New South Wales, Conway's maverick ways were guaranteed to upset. Tempers settled, a little, when he agreed the last place in the XI should be taken by a New South Welshman, ensuring Sydney-based players a sixth invitation and Melbourne five. But the balance altered when Evans was unavailable and Spofforth withdrew in pique after 'his' wicketkeeper Murdoch had been overlooked. The Combined XI's frontline options were further lessened when Victorian Frank Allan, known as the 'Bowler of the Century', claimed a prior commitment in Warrnambool. When it was discovered he was merely meeting friends at a local agricultural show, the Melbourne press went into overdrive: 'Great as is this player's value in the field,' said one newspaper, 'his capriciousness is still greater and we trust that for the future he will be studiously left in that retirement which he always professes to be so loath to leave.'[1]

Allan's replacement was young round-arm bowler John Hodges, who had started the season at junior metropolitan level with the Capulets before showing considerable promise with Richmond, one of the senior inner-city clubs. Like his Richmond colleague and fellow left-armer Tommy Kendall – noted for dismissing Dr W.G. Grace in 1873–74 – Hodges had never previously played inter-colonial cricket. And the youngest chosen, 18-year-old Tom Garrett from Newington College in Sydney, had played only once. He was particularly elated at his unexpected promotion. The £20 match fee was the equivalent of two months' wages for most working men.[2]

England was unable to include the in-disgrace Pooley, John Selby acting as substitute wicketkeeper as well as opening the innings. The tourists also included 49-year-old James Southerton, who remains Test cricket's oldest debutant.

Many of Melbourne's well-to-do and social set were among the crowd of 1,500 gathered for the start of play on a magnificent autumn afternoon on 15 March 1877. By 4 p.m. the numbers had swelled to 4,500 when Charles Bannerman completed a masterly century, the first and still one of the most dominant in Test annals. Ten thousand attended on the Saturday, paying a premium to sit in the MCC's pride-and-joy reversible grandstand on the northern flank of the ground. It seemed the whole colony was transfixed by the cricket.

England had started the game as clear favourites and there was disappointment among the pro-English punters when the team failed to chase down a fourth-innings target of just 154, Kendall, bowling from just two steps, taking 7-55 in the performance of his life.

When Lillywhite's team hit back to win the second 'international' a fortnight later, the punting fraternity accused them of playing 'dead' in the first match. The dismissal of Bannerman for just 10 in the Australian first innings was a key, Lillywhite later writing: 'We were rather pleased to see the back of this dangerous customer.'[3]

In the second innings, on his way to a better-than-even-time 30, Bannerman had become the first Australian to hit a fiver, a straight hit from Lillywhite, which soared over the heads of the spectators.

An epic tour of Australia, New Zealand, England and America was to follow under the captaincy of Dave Gregory, the programme extending for an unprecedented fourteen months. Most of the games were against odds.

In the eleven-a-side matches, Charles Bannerman and Spofforth were the standouts, Bannerman accelerating to the only first-class century of the tour, at Leicester. The sheer volume of cricket exhausted even the hardiest in the Australian XII and manager Conway was one of several to fill in. On the way home from England, the Australians tumbled to an embarrassing 32-7 against New York and were forced to have a second innings to win the match, the visitors being described by the *American Cricketer* magazine as being from 'a land as remote as Mars'.[4]

Gregory's tourists remained together until January 1879, when they contested the only Test match of their time together in Melbourne against 'The Gentlemen of England', led by the formidable and influential Lord Harris, who was both captain and secretary at Kent.[5]

The only professionals in his Lordship's team were Yorkshiremen 'Happy Jack' Ulyett and Tom Emmett, and the Australians, comprising ten of the 1878 side plus an additional batsman in Irishman Tom Kelly, won easily. The irrepressible Spofforth took 13 wickets, including a hat-trick. Frank Allan, on debut, claimed four wickets, the same newspapers who had previously ridiculed him handing out special praise!

The Englishmen were unused to the heat or the ultra-bright sunshine, one of their party, first-timer Charles Absolom, notable for never wearing a hat, claiming that the temperature in the opening match in Adelaide was 'frightful – between 150 and 160 degrees'.[6]

The tour was marred by a riot at the Association Ground (later named the Sydney Cricket Ground) during a second match against New South Wales. The trouble started on the opening day when Harris was given not out by the umpire he had appointed, Victorian George Coulthard. 'It was said the snick ... had been heard all over the ground and the barracking became particularly bad, especially from bookmakers in the grandstand,' said Harris's biographer James Coldham.[7]

The English established a 90-run first innings lead, despite Murdoch becoming the first to carry his bat, for 82. NSW had to follow-on and when Murdoch, on 10, was adjudged run out by Coulthard, despite seeming to be well past his crease, it so riled major sections of the 10,000 present that they stood and began hooting and jeering. Local captain Gregory was also horrified and refused to send in the next batsman, Nat Thomson. As Lord Harris marched towards the pavilion asking Gregory to continue the game, Gregory demanded that Coulthard be stood down. Harris refused and as the two skippers argued, enraged spectators jumped the fence and invaded the wicket. As Harris backtracked, in part to protect the umpires, he was struck by an assailant with a stick. 'Let me have a go at him, my Lord,' said the burly Ulyett, who had grabbed two stumps to defend his captain.

'No, no, George,' said Harris.[8] Emmett, too, had seized a stump and also had to be restrained. 'Monkey' Hornby had his shirt ripped as he grabbed the offender and marched him off the ground into police custody.

There was no more play that afternoon, the crowd invading again after Harris later walked his team onto the field, still flanked by Coulthard.

Tempers had settled by nightfall and the fixture continued after the obligatory Sunday off, the English winning by an innings and 41 runs. The riot had later scheduling repercussions for the next Australian team to England, the formidable Harris still disgusted by the barbaric behaviour of the colonials, triggered, he believed, by the larrikinism of the bookmaking element so inherent in the colonies. He wrote: 'We never expect to see such a scene of disorder again – we can never forget this one.'[9]

Man of the Decade: *Charles Bannerman*

Charles Bannerman, Australia's first great batsman, was twenty-five and at the height of his powers when he made a captivating, unbeaten century against James Lillywhite's touring professionals on the opening day of what later was acknowledged as the first Test match.

One of five born-and-bred Brits in Australia's first Test XI, Bannerman was from the south of London and had been in Australia only five years.

Of medium build, just a shade taller than Don Bradman, who he used to watch years later at the Sydney Cricket Ground, Bannerman favoured front-foot shots and rarely hit the ball in the air. His timing and placement was unsurpassed.

His 165 retired hurt was scored out of 245 and remains one of the most dominant solos of them all. No one else in the NSW–Victoria Combine made 20.

But for ill-health, which saw him retire at twenty-nine, he may have matched at least some of the feats of his younger brother Alick, who was to play twenty-eight Tests and tour England five times in the 1880s and early 1890s.

During his one and only visit to England with the 1878 Australians – a tour which was to extend fourteen months and also include matches in America, Canada and New Zealand – Bannerman amassed almost 800 first-class runs in bowler-friendly conditions at a substantial average of 25.

Bannerman had been coached by the noted Englishman William Caffyn, who regarded him as the finest Australian player of the nineteenth century.

Leading into the match of his life, in Melbourne, Bannerman had played only eight inter-colonial matches.

From his first game, when he made a polished 32, having been sent in at No. 8, he had been described as 'a premier bat'[10] by the writer from the *Town and Country Journal* and he rarely again batted lower than the first three.

Others in this period may have appeared and toured more often, but none were as polished or, during this golden week in March 1877, as charming a strokemaker.

On the first day, Bannerman scored 126 in a team score of 166-6 and when forced to retire hurt on the second, having split a finger, he was 165 out of 240-7. His innings represented almost 70 per cent of Australia's score, a phenomenal domination still unsurpassed 130 years on.

Ironically, Bannerman's century in Melbourne was one of only two tons he was to make in major cricket. The other was against Leicestershire in 1878, the first by an Australian overseas in eleven-a-side cricket. '[It was] an innings absolutely without a fault and one which for fine, clean, well-timed batting has never been surpassed,' said Lillywhite's annual.[11]

Charles Bannerman v. England

rh retired hurt
* not out

Season	Scores	Runs	Ave
1876–77	165rh, 4, 10, 30	209	69.66
1878–79	15, 15*	30	30.00

Tests:	3 (all v. England)
Runs:	239
Average:	59.75
Highest score:	165 retired hurt, Melbourne, 1876–77
100s:	1

Match of the decade: *Melbourne, 1879*

Fred 'The Demon' Spofforth truly announced himself as a hostile bowling force with 13 wickets for the match, including eight bowled, as Australia clinched victory by 10 wickets in the third international match at the Melbourne Cricket Ground. There was a fierce morning hailstorm on the opening day and Lord Harris batted when he should have bowled and the Gentlemen of England, as they were billed, collapsed in under two hours for 113 after at one stage being 26-7. Spofforth became the first to take a Test hat-trick when he dismissed Francis Mackinnon, Vernon Royle and left-hander Tom Emmett with consecutive deliveries.

Match scores: Australia 256 (A. Bannerman 73, Emmett 7-68) and 19-0 defeated England 113 (Absolom 52, Spofforth 6-48) and 160 (Spofforth 7-62) by 10 wickets

Odd spot: *Cricket's first substitute*

The Melbourne Cricket Club's professional William Newing became Test cricket's first substitute when he fielded for the injured Charles Bannerman during the historic first Test match in Melbourne. He also 'subbed' in the second Test a fortnight later when wicketkeeper Jack Blackham was indisposed with sunstroke.

Looking back: *Alfred Shaw, Melbourne, 1877*

'We had only landed the day before the [first Test] match commenced from our New Zealand trip . . . not one of us was fit to play cricket . . . we were delayed on the voyage and the accommodation on shipboard was so bad that some of us had to sleep on deck. I was simply spun out myself.'[12]

Shaw bowled the first ball in Test cricket, captained a team to Australia and was joint promoter of four other tours down-under.

One for the statisticians: *Still the youngest*

Selected by default when other more experienced players refused invitations, 18-year-old clerk Tom Garrett was the youngest player in the Combined Match and still is the youngest ever to play an Anglo-Australian Test.

Tests 1876–77 to 1878

KEY: M Matches **I** Innings **NO** Not out innings **HS** Highest score **BB** Best bowling
5wI 5-wicket innings **10wM** 10-wicket match * Not out # Second innings **rh** Retired hurt

Series results

	Tests	Aust	Eng	Drawn
1876–77 (Aust)	2	1	1	0
1878–79 (Aust)	1	1	0	0
Total	3	2	1	0

Summary

	Runs	Wkts	Ave
Australia	1,005	49	27.50
England	960	56	17.14

Highest innings totals

Australia		England	
259	Melbourne 1876–77 (2nd Test)#	261	Melbourne 1876–77 (2nd Test)
256	Melbourne 1878–79 (Only Test)		

Lowest completed innings totals

Australia		England	
104	Melbourne 1876–77 (1st Test)#	108	Melbourne 1876–77 (1st Test)#
122	Melbourne 1876–77 (2nd Test)	113	Melbourne 1878–79 (Only Test)

Leading run scorers

	M	I	NO	Runs	HS	Ave	100	50
Australia								
C. Bannerman	3	6	2	239	165rh	59.75	1	–
England								
G. Ulyett	3	6	0	163	63	17.16	–	2

Hundreds

Australia (1)		England
1	C. Bannerman	No instance

Highest individual scores

Australia	
165rh	C. Bannerman at Melbourne 1876–77 (1st Test)
73	A. C. Bannerman at Melbourne 1878–79 (Only Test)
England	
63	H. Jupp at Melbourne 1876–77 (1st Test)
63	G. Ulyett at Melbourne 1876–77 (2nd Test)#

Hundred partnerships

No instance. Highest were as follows:

Australia		
88	1st	N. F. D. Thomson and D. W. Gregory at Melbourne 1876–77 (2nd Test)#
77	4th	C. Bannerman and B. B. Cooper at Melbourne 1876–77 (1st Test)
England		
74	6th	G. Ulyett and T. Emmett at Melbourne 1876–77 (2nd Test)

Leading wicket-takers

	Tests	Balls	Mdns	Runs	Wkts	Ave	BB	5wI	10wM
Australia									
F. R. Spofforth	2	416	34	221	17	13.00	7-62	2	1
T. K. Kendall	2	563	56	215	14	15.35	7-55	1	–
W. E. Midwinter	2	429	44	156	8	19.50	5-78	1	–
England									
Jas Lillywhite Jnr	2	340	37	126	8	15.75	4-70	–	–
A. Shaw	2	655	96	146	8	18.25	5-38	1	–

Five wickets in an innings

Australia (4)		England (2)	
2	F. R. Spofforth	1	T. Emmett
1	T. K. Kendall		A. Shaw
	W. E. Midwinter		

Best individual bowling

Australia

7-55	T. K. Kendall at Melbourne 1876–77 (1st Test)#
7-62	F. R. Spofforth at Melbourne 1878–79 (Only Test)#
6-48	F. R. Spofforth at Melbourne 1878–79 (Only Test)

England

7-68	T. Emmett at Melbourne 1878–79 (Only Test)

10 wickets in a match

Australia (1)

13-110	F. R. Spofforth (6-48 and 7-62) at Melbourne 1878–79 (Only Test)

England

No instance

Hat-trick

F. R. Spofforth (Aust) at Melbourne 1878–79 (Only Test)
    (V. P. F. A. Royle b, F. A. Mackinnon b, T. Emmett c T. P. Horan)

Leading wicketkeeper

	Tests	Dismissals	Catches	Stumpings
J. M. Blackham (Aust)	3	6	4	2

Leading fieldsmen

	Tests	Catches		Tests	Catches
Australia			**England**		
F. R. Spofforth	2	4	T. Emmett	3	4

Captains

	Tests	Won	Lost	Drawn	Toss won
Australia					
D. W. Gregory	3	2	1	0	2
England					
Jas Lillywhite Jnr	2	1	1	0	0
Lord Harris	1	0	1	0	1

Most appearances

Australia (17 players)		England (20 players)	
3	C. Bannerman	3	T. Emmett
	J. M. Blackham		G. Ulyett
	T. W. Garrett		
	D. W. Gregory		

C.T.B. 'Terror' Turner, Australia's finest bowler throughout the 1880s. *Ken Piesse Collection*

1880s

REBUILDING BRIDGES

••

'. . . the excitement was so tremendous that one man dropped dead, some fainted and the vast crowd afterwards rushed the ground.'

So furious was Lord Harris at being attacked in Sydney and so significant and far-reaching was his influence that the 1880 Australians, star-studded as they were, had to resort to advertising for matches. Despite the efforts of Jim Lillywhite and Surrey's secretary Charles Alcock to extend the fixture list, only six games against the counties, including two each against Yorkshire and Derbyshire, were scheduled before September. Most of the other games were inconsequential matches against odds. Dr W.G. Grace proposed a fixture at Lord's, but the game's powerbrokers refused. The Australians were accruing considerable debts and the tour would have been a total failure but for Alcock approaching Harris and suggesting a one-off match between the Australians and a truly-representative All-England XI.

Alcock, 'The Prince of Secretaries', was at his persuasive best. He told Harris a resumption of friendly relations was crucial for the game to advance. The tourists' captain was Billy Murdoch and *not* Dave Gregory, with whom Harris had warred in Sydney. Furthermore, if his Lordship agreed to lead the English XI, it would be undeniable proof that the events of Sydney eighteen months earlier, while not forgotten, had at least been forgiven. Harris may have been autocratic, but he was a good listener. He respected Alcock and admired his work ethic and vision. After a pause he said: 'You find the timber and we will find the workmen to build a bridge which will last forever.'[1]

Had Alcock not been so convincing and Harris not so conciliatory, the first Test match in England may have been delayed for years. The three-day game began at The Oval on 6 September, the date originally set aside for the Australians' fixture with Sussex. A century from Dr W.G. Grace, one of three Grace brothers to be selected, helped England to a five-wicket victory, the Australians weakened by the absence of their champion Fred Spofforth with a finger injury. In all matches on tour, 'The Demon' amassed 391 wickets. Some reckoned his absence 'tipped the balance in the Test match'.[2]

The crowds were immense, 20,000 attending on each of the first two days ensuring a much-needed and belated profit for the tourists. The Australians fought courageously after being hopelessly behind and forced the match into a fourth innings. At one stage in the pursuit of just 57, England was 32-5 before Frank Penn and 'W. G.' ensured the victory.

The game re-energised Anglo-Australian cricket relations and while there were storms and tempests aplenty in the years to follow, the game was rarely anything but the winner.

Betting in cricket and the prominence of bookmakers at grounds was to remain a lifelong abhorrence for Lord Harris. He felt some of the very best cricketers would become irreversibly tangled and discredit the game.

Ironically, on the very next tour to Australia in 1881–82, several in the All-England XI were accused of trying to throw a match, against Victoria in Melbourne. It was alleged that professional trio George Ulyett, John Selby and William Scotton had been paid £100 to perform poorly.

Victoria needed only 94 runs to win and although it was a sticky wicket, bookmakers offered 30–1 against the Englishmen. So extravagant were the odds that touring captain Alfred Shaw broke a golden rule and wagered £1 on the result and insisted that everyone else in the team follow suit. In reply, the Victorians lost 7-6 before Harry Boyle's 43 lifted them to within range, England eventually winning by 18 runs. 'Certain cases of misfielding,' said Shaw, 'compelled me to come to the conclusion that the rumors were not without foundation'.[3]

The players said to be under the influence of the bookmakers all had a modest game, Ulyett making two and four, Selby six and 23, and Scotton 28 and two. Later the Australian-born Billy Midwinter, who had tipped Shaw off to the conspiracy, was involved in a shipboard scuffle with two of the accused.

Four 'Tests' were played, two being drawn in Melbourne and two, both won by Australia, in Sydney thanks mainly to the bowling of South Melbourne's G.H. 'Joey' Palmer who could break the ball back from leg at will, even on the most placid of wickets. He claimed 20 wickets in two matches and at the time was second only to Spofforth as Australia's leading bowler. In the opening Test in Melbourne, Australia named a 12th man for the first time, teenager John Edwards from Wesley College.

Throughout the thirty-match campaign, which included matches in America, Australia and New Zealand, the Englishmen used just eleven players, manager Lillywhite filling-in occasionally in the games against odds.

The intimidating, ultra-competitive Spofforth, the first of the truly great over-arm bowlers, and Lady Janet Clarke, Melbourne's leading socialite, were primarily responsible for the launching of the Ashes.

In a one-off Test at The Oval in August 1882, Spofforth mowed down the might of England's finest, triggering a remarkable Australian victory and giving cricket in the colonies new credibility and standing.

Spofforth rushed in on a curve from close to mid-off and bowled both fast and slow with a virtually identical action.

Set 85 to win, a full-strength English XI folded for 77, Dr W.G. Grace topscoring with 32. Twelve maiden overs were played in mid-innings before a single was deliberately forfeited to the Hon. Alfred Lyttelton to allow Spofforth to bowl at a different batsman. 'It looked a guinea to a gooseberry on the Old Country,' said Australia's Tom Horan (Felix of the *Australasian*).[4]

Ten of Spofforth's last eleven overs were maidens, his final figures 7-44 from twenty-eight unchanged overs. 'None dreamed that we should be beaten,' said one of England's premier players C.T. Studd, who was marooned at the non-striker's end.[5]

'Spofforth and Boyle bowled with such wonderful precision,' said Felix, 'that a strange hush fell upon that vast circling crowd ... [the English] could do nothing with Spoff and he was splendidly supported by Boyle who until he bowled (last man Ted) Peate seemed as cool as a cucumber. Then he jumped four feet into the air, gave a wild Bendigonian yell and set forth for the pavilion. The excitement was so tremendous that one man dropped dead, some fainted and the vast crowd afterwards rushed the ground, patted the Australians on the back and cheered them to the echo. That was the only time I ever saw W.G. Grace downcast. He said to me: "Well, well. I left six men to get 30–odd and they couldn't get them." '

Afterwards, several obituary notices were published, the most famous by journalist Reginald Brooks in the *Sporting Times* on 2 September 1882:

> In Affectionate Remembrance of ENGLISH CRICKET
> Which died at the Oval on 29th August, 1882.
> Deeply lamented by a large circle of sorrowing friends
> and acquaintances
> R.I.P.
> N.B. – The body will be cremated and the Ashes
> taken to Australia.

It was an astonishing victory, one thought impossible pre-match, given the statistical superiority of the English XI, which for the first time in the 'Great' matches was fully representative. Man for man, the Australians seemed out of their depth. Averages published in *Wisden Cricketers' Almanack* backed the claim that this was a boilover of the greatest magnitude:

First–class batting averages, late August 1882

	Australia		England	
1	A.C. Bannerman	23	Dr W.G. Grace	24
2	H.H. Massie	27	R.G. Barlow	29
3	W.L. Murdoch	36	G. Ulyett	30
4	G.J. Bonnor	19	A.P. Lucas	38
5	T. Horan	31	The Hon. A. Lyttelton	35
6	G. Giffen	21	C.T. Studd	34
7	J.M. Blackham	21	M. Read	24
8	T.W. Garrett	9	W. Barnes	30
9	H.F. Boyle	11	A.G. Steel	29
10	S.P. Jones	15	A.N. Hornby	29
11	F.R. Spofforth	9	E. Peate	11

First–class bowling averages, late August 1882

Australia		England	
Boyle	12	Barlow	11
Spofforth	13	Peate	11
Garrett	27	Ulyett	14
		Studd	16
		Steel	20
		Barnes	35

Later that year, on landing in the Antipodes, English captain The Hon. Ivo Bligh quipped that his XI had come to 'beard the kangaroo in his den and try to recover those ashes'.[6]

At the reception at the Melbourne Town Hall, Australia's captain Billy Murdoch replied in kind: 'Our boys fairly won the Ashes (in August) and we confidently rely on them to retain possession, at least for the present.'[7]

At this stage the Ashes were entirely mythical and talk of 'the Ashes' mere byplay between the two captains after Australia's unexpected win at The Oval. However, within weeks, a tiny clay urn was presented to Bligh following a picnic match on the grounds of Rupertswood, the newly built Sunbury mansion belonging to Sir William and Lady Clarke. Sir William, a millionaire grazier, was a member of the Legislative Assembly, president of the Melbourne Cricket Club and the colony's most generous and influential benefactor.

Eight of Bligh's party – he and seven fellow amateurs – were among Sir William's guests for Christmas in the country. Christmas Eve morning was spent in church and in the afternoon a social match was arranged between the English visitors and the other guests and staff. It was an impromptu, light-hearted game, but author Joy Munns says Sir William insisted on having servants camped around the boundaries to retrieve the many 4s and 5s and guard against lost balls.[8] As a joke, the affable Lady Clarke burnt one of the bails used during the game, put the ashes into a small clay urn and presented it as a memento to Bligh, the winning captain.

Three Tests had been scheduled that summer and when Bligh's XI won the decider in Sydney, a velvet bag, embroidered with '1883' was presented to him in which to house the urn. One hundred and twenty-five years on, the little urn – and bag – remains integral to the spirit, philosophy and competitiveness of Ashes cricket.

The first 'Ashes' series originally consisted of three representative matches. The initial scheduling had been rushed and was merely provisional, the dates and venues changing markedly from the time they were first aired in the London *Sportsman* on 5 September 1882, just a week after Australia's stunning triumph at The Oval.[9]

The series was billed as being between 'Mr. Murdoch's Eleven and The Hon. Ivo F.W. Bligh's Team'. A fourth game, also to be elevated to Test status, was contested, too, at the tour end, but not before Bligh was in full celebration and the Ashes urn in his keeping.

His team was strong, but as with most of the early touring teams from the UK was not truly representative. The Australians fielded the same XI that had toured England in 1882.

After Bligh agreed to an additional challenge match against a Combined Australia in Sydney, the colonials strengthened Murdoch's UK XI with the inclusion of three bowlers – Ted Evans, Harry Boyle and the globetrotting Midwinter, who, in a selection quirk, had previously represented Australia *and* England.

The prodigious hitting of the 198 cm (6 ft 6 in) George Bonnor was a feature of the summer. Known as the 'Colonial Hercules', he'd plant his substantial size 15s down the wicket and swing at anything within reach. It was so sunny in Melbourne the tourists complained about being dazzled and Bonnor was missed eight times on his way to 85, a remarkable innings which included five 4s and four 5s, at a time when five runs, rather than six, were awarded for hits over the fence.[10] One of Bonnor's huge smites zeroed beyond the roof of old Mac's curator's cottage and bounced off the fence at the park's outer extremities. Joey Palmer's 10 wickets for the match was equally important in Australia's much-celebrated opening win.

The second Test was also in Melbourne and visiting all-rounder Billy Bates claimed 14 wickets, including Bonnor first-ball to complete a hat-trick as England squared the series 1–1. Fourteen consecutive maidens were sent down by Englishmen Fred Morley and Dicky Barlow during this game. However, Walter Read's catch of Bonnor for Bates's hat-trick was the major talking point. 'Someone suggested that in the faint hope of securing a "hat" for Bates, we should bring [in] a silly mid-on,' said Allan Steel. 'Bates faithfully promised to bowl a fast shortish ball between the leg and the wicket and said he was quite certain that Bonnor would play slowly forward to it . . . in came the giant – loud were the shouts of welcome from the larrikins' throats – as Bates began to walk to the wicket to bowl, nearer and nearer crept our brave mid-on [Read]; a slow forward stroke to a fast shortish leg stump ball landed the ball in his hands not more than six feet from the bat. The crowd could not believe it and Bonnor was simply thunderstruck at mid-on's impertinence.'[11]

Noted stonewaller Alick Bannerman topscored with 94 in the third and deciding match in Sydney, but England won easily, Spofforth being so incensed at having his integrity questioned over his wearing of spiked shoes that he shaped up to Englishmen Barlow and the just-as-excitable Read before being calmed down.[12]

Bligh, twenty-three, was England's youngest-ever touring captain and while only a moderate performer, he was a fine ambassador and brilliant after-dinner speaker.

He bristled at insinuations that his English team had won the decider purely because of their good fortune at the toss allowed them first use of the best wicket, two pitches having been rolled for the match, one for each batting side.

Forced to bat last on a scuffed and pockmarked wicket, the Australians, set 153, were bowled out in just over two hours for 83. Only two made double figures, wicketkeeper Jack Blackham (26) and Hugh Massie (11). Barlow's seven-wicket haul in the Australian second innings made him England's hero of the hour and amid 'vociferous cheering'[13], he was presented to the crowd and given a collection.

In the fourth, additional match against Australia's very-best XI in Sydney, Bonnor opened the innings and continued on his dare-devil, tantalising ways to make 87, his big hits bringing whistles of admiration from an appreciative home crowd. In four Tests that summer he seven times cleared the boundary fences. Only the Golden Age's Albert Trott, who once hit a ball over the pavilion at Lord's, or the prodigious-hitting Englishman C.I. 'Buns' Thornton were in Bonnor's class as a hitter.

Bligh was to return to Australia the following year and marry Florence Morphy, Lady Clarke's companion and family governess, who he'd first met at Rupertswood. They were later to become Lord and Lady Darnley. Early in their marriage they lived in East Melbourne and friends remember seeing the tiny clay Ashes urn taking pride of place on their mantelpiece. It remained Bligh's most prized possession, donated to Lord's upon his death in 1927.

Tours were frequent in the 1880s, five being made both to and from Australia. England's domination saw the Ashes retained in seven consecutive series, a winning streak unequalled until modern times when Australia boasted the game's ultimate matchwinners Glenn McGrath and Shane Warne.

It was a troubled time for cricket, however, especially in the colonies, with a Murdoch-led Australian team going on strike and stormy relations escalating between Melbourne and Sydney authorities. Not everyone outside the powerful Melbourne Cricket Club regarded it as the club's unalienable right to be the game's leading promoter.

The warring elements undermined the strength and popularity of the game and Murdoch, Australia's finest batsman, went into a self-imposed exile, while others flicked back and forth between Sydney and Melbourne depending on where they felt they were most welcome.

On return from the UK, Murdoch and his 1884 Australians sought a larger slice of the game's lucrative gate monies, most of which, by custom, went to the touring team. Flushed by his own success at The Oval, where he made 211 and Australia amassed 551, Murdoch rated his Australian team at least the equal of any All-England XI and fought for what he believed should be a more equitable share. While easily beaten at Lord's, Murdoch felt an extra day's play would have been enough at The Oval for the Australians to have squared the series, his team batting well into the second day and forcing the English to follow-on. Amid the run orgy, all eleven Englishmen bowled, including wicketkeeper Lyttelton who took 4-19 with lobs, the only first-class wickets of his career. While England escaped defeat, it was a moral victory for Murdoch's Australians.

The power-broking Melbourne Cricket Club again funded the visit of the 1884–85 English team, managed this time by Shaw and captained by the outstanding Nottinghamshire professional Arthur Shrewsbury, England's principal batsman, who had toured under Shaw and Lillywhite in 1881–82.

The representative games were billed to be between 'Murdoch's Australian team and Shaw's English Team' and for the first time included an international in Adelaide. The match was promoted as 'the greatest treat ever offered to a South Australian public' featuring not only the game's elite players, but the ground's new scoring board, 'the largest in the world'.[14] Much work, too, had been done on the outer mounds, allowing the largest of crowds a full and uninterrupted view.

Much to Shaw's disbelief – and anger – Murdoch and his team demanded half the gate monies and it wasn't until the South Australian Cricket Association guaranteed the two teams 450 guineas each that the Cornstalks gathered for practice. The match went into a fourth day but the SACA lost heavily on the enterprise. Australia's formidable opening batsman Percy McDonnell became the first to score two centuries in a row – having also made a century at The Oval in August. England's tempestuous champion Billy Barnes made 134 and 28 not out, as well as taking three key wickets as the Australians collapsed in their second innings. The game was also notable for four Notts players: Wilfred Flowers, Scotton, Shrewsbury and Barnes filling the first four places in England's order as the winning runs were accumulated.

Never before had the Australians received £40 a match. It was the equivalent of a deposit on an inner-city house.

Approaching the second international in Melbourne, Murdoch again demanded an equal share of the gate but ran into a brick wall. The Victorian Cricketers' Association said they were controlling the game and told Murdoch he must play on *their* terms or not at all. When an offer of £20 per man was rejected, the Association directed selector George Major to go ahead and pick an alternate XI. Spofforth was one of several unavailable through injury or work commitments. Adelaide's Walter Giffen could not be coaxed into accepting an invitation, big brother George being one of Murdoch's men.

A totally different XI was fielded, including nine new to internationals. One was the first Tasmanian Test cricketer Samuel Morris, born in Hobart of West Indian parents. Opening batsman Sammy Jones and first-time captain Tommy Horan were the only two Australians who had previously played at representative level, but the replacements received enthusiastic support from Melburnians; Murdoch, a New South Welshman, being roundly condemned in the local press.

The Englishmen again won easily, this time by 10 wickets, bouncy Lancastrian Johnny Briggs, on the first of six tours, making 121 and dominating a tenth-wicket partnership of 98 with wicketkeeper Joe Hunter (39).

Billy Bruce, a standout as he both batted and bowled left-handed, opened both the batting and the bowling. Stand-in wicketkeeper A.H. 'Affie' Jarvis scored 82.

Bolstered by the return of rebels Alick Bannerman, Bonnor and H.J.H. 'Tup' Scott, as well as a fit-again Spofforth, the Australians hit back in the third match in Sydney, winning by six runs. Barnes, England's match-winner in Adelaide, refused to bowl in the English second innings, having not been used in the first. Spofforth's 6-90 from 48.1 overs was another inspired effort. He had disagreed with his teammates striking in Melbourne, believing they were being greedy.[15] He was happy to play again once fully fit.

Australia's third captain in as many matches, Massie, produced the ball which turned the match, a deceptively paced delivery, brilliantly held back, which bowled Read for 56 with England comfortably placed.

Australia won the fourth international, again in Sydney, thanks to the mighty Bonnor who made 128 in under two hours, coming in at No. 8. At that stage Australia was 134-7 chasing 269. The giant lifted his team into the lead in thrilling fashion, with four 5s and fourteen 4s. Of a 154-run stand with Jones, Bonnor made 120. Overnight rain so softened the wicket that Spofforth and Palmer were unplayable, the English being bowled out in just over an hour for 77.

England took the fifth and deciding match, Shrewsbury becoming the first English captain to score a century. It was yet another controversial match, umpire G.J. Hodges refusing to stand after tea on the third day following disagreements with the Englishmen, particularly Bobby Peel. Tom Garrett deputised for the final session and manager Lillywhite on the final day. Jim Phillips, one of the original umpires, was taken ill and replaced by J.C. Allen on the final two days.

England's 3–2 win confirmed their standing as the strongest visiting team to the colonies, despite the disqualifications and disputes that had unsettled the Australian XI.

The Marylebone Cricket Club, the game's lawmaker, expressed their official displeasure of the unedifying events at the summer-start by sending a cable in March saying all of the 1884 tourists, 'except for Spofforth', would not be welcome in England on the next tour.[16]

Lillywhite said the strike was ill-considered and did nothing but discredit the game in the colonies. 'The whole of them (Murdoch and co.) . . . were justly condemned by all right-thinking men throughout Australia,' he said.[17]

Lillywhite did not mention that three of the leading Englishmen including Shrewsbury had refused to play in the Players v. Australians fixture at Sheffield in 1884, a decision upsetting to Murdoch and his men as it rebounded against the gate.

Murdoch was not to play another important match for five years.

The Melbourne Cricket Club promoted the Australian visit to England in 1886, elevating its own 'Tup' Scott to the captaincy and naming secretary Ben Wardill as tour manager. The team even sported the club's colours. Of the thirteen, nine were from Victoria, with some of the biggest names, such as McDonnell, missing out. The tour was disastrous, *Wisden* describing the assembled party as 'feeble and spiritless'.[18] Key players were injured, others quarrelled among themselves, Scott's captaincy was castigated and his team lost each of the three internationals. One of the few positives was the all-round form of George Giffen, the South Australian rapidly gaining the reputation as Australia's 'W.G. Grace'.

There had been hopes of an Australian rebirth in 1886–87, especially with a more-representative side available, including two new frontline bowlers in C.T.B. 'Terror' Turner and the left-armer J.J. 'Jack' Ferris from Sydney. Charlie Turner was just nineteen when he first took all 10 wickets in an innings for a Bathurst XXII against a touring English team. His graceful, easy action belied his spirit and extraordinary skill, especially on any wicket offering even the slightest of assistance. Ferris was an ideal foil, tight and rarely collared, with constant drift and just enough away spin to worry even the most able players.

The English, known as 'Shaw's Team', were a formidable unit, the top-order including gifted batting aristocrat Shrewsbury and his Nottinghamshire teammates Billy Barnes, William Gunn and noted blocker Scotton.

The two internationals were gripping, England staging a remarkable comeback to win by 13 runs in Sydney before enjoying a more comfortable 57-run win in Melbourne.

Turner and Ferris were to become Australia's first truly great opening pair, even Spofforth being relegated to first-change duties in the second innings in Sydney after England, sent into bat for the first time in representative cricket, was bowled out for 45, still its lowest ever score. The two rookies were unchanged, Turner taking 6-15 and Ferris 4-27. They were also superb in Melbourne, gathering 18 more wickets between them to lift their combined aggregate to 35 in their first two internationals. Having triggered England's come-from-behind heroics in Sydney with a

Test-best 6-28 to castle Combined Australia, the rumbustious Barnes was involved in an altercation with NSW and Australian captain McDonnell. In attempting to throw a punch, he struck a brick wall and so badly damaged his thumb that he was unable to play again for weeks.

The tour was marred by rain, one of the first-time tourists, heavyweight wicketkeeper Mordecai Sherwin, telling Felix of the *Australasian*: 'Everywhere we went we were treated most hospitably, and during our travels we saw some very beautiful scenery. But the rain! I shall never forget it. It seemed to rain in every town we visited. The rain followed us around. That is what the people said, at any rate and they thanked us for breaking up the drought, and asked us to come again when another drought occurs. At Bowral we were above our ankles in water in our tent and cricket bags and boots were floating about us in a manner that was quite novel to us'.[19]

The Englishmen were rated the most powerful to ever visit the colonies, their only two defeats coming on indifferent, rain-affected wickets against New South Wales, matches in which 24-year-old Turner claimed 27 wickets.

The power plays between Melbourne and Sydney saw two teams from the UK tour in the ever-so-wet summer of 1887–88, the old firm of Alfred Shaw, Arthur Shrewsbury and Jim Lillywhite being invited by the Sydney Cricket Club and a rival group under the captaincy of The Hon. M.R. Hawke (later Lord Hawke) and the management of George Vernon, sponsored by the Melbourne Cricket Club.

The SCC tour was led by C. Aubrey Smith, known as 'Round the Corner' Smith for his habit of running up behind the umpire and suddenly veering towards the popping crease. He later became one of Hollywood's most acclaimed actors, appearing in more than 100 motion pictures, including *Rebecca* (with Laurence Olivier and Joan Fontaine) and *The Prisoner of Zenda* (Robert Colman and David Niven).

The touring groups were in conflict from the start and both suffered substantial losses. Vernon's tourists, which included a young Drewy Stoddart, lost almost £4,000 while the Shaw, Shrewsbury and Lillywhite enterprise lost £2,400, ending their touring ventures. 'At the finish,' said Shaw, years later, 'we were much worse off financially than when we had begun. The cricket rivalries in Melbourne and Sydney were our undoing.'[20] Amid the folly and strained friendships, Vernon's team won eleven matches, drew fourteen and lost only to a NSW team. The Shaw–Shrewsbury–Lillywhite team had fourteen victories and nine draws and lost to NSW twice. One Combined Match involving players from both tour groups was played in Sydney with Read named as the English XI's captain among the many compromises.

The Australians were led by Percy McDonnell, who gave the locals hope by winning the toss soon after very heavy rain. The Australian XI was weakened by the absence of Billy Bruce, George Giffen and Jarvis, who all declined invitations, while veteran Horan was among several who had withdrawn from the original nominated squad. The wicket was substandard and McDonnell sent the English into bat. They made just 113, but Combined Australia fared even worse, capitulating for 42, its lowest score in internationals until 1902 when it was bowled out for 36 at Edgbaston. George Lohmann and Bobby Peel each took five wickets. Eighteen wickets fell on the opening day before no play was possible on the scheduled days two and three. As it was, just 2,000 spectators attended the entire game, Australia losing by 126 runs after being bowled out a second time for 82. 'Towards this brilliant and gratifying result,' said *Wisden*, 'the splendid bowling of Lohmann and Peel mainly contributed, the two men taking 18 wickets between them.'[21] Shrewsbury's skilful 44 on the opening day remained the highest score in a game which saw 40 wickets fall in less than nine playing hours. Often Shrewsbury used his pads as a second line of defence against Turner, who was breaking the ball viciously.

Stoddart's 285 against Eighteen Melbourne Juniors was a preview of his skill and the highest score by a touring Englishman until Reggie Foster's 287 in 1903–04.

Amid more civil unrest, this time between the Victorian Cricketers' Association and the Melbourne Cricket Club, Australian teams toured the UK in 1888 and 1890 without notable success. They had trouble even against the counties and the missing big names including Spofforth, George Giffen, Billy Bruce and Hugh Trumble exposed the lack of depth among the reserves. Turner was the hero in 1888, taking 283 first-class wickets, including twenty-six five-wicket hauls. He and long-time partner Ferris became the first Australians accorded Cricketer of the Year status with the release of the 1889 edition of *Wisden Cricketers' Almanack*. In 1890,

Murdoch ended his self-imposed exile and returned as captain for a fourth tour. But for the first time a representative Australian team on tour lost more games than it won, the off-field unrest being as pronounced as the flighty performances in the middle. Australian cricket was to remain in a trough, too, until the cricket-loving Lord Sheffield acted as a white knight for the game down-under, not only giving the game's champion, Dr W. G. Grace a golden handshake ensuring his first visit to colonial shores in almost two decades, but helping fund a new inter-colonial competition that became the very heartbeat of Australian cricket.

Man of the Decade: *Fred 'Demon' Spofforth*

Deadly and destructive, spirited and skilled Fred Spofforth inspired the birth of the Ashes in 1882. In a one-off Test at The Oval, the inspirational Sydneysider was unchanged in taking 7-46 and 7-44 to trigger a massive upset. In a gripping finish, so fast did he bowl from eight paces that Jack Blackham, known as the 'Prince of Wicketkeepers', was forced to back away from the stumps for one of the few times in his career.[22]

Before England's extraordinary collapse, Spofforth declared in the rooms that 'this thing can be done'[23] and proceeded to bowl five players and have another caught and bowled, his victims being the who's who of All-England batsmanship: Dick Barlow, The Hon. Alfred Lyttelton, Alfred 'Bunny' Lucas, A. N. 'Monkey' Hornby, Allan Steel and Maurice Read. From 51-2, England capitulated, losing their last eight wickets for 26 to be beaten by seven runs. Spofforth was carried shoulder-high into the pavilion. Historian Harry Altham said: 'If ever a man made cricket history, it was he that day'.[24]

With his last 11 overs, Spofforth claimed four wickets for two runs, his vicious break-backs a feature. It was a remarkably stirring performance, which once and for all illustrated the mettle of the colonials at eleven-a-side cricket. And rather than future internationals being played on an ad-hoc basis, the first three-Test series were scheduled with the Ashes as the prize.

The first bowler noted for his change of pace, the 191 cm (6 ft 3 in) Spofforth possessed the highest action of his era, triggering the demise of the lob and round-arm bowlers. He was also headstrong and opinionated and refused to play in the inaugural Test because a Victorian had been chosen to keep wickets.

A frontline member of five Cornstalk touring teams to the United Kingdom, he took 94 wickets in just eighteen Tests at an average of more than five wickets per match before settling in England where he was still intimidating top-orders well into his 40s. Representing suburban team Wembley Park against Harry Trott's 1896 Australians, he took 11 wickets. The pitch was wet and under-prepared but, at forty-two years of age, Spofforth was still in a class of his own. Several months later, having inspected a green, grassy wicket prepared for the deciding Test of the series at The Oval, he pleaded with Trott to be included in Australia's XI, saying he'd have England out for less than 50.[25] Trott, a Melbur-nian, refused and Australia lost.

Spofforth v. England

Season	Analysis	Wkts	Ave
1876–77	3-67, 1-44	4	27.75
1878–79	6-48, 7-62	13	8.46
1881–82	1-92, 0-36	1	128.00
1882	7-46, 7-44	14	6.42
1882–83	1-56, 3-65, 0-57, 4-73, 7-44, 1-56, 2-57	18	22.66
1884	4-42, 2-52, 2-112, 2-81, 0-14	10	30.10
1884–85	4-54, 6-90, 2-61, 5-30, 2-71	19	16.10
1886	4-82, 2-40, 4-73, 4-65	14	18.57
1886–87	1-17	1	17.00

Tests:	18 (all v. England)
Wickets:	94
Average:	18.41
Best bowling:	7–44, The Oval, 1882
5-wicket Innings:	7
10-wicket Matches:	4
Strike-rate:	44
Average wkts per Test:	5.2

Match of the decade: *Sydney, 1887*

Bowled out for 45 in just over an hour in a dramatic opening session, Arthur Shrewsbury's English professionals snatched a remarkable victory after Australia, set just 111, was bowled out for 97, Billy Barnes taking 6-28. Hero of the very first Test, Charles Bannerman made his Test debut as an umpire and brother Alick, a noted stonewaller, batted an hour in Australia's second innings without scoring.

Match scores: England 45 (Turner 6-15, Ferris 4-27) and 184 (Ferris 5-76) defeated Australia 119 and 97 (Barnes 6-28) by 13 runs

Odd spot: *A foot in both camps*

When the volatile Billy Barnes punched himself out of the final Test of 1886–87, Reg Wood, an Englishman living in Melbourne, was co-opted into Arthur Shrewsbury's XI, making six and nought in his one and only Test match. Weeks earlier he had played for Victoria against the Englishmen, thereby becoming the first to appear both for and against a touring party in the same season.

Looking back: *Arthur Shrewsbury, Sydney, 1887*

'I have never played in a match that was literally pulled out of the fire as this one was. It was so entirely unexpected that the people out here could scarcely realise we had won. It was a glorious victory and I am sure the cricket public back home will be more than pleased with the result, considering the uphill game we had to fight.'[26]

> Shrewsbury was the first professional to captain England. He led two touring teams to the colonies.

One for the statisticians: *A century from No. 10*

With a triple century to his credit for Surrey, Walter Read was as well credentialed as most of the frontline English batsmen of the 1880s, yet found himself batting second last for England in the deciding Test of 1884 at The Oval. After Australia had started with 551, England slumped to 181-8 before Read made a matchsaving 117 against Spofforth and co. It remains the highest score in Ashes history from the No. 10 slot.

Tests 1880 to 1888

KEY: M Matches **I** Innings **NO** Not out innings **HS** Highest score **BB** Best bowling
5wI 5-wicket innings **10wM** 10-wicket match ***** Not out **#** Second innings **rh** Retired hurt

Series results

	Tests	Aust	Eng	Drawn
1880 (Eng)	1	0	1	0
1881–82 (Aust)	4	2	0	2
1882 (Eng)	1	1	0	0
1882–83 (Aust)	4	2	2	0
1884 (Eng)	3	0	1	2
1884–85 (Aust)	5	2	3	0
1886 (Eng)	3	0	3	0
1886–87 (Aust)	2	0	2	0
1887–88 (Aust)	1	0	1	0
1888 (Eng)	3	1	2	0
Total	**27**	**8**	**15**	**4**
Progressive	30	10	16	4

Summary

	Runs	Wkts	Ave
Australia	8280	469	17.65
England	9463	426	22.21

Highest innings totals

Australia		England	
551	The Oval 1884 (3rd Test)	434	The Oval 1886 (3rd Test)
327	The Oval 1880 (Only Test)#	420	The Oval 1880 (Only Test)
320	Melbourne 1881–82 (1st Test)	401	Melbourne 1884–85 (2nd Test)
309	Sydney 1884–85 (4th Test)	386	Melbourne 1884–85 (5th Test)
300	Melbourne 1881–82 (4th Test)	379	Lord's 1884 (2nd Test)
		369	Adelaide 1884–85 (1st Test)
		353	Lord's 1886 (2nd Test)

Lowest completed innings totals

Australia		England	
42†	Sydney 1887–88 (Only Test)	45^	Sydney 1886–87 (1st Test)
60	Lord's 1888 (1st Test)#	53	Lord's 1888 (1st Test)
63	The Oval 1882 (Only Test)	62	Lord's 1888 (1st Test)#
68	The Oval 1886 (3rd Test)	77	The Oval 1882 (Only Test)#
70	Manchester 1888 (3rd Test)#	77	Melbourne 1884–85 (4th Test)

† lowest total by Australia in Australia
^ lowest total by England against Australia

Leading run scorers

	M	I	NO	Runs	HS	Ave	100	50
Australia								
P.S. McDonnell	19	34	1	955	147	28.93	3	2
W.L. Murdoch	14	25	4	841	211	40.04	2	1
A.C. Bannerman	21	38	2	672	94	18.66	–	4
J.M. Blackham	23	40	4	580	66	16.57	–	3
G.J. Bonnor	17	30	0	512	128	17.06	1	2
England								
A. Shrewsbury	18	31	3	963	164	34.39	2	2
W. Barnes	19	30	2	706	134	25.21	1	5
G. Ulyett	19	29	0	664	149	22.89	1	4
W. Bates	15	26	2	656	64	27.33	–	5
A.G. Steel	13	20	3	600	148	35.29	2	–
W.W. Read	13	19	0	595	117	31.31	1	4
R.G. Barlow	17	30	4	591	62	22.73	–	2
W.G. Grace	11	18	1	542	170	31.88	2	–
W.H. Scotton	15	25	2	510	90	22.17	–	3

Hundreds

Australia (8)		England (10)	
3	P.S. McDonnell	2	W.G. Grace
2	W.L. Murdoch		A. Shrewsbury
1	G.J. Bonnor		A.G. Steel
	T.P. Horan	1	W. Barnes
	H.J.H. Scott		J. Briggs
			W.W. Read
			G. Ulyett

Highest individual scores

Australia

211	W.L. Murdoch at The Oval 1884 (3rd Test)
153*	W.L. Murdoch at The Oval 1880 (Only Test)#
147	P.S. McDonnell at Sydney 1881–82 (3rd Test)

England

170	W.G. Grace at The Oval 1886 (3rd Test)
164	A. Shrewsbury at Lord's 1886 (2nd Test)
152	W.G. Grace at The Oval 1880 (Only Test)
149	G. Ulyett at Melbourne 1881–82 (4th Test)
148	A.G. Steel at Lord's 1884 (2nd Test)

500 runs in a series

	Season	M	I	NO	Runs	HS	Ave	100	50
Australia									
No instance – best:									
P.S. McDonnell	1881–82	4	7	1	299	147	49.83	1	1
England									
No instance – best:									
G. Ulyett	1881–82	4	8	0	438	149	54.75	1	3

Hundred partnerships

Australia (6)

Partnerships of 150 and over:

207	3rd	W. L. Murdoch and H. J. H. Scott at The Oval 1884 (3rd Test)
199	4th	A. C. Bannerman and P.S. McDonnell at Sydney 1881–82 (3rd Test)
154	8th	G. J. Bonnor and S. P. Jones at Sydney 1884–85 (4th Test)

England (11)

Partnerships of 150 and over:

175	3rd	W. H. Scotton and W. Barnes at Adelaide 1884–85 (1st Test)
170	1st	W. G. Grace and W. H. Scotton at The Oval 1886 (3rd Test)
161	3rd	A. Shrewsbury and W. Barnes at Lord's 1886 (2nd Test)
151	9th	W. H. Scotton and W.W. Read at The Oval 1884 (3rd Test)
		(English 9th wicket record against Australia)

Leading wicket-takers

	Tests	Balls	Mdns	Runs	Wkts	Ave	BB	5wI	10wM
Australia									
G. E. Palmer	17	4,517	452	1,678	78	21.51	7-65	6	2
F. R. Spofforth	16	3,769	382	1,510	77	19.61	7-44	5	3
C.T. B. Turner	6	1,727	207	509	50	10.18	6-15	8	2
J. J. Ferris	6	1,465	174	513	35	14.65	5-26	3	–
T.W. Garrett	16	2,569	279	886	33	26.84	6-78	2	–
H. F. Boyle	11	1,672	168	614	30	20.46	6-42	1	–
G. Giffen	17	2,148	208	947	29	32.65	7-117	1	–
England									
R. Peel	9	2,211	264	690	54	12.77	7-31	3	1
W. Bates	15	2,364	282	821	50	16.42	7-28	4	1
G. A. Lohmann	9	1,496	187	524	49	10.69	8-35	4	2
W. Barnes	19	2,225	266	767	49	15.65	6-28	3	–
G. Ulyett	19	1,921	223	756	40	18.90	7-36	1	–
J. Briggs	14	1,158	145	336	34	9.88	6-45	3	1
R. G. Barlow	17	2,456	325	767	34	22.55	7-40	3	–
E. Peate	9	2,096	250	683	31	22.03	6-85	2	–
A. G. Steel	13	1,408	108	605	29	20.86	3-27	–	–

Five wickets in an innings

Australia (28)		England (25)	
8	C.T.B.Turner	4	W. Bates
6	G. E. Palmer		G.A. Lohmann
5	F.R. Spofforth	3	R. G. Barlow
3	J.J. Ferris		W. Barnes
2	T.W. Garrett		J. Briggs
1	H. F. Boyle		R. Peel
	W. H. Cooper	2	E. Peate
	G. Giffen	1	W. Flowers
	T. P. Horan		F. Morley
			G. Ulyett

Best individual bowling

Australia

7-43	C.T. B. Turner at Sydney 1887–88 (Only Test)#
7-44	F. R. Spofforth at The Oval 1882 (Only Test)#
7-44	F. R. Spofforth at Sydney 1882–83 (3rd Test)#
7-46	F. R. Spofforth at The Oval 1882 (Only Test)
7-65	G. E. Palmer at Melbourne 1882–83 (1st Test)
7-68	G. E. Palmer at Sydney 1881–82 (2nd Test)
7-117	G. Giffen at Sydney 1884–85 (4th Test)
6-15	C.T. B. Turner at Sydney 1886–87 (1st Test)
6-40	T. P. Horan 1884–85 at Sydney (3rd Test)
6-42	H. F. Boyle at Manchester 1884 (1st Test)
6-78	T.W. Garrett at Sydney 1881–82 (3rd Test)#
6-90	F. R. Spofforth at Sydney 1884–85 (3rd Test)#
6-111	G. E. Palmer at Lord's 1884 (2nd Test)
6-112	C.T. B. Turner at The Oval 1888 (2nd Test)
6-120	W. H. Cooper at Melbourne 1881–82 (1st Test)#

England

8-35	G.A. Lohmann at Sydney 1886–87 (2nd Test)
	(best innings analysis for England in Australia)
7-28	W. Bates at Melbourne 1882–83 (2nd Test)
7-31	R. Peel at Manchester 1888 (3rd Test)
7-36	G. Ulyett at Lord's 1884 (2nd Test)#
7-36	G. A. Lohmann at The Oval 1886 (3rd Test)
7-40	R. G. Barlow at Sydney 1882–83 (3rd Test)
7-44	R. G. Barlow at Manchester 1886 (1st Test)#
7-74	W. Bates at Melbourne 1882–83 (2nd Test)#
6-28	W. Barnes at Sydney 1886–87 (1st Test)#
6-31	W. Barnes at Melbourne 1884–85 (2nd Test)#
6-45	J. Briggs at Lord's 1886 (2nd Test)#
6-85	E. Peate at Lord's 1884 (2nd Test)

10 wickets in a match

Australia (7)

14-90	F. R. Spofforth (7-46 and 7-44) at The Oval 1882 (Only Test)
12-87	C. T. B. Turner (5-44 and 7-43) at Sydney 1887–88 (Only Test)
11-117	F. R. Spofforth (4-73 and 7-44) at Sydney 1882–83 (3rd Test)
11-165	G. E. Palmer (7-68 and 4-97) at Sydney 1881–82 (2nd Test)
10-63	C. T. B. Turner (5-27 and 5-36) at Lord's 1888 (1st Test)
10-126	G. E. Palmer (7-65 and 3-61) at Melbourne 1882–83 (1st Test)
10-144	F. R. Spofforth (4-54 and 6-90) at Sydney 1884–85 (3rd Test)

England (5)

14-102	W. Bates (7-28 and 7-74) at Melbourne 1882–83 (2nd Test)
12-104	G. A. Lohmann (7-36 and 5-68) at The Oval 1886 (3rd Test)
11-74	J. Briggs (5-29 and 6-45) at Lord's 1886 (2nd Test)
11-68	R. Peel (7-31 and 4-37) at Manchester 1888 (3rd Test)
10-87	G. A. Lohmann (8-35 and 2-52) at Sydney 1886–87 (2nd Test)

Hat-trick

W. Bates (Eng) at Melbourne 1882–83 (2nd Test)
(McDonnell b, G. Giffen c and b, G. J. Bonnor c W. W. Read)

25 wickets in a series

	Season	Tests	Balls	Mdns	Runs	Wkts	Ave	BB	5wI	10wM
Australia										
No instance – best:										
G. E. Palmer	1881–82	4	1,462	145	522	24	21.75	7-68	2	1
England										
No instance – best:										
R. Peel	1888	3	446	48	181	24	7.54	7-31	1	1

Leading wicketkeepers

	Tests	Dismissals	Catches	Stumpings
Australia				
J. M. Blackham	23	39	23	16
England				
R. Pilling	8	13	9	4
J. Hunter	5	11	8	3
E. F. S. Tylecote	6	10	5	5

Leading fieldsmen

Australia	Tests	Catches	England	Tests	Catches
G. J. Bonnor	17	16	W. G. Grace	11	26
A. C. Bannerman	21	14	A. Shrewsbury	18	26
G. E. Palmer	17	13	W. Barnes	19	17
S. P. Jones	12	12	R. G. Barlow	17	14
W. L. Murdoch	13	10	G. Ulyett	19	14
			G. A. Lohmann	9	12
			W. W. Read	13	11

Captains

Australia	Tests	Won	Lost	Drawn	Toss won
W. L. Murdoch	14	5	5	4	5
P. S. McDonnell	6	1	5	0	4
H. J. H. Scott	3	0	3	0	1
T. P. Horan	2	0	2	0	1
J. M. Blackham	1	1	0	0	0
H. H. Massie	1	1	0	0	1
England					
A. Shrewsbury	7	5	2	0	3
Hon. I. F. W. Bligh	4	2	2	0	3
A. Shaw	4	0	2	2	4
A. G. Steel	4	3	1	0	2
Lord Harris	3	2	0	1	1
W. G. Grace	2	2	0	0	1
A. N. Hornby	2	0	1	1	1
W. W. Read	1	1	0	0	0

Most appearances

Australia (44 players)		England (47 players)	
23	J. M. Blackham	19	W. Barnes
21	A. C. Bannerman		G. Ulyett
19	P. S. McDonnell	18	A. Shrewsbury
17	G. J. Bonnor	17	R. G. Barlow
	G. Giffen	15	W. Bates
	G. E. Palmer		W. H. Scotton
16	T. W. Garrett		
	F. R. Spofforth		
	D. W. Gregory		

Prince Ranjitsinhji captivated Australian crowds in 1897–98 with his wristiness and flair. *Famous Cricketers and Cricket Grounds* by C.W. Alcock, 1895

FORWARD TO
FEDERATION

• •

'. . . the value of Brockwell's success in those few miraculous overs was inestimable. His three sledge-hammer blows made the pavilion windows shake . . .'

Henry Holroyd, the third Earl of Sheffield, granted cricket a monumental favour when he convinced the game's foremost celebrity, Dr William Gilbert Grace, to tour for the first time in almost twenty years as part of his revivalist blueprint for the game in the Great Southern Land. Grace's fee was extraordinary, £3,000 plus expenses, the equivalent of £125,000 today, but his Lordship felt Grace's presence crucial if the tour and cricket down-under was to truly benefit. He had been perturbed and saddened by the events of 1890, when the Australians, as disjointed a unit as any to visit England, had been thrashed by even the weaker counties. The reports of drunkenness and fisticuffs only increased his desire to lure 'W.G.', who at forty-three was well beyond his best, but still the game's ultimate drawcard. As Lord Sheffield had hoped, Grace was feted everywhere the team trekked. In the match against Victoria at the Melbourne Cricket Ground the champion walked to the wicket to the strains of 'See the Conquering Hero Comes'. In Adelaide, newspaper billboards advertising the game simply read 'W.G. GRACE'.[1]

As part of his lifeline, Lord Sheffield also donated £150 to the three major colonies, New South Wales, Victoria and South Australia, leaving it to their discretion on how best to spend it. After spirited, extended debate, a motion was finally passed six votes to five to start an inter-colonial competition, named in his Lordship's honour.

With the first major controlling body, the Australasian Cricket Council being formed, albeit with teething problems, the game down-under was starting to develop a fresh strength and stability that was to hasten the game's wonderful Golden Age.

Lord Sheffield's team was representative of the best players in the UK, although northern professionals Arthur Shrewsbury and Billy Gunn had both baulked at the terms offered the rank-and-file, ten times less than their ageing captain. While they were to lose two of the three 'Tests', the English remained unbeaten in their other twenty-four games.

'At the outset there did not seem to be any chance of failure,' wrote Jim Lillywhite.[2]

The Englishmen felt their top-order could combat the two Australian champions Charlie 'Terror' Turner and Jack Ferris and expected their own opening bowlers George Lohmann and Johnny 'Boy' Briggs to master the heat and even the most batsman-friendly Australian wickets.

Six-ball overs (rather than four) were employed for the first time and the English started convincingly with victories against South Australia, New South Wales and Victoria. They remained undefeated, too, until the first international in Melbourne from 1 January 1892. Veteran wicketkeeper Jack Blackham, thirty-seven, led the Australians. He had a nice blend of youth and experience, with three players making their Ashes debut: Syd Callaway, Robert McLeod and H. 'Harry' Donnan. McLeod, a rangy lighterman from working-class Port Melbourne, caused an early sensation when he took five wickets. He also appeared to bowl Grace, the great man taking a step or two towards the pavilion before resuming his stance to widespread merriment from the players and the large holiday crowd. The spectator count was in excess of 20,000 on each of the first two days, most drawn by the prospect of seeing the old champion. Grace scored 50 and 25, but his team was narrowly beaten, the Australians enjoying superior batting conditions.

Blackham also won the toss in the second international in Sydney only for his side to be dismissed for 145 and concede a sizeable first-innings lead. But Alick Bannerman, who batted seven hours for 91, and the South Australian hitter Jack Lyons resurrected Australia's hopes. So intent was Bannerman on defence that Grace at point crept so close that one barracker exclaimed: 'Look out Alick, W.G.'ll have his hand in your pocket!'[3] Grace took no such liberties with Lyons, who in the first innings had crashed a ball from Lohmann onto the roof of the Ladies' Stand. The South Australian continued to blaze in the second innings, careering to his only Test century in just over two hours and lifting the Australians to 391. Rain on the fourth day transformed the wicket into an old-fashioned 'sticky'. Briggs finished the Australian innings off with a hat-trick and Walter Giffen, Callaway and last man Blackham fell in consecutive balls. The target of 229 seemed modest enough before the rain, but Turner and George Giffen excelled, sharing all 10 wickets as Australia clinched victory by 72 runs. Australia's 2–0 lead also secured the Ashes for the first time since 1882. On Day 2 of the game, a Saturday that attracted more than 20,000, England's opening batsman Bobby Abel, 'The Little Guvnor', carried his bat for 132, 'a perfect display' according to George Giffen.[4]

So paranoid was Grace about Blackham's early luck at the toss that he refused to allow the Australian to use his 'lucky' coin in the third international in Adelaide and the Englishmen won easily, the gifted A.E. 'Drewy' Stoddart's 134 lifting England to a new Test high of 499. The England tail batted in heavy rain, the Australians then forced to bat in inferior conditions. The wicket was diabolical and the Australians could manage only 100 and 169.

While Lord Sheffield lost £2,000 on his venture, he had effectively revitalised the game in the colonies with some of the great Test series of all time taking place in the following decades. Significantly, too, there was to be a new unison within Australia – the administrators from Sydney and Melbourne finally declaring a truce.

After the 1893 Australians had lost 1–0 in England, the Melbourne Cricket Club and the trustees of the Sydney Cricket Ground combined to bring the 1894–95 England team to Australia. The tour was an outstanding success, England triumphing in the deciding match to take the series 3–2. For the first time the term 'Test' cricket was widely used. There was phenomenal interest from the start, Stoddart leading a confident, assured team with jauntiness and aplomb. While old W.G. tended at times to be moody and bombastic, Stoddart was cheery and open. He advocated attacking, risk-taking cricket, which cemented the game's standing and popularity once and for all.

The first Test of the series was monumental and set the tone for one of the finest summers of all.

Scoring rates accelerated and George Giffen was responsible for one of the great all-round performances. For the series he made 475 runs and took 34 wickets. The games were thrilling from the opener in Sydney. Despite beginning with 586, the Australians were beaten by 10 runs in a massive turnaround. Youngsters including Joe Darling (who fell first ball in the first innings), Ernie Jones and Frank Iredale were among Australia's first-gamers. For England, one of its greatest Golden Age batsmen, Archie MacLaren, played for the first time. Strong in defence he was also a polished strokemaker and was to be respected by all the Australians as the most prized wicket of all.[5]

Approaching the final day, the Australians were 113-2, just 63 runs short of what seemed an inevitable victory. But there was an overnight deluge followed by hot morning sun, and the wicket flaked and turned square. Bobby Peel and Briggs, the two left-armers, were unplayable, the Australians losing their last eight wickets for just 36. Spectators rushed onto the ground when Peel captured the last wicket, some scooping up souvenirs of the wicket. Those in the city and unable to attend flocked around shop windows displaying regular score updates. There was general disbelief at the collapse. This was the first-ever six-day Test and the first time a team had won following-on. Stoddart considered it an amazing Christmas bonus, the result heralding a phenomenal interest in the game throughout the colonies and back in the Mother Country and the rest of the series was greeted with fanatical enthusiasm.

The second Test, which started at the MCG on 29 December, had far different weather conditions for the start of play. The wicket was rain-affected and England managed only 75 in the first innings. But Australia fared little better, being dismissed for 123. The wicket improved, Stoddart playing the innings of his life for 173, allowing England to reach 475 and set Australia 400-plus. Harry Trott and Billy Bruce began well with 98 for the first wicket and at 191-1, another gripping finish beckoned before Surrey's Billy Brockwell, better known as a high-order batsman, became the hero of the hour, dismissing three of the Australian top-order in a matchwinning spell. 'The spectators were not inclined to regard Brockwell's bowling very seriously,' said author Richard Binns, 'and when suddenly he held a return from Harry Trott they applauded the outgoing batsman and thought no more of it. 191 for two was a good enough score anyway. But Brockwell next tempted Giffen to make a present of a catch to (Jack) Brown and proceeded to wreck Darling's stumps when the latter had scored five – three mighty valuable wickets at the bargain price of 30-odd runs for the lot! . . . the value of Brockwell's success in those few miraculous overs was inestimable. His three sledge-hammer blows made the pavilion windows shake . . . '[6] The match-turning Brockwell was later presented with the ball, but it was Stoddart who had led the revival, his monumental 173 remaining the highest Ashes score by a visiting English captain until Mike Denness's 188, also in Melbourne, in 1974–75. 'Nothing I have ever done in cricket gives me the same lasting pleasure [as] to look back on that innings,' wrote Stoddart.[7]

They had been two of the most marvellous Tests, every bit as thrilling as the opening two from Australia's 2005 tour, and the thrills were to continue, too, with Australia responding with victories in Adelaide and Sydney to square the series 2–2 with one Test to play. The Sydney win belonged to 24-year-old H. 'Harry' Graham, a youngster from Berwick Grammar School, who made 105 in his first Test on Australian soil after Australia was 26-3 having been sent into bat. In Lord's in 1893, he'd made a century in his first appearance for Australia.

The dropping of the celebrated Turner, just days after he had become the first Australian to tally 100 Test wickets, remains one of the most stunning selection decisions in Ashes annals. He'd taken seven wickets in Sydney and 18 wickets for the summer, but leading into the decider in Melbourne he lost his place to rookie Tom McKibbin, having been outvoted by his fellow selectors Blackham and Giffen. Like Turner and George Bonnor, 23-year-old McKibbin hailed from Bathurst in country NSW. He'd forced his way ahead of the legend with some startling performances. In three games between the fourth and fifth Tests he took 34 wickets:

- 5-19 and 9-68 v. Queensland, Exhibition Ground, Brisbane
- 1-49 and 5-98 v. Stoddart's English XI, Exhibition Ground, Brisbane
- 6-123 and 8-66 v. South Australia, Sydney.

McKibbin had been playing representative cricket only since November and his selection at Turner's expense triggered a furore. Bowling right-arm medium pace he could jag the ball at will, but the fairness of many of his deliveries was questioned[8] and while he was the in-form bowler in the country, it was a massive stage on which to suddenly be thrust.

Melbourne was the venue for the final showdown and the crowds were huge, for the first time more than 100,000 attending the five days, including almost 30,000 on the Saturday. Replying to Australia's 414, England made 385, MacLaren excelling with 120. Lion-hearted Tom Richardson, the premier fast bowler in the world, took 6-104 to restrict the Australians to 267, an overall lead of 296. Brockwell fell close to stumps on the fourth night, confirming Australia's favouritism. It was grey and overcast with a persistent Scotch mist on the fifth day. The Australian bowlers struggled with the damp ball and Yorkshireman Brown played superlatively to wrest the momentum, his first 50 coming in just twenty-eight minutes and his second in sixty-seven. Albert Ward's patient 93 was equally valuable as England clinched a six-wicket win, having taken just three and a half hours to score almost 300. Albert Trott was the only frontliner not to concede more than three an over. Australia's defeat triggered ferocious criticism of the selectors, new boy McKibbin taking just 1-73 and 1-47. The game marked Trott's second-last appearance for Australia before shifting to the UK. While omitted from the 1896 touring party to England, a team captained by his brother Harry, he did act as a substitute fieldsman during the Lord's Test. He was to become an institution at Middlesex with his big-hitting and good humour. In 1899, he reserved a permanent place in Lord's lore when he lifted Australian M.A. 'Monty' Noble over the pavilion.

England's supremacy continued approaching a second Stoddart-led tour of the colonies in 1897–98, Harry Trott's 1896 Australians being defeated 2–1 in a series most notable for the stunning debut of Indian Prince Kumar Shri Ranjitsinhji. Ranji's debut match at Old Trafford was riveting. He made 62 and 154 not out with joyous all-around-the-wicket strokes to stamp an immediate authority on Test-match cricket. Australia's first great left-hander, Clem Hill from Adelaide, also played his first Tests in 1896.

'Ranji' was the 'name' player in Stoddart's combine, the NSW Government having waived a £100 deterrent tax on coloured immigrants so that Ranji could tour.

When George Giffen declined the offered terms for the Tests, Stoddart claimed that he couldn't imagine any Australian team without the South Australian.

Stoddart's personal misfortunes were to mar the tour. He had continued bad luck with tosses even in the minor matches, had his watch and chain stolen by a pickpocket in Brisbane and in early December, just forty-eight hours before the scheduled start of the first Test in Sydney, learnt that his mother Elizabeth had died. Grief stricken, he did not take part in the series until the third Test and even then showed little interest in the proceedings.

A further complication for the team was Ranjitsinhji's battle with tonsillitis. He seemed certain to miss the opening Test, but persistent rains delayed the start for three days, giving Ranji sufficient time to rest and recuperate. Held back in the order, he scored 175 from No. 7. Acting captain MacLaren opened with 109 and England tallied 551, enough to win by nine wickets. The run out of Australia's Charlie McLeod for 26 caused a storm, McLeod being bowled from a no-ball. Partially deaf, he did not hear the call and walked from the crease. England's Bill Storer pulled out a stump and ran McLeod out, much to the disgust of the Australians, who felt the English had ignored the spirit of the game.

The second Test in Melbourne was played in fierce heat, with Australia making 520. Ranjitsinhji was absent in the first session through a throat infection. The Englishmen wilted and were beaten by an innings, with Australian expressman Ernie Jones being called for throwing by fellow South Australian 'Dimboola Jim' Phillips.

Stoddart, his thoughts far away, watched on from the men-only pavilion. Many women at the Test wore England's colours in their buttonholes and queued for a glimpse of England's bachelor captain, a firm favourite even if he was in mourning.[9] The cracks in the wicket by the final sessions became wide and deep enough to insert several walking sticks.

The heat was also excessive in Adelaide for the third Test, the Australians again making a mammoth first-innings score and England easily beaten after having to follow on. On his return, Stoddart, at No. 8, made 15 and 24. Darling was superb in attaining his second century of the summer, batting through the entire first day for 178. The English struggled in the field with Ranji dislocating a finger early in the match and frontline bowlers George Hirst and Richardson less than fully fit.

The Australian domination continued in the fourth Test in Melbourne. Twenty-year-old maestro Hill scored 182 not out on the opening day, a solo record unsurpassed among Australians until Don Bradman's 192 runs in a day in 1936–37. Hill rescued Australia from 58-6 to 323 all out, the Australians winning by nine wickets to take a 3–1 series lead. Smoke from nearby bushfires and the continuing fierce heat made conditions barely tolerable for both the players and the spectators.

MacLaren was England's acting captain again in the final Test in Sydney, a despondent Stoddart having lost all focus. The thirst for cricket was immense, more than 36,000 spectators attending the opening day. In winning by six wickets, the Australians claimed a 4–1 series victory. Darling's second-innings century, his third of the summer, included a record thirty 4s.

Stoddart was upset by the barracking of the crowds and told the Sydney *Referee*: 'If allowed to go on, it [barracking] will inevitably reduce cricket to a low level, for your better class players, with any sense of feeling, cannot keep on playing under such circumstances'.[10]

A darling of the crowds just three years earlier, Stoddart was considered by most to be a good winner, but a poor loser. He had played his last Test match and was to take his own life, aged fifty-two. The mystical Ranji, too, was not to be seen on Australian shores again. He became a Maharajah and represented his country on the League of Nations. Despite his constant health problems, Ranji's series aggregate of 457 runs was surpassed by only one other Englishman, MacLaren with 488. Richardson, 'the Surrey Catapult', bowed out of Test cricket having taken 22 wickets in the five internationals, including an 8-94 in his last appearance, figures unsurpassed by any bowler on either side.

Such a comprehensive victory was gratifying and appropriate, too, according to the political commentators, with Australia verging on Federation. And when Darling's side retained the Ashes in England in 1899, introducing to Test cricket a young man from Sydney by the name of Victor Trumper, it hastened a riveting, unprecedented golden era for the game of Empire.

Man of the Decade: *Kumar Shri Ranjitsinhji*

No visiting cricketer, not even the mighty Dr W.G. Grace, provoked the heady acclamation or enjoyed the celebrity status of Indian genius Kumar Shri Ranjitsinhji upon his arrival down-under in 1897. Mysterious, colourful and captivating, at his best on faster wickets, 'Ranji' defied traditional textbooks with a sublime artistry that had the veteran professionals shaking their heads in wonderment.

Ranji claimed he 'saw' the ball earlier than most[11] and like Don Bradman years later, his presence at the crease guaranteed 'house full' signs throughout England.

On his celebrated debut at Old Trafford in 1896, Ranji made 62 and 154 not out against a crack Australian attack that included the expresses of Ernie Jones, the seam and guile of Hugh Trumble and the clever change of pace of George Giffen. On the third and final morning with England sinking fast, he accelerated from 41 to 154 with a dazzling array of strokes, including his sublime leg-side flick, which sent even good-length balls on off-stump skidding to the square leg ropes. 'He had the Australian bowlers quite at his mercy,' said Wisden.[12]

His wizardry saw him stroke 47 from 12 balls for the Gentlemen versus the Players at Lord's in a performance rated the finest ever cameo at the home of cricket. His biographer Roland Wild said: 'For years afterwards the cricketing world was divided into two sects – those who *had* and those who had *not* seen Ranji play those twelve balls'.[13]

Ranji fever engulfed all Australia upon his arrival in Adelaide with Drewy Stoddart's team in 1897–98. Australia's White Australia Policy was waived to allow his temporary entry and profiteers moved in for the kill, marketing Ranji matches, Ranji ginger-beer and even Ranji hair restorer. On witnessing his classic 189 on his Australian-soil debut at the Adelaide Oval, an appreciative old miner presented the Indian prince with a small gold nugget.

Ranji's thrilling form continued, too, from the first Test in Sydney when he freewheeled to 175 despite acute tonsillitis, which forced him to bat lower in the order.

Ranji also wrote for the newspapers and created a stir when he suggested Jones's action was anything but pure.

The 1897–98 visit was to be his only trip to Australia. However, he continued to play Tests in England, his average of almost 45 on uncovered wickets being among the highest in the first twenty-five years of Test cricket.

'He was a marvel,' said contemporary Clem Hill. 'It was almost uncanny to watch some of his risky cuts and shots. On a fast and fiery wicket I feel almost inclined to compare him with Trumper (in my opinion the greatest batsman I ever saw) but the New South Welshman was better on a sticky or bad wicket.'[14]

Ranjitsinhji v. Australia

Season	Scores	Runs	Ave
1896	62, 154*, 8, 11	235	78.33
1897–98	175, 8*, 71, 27, 6, 77, 24, 55, 2, 12	457	50.77
1899	42, 93*, 8, 0, 11, 21, 49*, 54	278	46.33
1902	13, 0, 2, 4	19	4.75

* not out

Tests:	15 (all v. Australia)
Runs:	989
Average:	44.95
Highest score:	175, Sydney, 1897–98
100s:	2

Match of the decade: *Sydney, 1894*

In making almost 600 in the first innings, Australia should presumably have won the first Test easily, but the Englishmen under the captaincy of the much-loved Drewy Stoddart refused to buckle in a game noted by an extraordinary all-round contribution from George Giffen. Set 177 to win, Australia made just 166, England's dead-eye-dick left-armers Johnny Briggs and Bobby Peel taking full advantage of a wet spot on the wicket on the sixth and final day.

> **Match scores:** England 325 (Ward 75, Briggs 57, Giffen 4-75) and 437 (Ward 117, Brown 53, Giffen 4-164) defeated Australia 586 (Gregory 201, Giffen 161, Richardson 5-181) and 166 (Darling 53, Giffen 41, Peel 6-67) by 10 runs

Odd spot: *A teetotaller no more*

One of Australia's foremost batsmen Frank Iredale was so short on form he missed selection in the first Test at Lord's in 1896. He failed again in the first innings of the next county match at Nottingham and, as he was preparing to bat in the second innings, legend has it that Australia's captain Harry Trott prescribed a pick-me-up to calm Iredale's nerves. 'We did not know what that stimulant was,' said Iredale's Australian teammate Clem Hill. 'Harry kept it a secret. But later we heard that it was good old brandy and soda . . . and Frank was a

TRAILBLAZERS: The first English team to the Antipodes, 1862. From left: George Wells, Mr Spiers, George Bennett (seated), William Mortlock, Roger Iddison, Billy Caffyn, Mr Mallam, H. H. Stephenson (captain, seated), Tom Sewell, George Griffith, William Mudie, Ned Stephenson (seated), Mr Pond, Charles Lawrence, Tom Hearne.

COLONIAL IMPORT: George Marshall, 31, captained the Victorians in the first 'Grand Match' at the MCG, making 27 and nought and taking 8–0. He was originally from Nottingham.

ADVENTURERS: The first white Australian team to England, 1878. Top row (l–r): Fred Spofforth, Jack Blackham, Charles Bannerman, Billy Murdoch, Tom Kendall. Middle: Dave Gregory (captain), Jack Conway (manager), Harry Boyle. Bottom: Alick Bannerman, Tom Garrett, Tommy Horan, Frank Allan and Joey Palmer.

MAGNIFICENT: The Melbourne Cricket Ground in the lead-up to the first international match, later proclaimed the first Test, in 1877. Its pride and joy, the state-of-the-art grandstand, burnt down just seven years later.

ASHES ORIGINS (below): The mock obituary to English cricket, first published in the *Sporting Times* after Fred Spofforth had inspired a remarkable Australian victory at The Oval in 1882.
Right: The 1882 Australians who won the famous match by seven runs.

In Affectionate Remembrance
OF
ENGLISH CRICKET,
WHICH DIED AT THE OVAL
ON
29th AUGUST, 1882,
Deeply lamented by a large circle of sorrowing
friends and acquaintances.

R. I. P.

N.B.—The body will be cremated and the
ashes taken to Australia.

STALWARTS ALL: Seven of the principals in James Lillywhite's 1881–82 venture, from left: batsman John Selby, left-arm 'expressman' Tom Emmett, captain Lillywhite, entrepreneur Alfred Shaw, stonewaller William Scotton, classy wicketkeeper Richard Pilling and feisty all-rounder George Ulyett.

LIONHEART: Tom Richardson averaged more than five wickets per Test match during two tours in the mid-1890s. He loved the harder wickets of Australia and bowled fast even if it was a heatwave.

INFLUENTIAL: The fourth Lord Harris, George Robert Canning Harris, was a formidable cricketer and even more forceful personality who was horrified by the 'barbaric' pitch invasion in Sydney in 1878–79.

FIRST TIMERS (above): The 1884 Australians who contested the first Test at Lord's, the home of cricket. Top (l–r): George Bonnor, Joey Palmer, Jack Blackham, Harry Boyle. Centre: Fred Spofforth, Billy Murdoch, Alick Bannerman. Bottom: William Cooper, Percy McDonnell, George Giffen, Tup Scott. Billy Midwinter also represented Australia in this series.

GLOBETROTTER (right): All-rounder Harry Trott made four tours to England and was regarded as one of Australia's most astute early captains. He was also a capital field at point.

LONGEVITY (below): Diminutive Syd Gregory's Ashes experience spanned three decades. He was the first to play fifty Ashes Tests. His father Ned also represented Australia.

THE TEAM OF '88: Percy McDonnell's tourists won at Lord's before losing the next two Tests. Back row (l–r): Jack Ferris, Sam Jones, Affie Jarvis, Jack Worrall, Mr Beal (manager), Jack Lyons, Jack Blackham, Harry Boyle, John Edwards. Front: George Bonnor, Charlie 'Terror' Turner, McDonnell (captain), Harry Trott, Alick Bannerman.

A TRIO OF CHAMPIONS: Influential Lord Hawke (left), popular Joe Darling and little Johnnie Briggs, a perennial visitor to Australian shores.

ENGLAND'S GREATEST: Sydney Barnes played when and where he wanted, and marked the fiftieth anniversary of English visits down-under with his riveting spell of 6–5 in Melbourne in 1911–12.

MACLAREN'S MEN: The 1901–02 English tourists included for the first time master-bowler-to-be Sydney Barnes. Standing (l–r): Johnny Tyldesley, Len Braund, Harold Garnett, Major Wardill (secretary, Melbourne Cricket Club), Charles Robson, Barnes, Colin Blythe, John Gunn, Willie Quaife. Sitting: Gilbert Jessop, Tom Hayward, Archie MacLaren (captain), Arthur Jones, Charlie McGahey, Dick Lilley.

HOBBS ARRIVES: Jack Hobbs, Wilfred Rhodes and Ken Hutchings were among an exciting band of youngsters to contest the Ashes in 1907–08. Top row (l–r): Arthur Fielder, Ernie Hayes, Joe Hardstaff, Syd Barnes. Middle: Jack Crawford, Hutchings, Arthur Jones (captain), Freddie Fane, Dick Young. Bottom: Len Braund, Joe Humphries, Hobbs, Colin Blythe, Rhodes.

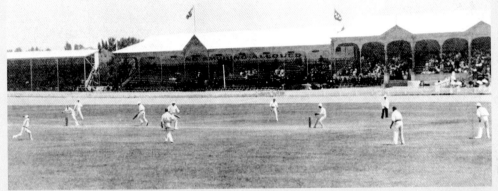

ADELAIDE BLISS (above): Adelaide was the third mainland venue granted an Ashes Test. This one, from 1901–02, sees England's Gilbert Jessop (left) looking to run out Hugh Trumble on the final day. Also caught in mid-pitch is local hero Joe Darling. The Australians chased down 315 in a game which went six days and was notable for Syd Barnes' breakdown.

THREE MORE VISITING GREATS: All-rounder Wilfred Rhodes (left), leg-spinner Len Braund and opening batsman Bobby Abel, who was known for his diminutive stature and waddle to the wicket.

A COLOSSEUM IN THE MAKING (above): The Melbourne Cricket Ground during Barnes' match in 1911–12. Below: One of the rare guides produced for the tour, marking fifty years since the inaugural tour by H.H. Stephenson's All-England Eleven. *John O'Sullivan Collection*

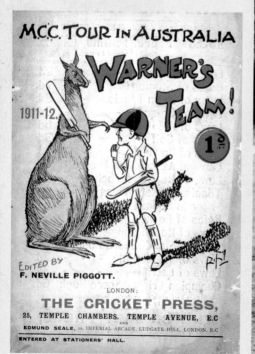

M.C.C. TOUR IN AUSTRALIA

WARNER'S TEAM!

1911-12.

1d.

EDITED BY
F. NEVILLE PIGGOTT.

LONDON:
THE CRICKET PRESS,
25, TEMPLE CHAMBERS, TEMPLE AVENUE, E.C
AND
EDMUND SEALE, 10, IMPERIAL ARCADE, LUDGATE HILL, LONDON, E.C

ENTERED AT STATIONERS' HALL.

ASHES GREATS: The googly bowler Bernard Bosanquet, a Golden Age revelation (opposite), and three early Australian heroes of the new century: Charlie Macartney (left) Warwick Armstrong and Monty Noble (right).

John O'Sullivan Collection

ALL CONQUERING: The 1921 Australians were unbeaten in the Tests under the 'Big Ship', Warwick Armstrong. Below: A smiling Jack Hobbs (with cap, looking down, centre right) is pictured with fellow members of the 1920–21 side.

STAR DEBUTANT (top): Bill Woodfull on strike to Yorkshire's slow-seamer George Macauley at Leeds, 1926. The Victorian schoolteacher was one of the finds of the tour.
Gerry McGinley Collection

Above: Mature-age Jack Hobbs dominated the 1920s, building a particularly formidable record in Melbourne.

A CENTURY BEFORE LUNCH: Legendary Charlie Macartney raced to one of the most memorable Ashes centuries of all after being dropped fourth ball by England's captain Arthur Carr at Headingley in 1926. He was 112 not out at lunch, one of his three centuries on his farewell tour.
Gerry McGinley Collection

OLD MASTERS: Jack Hobbs (left) and Herbert Sutcliffe remain Ashes cricket's most successful set of openers, averaging 86 runs per innings and famously batting through an entire day's play in Melbourne in January 1925.
Gerry McGinley Collection

PRIDE OF ENGLAND (opposite): The 1926 Englishmen played four consecutive draws before winning the last Test under first-time captain Percy Chapman at The Oval, a game notable for the recall of 48-year-old Wilfred Rhodes and six wickets from the Notts express Harold Larwood.

ENGLAND
V
AUSTRALIA

THIRD TEST MATCH

LEEDS.

July 10. 12 & 13. 1926.

LIGHTNING: Bert Oldfield ends a 126-run opening partnership between Jack Hobbs and Herbert Sutcliffe with the leg-side stumping of Hobbs (66) from the bowling of Jack Ryder, on the opening day in Melbourne, 1924–25.
Jim Rutherford Collection

HAMSTRUNG: Arthur Gilligan was MCC's captain and a key new ball bowler in the 1924–25 summer, unable through illness to reproduce his best deeds from the 1924 English summer.

TEMPTING: Don 'Rock' Blackie becomes another victim of the enticing short square boundaries at Adelaide, holing out to Harold Larwood from the bowling of Jack White, handing England a 12-run victory in a seven-day Test in February 1929.

teetotaller too! He made 90-odd not out and followed with three centuries, each we presumed kicked off by the stimulant.'[15]

Looking back: *Clem Hill, Adelaide, 1898*

'In the third Test [1897–98] Joe [Darling] was approaching his century when Johnny Briggs pitched up a ball just outside his leg stump. Darling connected and with a mighty hit sent it square over the eastern gate at the Adelaide Oval. I was told afterwards that the ball bounced and then skimmed along the top of an ice-cream vendor's stall and smashed all of his glasses. I was at the other end and recall we had to wait for some minutes while the ball was being discovered.'[16]

> Clem Hill was Australia's first champion left-hander and the first to aggregate 10,000 first-class runs in Australia.

One for the statisticians: *'The Ashes'*

The term 'the Ashes' was an integral part of cricket reporting in Australia from the mid-1890s. It wasn't freely used in England, however, until 1903–04, when England captain P. F. 'Plum' Warner penned his famous tour account *How We Recovered the Ashes*.

Tests 1890 to 1899

KEY: M Matches **I** Innings **NO** Not out innings **HS** Highest score **BB** Best bowling
5wI 5-wicket innings **10wM** 10-wicket match ***** Not out **#** Second innings **rh** Retired hurt

Series results

	Tests	Aust	Eng	Drawn
1890 (Eng)	2†	0	2	0
1891–92 (Aust)	3	2	1	0
1893 (Eng)	3	0	1	2
1894–95 (Aust)	5	2	3	0
1896 (Eng)	3	1	2	0
1897–98 (Eng)	5	4	1	0
1899	5	1	0	4
Total	**26**	**10**	**10**	**6**
Progressive	56	20	26	10

† *The Test match at Manchester was abandoned without a ball bowled and is excluded.*

Summary

	Runs	Wkts	Ave
Australia	12,020	442	27.19
England	11,566	429	26.96

Highest innings totals

Australia		**England**	
586	Sydney 1894–95 (1st Test)	576	The Oval 1899 (5th Test)
573	Adelaide 1897–98 (3rd Test)	551	Sydney 1897–98 (1st Test)
520	Melbourne 1897–98 (2nd Test)	499	Adelaide 1891–92 (3rd Test)
421	Lord's 1899 (2nd Test)	483	The Oval 1893 (2nd Test)
414	Melbourne 1894–95 (5th Test)	475	Melbourne 1894–95 (2nd Test)#
412	Manchester 1896 (2nd Test)	437	Sydney 1894–95 (1st Test)
411	Adelaide 1894–95 (3rd Test)#		
408	Sydney 1897–98 (1st Test)#		

Lowest completed innings totals

Australia		**England**	
44	The Oval 1896 (3rd Test)#	65	Sydney 1894–95 (4th Test)
53	Lord's 1896 (1st Test)		(one batsman absent)
75	Melbourne 1894–95 (2nd Test)	72	Sydney 1894–95 (4th Test)#
84	The Oval 1896 (3rd Test)		(one batsman absent)
91	The Oval 1893 (2nd Test)		
92	The Oval 1890 (2nd Test)		

Leading run scorers

	M	I	NO	Runs	HS	Ave	100	50
Australia								
J. Darling	18	33	1	1139	178	35.59	3	4
S. E. Gregory	24	42	3	1096	201	28.10	3	4
G. H. S. Trott	21	36	0	884	143	24.55	1	4
F. A. Iredale	14	23	1	807	140	36.68	2	4
C. Hill	11	19	0	783	188	41.21	2	5
G. Giffen	14	26	0	775	161	29.80	1	5
J. J. Lyons	12	23	0	666	134	28.95	1	3
England								
K. S. Ranjitsinhji	12	22	4	970	175	53.88	2	6
A. E. Stoddart	15	28	2	963	173	37.03	2	3
A. C. MacLaren	16	30	3	933	124	34.55	3	3
T. W. Hayward	12	20	2	787	137	43.72	2	3
F. S. Jackson	10	16	1	612	118	40.80	2	2

Hundreds

Australia (17)		England (16)	
3	J. Darling	3	A. C. MacLaren
	S. E. Gregory	2	T. W. Hayward
2	H. Graham		F. S. Jackson
	C. Hill		K. S. Ranjitsinhji
	F. A. Iredale		A. E. Stoddart
1	G. Giffen	1	R. Abel
	J. J. Lyons		J. T. Brown
	C. E. McLeod		W. Gunn
	G. H. S. Trott		A. Shrewsbury
	V. T. Trumper		A. Ward

Highest individual scores

Australia

201	S. E. Gregory at Sydney 1894–95 (1st Test)
188	C. Hill at Melbourne 1897–98 (4th Test)
178	J. Darling at Adelaide 1897–98 (3rd Test)
161	G. Giffen at Sydney 1894–95 (1st Test)
160	J. Darling at Sydney 1897–98 (5th Test)#
143	G. H. S. Trott at Lord's 1896 (1st Test)#
140	F. A. Iredale at Adelaide 1894–95 (3rd Test)#

England

175	K. S. Ranjitsinhji at Sydney 1897–98 (1st Test)
173	A. E. Stoddart at Melbourne 1894–95 (2nd Test)#
154*	K. S. Ranjitsinhji at Manchester 1896 (2nd Test)#
140	J. T. Brown at Melbourne 1894–95 (5th Test)#

Carrying bat through completed innings

J. E. Barrett	67* out of 176 for Australia at Lord's 1890 (1st Test)#
R. Abel	132* out of 307 for England at Sydney 1891–92 (2nd Test)#

500 runs in a series

	Season	M	I	NO	Runs	HS	Ave	100	50
Australia									
J. Darling	1897–98	5	8	0	537	178	67.12	3	–
Also note:									
G. Giffen	1894–95	5	9	0	475	161	52.77	1	3
England									
No instance – best:									
A. C. MacLaren	1897–98	5	10	1	488	124	54.22	2	2

Hundred partnerships

Australia (17)

Partnerships of 150 and over:

221	4th	G. H. S. Trott and S. E. Gregory at Lord's 1896 (1st Test)#
193	3rd	J. Darling and J. Worrall at Sydney 1897–98 (5th Test)#
174	2nd	A. C. Bannerman and J. J. Lyons at Sydney 1891–92 (2nd Test)#
171	4th	G. Giffen and F. A. Iredale at Sydney 1894–95 (1st Test)
165	7th	C. Hill and H. Trumble at Melbourne 1897–98 (4th Test)
		(Australian 7th wicket record against England)
154	9th	S. E. Gregory and J. M. Blackham at Sydney 1897–98 (1st Test)
		(Australian 9th wicket record against all countries)

England (17)

Partnerships of 150 and over:

210	3rd	A. Ward and J. T. Brown at Melbourne 1894–95 (5th Test)#
185	1st	F. S. Jackson and T. W. Hayward at The Oval 1899 (5th Test)
162	5th	A. C. MacLaren and R. Peel at Melbourne 1894–95 (5th Test)
152	2nd	A. Shrewsbury and W. Gunn at Lord's 1893 (1st Test)#
151	1st	W. G. Grace and A. E. Stoddart at The Oval 1893 (2nd Test)

Leading wicket-takers

	Tests	Balls	Mdns	Runs	Wkts	Ave	BB	5wI	10wM
Australia									
G. Giffen	14	4,243	226	1,844	74	24.91	7-128	6	1
H. Trumble	19	4,057	241	1,615	63	25.63	6-30	3	1
E. Jones	14	3,064	130	1,519	56	27.12	7-88	3	1
C. T. B. Turner	11	3,452	250	1,161	51	22.76	6-67	3	–
M. A. Noble	9	1,758	106	791	32	24.71	6-49	2	–
G. H. S. Trott	21	1,863	45	994	29	34.27	4-71	–	–
England									
T. Richardson	14	4,498	191	2,220	88	25.22	8-94	11	4
J. Briggs	17	3,783	189	1,658	63	26.31	6-49	4	2
J. T. Hearne	11	3,005	209	1,070	48	22.29	6-41	4	1
R. Peel	11	2,937	180	1,025	47	21.80	6-23	2	–
G. A. Lohmann	6	1,812	139	478	28	17.07	8-58	1	1
W. H. Lockwood	8	1,486	82	677	26	26.03	7-71	2	–

Five wickets in an innings

Australia (23)		England (28)	
6	G. Giffen	11	T. Richardson
3	E. Jones	4	J. Briggs
	H. Trumble		J. T. Hearne
	C. T. B. Turner	2	W. H. Lockwood
2	M. A. Noble		F. Martin
1	S. T. Callaway		R. Peel
	J. J. Ferris	1	W. M. Bradley
	J. J. Lyons		G. A. Lohmann
	C. E. McLeod		J. W. Sharpe
	R. W. McLeod		
	A. E. Trott		

Best individual bowling

Australia

8-43	A. E. Trott at Adelaide 1894–95 (3rd Test)#
7-88	E. Jones at Lord's 1899 (2nd Test)
7-128	G. Giffen at The Oval 1893 (2nd Test)
6-30	H. Trumble at The Oval 1896 (3rd Test)#
6-49	M. A. Noble at Melbourne 1897–98 (2nd Test)#
6-59	H. Trumble at The Oval 1896 (3rd Test)
6-67	C. T. B. Turner at Lord's 1893 (1st Test)
6-72	G. Giffen at Sydney 1891–92 (2nd Test)#
6-82	E. Jones at Sydney 1897–98 (5th Test)
6-155	G. Giffen at Melbourne 1894–95 (2nd Test)#

England

8-58	G. A. Lohmann at Sydney 1891–92 (2nd Test)
8-94	T. Richardson at Sydney 1897–98 (5th Test)
7-71	W. H. Lockwood at The Oval 1899 (5th Test)
7-168	T. Richardson at Manchester 1896 (2nd Test)
6-23	R. Peel at The Oval 1896 (3rd Test)
6-39	T. Richardson at Lord's 1896 (1st Test)
6-41	J. T. Hearne at The Oval 1896 (3rd Test)
6-49	J. Briggs at Adelaide 1891–92 (3rd Test)
6-50	F. Martin at The Oval 1890 (2nd Test)
6-52	F. Martin at The Oval 1890 (2nd Test)#
6-67	R. Peel at Sydney 1894–95 (1st Test)#
6-76	T. Richardson at Manchester 1896 (2nd Test)#
6-84	J. W. Sharpe at Melbourne 1891–92 (1st Test)
6-87	J. Briggs at Adelaide 1891–92 (3rd Test)#
6-98	J. T. Hearne at Melbourne 1897–98 (4th Test)
6-104	W. H. Lockwood at Lord's 1893 (1st Test)
6-104	T. Richardson at Melbourne 1894–95 (5th Test)#

10 wickets in a match

Australia (3)

12-89	H. Trumble (6-59 and 6-30) at The Oval 1896 (3rd Test)
10-160	G. Giffen (4-88 and 6-72) at Sydney 1891–92 (2nd Test)
10-164	E. Jones (7-88 and 3-76) at Lord's 1899 (2nd Test)

England (9)

13-244	T. Richardson (7-168 and 6-76) at Manchester 1896 (2nd Test)
12-102	F. Martin (6-50 and 6-52) at The Oval 1890 (2nd Test)
12-136	J. Briggs (4-49 and 6-87) at Adelaide 1891–92 (3rd Test)
11-173	T. Richardson (6-39 and 5-134) at Lord's 1896 (1st Test)
10-60	J. T. Hearne (6-41 and 4-19) at The Oval 1896 (3rd Test)
10-142	G. A. Lohmann (8-58 and 2-84) at Sydney 1891–92 (2nd Test)
10-148	J. Briggs (5-34 and 5-114) at The Oval 1893 (2nd Test)
10-156	T. Richardson (5-49 and 5-107) at Manchester 1893 (3rd Test)
10-204	T. Richardson (8-94 and 2-110) at Sydney 1897–98 (5th Test)

Hat-tricks

J. Briggs (Eng) at Sydney 1891–92 (2nd Test)#
   (W. F. Giffen b, J. M. Blackham lbw, S. T. Callaway c W. G. Grace)
J. T. Hearne (Eng) at Leeds 1899 (3rd Test)#
   (C. Hill b, S. E. Gregory c A. C. MacLaren, M. A. Noble c K. S. Ranjitsinhji)

25 wickets in a series

	Season	Tests	Balls	Mdns	Runs	Wkts	Ave	BB	5wI	10wM
Australia										
G. Giffen	1894–95	5	2,126	111	820	34	24.11	6-155	3	–
E. Jones	1899	5	1,276	73	657	26	25.27	7-88	2	1
England										
T. Richardson	1894–95	5	1,748	63	849	32	26.63	6-104	4	–
R. Peel	1894–95	5	1,831	77	721	27	26.70	6-67	1	–
Also note:										
T. Richardson	1896	3	876	58	439	24	18.29	7-168	4	2

Leading wicketkeepers

	Tests	Dismissals	Catches	Stumpings
Australia				
J. J. Kelly	13	18	13	5
J. M. Blackham	9	16	10	6
England				
G. MacGregor	8	17	14	3
A. A. Lilley	7	23	22	1

Leading fieldsmen

Australia	Tests	Catches	England	Tests	Catches
H. Trumble	19	26	W. G. Grace	11	13
G. H. S. Trott	21	21	K. S. Ranjitsinhji	12	13
G. Giffen	14	20			
F. A. Iredale	14	16			
J. Darling	18	15			
S. E. Gregory	24	15			
E. Jones	14	14			
W. Bruce	10	11			

Captains

	Tests	Won	Lost	Drawn	Toss won
Australia					
G. H. S. Trott	8	5	3	0	5
J. M. Blackham	7	2	3	2	4
J. Darling	5	1	0	4	2
G. Giffen	4	2	2	0	3
W. L. Murdoch	2	0	2	0	2
England					
W. G. Grace	11	6	3	2	3
A. E. Stoddart	8	3	4	1	2
A. C. MacLaren	7	1	3	3	5

Most appearances

Australia (38 players)		England (50 players)	
24	S. E. Gregory	17	J. Briggs
21	G. H. S. Trott	16	A. C. MacLaren
19	H. Trumble	15	A. E. Stoddart
18	J. Darling	14	T. Richardson
14	G. Giffen		
	F. A. Iredale		
	E. Jones		

Hat-trick specialist **Hugh Trumble** (left) dwarfs his Australian teammates **Alick Bannerman** and **Billy Bruce**, Oxford University, 1893.
Trumble Family Archives

1900s
GOLDEN TIMES

• •

'This performance of theirs will ever remain a shining example of grit and courage and a glorious tradition for future generations . . .'

So smitten was Australia's captain Joe Darling by the talents of batting virtuoso Victor Trumper during his first tour of England in 1899 that often he'd ask: 'Is Vic aboard?' before allowing the Australians' stagecoach to leave for the ground each morning. The genius of Trumper was to dominate home and away at the turn of the century, his breathtaking assaults at the head of the order giving the Australian XI a new powerful edge.

At his exhilarating best, Trumper was worth two and three men. While others often failed to cope with the wet and sticky wickets of the time, Trumper played with unconcerned majesty, decimating attacks with thrilling shots all around the wicket. Along with left-handers Darling and Clem Hill and the champion and influential all-rounder M.A. 'Monty' Noble – who admired him like no other – Trumper was the cornerstone of one of Australia's most powerful top sixes in the first fifty years of Test cricket.

Noble described Trumper, the player, as 'a genius without compare, the finest and most-loved player of his time, whose modesty and generosity off the field was just as praiseworthy'.[1]

'Coming out of the London Coliseum one cold, wet night he saw a boy shivering in a doorway selling music,' said Noble. 'Victor broke away from the rest of us, spoke to the lad, bought the whole of his stock-in-trade and sent the youngster home happy.'[2]

England's Golden Age teams included a young Sydney Barnes, but even the Staffordshire wizard struggled to contain Trumper. Had he been blessed with a stronger constitution, his performances would have been lauded even more as there were days when he was unwell and lacking the vitality to play with his normal flair and flourish.

The Ashes battles were competitive, high-class contests in the first ten years after the six Australian colonies agreed to become a Commonwealth on 1 January 1901. And they featured some of the most celebrated players in the annals of Anglo-Australian cricket.

In 1901–02, master batsman Archie MacLaren led the last privately organised England team to play Tests in Australia. The Melbourne Cricket Club was again the promoter. Not only cricket was on the agenda, but an early soccer match or two, first-time tourist Colin 'Charlie' Blythe being awarded a gold medal for his man-of-the-match efforts across half-back in an impromptu England v. Fremantle game.[3]

MacLaren had been disadvantaged from the start when Yorkshire's two leading bowlers Wilfred Rhodes and George Hirst bowed to committee pressure and refused invitations, the all-powerful Lord Hawke believing it more important that the pair be fully rested in preparation for Yorkshire's tilt at a third consecutive county championship. Others to also bypass the trip included distinguished amateurs such as the Hon. Stanley Jackson, later to captain England in the epic summer of 1905, C.B. Fry, J.R. Mason and R.E. 'Tip' Foster, a star two years later.

MacLaren had no choice but to blood the uninitiated. In the first Test in Sydney the results were beyond even his headiest expectations, with previously uncapped trio Barnes, Len Braund and Blythe taking all 20 wickets between them as Australia crashed to an innings' defeat.

Barnes's selection seemed an extraordinary gamble as he had played for Lancashire only once, instead preferring to play in local League cricket. He was twenty-eight and strictly fast medium, but he proved to be an inspired selection, helping to win the first Test in Sydney with six wickets. And in the next, in Melbourne, he took 13 more before his knee gave way, forcing him to miss the rest of the series. Braund was an all-round find, his leg-breaks netting him more than 100 wickets for the tour. And only MacLaren was ahead of him in the batting aggregate.

Blythe made a brilliant start with seven wickets on debut before he, too, was injured.

MacLaren batted with composure throughout, with 412 runs. The fielding was also excellent, every bit as athletic as the Australians, but with Barnes sidelined the tourists' bowling reserves were exposed, swinging the fortunes Australia's way. Noble's swerve and seam saw him amass 32 wickets including 7-17 in the New Year's Test in Melbourne. The imposing Hughie Trumble with 28 was equally menacing. He finished the Melbourne Test within an hour on the fourth morning with the hat-trick dismissal of John Gunn, Arthur Jones and Barnes.

England led on the first innings in four of the five Tests, only to be beaten 4–1, the same scoreline as in 1897–98 when MacLaren and Drewy Stoddart interchanged the leadership. Many in their team seemed to struggle with the relentless heat and the duration of games, too, most of the Tests going at least four days and one in Adelaide for six days.

Australia won a fourth series in a row in 1902, Trumper's displays superlative in a wet English summer. It was generally agreed that there had been no finer Australian batsman to visit the UK. And it was to be thirty-six years before his record of eleven on-tour centuries was surpassed, by Don Bradman in 1938.

There were some key changes to Australia's XI approaching the 1903–04 summer, the first to involve an English team as selected by the game's governor, the Marylebone Cricket Club. Darling was in temporary retirement, his place being taken by Noble, while Ernie Jones had played his last Test, leading to the promotion of young Sydney slinger Albert 'Tibby' Cotter.

The MCC was led for the first time by P.F. 'Plum' Warner, whose only Tests previously had been against South Africa. MacLaren had originally been commissioned by the Melbourne Cricket Club to arrange a tour, but with Barnes and Bill Lockwood, hero of the 1902 Old Trafford Test, unavailable, he asked for the tour to be postponed for twelve months. But the MCC was not prepared to delay and sought Marylebone's involvement, beginning the four-year cycle of English visits down-under.

One of Warner's newcomers was the Middlesex amateur, googly specialist Bernard Bosanquet, whose back-of-the-hand deliveries resulted in the ball mysteriously spinning back into, rather than away from, the right-handers. He'd had only a modest county summer, but six of his 26 championship wickets came in one innings in the final match of the season against star-studded Yorkshire at Lord's, compelling proof of his skill. While Rhodes returned the most extraordinary analysis of the tour, a 15-wicket haul on a rain-affected wicket in Melbourne, Bosanquet's spell of 5-12 in the fourth Test in Sydney effectively won back the Ashes. Warner had been responsible for unearthing Bosanquet five years previously and some felt the old Etonian's performances had not deserved a place, but his all-round contributions were crucial as England recovered the Ashes 3–2. He revelled on a fast Sydney wicket, his well-disguised googly zipping back rapidly to the discomfort of all. 'Except when Rhodes and (Ted) Arnold put Victoria out for 15,' said Warner, 'nothing more startling was done with the ball during the tour. Unkind people have said that I "ran" Bosanquet into this team because he was a friend of mine, but on his day he rivalled [George] Hirst and Braund as an allround cricketer . . . and when he gets a length, he is, on hard wickets, about the most difficult bowler there is.'[4]

Rain shaped many of the finishes, the feature game of the tour being the first in Sydney. Foster, on his long-awaited debut, scored a massive 287, the highest in the first fifty years of Test cricket; Trumper replied with a joyous 185 not out when all seemed lost. The English ran down almost 200 in the fourth innings to win by five wickets, opener Tom Hayward's chanceless 91 pivotal in the win. Foster, the 25-year-old son of a clergy-man, made a record 214 runs on the third day, the last two English wickets adding 245 in a rare run spree. Three of the Australians – Jack Saunders, Bill Howell and Frank Laver – each conceded 100-plus runs. The run out of Hill in Australia's second innings caused such a furore that Warner threatened to take his players from the field. Hill had attempted a risky fifth run and was clearly upset by umpire Bob Crockett's decision. The English fielders side-on to the wicket felt the Australian short of his crease by a foot. The barracking was loud and vociferous and continued unabated on resumption, one yelling: 'How much did you pay Crockett, Warner?'[5]

Warner said the 'yelling and hissing' was so loud that even 'hardened Test match players Hirst and Rhodes were quite upset'.[6]

'There was absolutely no excuse for this demonstration which was as disgraceful as it was unwarranted,' Warner said. 'It was started [too] from the member's pavilion, from which point it was impossible to see what had occurred.'

Writing in the *Daily Mail*, former Australian Frank Iredale said Warner had fuelled the demonstration by walking towards the pavilion.

Trumper's spectacular batting after the tea interval saw him advance his score from seven to 119 in a 100-minute session, 64 of the runs coming in the last forty minutes.

The six-day Test remains one of the finest ever contested at the Sydney Cricket Ground. 'The Australians deserved as much credit as we did,' said Warner, 'for I cannot recollect another instance of a side which, going in 292 in arrears, eventually sets its opponent nearly 200 runs to win. This performance of theirs will ever remain a shining example of grit and courage and a glorious tradition for future generations.'[7]

With 31 wickets and 126 runs, Rhodes was England's outstanding player and the difference between the teams.

After the Englishmen confirmed their superiority in 1905 with a 2–0 series win, a new-look Australia, including four debutants, played with increasing command to all but inflict the biggest ever defeat upon a touring team from the old country. Arthur Jones's 1907–08 Englishmen were beaten 4–1, mirroring the series results of 1897–98 and 1901–02. Jones fell ill and figured in only the final two Tests, England's replacement captain being Freddie Fane.

In Melbourne, where the tourists won by one wicket, the game could easily have been tied at 663 runs each but for a wild shy from a teenage Gerry Hazlitt, which allowed England's last pair of Barnes and Arthur Fielder to scamper the winning run. Racing in from cover, all Hazlitt had to do was flick the ball back to wicketkeeper H. 'Sammy' Carter and Fielder, who had hesitated, would have been run out by yards. But in the excitement of the moment, Hazlitt's death-or-glory throw missed everything and Fielder, having made his ground, continued to run flat out towards the pavilion before being mobbed by his teammates. Jack Hobbs, playing his first Test, said: 'No Derby, no race won produced a greater thrill.'[8]

Five of England's top six batsmen from 1905, including captain F.S. Jackson, the hero of the hour, were unavailable for the tour and the weakened line-up could not deliver the knockout blow, despite being in winning positions in virtually every match. George Gunn, co-opted into the side on the eve of the first Test, and Hobbs, who turned twenty-five in mid-tour, were the only two to make any consistent headway against the left-armer Saunders, who took 31 wickets in five Tests in the summer of his life.

Among the Australians new to Test cricket, Charles Macartney, Carter and Vernon Ransford were all to have auspicious careers. The menacing Cotter continued to emerge, too, before being sidelined in mid-series.

The most remarkable Test was in Adelaide in mid-January, temperatures soaring beyond 40 degrees. England had established a 78-run lead on the first innings and had Australia 180-7 on the fourth day before seasoned Queenslander Roger Hartigan, making his debut, and Clem Hill, held back to No. 9 after a bout of influenza, shared a matchwinning eighth wicket stand of 243 in four hours, a record for any wicket at the time. Hartigan's polished 116 included three chances, one to Melbourne hero Fielder when he'd made just 32. So overcome was Hill (160) by illness and the heat that he was vomiting and on the verge of collapse in his last hour at the crease. He did not field in the final innings, his place being taken by his brother Roy. He too had been dropped early, at 22, by Barnes. When Hill square cut Rhodes to the boundary to reach one of the great Test 100s, 'the crowd threw hats and sticks in the air with wild abandon'.[9]

Hartigan, twenty-eight, worked for a Brisbane auction house and had been granted only a week's leave. He had reached 105 not out at the end of day four and was relieved when his employers sent a telegram: 'Stay as long as you are making runs.'[10]

Set 429, England was bowled out for 183, having at one stage been 15-3. Hobbs was among the early ones to exit, too, having retired hurt after being struck first ball by Saunders. Both Saunders and local boy, debutant Jack O'Connor, a late inclusion for the injured Cotter, took five wickets.

In Melbourne, when Australia reclaimed the Ashes, Trumper was out for a pair. But he hit back in the final Test in Sydney with 166 in four breathtaking hours as Australia again came from behind to win.

Australians Warren Bardsley and Bill Whitty and the emerging Kent left-hander Frank Woolley were among those promoted into Test ranks during Australia's 1909 tour, which saw the Ashes retained 2–1. England had won the first Test at Edgbaston after left-arm pair George Hirst and Blythe shared all 20 wickets between them – shades of Turner and Ferris years before.

This was to be Trumper's fourth and final tour. It was also 'Monty'

Noble's English farewell. He led with great flair and acumen and also was blessed at the toss, calling correctly five times in a row. In Armstrong and Bardsley, the first Australian to amass more than 2000 runs on tour, Noble also possessed the two leading players on either side.

Trouble was looming, however, with the players bucking at the cricket board's power plays, resulting, in 1912, in Australia's best six cricketers, including everyone's hero Trumper, all standing down from the Triangular Tests, an impasse which dismayed cricket lovers at home and throughout the Mother Country.

Man of the decade: *Victor Trumper*

Victor Trumper's reputation as the outstanding wet-weather batsman of the Golden Age advanced to a heady new stratosphere during the 1902 tour of England when he amassed eleven centuries on his way to more than 2,500 runs. Included was a thrilling century before lunch on a sticky wicket on the opening day at Old Trafford where Australia triumphed in one of the finest finishes of all.

No Australian of his era played with Trumper's flair or effortless majesty. He so dictated that England's master bowler Sydney Barnes considered it a feat to keep Trumper quiet, let alone dismiss him. 'He played as he liked, not as you liked,' Barnes said.[11]

Trumper's career average was under 40, but in the era of uncovered wickets batting was tough, especially in England. 'Throughout the [1902] season he played the best bowling on the worst wickets with consummate ease and breathtaking brilliance,' according to author Patrick Morrah. 'It is significant that although he made eleven centuries, his highest score was 128. Time and again he threw away his wicket when there was no particular reason for keeping it.'[12]

The most modest of champions, Trumper seemed genuinely embarrassed by the acclamation his feats generated, especially in his home town Sydney where he made three of his six Ashes centuries including 185 not out during his prolific 1903–04 summer. Out for just one in the first innings of the opening Test of the series, his audacious 185 in the second innings, having been shuffled down the order to No. 5, was a dazzling exhibition, his century coming in better than even time. Twice he hit four 4s in an over, Len Braund's fifth over going for 20. From being hopelessly behind on the first innings, Trumper's exciting solo gave Australia a sniff of an improbable victory, the Englishmen losing four early wickets chasing 194 before steadying.

In the following rain-plagued Test in Melbourne, the game in which the wily Yorkshireman Wilfred Rhodes claimed 15 wickets, Trumper topscored in each innings with 74 and 35, the Australians being bowled out in under two hours in both the first and second innings.

Biographer and ex-Australian Jack Fingleton claimed Trumper to even be Bradman's superior, 'classically dissecting everything that was offered against him'.[13] Even taking into account the enmity that existed between Fingleton and Bradman, it was extraordinary praise that cannot be dismissed lightly given Fingleton's standing as Australia's leading cricketer-writer. 'No cricketer, surely, has known such love and abject affection from his fellow men,' wrote Fingleton.[14]

Trumper v. England   * not out

Season	Scores	Runs	Ave
1899	0, 11, 135*, 12, 32, 14, 63, 6, 7	280	35.00
1901–02	2, 34, 0, 16, 65, 25, 7, 25, 27, 18	219	21.90
1902	18, 15, 1, 62, 104, 4, 42, 2	247	30.88
1903–04	1, 185*, 74, 35, 113, 59, 7, 12, 88, 0	574	63.77
1905	13, 0*, 31, 8, 0, 11, 30, 4, 28	125	17.85
1907–08	43, 3, 49, 64, 4, 0, 0, 0, 10, 166	338	33.80
1909	10, 1, 28, 27*, 2, 2, 48, 73, 20	211	26.37
1911–12	113, 14, 13, 2, 26, 1*, 17, 28, 5, 50	269	29.88

Tests v. England:	40 (48 overall)
Runs:	2,263 (3,163)
Average:	32.79 (39.04)
Highest score:	185 not out, Sydney, 1903–04 (214 not out)
100s:	6 (8)

Match of the decade: *Melbourne, 1907–08*

Jack Hobbs's debut Test ended in pandemonium when tailenders Sydney Barnes and Arthur Fielder stole a suicide single to give England a series-squaring one-wicket victory. The match would have been tied had cover point Gerry Hazlitt simply flicked the ball to the wicketkeeper, rather than trying to throw the stumps down himself. His throw was wide and the winning run stolen. Barnes had met No. 11 Fielder as he came to the wicket and said: 'C'mon Pip, we'll knock 'em off now'.[15] Set 282, the Englishmen were 209-8 and then 243-9 before the famous last stand triggered the most gripping of finishes.

Match scores: England 382 (Hobbs 83, Hutchings 126, Cotter 5-142) and 9-282 (Fane 50) defeated Australia 266 (Noble 61, Crawford 5-79) and 397 (Trumper 63, Macartney 54, Noble 64, Armstrong 77, Carter 53, Barnes 5-72) by 1 wicket

Odd spot: *One-Test wonder*

Googly specialist Douglas Carr was thirty-seven and in his first season of county cricket with Kent when selected for the first time against the 1909 Australians at The Oval.

Opening the bowling, he claimed 3-19 in his first seven overs (Syd Gregory, 'Monty' Noble and Warwick Armstrong) before being collared and finishing with match figures of 7-282. He was not selected again.

Looking back: *Charlie Macartney, Sydney, 1907*

'The first surprise of the game came after the fall of the first wicket . . . to my astonishment the name of GUNN came up on the board. I have no doubt that Noble, our skipper, knew he had been included in the opposing team, but several of us did not and personally I wondered who this person could be. However, George Gunn did not let us forget him, as we did not get rid of him until he had compiled 119 by splendid cricket, the chief feature of his batting being the extraordinarily easy method he had of dealing with fast bowling. Gunn came out to Australia with the English team for a health trip and it was not expected that he would play at all . . . [and] he played in every Test of the series that year.'[16]

Macartney, twenty-one, was playing the first of his 35 Tests. Among his many distinctions was a century before lunch in the 1926 Ashes Test at Leeds.

One for the statisticians: *An unforgettable entry*

R. E. 'Tip' Foster's 287 in Sydney in 1903–04 remains the highest individual score by any player on his Test debut. It is also the highest Test score by a visiting Englishman to Australia and was the highest score in all Test cricket until 1929–30. His match aggregate of 306 runs on debut is also an Ashes record.

Tests 1901–02 to 1909

KEY: M Matches **I** Innings **NO** Not out innings **HS** Highest score **BB** Best bowling
5wI 5-wicket innings **10wM** 10-wicket match ***** Not out **#** Second innings **rh** Retired hurt

Series results

	Tests	Aust	Eng	Drawn
1901–02 (Aust)	5	4	1	0
1902 (Eng)	5	2	1	2
1903–04 (Aust)	5	2	3	0
1905 (Eng)	5	0	2	3
1907–08 (Aust)	5	4	1	0
1909 (Eng)	5	2	1	2
Total	30	14	9	7
Progressive	86	34	35	17

Summary

	Runs	Wkts	Ave
Australia	13, 229	523	25.29
England	13, 248	495	26.76

Highest innings totals

Australia		England	
506	Adelaide 1907–08 (3rd Test)#	577	Sydney 1903–04 (1st Test)
485	Sydney 1903–04 (1st Test)#	464	Sydney 1901–02 (1st Test)
422	Sydney 1907–08 (5th Test)#	446	Manchester 1905 (4th Test)
421	Lord's 1899 (2nd Test)	430	The Oval 1905 (5th Test)
		426-5 dec	Nottingham 1905 (1st Test)#

Lowest completed innings totals

Australia		England	
36^	Birmingham 1902 (1st Test)	61	Melbourne 1903–04 (5th Test)
74	Birmingham 1909 (1st Test)	61	Melbourne 1901–02 (1st Test)
86	Manchester 1902 (4th Test)#	87	Leeds 1909 (5th Test)#
			(one batsman absent)
		99	Sydney 1901–02 (4th Test)#

^ *lowest total in Australia v. England Tests*

Leading run scorers

	M	I	NO	Runs	HS	Ave	100	50
Australia								
V. T. Trumper	30	55	3	1714	185*	32.96	4	7
C. Hill	25	47	1	1603	160	34.84	2	9
M. A. Noble	30	54	3	1432	133	28.07	1	11
W. W. Armstrong	27	48	7	1232	133*	30.04	1	3
R. A. Duff	19	34	1	1079	146	32.69	2	5
S. E. Gregory	24	45	4	1013	112	24.70	1	4
V. S. Ransford	10	19	4	641	143*	42.73	1	3

	M	I	NO	Runs	HS	Ave	100	50
England								
J. T. Tyldesley	24	42	1	1339	138	32.65	3	8
A. C. MacLaren	19	31	1	998	140	33.26	2	3
T. W. Hayward	17	31	0	960	91	30.96	–	9
L. C. Braund	20	36	3	830	103*	25.15	2	2
Hon. F. S. Jackson	10	17	3	803	144*	57.35	3	4
W. Rhodes	23	38	12	712	69	27.38	–	3

Hundreds

Australia (15)		England (17)	
4	V. T. Trumper	3	Hon. F. S. Jackson
2	W. Bardsley		J. T. Tyldesley
	R. A. Duff	2	L. C. Braund
	C. Hill		G. Gunn
1	W. W. Armstrong		A. C. MacLaren
	S. E. Gregory	1	R. E. Foster
	R. J. Hartigan		C. B. Fry
	M. A. Noble		K. L. Hutchings
	V. S. Ransford		G. L. Jessop
			J. Sharp

Highest individual scores

Australia

185*	V. T. Trumper at Sydney 1903–04 (1st Test)#
166	V. T. Trumper at Sydney 1907–08 (5th Test)#
160	C. Hill at Adelaide 1907–08 (3rd Test)#
146	R. A. Duff at The Oval 1905 (5th Test)
143*	V. S. Ransford at Lord's 1909 (2nd Test)

England

287	R. E. Foster at Sydney 1903–04 (1st Test)
	(highest individual score for England in Australia and the record by any batsman on Test debut)
144*	F. S. Jackson at Leeds 1905 (3rd Test)
144	C. B. Fry at The Oval 1905 (5th Test)
140	A. C. MacLaren at Nottingham 1905 (1st Test)#

Century in each innings

136 and 130	W. Bardsley (Aust) at The Oval 1909 (5th Test)
	(first instance in Test cricket)

500 runs in a series

	Season	M	I	NO	Runs	HS	Ave	100	50
Australia									
V. T. Trumper	1903–04	5	10	1	574	185*	63.77	2	3
C. Hill	1901–02	5	10	0	521	99	52.10	–	4
England									
No instance – best:									
Hon. F. S. Jackson	1905	5	9	2	492	144*	70.28	2	2
R. E. Foster	1903–04	5	9	1	486	287	60.75	1	–

Hundred partnerships

Australia (17)

Partnerships of 150 and over:

243	8th	R. J. Hartigan and C. Hill at Adelaide 1907–08 (3rd Test)#
		(Australian 8th wicket record against all countries)
180	1st	S. E. Gregory and W. Bardsley at The Oval 1909 (5th Test)#
162	4th	M. A. Noble and S. E. Gregory at Adelaide (3rd Test)#

England (28)

Partnerships of 150 and over:

192	5th	R. E. Foster and L. C. Braund at Sydney 1903–04 (1st Test)
158	6th	J. T. Tyldesley and R. H. Spooner at The Oval (5th Test)#
154	1st	A. C. MacLaren and T. W. Hayward at Sydney 1901–02 (1st Test)
151	4th	C. B. Fry and Hon. F. S. Jackson at The Oval 1905 (5th Test)
Also note:		
130	10th	R. E. Foster and W. Rhodes at Sydney 1903–04 (1st Test)
		(English 10th wicket record against all countries)

Leading wicket-takers

	Tests	Balls	Mdns	Runs	Wkts	Ave	BB	5wI	10wM
Australia									
M. A. Noble	30	5,087	247	2,069	83	24.92	7-17	7	2
H. Trumble	12	3,838	207	1,330	78	17.05	8-65	6	2
J. V. Saunders	12	3,268	108	1,620	64	25.31	5-28	5	–
A. Cotter	12	2,468	36	1,368	55	24.87	7-148	6	–
W. W. Armstrong	27	4,530	246	1,538	48	32.04	6-35	3	–
F. J. Laver	11	2,201	114	894	33	27.09	8-31	2	–
C. G. Macartney	10	1,377	54	524	26	20.15	7-58	1	1
England									
W. Rhodes	23	3,960	146	1,801	81	22.23	8-68	6	1
S. F. Barnes	12	3,,595	172	1,388	67	20.71	7-60	8	1
G. H. Hirst	16	2706	87	1,219	46	26.50	5-48	3	–
L. C. Braund	20	3,733	140	1,769	46	38.45	8-81	3	–
C. Blythe	9	2,085	99	877	41	21.39	6-44	3	1
J. N. Crawford	5	1,426	36	742	30	24.73	5-48	3	–
A. Fielder	6	1,491	42	711	26	27.34	6-82	1	–
B. J. T. Bosanquet	7	970	10	604	25	24.16	8-107	2	–
E. G. Arnold	8	1,365	47	689	25	27.56	4-28	–	–

Five wickets in an innings

Australia (32)		England (38)	
7	M. A. Noble	8	S. F. Barnes
6	A. Cotter	6	W. Rhodes
	H. Trumble	3	C. Blythe
5	J. V. Saunders		L. C. Braund
3	W. W. Armstrong		J. N. Crawford
2	F. J. Laver		G. H. Hirst
1	C. G. Macartney		W. H. Lockwood
	C. E. McLeod	2	B. J. T. Bosanquet
	J. D. A. O'Connor	1	W. Brearley
			D. W. Carr
			A. Fielder
			J. R. Gunn
			F. S. Jackson
			A. E. Relf
			A. Warren

Best individual bowling

Australia

8-31	F. J. Laver at Manchester 1909 (4th Test)
	(best innings analysis for Australia in England)
8-65	H. Trumble at The Oval 1902 (5th Test)
7-17	M. A. Noble at Melbourne 1901–02 (2nd Test)
7-28	H. Trumble at Melbourne 1903–04 (5th Test)#
7-58	C. G. Macartney at Leeds 1909 (3rd Test)
7-64	F. J. Laver at Nottingham 1905 (1st Test)
7-100	M. A. Noble at Sydney 1903–04 (4th Test)
7-148	A. Cotter at The Oval 1905 (5th Test)
6-35	W. W. Armstrong at Lord's 1909 (2nd Test)#
6-40	A. Cotter at Melbourne 1903–04 (5th Test)
6-52	M. A. Noble at Sheffield 1902 (3rd Test)#
6-53	H. Trumble at Manchester 1902 (4th Test)#
6-60	M. A. Noble at Melbourne 1901–02 (2nd Test)#
6-74	H. Trumble at Adelaide 1901–02 (3rd Test)#
6-95	A. Cotter at The Oval 1909 (5th Test)
6-98	M. A. Noble at Melbourne 1901–02 (5th Test)#
6-101	A. Cotter at Sydney 1907–08 (1st Test)

Best individual bowling

England

8-68	W. Rhodes at Melbourne 1903–04 (2nd Test)#
8-81	L. C. Braund at Melbourne 1903–04 (5th Test)
8-107	B. J. T. Bosanquet at Nottingham 1905 (1st Test)#
7-17	W. Rhodes at Birmingham 1902 (1st Test)
7-56	W. Rhodes at Melbourne 1903–04 (2nd Test)
7-60	S. F. Barnes at Sydney 1907–08 (5th Test)
7-121	S. F. Barnes at Melbourne 1901–02 (2nd Test)#
6-42	S. F. Barnes at Melbourne 1901–02 (1st Test)
6-44	C. Blythe at Birmingham 1909 (1st Test)
6-48	W. H. Lockwood at Manchester 1902 (4th Test)
6-49	S. F. Barnes at Sheffield 1902 (3rd Test)
6-51	B. J. T. Bosanquet at Sydney 1903–04 (4th Test)#
6-63	S. F. Barnes at Leeds 1909 (3rd Test)#
6-82	A. Fielder at Sydney 1907–08 (1st Test)

10 wickets in a match

Australia (5)

13-77	M. A. Noble (7-17 and 6-60) at Melbourne 1901–02 (2nd Test)
	(best match analysis for Australia in Australia)
12-173	H. Trumble (8-65 and 4-108) at The Oval 1902 (5th Test)
11-85	C. G. Macartney (7-58 and 4-27) at Leeds 1909 (3rd Test)
11-103	M. A. Noble (5-651 and 6-52) at Sheffield 1902 (3rd Test)
10-128	H. Trumble (4-75 and 6-53) at Manchester 1902 (4th Test)

England (4)

15-124	W. Rhodes (7-56 and 8-68) at Melbourne 1903–04 (2nd Test)
	(best match analysis for England in Australia)
13-163	S. F. Barnes (6-42 and 7-121) at Melbourne 1901–02 (2nd Test)
11-76	W. H. Lockwood (6-48 and 5-28) at Manchester 1902 (4th Test)

Hat-tricks

H. Trumble (Aust) at Melbourne 1901–02 (2nd Test)#
  (A. O. Jones c J. Darling, J. R. Gunn c E. Jones, S. F. Barnes c and b)
H. Trumble (Aust) at Melbourne 1903–04 (5th Test)#
  (B. J. T. Bosanquet c D. R. A. Gehrs, P. F. Warner c and b, A. A. Lilley lbw)

25 wickets in a series

	Season	Tests	Balls	Mdns	Runs	Wkts	Ave	BB	5wl	10wM
Australia										
M. A. Noble	1901–02	5	1,380	68	608	32	19.00	7-17	4	1
J. V. Saunders	1907–08	5	1,603	52	716	31	23.09	5-28	3	–
H. Trumble	1901–02	5	1,604	93	561	28	20.03	6-74	2	–
H. Trumble	1902	3	1,036	55	371	26	14.26	8-65	2	2
Also note:										
H. Trumble	1903–04	4	1,198	59	398	24	16.58	7-28	2	–

	Season	Tests	Balls	Mdns	Runs	Wkts	Ave	BB	5wl	10wM
England										
W. Rhodes	1903–04	5	1,032	36	488	31	15.74	8-68	3	1
J. N. Crawford	1907–08	5	1,426	36	742	30	24.73	5-48	3	–
A. Fielder	1907–08	4	1,299	31	627	25	25.08	8-82	1	–
Also note:										
S. F. Barnes	1907–08	5	1,640	74	626	24	26.08	7-60	2	–

Leading wicketkeepers

	Tests	Dismissals	Catches	Stumpings
Australia				
J. J. Kelly	20	37	26	11
H. Carter	10	21	14	7
England				
A. A. Lilley	25	61	43	18

Leading fieldsmen

	Tests	Catches		Tests	Catches
Australia			**England**		
W. W. Armstrong	27	25	L. C. Braund	20	37
M. A. Noble	30	22	A. C. MacLaren	19	22
H. Trumble	12	19	W. Rhodes	23	22
V. T. Trumper	30	18	A. O. Jones	11	13
C. Hill	25	17	J. T. Tyldesley	24	12
R. A. Duff	19	13	G. H. Hirst	16	11

Captains

	Tests	Won	Lost	Drawn	Toss won
Australia					
M. A. Noble	15	8	5	2	11
J. Darling	13	4	4	5	3
H. Trumble	2	2	0	0	1
England					
A. C. MacLaren	15	3	8	4	6
Hon. F. S. Jackson	5	2	0	3	5
P. F. Warner	5	3	2	0	2
F. L. Fane	3	1	2	0	1
A. O. Jones	2	0	2	0	1

Most appearances

Australia (28 players)		England (47 players)	
30	M. A. Noble	25	A. A. Lilley
	V. T. Trumper	24	J. T. Tyldesley
27	W. W. Armstrong	23	W. Rhodes
25	C. Hill	19	A. C. MacLaren
24	S. E. Gregory		
20	J. J. Kelly		
19	R. A. Duff		

Batting virtuoso **Victor Trumper** (left) with fellow Australian tourists to the UK, 1899. *Trumble Family Archives*

1910s
AN UNHOLY ROW

••

'. . . Hill leant across the table and struck McAlister, beginning an infamous fifteen-minute brawl . . . and both men left bloodied and bruised.'

As bunfights go, this was the full monty. In Victor Trumper, Clem Hill, Warwick Armstrong and co., Australia boasted some of the most formidable and celebrated cricketers in its history; true champions of the Dominion who hastened the good times and ensured cricket's standing as the sport of Empire. Trumper and Hill, in particular, were the personality and face of the game down-under, commanding enormous popularity, power and clout.

For the first thirty years of Australian Test cricket, the players had selected their own teams, negotiated their own tours and held financial control. In 1905, however, the Board of Control was established and gradually expanded, leading to a more democratic voice. Keen to flex its new standing, the Board suspended the entire New South Wales XI for daring to be a party to the Melbourne Cricket Club's attempts to organise another trip to England. While the ban was soon lifted and the players again promised the equal split of profits they had previously enjoyed on tours of the UK, it was agreed that the Board of Control and *neither* the MCC *nor* the NSW Cricket Association would be responsible for organising future tours, a crucial leverage point that triggered the deepest of rifts.

Provocatively, the Board appointed its own selection chairman in ex-player Peter McAlister, who as a 40-year-old had not only named himself in the 1909 touring party, but had appointed himself vice-captain and treasurer. Hill was so disgusted he immediately withdrew. Until then, Australian teams had been chosen by the captain and the two next most senior players. Hill and others felt McAlister had merely been planted as a stool pigeon, reporting back to officialdom. Well past his best as a player, McAlister was included in only two Tests, which were both won by Australia, and averaged 16.

The elite players were further incensed when the Board refused to ratify Frank Laver's re-appointment as manager of the 1912 team to England. Six went on strike: Hill, Trumper, Armstrong, Vernon Ransford, H. 'Sammy' Carter and A. 'Tibby' Cotter.

Months earlier the uneasy, festering relationship between administration and players had plummeted to a new low when McAlister and Hill fought like wild dogs on the third-floor boardroom of the NSW Cricket Association. They were supposed to have been selecting Australia's next Test team. Sunny-natured and normally implacable, Hill's temper boiled over when McAlister boasted he was a superior captain to Hill, Armstrong and Victor Trumper. Furthermore, monumental tactical errors by Hill in Adelaide, he said, had handed victory on a plate to England.

The next twenty minutes were as explosive as any in Australian cricket history as McAlister and Hill traded barbs leading to an all-in.

McALISTER: You're the worst captain I've seen.

HILL: You have been asking for a punch in the jaw all
night . . . and I'll give you one.[1]

According to *The Australasian*, Hill leant across the table and struck McAlister, beginning an infamous fifteen-minute brawl, which resulted in papers being strewn around the room, furniture upturned and both men left bloodied and bruised.

It was an extraordinary backdrop to an enthralling Ashes battle, which for the first time down-under saw the Englishmen win four Tests in a row. They had been 1–0 down after the opening match in Sydney. It was a comeback to savour, especially with England's captain and leading batsman P.F. 'Plum' Warner falling seriously ill after the opening match in Adelaide and failing to take any part in the Tests. He'd been hospitalised after making 151 and had to spend six weeks convalescing in a Sydney nursing home. 'I was desperately ill,' he wrote later, 'and I owe my life to the skill of Mr [Sir Charles] Blackburn and the most devoted nursing and care.'[2]

On Warner's recommendation, Johnny Douglas, a one-Test medium pacer, was named as his replacement. 'I know of no cricketer who is a finer or keener fighter,' said Warner. 'All his energy and determination are thrown into the game and he never knows when he is beaten. He inspired the side with remarkable zeal.'[3]

Having lost the opening Test when Douglas, a medium-pacer of modest skill but unflinching endeavour, dared open the bowling ahead of England's Rolls-Royce Sydney Barnes, England was to win the next four matches in a row, in Melbourne (twice), Sydney and Adelaide, where the South Australian Cricket Association proudly unveiled its new modern scoreboard, the equal of any in the east.

It was a remarkable transformation by the visitors, and while Douglas was overshadowed by the deadly pairing of Frank Foster and Barnes, his 5-46 from third change in the fourth Test in Melbourne enabled England to win by an innings and gave it an unassailable 3–1 series lead. This was the game in which Jack Hobbs and Wilfred Rhodes opened with a record 323 for the first wicket, being separated only late on the second day as England totalled an unassailable 589.

While Barnes's onslaught on the opening morning of the second Test was the tour highlight – he took 4-1 from his first seven overs – there were some other great moments, E.J. 'Tiger' Smith's pre-planned leg-side stumping of Hill in Adelaide, Hobbs's three centuries in three Tests and gifted left-hander Frank Woolley's 133 in the final Test in Sydney.

The Englishmen won twelve and drew five of their eighteen games, their only loss all tour coming in the first Test dominated by Trumper, who made a chanceless 113 from No. 5, and the mature-age leg-spinner H.V. 'Ranji' Hordern, who claimed 12 wickets in one of the great Ashes debuts. Overall, the 28-year-old dentist collected 32 wickets, just two behind Barnes. The fifth Test in late February in Sydney spilled into a seventh day, two full days being washed out. In what proved to be their farewell Tests, Trumper made five and 50 and Hill 20 and eight.

The recalled Sid Gregory, then forty-one, was to lead the 1912 Australians in the absence of the rebels. It was to be an ill-fated venture and Australia's last tour before World War I. A team to tour South Africa in 1914–15 was also chosen under the captaincy of Armstrong; Hill, Trumper, Hordern and Vernon Ransford were among those unavailable. The tour was soon abandoned with the outbreak of war in Europe.

Trumper's health, always a concern, was declining rapidly and in 1915 he was to die of Bright's disease, aged thirty-seven, his funeral bringing Sydney to a standstill. There had been no more loved or admired player of the mighty Golden Age.

Man of the decade: *Sydney Barnes*

Temperamental, enigmatic and mercurial, Sydney Barnes was an extraordinarily fine bowler, maybe the greatest ever, a master of seam and swerve. His old captain Archie MacLaren once declared all he ever had to do was hand the ball to Barnes and his troubles were over.[4] On one humid Melbourne Saturday in 1911–12, Barnes was responsible for the most sensational Ashes burst of them all when five frontline Australians succumbed for six in eleven overs: Warren Bardsley first-ball for nought, Clem Hill four, Charlie Kellaway two, Warwick Armstrong four and Roy Minnett two.

In atmospheric conditions, ideal particularly on the first morning for swing bowling, Australia was bowled out for 184 and 299, England squaring the series 1–1.

With 5-44 and 3-96, Barnes was the mastermind behind England's eight-wicket win and their 4–1 Ashes victory. Then thirty-eight, Barnes took 34 wickets and his junior partner, left-arm seamer Frank Foster, took 32.

Barnes had been miffed at being relegated to first-change duties in the opening Test in Sydney, a decision crucial in the match fortunes. England's stand-in captain Johnny Douglas did not repeat his mistake in Melbourne and Barnes was supreme, dodging and hooping the ball like it was a two-piecer. Australian captain Hill, the world's No. 1 batsman, received in succession: an off-break, an inswinger, an outswinger and an off-cutter, which pitched on his leg-stump and hit off. Afterwards he said he'd never before faced such an over[5] and had the conditions not improved, 'he [Barnes] would have dismissed the best 11 batsmen in the world for under 100'.[6]

Many rate Barnes as England's finest ever bowler, dwarfing Maurice Tate, Alec Bedser, Freddie Trueman and any of the moderns.

Not only could he move the ball in the air and off the pitch, he had a quick leg-break, spun so venomously that it was known to tear lumps out of the turf.[7]

Remarkably, Barnes was plucked directly from Lancashire League ranks into the 1901–02 Australian tour. Years later he told his biographer Leslie Duckworth: 'I don't think I ever got over the questions which were asked when [captain] Archie MacLaren surprised everybody by picking me straight from

Burnley. I determined to show them; I resolved to vindicate MacLaren. I bowled hard all the time. I couldn't bear the idea of letting myself or MacLaren down.'[8]

He was presented with the match ball after each of his first two Tests when he claimed 19 wickets, including Victor Trumper and Hill three times in four innings.

Much of his best work was done overseas, on three tours of Australia, where he amassed 77 of his 106 Ashes wickets, and in South Africa in 1913–14, where he claimed a record 49 wickets in four Tests on matting before refusing to play in the fifth.

When international cricket resumed in 1920–21, Barnes was 47 yet still in demand to join the winter tour to Australia. But he withdrew after permission for his wife to accompany him was not forthcoming.

Tall and slim at 185 cm (6 ft 1 in) Barnes had a lively run-up and while his pace was only medium to medium fast, no bowler of his time was as unplayable. And only once during that 1911–12 series, when the renowned Australian hitter A. 'Tibby' Cotter was swinging lustily, did he bother with an outfielder.

At The Oval in 1912 during the triangular Tests, Barnes took 8-29 before lunch on the second day against the South Africans, spectacular striking unequalled almost 100 years on. 'Barnes surpassed himself,' said *Wisden*, 'bowling in even more deadly form than in any of the previous Test matches. He broke both ways and his length was irreproachable.'[9]

Champion teammate Jack Hobbs said Barnes's career figures would have been even more impressive had he had the opportunity to bowl at taller sets of stumps, which were adopted from 1931.[10] 'He would have reaped a rare harvest . . . for most of his balls lifted a little too high,' said Hobbs.[11]

In his last playing year, as a 50-year-old in the Bradford League, Barnes took 62 wickets at an average of 4.18, many considering him world-class even then.

English Testman C. H. 'Ciss' Parkin modelled his bowling on Barnes, who he regarded as incomparable. 'His length is wonderful,' he said, in 1924. 'And he can turn the ball both ways. His best ball is almost unplayable; it is fast and pitches on the middle and leg sticks and breaks across to the off. You dare not leave it alone because it keeps too close to the wicket. And the way he makes the ball nip off the turf! You would think an imp is inside the leather!'[12]

Barnes v. Australia

Season	Analysis	Wkts	Ave
1901–02	5-65, 1-74, 6-42, 7-121, 0-21	19	17.00
1902	6-49, 1-50	7	14.14
1907–08	1-74, 2-63, 0-30, 5-72, 3-60, 3-83, 1-37, 1-69, 7-60, 1-78	24	26.08
1909	1-37, 6-62, 5-56, 1-66, 2-57, 2-61	17	20.00
1911–12	3-107, 1-72, 5-44, 3-96, 3-71, 5-105, 5-74, 2-47, 3-56, 4-106	34	22.88
1912	0-74, 5-30, 0-18	5	24.40

Tests v. Australia:	20 (27 overall)
Wickets:	106 (189)
Average:	21.58 (16.43)
Best bowling:	7-121, Melbourne, 1901–02 (9-103)
5-wicket Innings:	12 (24)
10-wicket Matches:	1 (7)
Strike-rate:	54 balls per wkt (41)
Average wkts per Test:	5.3 (7)

Match of the Decade: *The Oval, 1912*

England became cricket's first world champion in the 'final' of the nine-match Triangular Test series, the first-ever Test played to a finish in England. Fielding a star-studded array of Golden Age stars and captained for the first time that summer by the commanding C.B. Fry, the Englishmen outbatted the weakened Australians on a wicket that at times spun viciously. Fry's second-innings 79 and Woolley's all-round feats were the match highlights.

Match scores: England 245 (Hobbs 66, Woolley 62, Whitty 4-69) and 175 (Fry 79, Hazlitt 7-25) defeated Australia 111 (Barnes 5-30, Woolley 5-29) and 65 (Woolley 5-20, Dean 4-19) by 244 runs

Odd spot: *A true all-sportsman*

Before standing-in as England's captain in 1911–12, Johnny Douglas won the middleweight boxing title at the 1908 London Olympic Games. The 25-year-old defeated Australia's 'Snowy' Baker in a final described by *The Times* as 'one of the most brilliant exhibitions of skilful boxing, allied to tremendous hitting, ever seen'.[13]

Looking back: *Charles Fry*

'The combined success of Frank Foster and Sydney Barnes in Australia [in 1911–12] was due to the pace of the Australian wickets exactly suiting their style. Both of them could pitch the ball a foot or two shorter there for a good length than in England. This especially applied to Barnes. The one way of getting on top of Barnes – it was not often done – was to drive him over his head. But in Australia this was more difficult to do . . . the opinion in the cricket world of Australia is that Barnes is the greatest bowler England ever sent to Australia and they rank him with their own F. R. Spofforth . . .'[14]

> England's ultimate Golden Age sporting hero, Charles Fry was captain throughout the 1912 Triangular Test series.

One for the statisticians: *He batted first and last*

Golden Age great Wilfred Rhodes is the only English cricketer to go in first *and* last. He still shares two of the oldest Ashes partnership records of all: 323 for the first wicket with Jack Hobbs in Melbourne in 1911–12 and 130 for the last with R. E. 'Tip' Foster in Sydney in 1903–04.

Tests 1911–12 to 1912

KEY: M Matches **I** Innings **NO** Not out innings **HS** Highest score **BB** Best bowling
5wI 5-wicket innings **10wM** 10-wicket match ***** Not out **#** Second innings **rh** Retired hurt

Series results

	Tests	Aust	Eng	Drawn
1911–12 (Aust)	5	1	4	0
1912 (Eng)	3	0	1	2
Total	8	1	5	2
Progressive	94	35	40	19

Summary

	Runs	Wkts	Ave
Australia	3,151	127	24.81
England	3,766	110	34.23

Highest innings totals

Australia		England	
476	Adelaide 1911–12 (3rd Test)#	589	Melbourne 1911–12 (4th Test)
447	Sydney 1911–12 (1st Test)	501	Adelaide 1911–12 (3rd Test)

Lowest completed innings totals

Australia		England	
65	The Oval 1912 (3rd Test)#	175	The Oval 1912 (3rd Test)#
111	The Oval 1912 (3rd Test)		

Leading run scorers

	M	I	NO	Runs	HS	Ave	100	50
Australia								
W.W. Armstrong	5	10	0	324	90	32.40	–	2
R.B. Minnett	6	12	0	309	90	25.75	–	3
England								
J.B. Hobbs	8	13	1	886	187	73.83	4	2
W. Rhodes	8	13	1	667	179	55.58	1	5
F.E. Woolley	8	11	1	388	133*	38.80	1	2
G. Gunn	5	9	0	381	75	42.33	–	4
J.W. Hearne	8	13	2	326	114	29.63	1	1

Hundreds

Australia (1)		England (7)	
1	V.T. Trumper	4	J.B. Hobbs
		1	J.W. Hearne
			W. Rhodes
			F.E. Woolley

Highest individual scores

Australia	
113	V.T. Trumper at Sydney 1911–12 (1st Test)

England	
187	J.B. Hobbs at Adelaide 1911–12 (3rd Test)
179	W. Rhodes at Melbourne 1911–12 (4th Test)
178	J.B. Hobbs at Melbourne 1911–12 (4th Test)

500 runs in a series

	Season	M	I	NO	Runs	HS	Ave	100	50
Australia									
No instance – best:									
W.W. Armstrong	1911–12	5	10	0	324	90	32.40	–	2
England									
J.B. Hobbs	1911–12	5	9	1	662	187	82.75	3	1

Hundred partnerships

Australia (4)

Partnership of 150 and over:

| 157 | 3rd | H. Carter and C. Hill at Adelaide (3rd Test)# |

England (8)

Partnership of 150 and over:

| 323 | 1st | J. B. Hobbs and W. Rhodes at Melbourne 1911–12 (4th Test) |
| | | (English 1st wicket record against Australia) |

Also note:

| 143 | 7th | F. E. Woolley and J. Vine at Sydney 1911–12 (5th Test) |
| | | (English 7th wicket record against Australia) |

Leading wicket-takers

	Tests	Balls	Mdns	Runs	Wkts	Ave	BB	5wl	10wM
Australia									
H. V. Hordern	5	1,665	42	780	32	24.37	7-90	4	2
G. R. Hazlitt	4	939	44	345	16	21.56	7-25	1	–
W. J. Whitty	5	1,170	68	437	15	29.13	4-43	–	–
England									
S. F. Barnes	8	2,154	90	900	39	23.07	5-30	4	–
F. R. Foster	8	1,894	76	742	34	21.82	6-91	3	–
F. E. Woolley	8	549	20	264	18	14.66	5-20	2	1
J. W. H. T. Douglas	6	839	30	355	15	23.66	5-46	1	–

Five wickets in an innings

Australia (5)		**England (10)**	
4	H. V. Hordern	4	S. F. Barnes
1	G. R. Hazlitt	3	F. R. Foster
		2	F. E. Woolley
		1	J. W. H. T. Douglas

Best individual bowling

Australia

| 7-25 | G. R. Hazlitt at The Oval 1912 (3rd Test)# |
| 7-90 | H. V. Hordern at Sydney 1911–12 (1st Test)# |

England

| 6-91 | F. R. Foster at Melbourne 1911–12 (2nd Test)# |

10 wickets in a match

Australia (2)

| 12-175 | H. V. Hordern (5-85 and 7-90) at Sydney 1911–12 (1st Test) |
| 10-161 | H. V. Hordern (5-95 and 5-66) at Sydney 1911–12 (5th Test) |

England (1)

| 10-49 | F. E. Woolley (5-29 and 5-20) at The Oval 1912 (3rd Test) |

25 wickets in a series

	Season	Tests	Balls	Mdns	Runs	Wkts	Ave	BB	5wl	10wM
Australia										
H.V. Hordern	1911–12	5	1,665	42	780	32	24.37	7-90	4	2
England										
S.F. Barnes	1911–12	5	1,782	64	778	34	22.88	5-44	3	–
F.R. Foster	1911–12	5	1,660	58	692	32	21.62	6-91	3	–

Leading wicketkeepers

	Tests	Dismissals	Catches	Stumpings
Australia				
H. Carter	5	9	7	2
England				
E.J. Smith	7	13	12	1

Leading fieldsmen

	Tests	Catches		Tests	Catches
Australia			**England**		
C. Hill	5	8	F.E. Woolley	8	9
C. Kelleway	7	6	W. Rhodes	8	7

Captains

	Tests	Won	Lost	Drawn	Toss won
Australia					
C. Hill	5	1	4	0	3
S.E. Gregory	3	0	1	2	0
England					
J.W.H.T. Douglas	5	4	1	0	2
C.B. Fry	3	1	0	2	3

Most appearances

Australia (21 players)		England (19 players)	
7	W. Bardsley	8	S.F. Barnes
	C. Kelleway		F.R. Foster
6	R.B. Minnett		J.W. Hearne
			J.B. Hobbs
			W. Rhodes
			F.E. Woolley
		7	E.J. Smith
		6	J.W.H.T. Douglas

Jack Hobbs was England's outstanding batsman of the 1920s. *Ken Piesse Collection*

1920s

GELIGNITE JACK
ARRIVES

• •

'. . . the poker-faced White enjoyed his finest hour and despite having bowled more than 120 overs . . . could still summon enough energy to do a series of victory handstands on the overnighter from Adelaide to Ballarat!'

He was known as 'Gelignite Jack' and from the time he first kangaroo-hopped to stardom as the champion of the Australian Imperial Forces squad, Jack Gregory was a headliner and new hero to millions as cricket helped to cast aside the gloom and pessimism created by World War I.

Australia's fast bowler A. 'Tibby' Cotter and England's slow left arm bowler Colin Blythe were among thousands of young men to have died serving overseas. An epidemic of Spanish pneumonia had claimed thousands more in Australia. With six years' break between internationals, many of Australia's most distinguished were too old to resume. England, however, still had many of their post-war team still playing.

But so compelling was Gregory's rise and so irresistible were his skills that an army of new supporters were soon attracted to the game, thrilling in his buccaneering big-hits, razor-sharp reflex catching and especially his blistering bat-breaking pace – bettered in the first fifty years of Test cricket by only one other, 'the Notts Express' Harold Larwood. The strapping 189 cm (6 ft 2½ in) Gregory had a family link with Australia's first

Test captain Dave Gregory, but other than captaining Shore's first XI, he had played little cricket of note. He hadn't even appeared at first-grade level for his club team Sydney.[1]

His performances with the AIF team were a revelation and in all but doing the double (1,000 runs and 100 wickets), the athletic 23-year-old outshone notables including captain Herbie Collins, Johnnie Taylor, C.E. 'Nip' Pellew and Charlie Kelleway, all of whom had already played representative cricket.

Recommended to the AIF combine by NSW batsman Frank Buckle[2], Gregory was raw, erratic and the quickest bowler in all-England in 1919, responsible for 131 wickets and 942 runs. He had tremendous vitality and magnetism and a charismatic presence like few before or since.

Sightscreens needed to be taller when Gelignite Jack was approaching the popping crease, his fearsome final leap allowing him to propel the ball from almost seven feet. His steepling bounce intimidated even the old 'uns. He tore through Yorkshire with 13 wickets for the match, grabbed 11 against Worcester and finished the tour at Scarborough with 10 more against C.I. Thornton's XI, representative of the best England had to offer.

At Northants, Collins elevated the young artilleryman to the head of the batting order and he responded with 115 and 49 in a low-scoring match. Coupled with his eight wickets and a catch or three, he had quite a match of it. Those who hadn't closely followed the fortunes of the AIF team in England or South Africa soon learnt that Australian cricket had a vibrant new star. In Sydney, against a NSW XI that included Warren Bardsley, Alan Kippax, H. 'Sammy' Carter and Arthur Mailey, Gregory opened with 122 after Collins was out first ball. In the second innings he made 102. As usual, more than 60 per cent of his runs came in boundaries, most with imperious front-foot thumps. Characteristically, too, he refused to wear batting gloves, saying they interfered with his 'feel' on the bat.

Australia had not had a game-breaking all-rounder to compare since its own 'W.G.', George Giffen, and Gregory was to dominate as Australia won the first three series after the War.

As early as 1919, Australian authorities looked to broker a Marylebone visit. But such was the devastation in London, the MCC delayed sending a team until the following summer. Johnny Douglas again led, captain-elect Reggie Spooner having withdrawn.

There had been almost ten years between Ashes tours and with Gregory and the silky-smooth southerner Ted McDonald paired from mid-summer, Australia played with growing authority, despite the presence in the English ranks of seasoned quartet Jack Hobbs, Frank Woolley, Wilfred Rhodes and Douglas.

From the opening Test in Sydney, the tourists struggled to combat Gregory's expresses and Arthur Mailey's each-way wrist spin. Fielding at slip, Gregory snared a record fifteen catches in the five Tests, including six in the final Test in Sydney where Australia for the first time completed a clean sweep, five wins from five. Eight of Mailey's record 36 wickets were caught by Gregory, several at leg-slip after he'd spotted Mailey's googly early and dashed behind the wicketkeeper and dived to complete miraculous one-handers. Once he went to leg-slip after a between-overs chat with Mailey, in anticipation of a wrong-un. But Mailey forgot the ploy, instead delivering a perfect, curving leg-break to Hobbs, which Gregory sighted at the last minute and lunging back to first slip took the catch, just a metre or so from the crease. Asked later what had happened, Hobbs said: 'Not sure, but I heard a devil of a scramble going on behind the stumps!'[3]

The Englishmen struggled, too, in matching Australia's out-cricket, the mobility and strong throwing arms of the Australians a delight. Many first-time tourists found the bright light and heat overpowering.

Hobbs, however, was such a menace at cover point that in mid-series the Australians decided not to run if he was anywhere near the ball.[4] E.A. 'Patsy' Hendren, too, was brilliant. 'Jack Hobbs had a roving commission,' said Mailey, 'and like a wicketkeeper was allowed to operate where he decided he could be of best use ... he loved to lull the batsmen (running between the wickets) into a false sense of security.[5]

Gregory was among five debutants from New South Wales and seven overall named in Australia's XI for the opening Test in Sydney. There had not been such an unfamiliar roll call since the Melbourne strike of 1884–85.

The captaincy moved to the heavyweight Victorian Warwick Armstrong, who at 20-plus stone was almost as broad as a Moreton Bay fig and just as imposing. Young club cricketers like Testman-to-be Leo O'Brien remembered facing Armstrong's leg-breaks in District matches and the old man calling 'Hit it, hit it' if he happened to overpitch.

Armstrong bowled little against the English, except in the second Test in Melbourne when Mailey's arm was sore. But he was unstoppable with the bat, scoring three centuries and striking the ball with such ferociousness that fielding even at mid-off was a health hazard.

Armstrong was the canniest of leaders and whenever Douglas, normally a competent No. 7, came to the crease, he would re-employ Mailey, knowing Douglas's dislike of wrist spin.

Tossing the ball ostentatiously into the air, Mailey dismissed Douglas six times and it wasn't until mid-series that the Englishman made any decent scores. So hesitant had he been initially against Mailey's wafting, tempting leg-breaks that he resorted to stonewalling, his back foot firmly anchored behind the crease. The agony was too much for one wag who dubbed him 'Johnny Won't Hit Today', after his four initials J.W.H.T!

After Armstrong's thunderous 158 took the game away from England in Sydney, Gregory's 100 (from 115 balls) and eight wickets triggered an innings victory in Melbourne, diminutive 'Nip' Pellew's 116 from No. 7 qualifying him for a pound per run bonus for every run scored *over* 100 on offer from a local businessman.[6]

It took Australia just fifteen days to re-win the Ashes, historian Harry Altham dubbing it 'a disaster unparalleled in the history of English cricket'.[7]

But the English did play some memorable cricket, especially early in the Adelaide Test where they led by almost 100 runs at the change of innings only to be beaten by 119. Gregory's five wickets, including the left-handed Woolley in both innings, were crucial breakthroughs. Early on the third morning when his lethal spell changed the course of the match, he bounced one at the willowy Englishman and to avoid being hit in the face, Woolley turned his back at the last moment only to be struck a tremendous blow high on his spine. He collapsed onto his knees and while he showed courage in finally continuing, he was soon out to a limp shot to gully. No one was responsible for more direct hits on English batsmen than Gelignite Jack Gregory.[8]

Hobbs played with marvellous assurance throughout the one-sided summer, his second-innings century in Adelaide a chanceless affair and against an absolute crack attack. So impressed was South Australia's Governor Lieut.-Colonel Sir Geoffrey Weigall that he sent Hobbs a congratulatory letter, complete with an opal tie-pin. 'My dear Hobbs,' he wrote. 'I hope you will accept this tiny souvenir of a perfect innings and as a slight recognition of the great pleasure it gave.'[9]

While Australia's winning margin was comfortable enough, the match aggregate of 1,753 runs was the highest for any Test in Australia until 1968–69.[10] And had Kelleway been caught third ball from paceman Harry Howell on the third evening, Australia may well have been beaten. Kelleway hadn't scored at the time and went on to make a Test-best 147. He batted laboriously through the entire five hours' play for just 95 on Day 4 as Australia retrieved lost ground. 'He was painfully slow,' said Percy Fender, playing in his first game. 'One cannot help wonder what would happen to cricket if innings of this type were common.'[11]

Mailey captured 10 wickets in this game at a cost of more than 300 runs. His innings figures of 5-160 and 5-142 are still among the most extravagant in Test cricket. Three weeks later in Melbourne, Mailey returned the best-ever Ashes analysis by an Australian: 9-121 from 47 overs, three being stumped, two lbw, two caught by Gregory at slip and two others caught elsewhere.

Hendren was the only wicket he missed. Ironically, he had been dropped from Mailey's bowling earlier in his innings before falling at the opposite end to the swerve of Kelleway. From his last 19 balls, Mailey took 5-13.

Collins also enjoyed an imposing maiden summer with 557 runs including 70 and 104 in the opening Test. At thirty-two, he was the oldest of five Australian debutants to score a century in Ashes contests.

In the final Test in Sydney, Charlie Macartney raced to an imperious 170. 'The great little batsman had given a really great display,' said Fender, who finally took his wicket, one of his five for the innings.

'All shots and all bowling seemed to come alike to him.'[12]

One of the hero-worshippers in the crowd was a 12-year-old Don Bradman, who told his father he would never be satisfied until he, too, stepped onto the historic arena.

Collins assumed the captaincy after Armstrong led the 1921 Australians to a 3–0 series win. England was so unbalanced for its first home series in almost a decade that it employed a record thirty players in five Tests, including sixteen new to Ashes battle.

Gregory and McDonald were unstoppable, Gregory's bounce and vitality complemented by McDonald's magnificent rhythm and line. Invariably he'd bowl within himself but when opposed by champions like Hobbs, he would lift and bowl genuinely fast. In England in 1921,

McDonald gathered 27 wickets and took 10 more on the way home in South Africa. His acceptance of professional terms in England was to prematurely end his Australian career just as it was blossoming.

Gregory's new partner for the 1924–25 English visit was the versatile Kelleway, who dropped down the batting list with the extra new-ball responsibilities.

Australia may have enjoyed another commanding victory in the first summer of eight-ball overs, but the form of England's two openers, Hobbs and first-timer Herbert Sutcliffe, consistently saw the tourists away to comfortable starts.

In the opening Test in Sydney, they started with 157 and 110 and in Melbourne a week later became the first to bat through an entire day's play. It was an extraordinary feat on a testing wicket after Australia had batted the first two days and made 600.

In an enthralling game, England was 254-4 chasing 372 in the fourth innings before Gregory bowled Hendren, changing the face of the game.

At forty-two, Hobbs was a marvel, scoring three centuries for the summer, while his 30-year-old partner Sutcliffe made four, including three in a row. In the second Test from 1 January, the unflappable Yorkshireman batted through the third and fifth days. His extraordinary run continued, too, in the return Test in Melbourne five weeks later when he was unconquered through the first day's play for yet another ton. It wasn't until his final Test innings of the tour that everyone else's tormentor Gregory managed to rifle through Sutcliffe's defences. His record aggregate of 734 runs remains unequalled by a visiting opening batsman. And few have shown his patience or courage under adversity.

England also had the standout bowler in the series in genial medium-pacer Maurice 'Chub' Tate who amassed 38 wickets, eclipsing even the best of Syd Barnes.

With his willing smile and love of life, Tate was a hero for thousands, especially one young knee-high-to-a-grasshopper Melburnian Phillip Opas, who was foxing balls at the nets for the tourists in Melbourne when Tate asked him if he wanted to come and have a bowl.

'He introduced me to [captain] Arthur Gilligan,' Phil Opas recalled 'and asked if I would like to be a guest of the English cricket team at the Test match.

'I said, "Would I!"'

'"Okay, wait for me at the gates at 9.30 in the morning at the member's entrance." He saw me there, took me in and I watched the game from the dressing rooms. I asked him home for dinner and he said he couldn't while the Test is on but when we come back to play Victoria he would.

'They came back from Adelaide on the Overlander and I was waiting at Spencer Street Station, and he said, "I haven't forgotten" and came out and had tea with us. In the backyard he showed us how to hold the ball for swing.

'We collected the old cigarette cards with biographies on the back and I sent one with a letter for his birthday to "Mr M Tate, the best bowler in the world, England". And it got there!

'Maurice came out with Percy Chapman's team too, and again in 1932–33, not that he got a look-in that summer.'

A master of swing and seam and with a heart as big as a cabbage, 20 of Tate's wickets came in the first two Tests, which extended into a seventh day. The third Test in Adelaide also went seven days, Australia winning narrowly to extend their series lead to an unassailable 3–0.

Prominent newcomers included Victoria's batting virtuoso Bill Ponsford and the brilliant South Australian all-sportsman Victor Richardson.

Ponsford already had a 400 in his CV and was to make back-to-back 100s on debut, a feat unmatched in Ashes battles until 1965–66 when a teenage Doug Walters made his irresistible entry into Test cricket. Richardson scored a ton in his second appearance. He was to support Bill Woodfull resolutely during the fiery Bodyline summer almost a decade later.

Ponsford couldn't fathom Tate's early movement. Neither could the English wicketkeeper Herbert Strudwick who twice conceded four byes. While only operating off a short run-up, Tate fizzed the ball disconcertingly, Ponsford repeatedly fanning at thin air.

Strudwick, a veteran of three tours, said Ponsford could have been bowled six times in his first two overs. At one stage the young Ponny turned to Strudwick and said: 'I've never played against such bowling before!'

'No, it does not look like you have!' said the affable 'Struddy'.[13]

Somehow Ponsford survived, the more-experienced Collins taking Tate almost exclusively until the youngster had truly settled. 'I don't think I ever bowled better in my life than I did that morning before lunch,' said

Tate, 'and I sent down 19 overs for about 45 runs but didn't get a single wicket!'[14]

It was a testimony to Ponsford's inner strength that he was able to ignore his embarrassing beginnings and play with such authority later. England's back-up bowlers included for the first time 36-year-old A.P. 'Tich' Freeman and Ponsford's dancing feet repeatedly took him to the pitch of the ball, effectively negating the Freeman googly and allowing a freewheeling range of front-foot shots.

Both he and Collins made centuries and when the Victorian was dismissed inside the final ten minutes, he immediately went to Collins in the rooms, saying without him such a fairytale start would have been impossible.[15] It was the beginning of an auspicious career that was to culminate a decade later in the greatest partnership in the history of the Ashes.

Tate lacked support all tour, captain Arthur Gilligan able to bowl only at a military medium pace after being struck over the heart while batting the previous English summer. At Edgbaston just months earlier, he'd taken 6-7 as South Africa was bundled out for 30 but he was never able to recapture that form in Australia. Later, however, he was to return many times as a commentator.

With the Ashes already lost, the tourists won by an innings in the return match in Melbourne, only to go down by a massive 307 runs in Sydney, a little leg-spinner by the name of Clarrie Grimmett making a remarkable entry with 11 wickets for the game. Had Mailey not been so prominent, the Dunedin-born Grimmett may well have been selected years earlier, when he played an integral role in three consecutive District cricket premierships with Prahran. It was during his time in Melbourne that Grimmett trained his black and white fox terrier, Joe, to remain motionless while he bowled eight balls on his backyard pitch before each would be retrieved and placed back at Grimmett's feet. One Sunday morning some of Grimmett's Sheffield Shield teammates visited and Jack Ellis grabbed a ball and called Joe to do his thing. The dog remained motionless. It wasn't until Clarrie stood up and stepped out his run that Joe stopped sunning himself and showed even a half-interest in the proceedings. To the delight of the guests, just as Clarrie bowled his eighth ball, Joe sprang to life, racing back and forth until all eight balls were again at the top of Clarrie's mark! Down at the local shops, Mrs Lizzy Grimmett became used to hearing her husband referred to as 'that mad bloke with the dog'.[16] Clarrie and Joe spent hours at play, the regular sessions crucial in Grimmett developing the extraordinary accuracy and the each-way side-spin of a conjurer. He was to be Australia's No. 1 spinner in almost all of the next five Ashes battles – and was the first to 200 Test wickets.

After seeing their pride-and-joy XI beaten so consistently in the first years after World War I, there was widespread jubilation throughout England when first-time captain Percy Chapman won the final Test at The Oval in 1926, giving England a 1–0 series win after the first four Tests were drawn. It was the only blemish for the Australians, who otherwise were undefeated for almost five months and forty matches.

The fallout was immediate, Collins being stripped of the captaincy, his first-class career over. Macartney farewelled Test cricket with three 100s in a row including one before lunch at Manchester. Warren Bardsley, at forty-three, was also finished, but young Victorian Woodfull, on his first tour, impressed as having the mettle to be a long-termer. Wicketkeeper Bert Oldfield also made a wonderful impression.

The choice of the Nottinghamshire tearaway Harold Larwood for his first Test matches was heralded as being England's most significant selection in years. In the decider at The Oval his hustling pace was responsible for six important wickets, all in the Australian top-six including Macartney, Australia's outstanding player on tour, in the second innings. Chasing 400-plus, the Australians were bundled out for just 125 triggering an ever-so-joyous ground invasion. Thousands gathered at the pavilion where the victorious Englishmen were feted like returning war heroes.

Larwood was just 171 cm (5 ft 7½ in) but he was strong and already very whippy. His emergence had been as meteoric as Gregory's just a few years earlier and he was to be as important, too, in the years ahead, especially on Australian wickets where the firmer run-ups encouraged maximum momentum at the crease.

In 1928–29, Larwood made the first significant strikes of the summer in the inaugural Test in Brisbane, an extraordinarily lopsided game, which a powerful, well-balanced England won by a record 675 runs. With 6-32 and 2-30, Larwood tore through the Australian top-order in a match also notable for being Gregory's last and young Don Bradman's first. How the four Australian selectors, including the just-retired Bardsley, could possibly have omitted 20-year-old Bradman after just one trial remains a blunder of monumental proportions. At best, it was ill-advised and left his replacement Otto Nothling and Ponsford, at twenty-eight, the juniors in an ageing outfit.

Just two years earlier, Bradman had been playing bush cricket in Bowral before his astonishing Boys' Own elevation into representative-level cricket. Leading into his first Test selection, Bradman's scores for New South Wales were: 131, 133 not out, 87, 132 not out, 58 not out and 18. Later that season he was to set a new Sydney Cricket Ground record with 340 not out for NSW against Victoria. Walking from the ground, he seemed as fresh as he had been at the beginning of his epic.[17] His season tally of 1,690 first-class runs set a new high by an Australian.

England's defence of the Ashes was completed in just eighteen days, even the team's catching and fielding was superior to that of the Australians. In Brisbane, Woodfull fell for a fourth-ball duck after Chapman, in the gully, took a spectacular one-handed catch diving full stretch to his left. It helped set the tone for the rest of the summer.

Walter Hammond was a revelation, carving up a pedestrian attack that lacked punch with Gregory sidelined, the old champion's knee having buckled in Brisbane. The powerful 25-year-old from Gloucester had notched a triple century in his mid-teens at school and debuted for his county at seventeen. Tall for the time, he played with unequalled presence and power through the offside and in the summer of his life gorged himself on the shirtfront wickets with four centuries, including two doubles on his way to 905 runs at an average of 113. Eighty years on it's still an Ashes record down-under.

Hobbs, Sutcliffe and the crowd favourite Hendren shared in another 1,200-plus runs between them, while the sustained accuracy, endurance and guile of Somerset's Jack 'Farmer' White resulted in him taking a series-high 25 wickets with what seemed to be, from the stands, the most innocuous of left-arm slows.

The average age of the English team was thirty-two. They were a match-hardened band and it wasn't until the tumultuous Christmas Test in Melbourne (beginning 29 December 1928) that England was seriously challenged, yet they still chased down 332 on a seventh-day wicket affected early by rain. All but batting through, Sutcliffe played the finest innings of his career. He shared an important century stand with Hobbs, the pair defying a treacherous, pock-marked wicket and an array of close-in fieldsmen in another masterful display on a sticky wicket. A young Don Bradman watching from the covers marvelled at Sutcliffe's calm demeanour and lightning reflexes in consistently avoiding wicked, lifting deliveries from just short of a good length. 'Sutcliffe's exhibition that day was the nearest approach to mastery on a sticky wicket I saw throughout my career.'[18] Years later Sutcliffe described the wicket as 'a nightmare'.[19]

In Adelaide, Hobbs's slick run out of Bradman (for 58) in Australia's second innings was pivotal in England's 12-run win. Again the Test carried into a seventh day. Australia needed less than 30 with three wickets left when Oldfield called for a suicidal single to Hobbs at cover point. Bradman thought about refusing but realised Oldfield was coming no matter what. He desperately sprinted back up the wicket only for wicket-keeper George Duckworth to catch him just short of his ground. Duckworth's tremendous whoop of delight left no one in doubt as to which way he believed the decision should go. Bradman later described it as 'a hair-splitting decision' but he stopped short of criticising Duckworth for what, in another era, may have been labelled as gamesmanship.[20] Australia's last man out was Don 'Rock' Blackie who had been included in his first Ashes series alongside his St Kilda new-ball partner H. 'Dainty' Ironmonger. Both were forty-six, Australia's oldest ever newcomers.

With 8-126, the poker-faced White enjoyed his finest hour and despite having bowled more than 120 overs, 60 in the first innings and 65 in the second, could still summon enough energy to do a series of victory handstands on the overnighter from Adelaide to Ballarat![21]

It was only the second time since 1877 that England XIs on tour had won four Ashes Tests in a row.

Included for the first time in that epic match was Balmain teenager Archie Jackson who replaced Vic Richardson at the head of the order and promptly made a century on debut, a remarkably poised performance after Australia had lost 19-3 chasing 334. At nineteen years and 154 days, he was the youngest Ashes centurion of all. In more than five hours of batting, Jackson didn't give even one chance. Umpire George Hele said the young New South Welshman looked as white as a sheet, but played all of the bowling from Larwood and Tate through to White and George Geary with aplomb, the kid's nerves being settled by Australia's captain Jack Ryder who kept telling him he was 'doing all right'.[22]

Jackson reached his century with a glorious cover drive from Larwood that whistled to the short square boundary and bounced back into the in-field.[23] 'That ball was delivered as fast as any I had ever bowled previously,' said Larwood years later. 'That glorious stroke has lived in my memory to this day for its ease and perfect timing.'[24] Hele said he never saw the ball at all until it rebounded fifty yards from the pickets behind point. Sadly, the popular cricketing Keats was to die just four years later from tuberculosis.

The only Test Australia won all summer was the last back in Melbourne when captain Chapman was among those to stand down so some of the team's reserves could also play in one of the important matches. Despite starting with 519, England was beaten by five wickets, Bradman making his second century of the summer. Maurice Tate had suggested to him earlier in the tour that he needed to 'keep that bat a bit straighter when you come to England, or you won't have much luck there'.[25]

After Bradman's modest debut in Brisbane, Tate had also playfully dubbed Bradman as his 'bunny'[26], throwaway lines the Don never forgot.

Man of the decade: *Jack Hobbs*

In an era of Australian domination, featuring, in 1928, the acclaimed arrival of 20-year-old Sydney prodigy Don Bradman, one player stood supreme for England: the Surrey colossus John Berry 'Jack' Hobbs.

Hobbs had been the batsman of the series in England's 4–1 victory down-under in 1911–12, a summer where his exploits included centuries in three consecutive Ashes Tests.

After World War I intervened, Hobbs's stellar performances continued. He excelled series after series, scoring eight of his twelve Ashes centuries and enhancing his reputation as the most accomplished batsman in the first fifty years of Test cricket. Not only was he sharp of eye, his athleticism was superb and fitness undeniable, and his feat of ninety-eight first-class centuries *after* his fortieth birthday is a remarkable achievement, unlikely to be surpassed.

Opening the batting from the mid-1920s with the poised Yorkshireman Herbert Sutcliffe, the pair amassed fifteen century partnerships. As soloists they were sublime; as a pair, scintillating. For the first time in Australian first-class history in Melbourne in 1924–25, they batted through an entire day's play, Hobbs scoring 154 and Sutcliffe 123. Former Australian captain M. A. 'Monty' Noble said it was 'English cricket at its best'.[27] Their defences were impregnable and judgement in stealing short singles impeccable.

Hobbs particularly loved the enormity of the MCG and big crowds attended the games, including more than 33 000 on that history-making Saturday.

His average bordered on 70 in ten Tests at cricket's mighty colosseum. Six times he shared in century stands, four for the first wicket, including a best of 323 with Wilfred Rhodes in 1911–12. Only Bradman was more prolific.

At 174 cm (5 ft 9½ in), and 73 kg (11 st 7 lb) he was rangy rather than powerful yet when in the mood could strike the ball astonishing distances.[28]

Hobbs contended he was a far superior, all-round batsman before the war and while he was not as dashing afterwards, having limited his shot selection, he was more prolific. When early in his career he would imperiously loft the new-ball bowlers back over their heads, he settled into a tighter, less-aggressive game. But his balance, footwork and timing remained exquisite.

John Arlott said Hobbs made batting look simple like no one else he ever saw. 'Often his genius was only apparent when one saw the difficulties of the batsman at the other end.'[29]

In 1953, Hobbs became the first professional to be knighted for his services to cricket. The members' gates at Kennington Oval were named in his honour in 1934.

Hobbs v. Australia

* not out

Season	Scores	Runs	Ave
1907–08	83, 28, 26, 23*, 57, 0, 72, 13	302	43.14
1909	0, 62*, 19, 9, 12, 30	132	26.40
1911–12	63, 22, 6, 126*, 187, 23, 178, 32, 45	662	82.75
1912	107, 19, 66, 32	224	56.00
1920–21	49, 59, 122, 20, 18, 123, 27, 13, 40, 34	505	50.50
1924–25	115, 57, 154, 22, 119, 27, 66, 0, 13	573	63.66
1926	19*, 119, 49, 88, 74, 37, 100	486	81.00
1928–29	49, 11, 40, 20, 49, 74, 1, 142, 65	451	50.11
1930	78, 74, 1, 19, 29, 13, 31, 47, 9	301	33.33

Tests v. Australia:	41 (61 overall)
Runs:	3,636 (5410)
Average:	54.26 (56.94)
Highest score:	187, Adelaide, 1911–12 (211)
100s:	12 (15)

Match of the Decade: *The Oval, 1926*

The appointment of a new captain (Percy Chapman) and the recall of a 48-year-old (Wilfred Rhodes) were integral in England's famous Ashes-snatching victory at Kennington Oval, where local hero Jack Hobbs made his one and only home-ground Test 100. Chapman led with flair and energy while in a remarkable Ashes farewell, Rhodes claimed 2-35 and 4-44, his wickets including 'the unbowlable' Bill Woodfull. After defeating Australia only once in the previous nineteen Tests, England triumphed by 289 runs, thanks mainly to their bold selections and a riveting 172-run opening stand on a rain-affected wicket between Hobbs and Herbert Sutcliffe.

> **Match scores:** England 280 (Sutcliffe 76, Mailey 6-138) and 436 (Hobbs 100, Sutcliffe 161) defeated Australia 302 (Collins 61, Gregory 73) and 125 (Rhodes 4-44) by 289 runs

Odd spot: *'Bob . . . they're still batting!'*

Unlike her husband, long-time Australian Prime Minister Robert Menzies, Dame Patti Menzies had little understanding of cricket.

Asked one day if she had actually been to a match, she said she had, in Melbourne in 1924–25 when Jack Hobbs and Herbert Sutcliffe batted through the entire day's play.

'I got bored and went home in the afternoon,' she said.

'We were in England in 1926 and Bob suggested I should see at least one game in England, so down to The Oval I went, Australia playing England and there they were again, Hobbs and Sutcliffe. They were still batting!'[30]

Looking back: *Don Bradman, Sydney, 1921*

'In that memorable (1921) Test match, I was privileged to see (Charlie) Macartney in all his glory, making 170 runs. I can picture his delicate leg glances and one flashing drive not through the covers but over the top . . . my father must have been amused when I said to him: "I shall not be satisfied until I play on this ground" '.[31]

> Don Bradman, then twelve, was attending his first Test match at the Sydney Cricket Ground. He was to become the most-prolific Test batsman of all.

One for the statisticians: *Ageless Wilfred*

Sentiment was not part of Wilfred Rhodes' recall for the deciding Test at The Oval in 1926. He may have been nearing his forty-ninth birthday, but he'd finished second on the first-class averages with 115 wickets at 14.86. He also made more than 1000 runs at an average of 35. Percy Chapman, England's new captain at The Oval, hadn't even been born when Rhodes first played for England.

Tests 1920–21 to 1928–29

KEY: M Matches **I** Innings **NO** Not out innings **HS** Highest score **BB** Best bowling
5wI 5-wicket innings **10wM** 10-wicket match ***** Not out **#** Second innings **rh** Retired hurt

Series results

	Tests	Aust	Eng	Drawn
1920–21 (Aust)	5	5	0	0
1921 (Eng)	5	3	0	2
1924–25 (Aust)	5	4	1	0
1926 (Eng)	5	0	1	4
1928–29 (Aust)	5	1	4	0
Total	**25**	**13**	**6**	**6**
Progressive	119	48	46	25

Summary

	Runs	Wkts	Ave
Australia	13,879	377	36.81
England	13,922	389	35.78

Highest innings totals

Australia		England	
600	Melbourne 1924–25 (3rd Test)	636†	Sydney 1928–29 (2nd Test)^
582	Adelaide 1920–21 (3rd Test)#	548	Melbourne 1924–25 (4th Test)
581	Sydney 1920–21 (1st Test)#	521	Brisbane# 1928–29 (1st Test)
499	Melbourne 1920–21 (2nd Test)	519	Melbourne 1928–29 (5th Test)
494	Leeds 1926 (3rd Test)	479	Melbourne 1924–25 (2nd Test)
491	Melbourne 1928–29 (5th Test)	475-3 dec	Lord's 1926 (2nd Test)
489	Adelaide 1924–25 (4th Test)	447	Adelaide 1920–21 (3rd Test)
452	Sydney 1924–25 (1st Test)#		
450	Sydney 1924–25 (1st Test)		

† highest total by England in Australia

Lowest completed innings totals

Australia		England	
66	Brisbane¹ 1928–29 (1st Test)#	112	Nottingham 1921 (1st Test)
	(two batsmen absent)	146	Sydney 1924–25 (5th Test)#
122	Brisbane¹ 1928–29 (1st Test)	147	Nottingham 1921 (1st Test)#
	(one batsman absent)		
125	The Oval 1926 (5th Test)#		

Brisbane¹ played at Brisbane Exhibition Ground (all subsequent Australia v. England Tests at Brisbane played at Woolloongabba)

Leading run scorers

	M	I	NO	Runs	HS	Ave	100	50
Australia								
J. Ryder	17	28	4	1060	201*	44.16	2	6
C. G. Macartney	12	18	3	1033	170	68.86	5	2
H. L. Collins	16	26	0	1012	162	38.92	3	5
J. M. Taylor	18	25	0	957	108	38.28	1	8
J. M. Gregory	21	30	3	941	100	34.85	1	6
W. Bardsley	18	28	4	911	193*	37.95	1	7
W. M. Woodfull	10	16	1	797	141	53.13	5	1
W. A. S. Oldfield	19	32	8	697	65*	29.04	–	2
W. W. Armstrong	10	13	2	616	158	56.00	3	1
England								
J. B. Hobbs	21	35	1	2015	154	59.26	8	7
H. Sutcliffe	14	23	1	1561	176	70.95	6	7
E. H. Hendren	27	38	4	1308	169	38.47	2	8
F. E. Woolley	20	33	0	1190	123	36.06	1	9
W. R. Hammond	5	9	1	905	251	113.12	4	–

Hundreds

Australia (33)

5	C. G. Macartney
	W. M. Woodfull
3	W. W. Armstrong
	H. L. Collins
2	D. G. Bradman
	C. E. Pellew
	W. H. Ponsford
	J. Ryder
1	W. Bardsley
	J. M. Gregory
	H. S. T. L. Hendry
	A. Jackson
	C. Kelleway
	A. F. Kippax
	A. J. Richardson
	V. Y. Richardson
	J. M. Taylor

England (27)

8	J. B. Hobbs
6	H. Sutcliffe
4	W. R. Hammond
3	A. C. Russell
2	E. H. Hendren
1	M. Leyland
	C. P. Mead
	J. W. H. Makepeace
	F. E. Woolley

Highest individual scores

Australia

201*	J. Ryder at Adelaide 1924–25 (3rd Test)
193*	W. Bardsley at Lord's 1926 (2nd Test)
170	C. G. Macartney at Sydney 1920–21 (5th Test)
164	A. Jackson at Adelaide 1928–29 (4th Test)
162	H. L. Collins at Adelaide 1920–21 (3rd Test)
158	W. W. Armstrong at Sydney 1920–21 (1st Test)#
151	C. G. Macartney at Leeds 1926 (3rd Test)
147	C. Kelleway at Adelaide 1920–21 (3rd Test)#
141	W. M. Woodfull at Leeds 1926 (3rd Test)

England

251	W. R. Hammond at Sydney 1928–29 (2nd Test)
200	W. R. Hammond at Melbourne 1928–29 (4th Test)
182*	C. P. Mead at The Oval 1921 (5th Test)
177	W. R. Hammond at Adelaide 1928–29 (4th Test)#
176	H. Sutcliffe at Melbourne 1924–25 (2nd Test)
169	E. H. Hendren at Brisbane# 1928–29 (1st Test)
161	H. Sutcliffe at The Oval 1926 (5th Test)
154	J. B. Hobbs at Melbourne 1924–25 (2nd Test)
143	H. Sutcliffe at Melbourne 1924–25 (4th Test)
142	J. B. Hobbs at Melbourne 1928–29 (5th Test)

Century in each innings

176 and 127	H. Sutcliffe (Eng) at Melbourne 1924–25 (2nd Test)
119* and 177	W. R. Hammond (Eng) at Adelaide 1928–29 (4th Test)

Carrying bat through completed innings

W. Bardsley	193* out of 383 for Australia at Lord's 1926 (2nd Test)
W. M. Woodfull	30* out of 66 for Australia at Brisbane# 1928–29 (1st Test)#
	(Australia batted two men short)

500 runs in a series

	Season	M	I	NO	Runs	HS	Ave	100	50
Australia									
H. L. Collins	1920–21	5	9	0	557	162	61.88	2	3
J. M. Taylor	1924–25	5	10	0	541	108	54.10	1	4
Also note:									
J. Ryder	1928–29	5	10	1	492	112	54.66	1	4
W. M. Woodfull	1928–29	5	10	1	491	111	54.55	3	1
England									
W. R. Hammond	1928–29	5	9	1	905	251	113.12	4	–
H. Sutcliffe	1924–25	5	9	0	734	176	81.55	4	2
J. B. Hobbs	1924–25	5	9	0	573	154	63.66	3	2
J. B. Hobbs	1920–21	5	10	0	505	123	50.50	2	1

Hundred partnerships

Australia (34)

Partnerships of 150 and over:

235	2nd	W. M. Woodfull and C. G. Macartney at Leeds 1926 (3rd Test)
215	2nd	W. M. Woodfull and H. S. T. L. Hendry at Sydney 1928–29 (2nd Test)#
198	4th	C. G. Macartney and J. M. Gregory at Sydney 1920–21 (5th Test)
194	4th	C. Kelleway and W. W. Armstrong at Adelaide 1920–21 (3rd Test)
192	2nd	W. M. Woodfull and C. G. Macartney at Manchester 1926 (4th Test)
190	2nd	H. L. Collins and W. H. Ponsford at Sydney 1924–25 (1st Test)
187	6th	C. Kelleway and W. W. Armstrong at Sydney 1920–21 (1st Test)#
183	5th	D. G. Bradman and A. G. Fairfax at Melbourne 1928–29 (5th Test)
173	8th	C. E. Pellew and J. M. Gregory at Melbourne 1920–21 (2nd Test)
161	4th	W. H. Ponsford and J. M. Taylor at Melbourne 1924–25 (2nd Test)
161	4th	A. F. Kippax and J. Ryder at Melbourne 1928–29 (3rd Test)

Also note:

127	10th	J. M. Taylor and A. A. Mailey at Sydney 1924–25 (1st Test)#
		(Australian 10th wicket record against all countries)

England (32)

Partnerships of 150 and over:

283	1st	J. B. Hobbs and H. Sutcliffe at Melbourne 1924–25 (2nd Test)
262	3rd	W. R. Hammond and D. R. Jardine at Adelaide 1928–29 (4th Test)#
		(English 3rd wicket record against Australia)
182	1st	J. B. Hobbs and H. Sutcliffe at Lord's 1926 (2nd Test)
172	1st	J. B. Hobbs and H. Sutcliffe at The Oval 1926 (5th Test)#
158	1st	A. C. Russell and G. Brown at The Oval 1921 (5th Test)#
157	1st	J. B. Hobbs and H. Sutcliffe at Sydney 1924–25 (1st Test)
156	1st	J. B. Hobbs and H. Sutcliffe at Leeds 1926 (3rd Test)

Also note:

124	8th	E. H. Hendren and H. Larwood at Brisbane# 1928–29 (1st Test)#
		(English 8th wicket record against Australia)

Leading wicket-takers

	Tests	Balls	Mdns	Runs	Wkts	Ave	BB	5wI	10wM
Australia									
A. A. Mailey	18	5,201	90	2,935	86	34.12	9-121	6	2
J. M. Gregory	21	4,472	109	2,364	70	33.77	7-69	3	–
C. V. Grimmett	9	3,805	160	1,520	47	32.34	6-37	5	1
E. A. McDonald	8	1,991	42	1,060	33	32.12	5-32	2	–
C. Kelleway	11	2,453	80	805	29	27.75	4-27	–	–
England									
M. W. Tate	15	6,005	248	1,966	68	28.91	6-99	5	1
C. H. Parkin	9	1,999	50	1,090	32	34.06	5-38	2	–
J. C. White	6	2,656	141	867	28	30.96	8-126	3	1
H. Larwood	7	2,125	60	976	27	36.14	6-32	1	–
F. E. Woolley	20	2,927	108	1,216	25	48.64	4-77	–	–

Five wickets in an innings

Australia (18)		England (15)	
6	A. A. Mailey	5	M. W. Tate
5	C. V. Grimmett	3	J. C. White
3	J. M. Gregory	2	P. G. H. Fender
2	E. A. McDonald		G. Geary
1	D. D. Blackie		C. H. Parkin
	T. W. Wall	1	H. Larwood

Best individual bowling

Australia

9-121	A. A. Mailey at Melbourne 1920–21 (4th Test)
	(best innings analysis for Australia in all Tests)
7-69	J. M. Gregory at Melbourne 1920–21 (2nd Test)
6-37	C. V. Grimmett at Sydney 1924–25 (5th Test)#
6-58	J. M. Gregory at Nottingham 1921 (1st Test)
6-94	D. D. Blackie at Melbourne 1928–29 (3rd Test)
6-131	C. V. Grimmett at Brisbane# 1928–29 (1st Test)#
6-138	A. A. Mailey at The Oval 1926 (5th Test)

England

8-126	J. C. White at Adelaide 1928–29 (4th Test)#
6-32	H. Larwood at Brisbane# 1928–29 (1st Test)
6-99	M. W. Tate at Melbourne 1924–25 (2nd Test)#
6-130	M. W. Tate at Sydney 1924–25 (1st Test)

10 wickets in a match

Australia (3)

13-236	A. A. Mailey (4-115 and 9-121) at Melbourne 1920–21 (4th Test)
11-82	C. V. Grimmett (5-45 and 6-37) at Sydney 1924–25 (5th Test)
10-302	A. A. Mailey (5-160 and 5-142) at Adelaide 1920–21 (3rd Test)

England (2)

13-256	J. C. White (5-130 and 8-126) at Adelaide 1928–29 (4th Test)
11-228	M. W. Tate (6-130 and 5-98) at Sydney 1924–25 (1st Test)

25 wickets in a series

	Season	Tests	Balls	Mdns	Runs	Wkts	Ave	BB	5wl	10wM
Australia										
A. A. Mailey	1920–21	5	1,465	27	946	36	26.27	9-121	4	2
E. A. McDonald	1921	5	1,235	32	668	27	24.74	5-32	2	–
Also note:										
A. A. Mailey	1924–25	5	1,464	20	999	24	41.62	5-92	1	–
England										
M. W. Tate	1924–25	5	2,528	62	881	38	23.18	6-99	5	1
J. C. White	1928–29	5	2,440	134	760	25	30.40	8-126	3	1

Leading wicketkeepers

	Tests	Dismissals	Catches	Stumpings
Australia				
W.A.S. Oldfield	19	43	26	17
H. Carter	6	22	14	8
England				
H. Strudwick	16	40	36	4
G. Duckworth	5	14	13	1

Leading fieldsmen

	Tests	Catches		Tests	Catches
Australia			**England**		
J.M. Gregory	21	30	F.E. Woolley	20	24
J. Ryder	17	15	E.H. Hendren	22	13
A.A. Mailey	18	12	A.P.F. Chapman	12	11
H.L. Collins	16	11	H. Sutcliffe	14	10

Captains

	Tests	Won	Lost	Drawn	Toss won
Australia					
W.W. Armstrong	10	8	0	2	4
H.L. Collins	8	4	2	2	5
J. Ryder	5	1	4	0	2
W. Bardsley	2	0	0	2	1
England					
J.W.H.T. Douglas	7	0	7	0	4
A.P.F. Chapman	5	5	0	0	3
A.E.R. Gilligan	5	1	4	0	1
A.W. Carr	4	0	0	4	2
Hon. L.H. Tennyson	3	0	1	2	2
J.C. White	1	0	1	0	1

Most appearances

Australia (33 players)		England (52 players)	
21	J.M. Gregory	22	E.H. Hendren
19	W.A.S. Oldfield	21	J.B. Hobbs
18	W. Bardsley	20	F.E. Woolley
	A.A. Mailey	16	H. Strudwick
	J.M. Taylor	15	M.W. Tate
17	J. Ryder	14	H. Sutcliffe
16	H.L. Collins		

Bill Woodfull is struck under the heart by Harold Larwood in Adelaide, 1932–33. His wife later claimed the force of the impact had shortened his life. *Cricketer magazine*

1930s
HUNTING THE DON
● ●

'. . . it was lucky for Jardine that we were in Adelaide. Had Bertie been struck in Melbourne and Sydney, the mob wouldn't have been waiting around. They would have tried to lynch him . . .'

In time, Don Bradman was to be dubbed the Eighth Wonder of the World. His vibrant beginnings in 1928–29 were the forerunner to a set of astonishing batting performances so stratospheric they still seem unconquerable. The Don so crushed opposing attacks that even Bill Ponsford thought it pointless trying to compete. His astonishing dominance on his first visit to England in 1930 saw the Ashes regained against a star-studded home team, one of the best ever fielded. In making almost 1,000 runs in five Tests, Bradman was unstoppable, playing with unprecedented authority. In mid-tour, a London newspaper banner proclaimed 'BRADMAN FAILS'. He'd made 79!

So insatiable was the Don's appetite for runs throughout the 1930 tour that England concocted its intimidating Bodyline attack with the sole aim to stop him. The tactics not only totally flaunted the spirit of the game, they threatened Imperial relations.

After everyone's favourite, little Bertie Oldfield, had his skull fractured by Harold Larwood operating to an orthodox field in Adelaide, the crowd all but rioted. Next-man-in Bill O'Reilly says having to make his way down the members' steps through the enraged crowd onto the oval provided the most dramatic, out-of-control minutes of his headlining career.

'There were mounted police everywhere trying to keep the crowd back,' O'Reilly recalled. 'Had one jumped, the whole lot would have come over. It was lucky for [England's captain Douglas] Jardine that we were in Adelaide. Had Bertie been struck in Melbourne and Sydney, the mob wouldn't have been waiting around. They would have tried to lynch him.'

The remorseless Jardine and his expressman Larwood were to be blacklisted for leading the most violent and volatile summer of all. While Jardine captained England at home in 1933 and was to take the first MCC touring party to India, where he callously re-launched Bodyline, Larwood was never selected again. Believing he'd been made a scapegoat, he took his family to Australia, where, he said, he was among genuine friends.

The genesis for the unprecedented, at-the-body attack came in the final Test at The Oval in August 1930. Bradman was careering towards another double-hundred when there was a rain delay. On resumption, well after 6 p.m., less than three overs were possible but Bradman was genuinely discomforted by several short deliveries. The next day, having made 175, he was struck hard on the chest by Larwood. There was a five-minute delay as the champion regained his composure. Afterwards, while his partner Archie Jackson defended without flinching, the Don was seen to back away. 'That's it!' said Hugo Weaving, who played Jardine in the mini-series *Bodyline*. 'He's yellow [scared].'[1]

Jardine had been a key member of the English middle-order during the run sprees of 1928–29 and feared being unable to contain Bradman on the flint-hard Australian pitches with time being of no consequence. After his breathtaking performances in 1930, Bradman had averaged 111 against the West Indians in 1930–31 and 201 against the South Africans in 1931–32.

Jardine suddenly felt he had hope. If Larwood could bowl fast and straight, directly *at* Bradman and the other leading Australians, they may be discomforted enough to sacrifice their wickets. There was nothing written into the rules forbidding fast leg theory. Bowlers could send down as many bouncers as they liked, and if batsmen were intimidated that wasn't Jardine's problem. He was interested only in the end result.

Jardine met with Nottinghamshire's captain Arthur Carr, Larwood, and his Notts new-ball partner, the burly Bill Voce, at London's Piccadilly Hotel in August 1932. The two professionals agreed that they could bowl leg theory – if that was what was required. Jardine told how their accuracy would be all-important. He would support them with a ring of close-in fieldsmen to catch the self-defence prods. Two fieldsmen would patrol the fine-leg boundary for the hook and pull shots. At the end of the night, it's said that Carr took Jardine aside, saying if any of the Australians were proving troublesome, he should tell 'Lol' (Larwood) that the Australians reckoned he wasn't nearly as fast as he used to be![2]

Jardine also consulted with Frank Foster, Syd Barnes's old opening partner, a fast left-armer, who had employed his 'death trap' (four short legs) against the Australians in 1911–12.

In the following months, Jardine was to drive the most violent stanza in the game's history. Touring MCC captains had previously been known for their affability and ambassadorship. Jardine was austere and fiercely focused and made little attempt to win friends. The tour was a conquest for the British Empire; the colonials needed to be taught a lesson. He told his players on the *Orontes* that to win they needed to hate the Australians. He was obsessed with winning and remains, in the Great South Land anyway, the most despised of all visiting captains.

Larwood had sent a bail spinning 66 yards in a county game in 1929. He could curve the ball away from the right-handers but once the shine went off the ball after four or five overs, he would bowl fast, but gun-barrel straight. If the new leg-theory tactics as prescribed by Jardine could possibly reduce Bradman's influence, why not try it out?

There were to be twenty-five instances of Australian batsmen being 'pinged', including Bradman, twice in the fifth Test in Sydney. The extreme speed cut into the profits, too. With Bodyline, there was no such thing as a seven-day Test. In 1928–29, the Ashes battles went thirty-three days; in 1932–33, they lasted just twenty-six. While there were several ground records established for a single day's play, the overall match attendance aggregates decreased by 20 per cent.[3]

After Carr led a few dress rehearsals in Nottinghamshire county circles, Bodyline was officially unveiled a fortnight before the first 1932–33 Test, when the full complement of England's pace bowlers – Larwood, Voce, Bill Bowes and G. O. 'Gubby' Allen – were included for the clash against an Australian XI. As opening batsman Leo O'Brien, a left-hander, called for 'two centres', he watched with growing puzzlement as virtually everyone walked behind him. Normally against the new ball there'd be four or five in the slips and only two or three on the leg. But this time there was just one fieldsman on the offside and eight on the leg. 'But I'm the left-hander!' he called in the direction of stand-in captain Bob Wyatt.

Larwood was to dismiss Bradman in both innings, lbw in the first and bowled in the second. Jardine's plans were unfolding nicely.

Ironically, Bradman was ill leading into the first Test in Sydney and was an enforced omission from the thirteen-man squad. The Don was also embroiled in a stand-off with the Australian Board of Control over his right to earn his living outside the game as a journalist.

Knowing Bradman was a withdrawal, Jardine agonised over his final XI before including a spinner, Hedley Verity, ahead of the in-form Bowes, who had taken 77 championship wickets in August alone. The Nawab of Pataudi – or, as some in the crowd dubbed him, 'The Nawab of Potato' – was to make a century on debut, but it was totally overshadowed by the furore over leg theory and a thrilling counter-attack from Australia's Stan McCabe, the boy from Grenfell, who had debuted in England in 1930.

The Australians knew this was to be a Test series with a difference and 22-year-old McCabe, in at No. 5, told his father not to allow his mother to jump the fence if he happened to be hit. Courage ran in the McCabe family. His grandmother, Catherine McCabe, was once confronted by bushrangers outside Albury, a single rifle the only protection for her and her three sleeping children. The men eyed Mrs McCabe and her children and rode off.[4] One of the sleeping children was William McCabe, Stan's father.

Young Stan McCabe may have been slender at just 63 kg (10 st) but he was brave and his inspirational innings rattled the Englishmen. His 187 not out included 100 in boundary shots. Fifteen of the 4s came from pull shots. Larwood worked up to a furious speed, umpire George Hele rating him 'five yards faster'[5] than in 1928–29. Later it was assessed via slow-motion film that Larwood had bowled upwards of 140 km/h (90 mph), faster than anyone in history, including the Australians Cotter and Gregory and the two Englishmen Knox and Kortright.

Woodfull, Ponsford and the veteran New South Welshman Alan Kippax were particularly discomforted, Ponny turning his back and taking a smarting blow on the rump. His love of cricket was to be dulled by

Bodyline and was the influencing factor in his premature retirement less than two years later.

McCabe was also struck, on the hip by Voce, but he continued to play his shots audaciously. One Voce over went for 14 to the unbridled joy of the crowd.

On song, McCabe could outpace even the Don and his domination momentarily exposed Jardine's tactics. The two English hitmen bowled with seven on the onside and just two on the off, prompting a ground-swell of boos, which Jardine studiously ignored.

So brilliant was McCabe's strokeplay and placement that he didn't give a chance until he was well past 150. During the action-packed second morning when the crowd swelled to almost 60,000, McCabe made 51 of a 55-run 10th wicket stand with Australia's No. 11 Tim Wall.

Later McCabe told umpire Hele that he was lucky and could never expect to do it again.[6]

Australia's all-out score of 360, however, given the strength of the tourists' line-up and the quality of the wicket, was never going to be enough. Larwood took 10 wickets for the match and the Australians were beaten easily.

Bradman was released from his media contract to allow him to take his place in the second Test. O'Brien had been included for the first time and was strapping on his pads on the first morning ready to go in at No. 3 when Bradman appeared. 'You don't seem to have much confidence in me, Leo,' said the Don, reaching for his gear.

'I've had a look at the batting order,' said O'Brien. 'I'm down for [number] three.'

Taken aback, Bradman put his gear back down and went out to the viewing room. O'Brien was dismissed just after lunch, and Bradman's appearance prompted a thunderous, prolonged reception all the way to the wicket and even after he'd taken his guard.

The Yorkshire giant Bowes was operating from the southern end and stopped in his run-up, waiting for the cheering to subside. He waited and tried again but still the commotion continued. He filled in time by moving one or two of his leg-side fieldsmen a yard either way.

Finally, there was quiet, and from his shortish, shuffling run Bowes delivered short and outside the off-stump. Stepping inside the line, looking to play a pull shot, Bradman was through his shot before the ball actually arrived and his inner-edge dragged the ball onto his leg-stump. Australia's hero was out – first ball!

A shocked 'O-OOH' reverberated around the ground. Bradman glanced at his broken wicket, quickly tucked his bat under his arm and walked off in absolute shocked silence. The man he had replaced, O'Brien, was still in the rooms taking off his pads. 'Fancy doing that,' Bradman said.

Historian David Frith said the disappointment at Bradman's freakish dismissal rebounded around the country. In Launceston, a chap named Hancock was so disgusted he turned off his radio and took himself off for a walk only to come across three young kids struggling in a nearby river. He dived in, fully clothed, and saved them from almost certain drowning.[7]

More than 63,000 – a world record attendance – had witnessed the dismissal, still the most dramatic in the first 130 years of Test cricket in Melbourne. Come day three, with Bradman due to bat again, a new world record of 70,000 attended. The Don made an unbeaten century as Australia squared the series. He was on 98 when joined at the wicket by last man Bert 'Dainty' Ironmonger. At fifty, he was Australia's oldest ever Test cricketer. 'Don't worry son,' said Bert. 'I won't let you down.'[8]

To squeals of excitement, the old man kept his bat in the blockhole and somehow survived the final two balls from the medium-paced Hammond before Bradman, back on strike to Voce, pierced the leg-side field with a front-of-the-wicket pull shot, giving him the runs he needed for his only ton of the summer. There was pandemonium, even members of the English XI applauding amid the tumultuous volleys of cheers with an intensity unprecedented in Test matches at the ground. Just forty-eight hours after his infamous duck, cricket's ultimate phenomenon had triumphed again. Set 251, England started well only to be bowled out for 139, the menacing 'Tiger' O'Reilly taking his second 5-wicket haul of the match.

The Melbourne wicket had been uncharacteristically slow. Verity's absence was crucial, as it deprived Jardine of a specialist spinner. Australia had three: O'Reilly, who opened, along with Ironmonger and Grimmett.

Jardine's Bodyline tactics had been repelled but not defeated, and it was to be Australia's only success of the nastiest of all summers. Jardine so intensified his leg-theory attack that the tour was all but called off after the fieriest match of all a week later in Adelaide, where England won by more than 300 runs. Oldfield had his skull fractured and Woodfull was

The Australasian
PICTORIAL

DON BRADMAN, THE
AUSTRALIAN CHAMPION.
(S. J. Hood photograph.)

INCOMPARABLE: Don Bradman, as pictured in the colour
supplement of *The Australasian* in November 1932.

COVER APPEAL: 'Gelignite Jack' Gregory graced the cover of the first issue of Sydney's *Amateur Sports Weekly* in 1928.

THE AUSTRALIAN CAPTAIN.

W. M. WOODFULL.

THE UNBOWLABLE: Australia's Bodyline season captain Bill Woodfull in 1932–33.

The Australasian, November 1932

SERIOUSLY FAST: Harold Larwood was stronger and fitter than ever before for the 1932–33 series, his 33 wickets a stunning blitzkrieg which caused enormous animosity. Ironically, he was to eventually settle in Australia, saying he was among friends.
The Australasian, November 1932

Not transferable
Yorkshire County Cricket Club.

England v. Australia

At HEADINGLEY GROUND, LEEDS,
On JULY 11th, 12th, 14th, and 15th, 1930.

Admit *Mr C. S. M. Wilson*

TO GROUND, PAVILION, AND COMMITTEE STAND.

R.S.V.P. (stating which day or days), to *Sir Frederick Toone, Secretary,*
The Secretary, Old Bank Chambers, Leeds.

A STAR IS BORN (top): Don Bradman, 20, was lifted into
Australia's team for the first time in 1928–29, playing four of the
five Tests and making two centuries in Melbourne, the most
prolific of all his Australian venues. Australia was outplayed all
summer, until the fifth Test when it defeated England by five
wickets. Standing (l–r): Bradman, Ted A'Beckett (12th man),
Tim Wall, Percy Hornibrook, Alan Fairfax, Clarrie Grimmett,
Archie Jackson, Bert Oldfield Sitting: Ron Oxenham, Jack Ryder
(captain), Bill Woodfull, Alan Kippax.
The Australasian

Above: One of the dream tickets of them all – the game in which
Don Bradman became the first to score 300 runs in a day, on his
way to his highest-ever Test score of 334, in the drawn third Test
at Headingley in 1930.

Left: Clarrie Grimmett was the outstanding leg-spinner in the
world in the late 1920s and early 1930s. In addition to being the
first to 200 Test wickets, he wrote three books on spin bowling,
including this one in 1934.

TIME OFF: The 1930 Australians enjoy some time off. At front, from left: Vic Richardson, Bill Woodfull, Alan Kippax (in a double-breaster) and youthful Stan McCabe (right), on his first of three tours of the UK.

SCINTILLATING STAN: Stan McCabe (right) resumes Australia's innings with Clarrie Grimmett on the Saturday of the opening Bodyline Test in Sydney in December 1932. He took his overnight score of 127 to 187 with a ferocious array of brave hooks and pulls which almost buried Bodyline even before the English could get at Don Bradman.

Gordon Vidler Collection

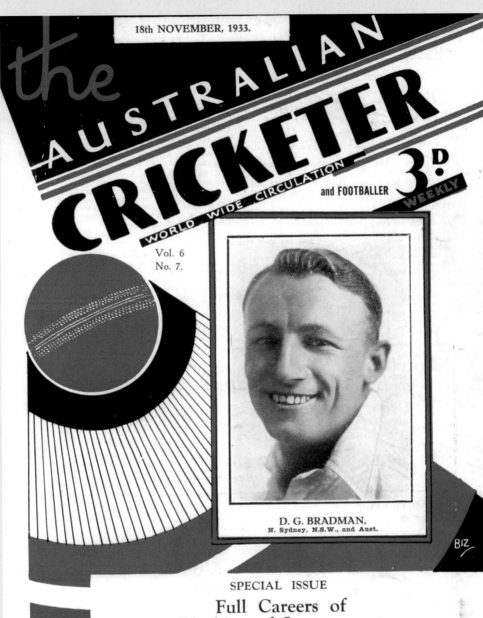

18th NOVEMBER, 1933.

the AUSTRALIAN CRICKETER

and FOOTBALLER

WORLD WIDE CIRCULATION

3D.
WEEKLY

Vol. 6
No. 7.

D. G. BRADMAN,
N. Sydney, N.S.W., and Aust.

BIZ

SPECIAL ISSUE

Full Careers of
Blackie and Ironmonger

RIGHTS VERSUS LEFTS FOR TESTS

Registered at G.P.O., Melbourne, for transmission
by post as a newspaper.

THE RECORDBREAKER: 'The Don'
on the front cover of the old *Australian
Cricketer* magazine.

AUSTRALIA'S BEST, 1932–33: After the violent Adelaide Test, the Australians named three first-timers for the fourth Test in Brisbane: Ernie Bromley, Len Darling and Hammy Love. Athletic South Australian Bert Tobin also made the XII for the only time in his career, and the Aussies were easily beaten. Standing (l–r): Tobin, Tim Wall, Bill O'Reilly, Bert Ironmonger, Bromley. Sitting: Love, Bill Ponsford, Vic Richardson, Bill Woodfull (captain), Stan McCabe, Don Bradman, Darling.

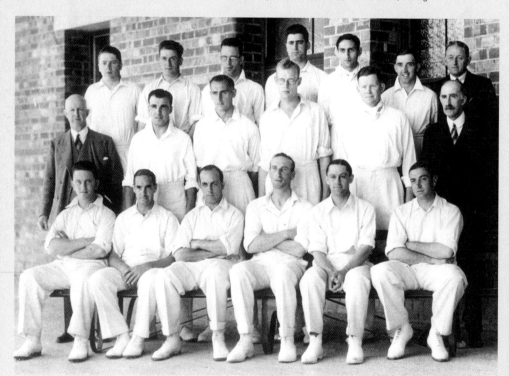

ENGLAND, 1932–33: Back row (l–r): George Duckworth, Harold Larwood, Tommy Mitchell, Bill Voce, The Nawab of Pataudi, Eddie Paynter, Bill Ferguson (scorer). Middle: Plum Warner (manager), Les Ames, Hedley Verity, Bill Bowes, Freddie Brown, Richard Palairet (co-manager). Sitting: Maurice Leyland, Herbert Sutcliffe, Bob Wyatt, Douglas Jardine (captain), Gubby Allen, Walter Hammond. Maurice Tate was also a member of the touring party.

John O'Sullivan Collection

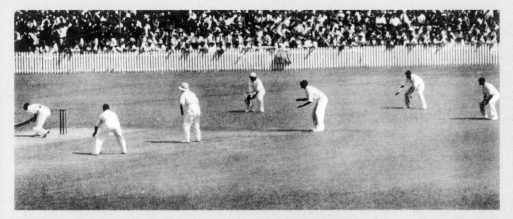

LEG THEORY: Bill Woodfull is struck in the ribs by a bouncer from Harold Larwood in Brisbane, five close-in fieldsmen waiting for a catch spooned in self-defence. The fielders from left are: Maurice Leyland, Gubby Allen, Douglas Jardine, Hedley Verity and Herbert Sutcliffe. The wicketkeeper is Les Ames.

South Australia's Champion---V. Y. Richardson

FIXTURES (above): One of the many fixture cards produced for the Bodyline summer, this one advertising State Express cigarettes.

OF STERN STUFF (left): Had no-nonsense Victor Richardson been captain and not vice-captain of the 1932–33 Australians, Bodyline would have been bowled by both teams.
The Adelaide News, *21 January 1933*

RECORDBREAKER: Bill Ponsford started his Ashes career with back-to-back centuries in 1924–25 and said farewell to the game ten years later with 181 at Headingley and 266 at The Oval.

NEWSMAKER: The arrival of Don Bradman in England was always front-page news.

FINAL HURRAH (right): Bill Woodfull (left) retired from representative cricket after the 1934 tour, citing his increased workload as a schoolteacher. He's pictured tossing the coin with England's Bob Wyatt during his final Ashes tour.

THE AUSTRALASIAN PICTORIAL

ENGLAND'S MASTER BATSMAN

Walter Hammond, England's champion batsman, who opened the tour of Australia with four consecutive centuries, posed in Melbourne especially for this portrait for "The Australasian."

PRIDE OF ENGLAND: Walter Hammond remained the outstanding English batsman in the world throughout the 1930s.

The Australasian, *November 1936*

GOODWILL SUMMER (top): The Wrigley's 1936–37 season souvenir featured opposing captains Don Bradman and Gubby Allen.

Above: The Savings Bank of South Australia produced a series of cricket fixture cards including this one for the 1934 Australian tourists to England.

John O'Sullivan Collection

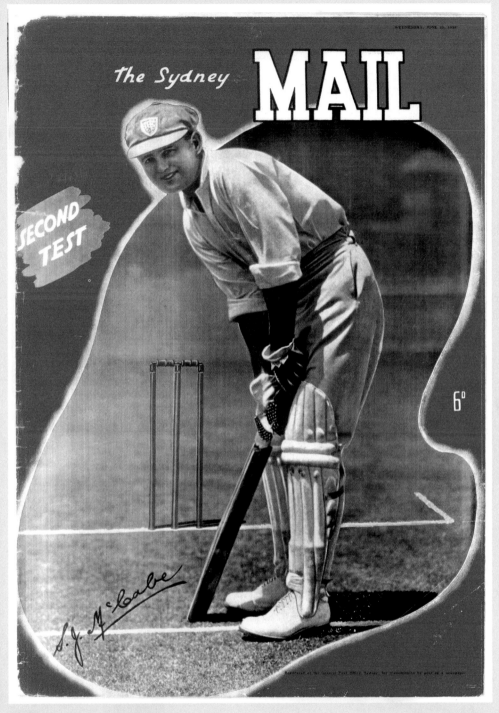

COURAGEOUS: Stan McCabe was featured on the front cover of the *Sydney Mail*
after making 232 and 39 in the drawn first Test at Trent Bridge in 1938.

Jim Rutherford Collection

OVERPOWERED: Rain-affected wickets triggered a series of topsy-turvy results early in the 1936–37 summer, the Australians losing by an innings in Sydney to go 2–0 down. Standing (l–r): Arthur Chipperfield, Ernie McCormick, Morrie Sievers, Bill O'Reilly, Frank Ward. Sitting: Ray Robinson (12th man), Leo O'Brien, Stan McCabe, Don Bradman (captain), Jack Fingleton, Bert Oldfield. Insert: Jack Badcock.

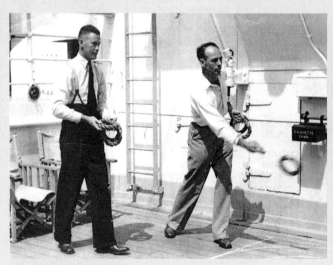

DECK QUOITS: Bill Brown and Jack Fingleton on board the *Orontes* on the way to England in 1938.

FRONTLINER: Paceman Ken Farnes took six for 96 in his final Australian appearance in the decider in Melbourne in 1936–37, only for Australia to make 600-plus and win by an innings.

IRRESISTIBLE (left): Don Bradman was the powerhouse of the 1930s, his 810 runs in the 1936–37 rubber the highest by an Ashes captain.

THE NURSERY (below): The Australians practise at Lord's soon after their arrival in England, April 1938.

IN DEMAND: Don Bradman's phenomenal success resulted in a string of companies seeking endorsement rights, from ice-cream manufacturers through to makers of cricket bats and trousers.

struck over the heart, a tremendous thump his widow believed ultimately shortened his life. A record 50,962 crammed into the oval on the Saturday, an enormous crowd for such a small city, and the action off the field was every bit as riveting as on. Australia's 12th man, O'Brien, was at the back of the rooms when Woodfull emerged from a shower with a towel draped around him. 'There are some terrible things happening out there, Leo,' he said.

Eyeing the two English team managers P.F. 'Plum' Warner and Dick Palairet who had come to sympathise, Woodfull made his famous remark: 'I don't want to see you Mr Warner. There are two teams out there. One is trying to play cricket. The other is not.'[9]

Within days the first of several terse cable messages were sent, the Australian Board of Control calling Jardine's tactics unsportsmanlike and warned that unless immediately stopped Bodyline may have severe repercussions for Anglo-Australian relations. Coverage of the Test battles back in England had centred purely on the success of Jardine's XI. To question the captain's integrity and sense of fair play was unthinkable.

'We, the Marylebone club, deplore your cable message,' came the reply. 'We depreciate your opinion that there has been unsportsmanlike play . . . (but) if you consider it desirable to cancel the remainder of the program, we would consent with great reluctance.'[10]

The series continued amid snowballing anti-British sentiment; the financial gains too important to ignore. On-field relations further plummeted, however. During one Test, one of the Australians referred to Jardine as a bastard, the worst possible insult at the time. When Warner came to the Australian dressing rooms to complain, vice-captain Vic Richardson answered the door and said: 'Which one of you blokes mistook Larwood for that bastard Jardine?'[11]

Australia lost each of the final three Tests to go down 4–1, Woodfull refusing to bow to those who wanted the Australian pacemen to retaliate. When debutant fast bowler Harry 'Bull' Alexander from Melbourne struck Jardine on the thigh in the final Test in Sydney the cheering was long and prolonged, Jardine having incited the crowd by wearing his elitist Harlequin cap, considered an emblem of Empire.

'It wasn't the game we knew,' said Bill Ponsford. 'It just wasn't cricket.' The recordbreaker was one of England's central targets. He was struck four times in Adelaide during his courageous 85 and twice in the final Test in Sydney. Rather than risk popping up a catch to the in-field, his way was to turn his back on the bouncers. Years later Bill, then seventy-nine, broke a long-running silence and agreed to our interview at the encouragement of his mate 'Mo' O'Brien. Modest to the extreme, he became very emotional talking about the battering he and his mates were subjected to that summer. 'Was it one of the reasons why you retired early Mr Ponsford?' I asked.

'Yes,' he said. 'It was.'

Bradman was criticised for making himself a moving target and for his unorthodox array of cross-batted shots. Writing in the London *Star* newspaper, Jack Hobbs commented that Bradman 'seemed to jib a bit'[12] while the vitriolic Warwick Armstrong in the London *Evening News* reckoned the Don was playing for himself, rather than the team.

He may have gone from being the *hunter* to the *hunted*, but he still topped the Australian averages with almost 400 runs. Only Hammond and Sutcliffe among the tourists made more. Larwood's 33 wickets were instrumental in England's reclaiming of the Ashes, but it was a victory without honour, the bitterness between the sides lingering for years.

Bodyline did not disappear with the final ball of the fifth Test. The West Indians bowled Bodyline at the Englishmen, most notably at Old Trafford in 1933. Despite the slowness of the wicket, Hammond had his chin cut by Learie Constantine. Returning after two stitches were inserted in the nick, he approached Constantine and said: 'Let's stick to cricket.'[13] Jardine's maiden Test century in that game was a high point. Struck several times on the body, never once did he stop to rub the spot.

Jardine was to unleash it, too, during the winter tour of India, defying the autocratic Lord Hawke, England's recalled selection chairman. In 1934, Voce bounced the visiting Australians with four short legs on his way to 8-for, before mysteriously developing 'shin soreness' and withdrawing in mid-match. Leg theory was the most contentious issue in cricket, yet it took almost a generation for procrastinating lawmakers to finally limit the number of fieldsmen allowed on the leg side.

The Voce onslaught came late on the 1934 tour, the Australians having again shown their superiority against a more orthodox line of attack. At Leeds, Bradman made another triple-century before sharing with Ponsford their famous 451-run partnership at The Oval. O'Reilly and Grimmett, with 53 wickets, were also superb, the pair being responsible for two-thirds of Australia's overs.

At Manchester after the ball was replaced during a drinks interval, O'Reilly took three wickets in four balls: Cyril Walters, Wyatt and Hammond. With his big bouncing leg-breaks and googlies and aggressive approach, O'Reilly was a revelation and was to be Australia's dominant bowler of the 1930s.

Sydney-born G. O. 'Gubby' Allen was England's leader in 1936–37. He had refused to bowl Bodyline four years earlier and resented being asked. Jardine had approached him even before the *Orontes* was out of the Bay of Biscay. He refused on the spot and was promptly told it didn't matter as Allen wouldn't be playing in the Tests anyway! In Melbourne, on the fateful morning Bradman was to fall for a first-ball duck, Jardine ordered Allen to bowl Bodyline, saying it was a legitimate, agreed team tactic – but he again refused, saying if Jardine didn't like the way he bowled he should pick someone else.[14]

Allen was to be included in every Test, his 21 wickets important in England's emphatic win. While he was to figure in only two Ashes Tests in 1934 through illness and injury, there was not a dissenter when he was named the MCC's touring captain. His mission was as much to heal the scars of 1932–33 and rebuild bridges as it was to win and he all but recaptured the Ashes in a wonderful, see-sawing series that were a reminder of the epic battles of the Great Test Series of 1894–95.

While Larwood was in martyrdom, despite amassing 300 wickets in three county seasons, Voce, his partner-in-pace at Notts, was chosen. In the opening rain-affected Tests in Brisbane and Sydney, Voce claimed 17 wickets, operating to orthodox fields.

Australia's captaincy had passed to Bradman and the spirit and goodwill between he and Allen was immediate.

Bradman was to be dismissed for two ducks in a row as England skipped to a surprise 2–0 lead, a patient double-century by Hammond in Sydney a flashback to his prolific days of 1928–29. Many wondered why Frank Ward's leg-breaks and googlies had been preferred to the seemingly evergreen Grimmett, especially after Sydney where Ward's figures ballooned to 2-132, with Hammond preying on the loose ones, one and two an over. Grimmett had captured 44 wickets the previous Test tour under

Vic Richardson in South Africa. Clearly he was not among Bradman's favourites.

The crowds in Melbourne for the third Test were large and vociferous, a world record of 350,000 fans attending over the six days. Included on the Monday was an unprecedented 87,798, many scrambling over barriers to watch from the uncompleted bays of the Melbourne Cricket Club's capacious new Southern Stand, which stretched from one end of the ground to the other. Bill Brown, then twenty-four, said so enthusiastic were the fans that they cheered wildly when catches were made – 'and we were only at fielding practice!'

England's back-to-back wins had created phenomenal interest and when Bradman declared Australia's innings closed at 200-9 after inclement weather, England firmed to favourite. The laws of cricket demanded that only the run-ups could be covered and the Melbourne wicket after rain and sun was as treacherous as any in the world.

On a spiced-up wicket, England limped to 76-9 before Allen, too, declared. In the context of the match, Hammond's 32 on a two-paced pitch was as good as his double century on a firm wicket in Sydney just weeks earlier. Maurice Leyland also relished the challenge. Both were to fall to extraordinary reflex catches at short leg by baseballer Len Darling, prompting one patron to lead a call for 'Three cheers for Lenny Darling'.

Allen had agonised over an earlier declaration but more rain threatened and the light was also murky so he carried on, the tall Victorian Morrie Sievers taking three wickets in an over on his way to 5-21. Four were in the top six. Sievers had only been included in Australia's XI at the eleventh hour after Ernie McCormick reported in ill. While only military medium, he made the ball rise dramatically off the pock marks. O'Reilly, too, whirled and snarled and was nigh on unplayable, confirming his status as Australia's finest bowler since the Golden Age.

Bradman hadn't wanted the Australians to bat again that night, so to protect his batting specialists he reversed his order, sending in tailenders O'Reilly and L.O. 'Chuck' Fleetwood-Smith, with Ward at three. While O'Reilly was out first ball, Fleetwood-Smith somehow survived, Australia going to stumps at 3-1, the game – and the Ashes – delicately poised.

Despite his misgivings at having to face the new ball on a dodgy, two-paced wicket, Fleetwood-Smith enjoyed his moment of batting fame.

He'd never opened in his life before, not even back home on the malthoid wickets at Stawell. Bradman felt if he struggled to hit them on a good batting wicket, he'd have no chance on a Melbourne sticky!

After fine weather on the Sunday, the rest day, Monday dawned bright and clear and by mid-afternoon the pitch had settled again and the batsmen resumed control, Bradman beginning an epic six-hour partnership with Jack Fingleton, which produced 346 runs. The Don scored 270, the highest of his nine MCG Test centuries, and Fingleton 136. In scoring 192 runs for the day, Bradman also passed Clem Hill's record mark of 182 on the first day of the MCG Test in 1897–98. Walter Hammond said Bradman 'more or less beat us off his own bat'.[15]

Australia made 564 to win by 365 runs, the first of three consecutive victories.

In Adelaide, a Fleetwood-Smith 'special' sunk the Englishmen on the sixth day when the game was evenly poised.

Bradman feared if Hammond (39 not out overnight) was able to re-settle and a partnership or two developed, England (148-3 chasing 392) may win the match and the series.

Hammond had delayed Fleetwood-Smith's introduction into Test cricket with a merciless hammering in a state game in Melbourne four years earlier. Brown said he can still picture Hammond running at Fleetwood-Smith and hammering him straight. 'We'd always stand a yard back for Hammond in the covers or at mid-off,' he said. 'He was a very powerful man and he loved to take on Fleetwood. He'd really make your fingers sting.'

In a see-sawing match, England had gained a narrow first-innings lead, only for a Bradman double century to ensure another sizeable target.

Going to Fleetwood-Smith on the final morning, Bradman suggested that now was as good a time as any for him to bowl 'his unplayable ball'.[16]

Fleetwood-Smith's second ball of the morning was a big-drifting chinaman, his natural wrist-spinner that was pitched full, curved and spun back wickedly through Hammond's defences and struck his off-stump. There was a roar of approval and Fleetwood-Smith sunk to his knees in jubilation. 'Was that what you wanted?' he said to Bradman.[17] The non-chalant, fun-loving womaniser had bowled the first Ball of the Century and England's champion was out. Fleetwood-Smith finished with six wickets for the innings and 10 for the game, the Australians winning comfortably. He was also given a souvenir stump by England's last man

Walter Robins who graciously said the delivery had swung the game. Earlier in the game the Englishmen had felt Fleetwood-Smith's erratic bowling looked like 'jam'.[18]

Allen reckoned Australia's good fortune in winning the toss in Melbourne and Adelaide had been the difference. But England's batting, bar Hammond and Leyland, had been fragile, especially on the flattest wicket of the summer in Adelaide where they were bowled out for just 330 and 243.

It had been more than forty years since there had been a decider and one cricket-loving English benefactor promised each member of Allen's team a new motor car if they could win the final Test. In a speech leading into the winner-take-all Test, Allen conceded he hadn't given his team 'a monkey's chance' at the tour start. Now he felt it highly capable of returning with the Ashes.[19]

The Australians had included champion footballer Laurie Nash in their thirteen and rumours that Nash would bounce the Englishmen à la Bodyline were so persistent that Allen told Bradman over lunch in the lead-ups that England would not tolerate any bowler who bowled directly at his batsmen.

According to Nash's biographer E.A. 'Ned' Wallish, Allen also approached umpire Jack Scott, accusing Nash of bowling Bodyline at his top-order in the Victoria-MCC game.[20] He warned Scott if there was a repeat he would call his batsmen from the field.[21] It led to an extraordinary situation with both captains meeting with the umpires and Board of Control members and being told that intimidatory bowling would not be tolerated.

Allen's biographer, E.W. 'Jim' Swanton, confirms the Englishman's angst approaching the decider. 'Determined that the last Test should maintain the hard but friendly nature of those preceding it, Gubby told the Don over lunch on the eve of the match that if Bodyline tactics were introduced, he would hold the Australian captain responsible and consider himself free to retaliate.'[22]

The match proved to be one-sided, Bradman's luck in winning the toss allowing the Australians to bat first in searing heat and amass an unassailable 604, a whirlwind third-wicket stand of 249 in under three hours between centurions Bradman and McCabe an unforgettable highlight on the opening day. While McCabe was dropped three times,

Bradman's superlative 100 was chanceless and took just 125 minutes. Later Ross Gregory, playing only his second Test, and Jack Badcock, playing his third, added 161 to effectively play England out of the game, the tourists' only bright light being tall paceman Ken Farnes who took 6-96.

Mentally and physically exhausted at the end of a long campaign, Allen had seriously considered withdrawing from the match. He dropped several important catches early in the innings and his figures of 0-99 were those of a captain whose tour had gone one Test too long. England was beaten by an innings.

Nash took five wickets for the game and hardly bowled a short ball. He also camped under the final catch, from Farnes, on the last morning, the ball a prize souvenir from his one and only Ashes Test match. The only bouncers came from McCormick, the recipient Wyatt making a joke of it all and brandishing his bat at McCormick as if he intended to hit him on the head.

Had England been prepared to select, in its original touring party, 20-year-old rookie Len Hutton, or play 42-year-old Sutcliffe one last time, the series could well have been won by England. From the time Stan Worthington was dismissed first ball of the series in Brisbane, the Englishmen struggled at the head of the order, Arthur Fagg being promoted in Sydney and Hedley Verity in Adelaide without marked success. England's highest opening stand all summer was just 53.

In scoring more than 800 runs in his first series as captain, Bradman had again emphasised his standing in the game as Australia's finest ever. Woodfull claimed him to be worth two batsmen; the Englishmen felt it was closer to three.

The Don was to maintain his form in England in 1938, where amid forming war clouds, the Ashes were retained 1–1 with two draws, the Manchester Test being abandoned without a ball being bowled.

Bradman made a century in every Test in which he batted before rolling his ankle at The Oval as England amassed 903-7 dec. and Hutton motored past Bradman's Test record score of 334. Fingleton was also injured and the Australians forced to bat two men short, Brown all but batting through the first innings, being the last man out before the follow-on. With more than 500 runs in four Tests, Brown enjoyed the season of his life and was to be rewarded immediately after World War II with the Australian captaincy, including a one-off Test in New Zealand.

Man of the decade: *Don Bradman*

When English maestro Walter Hammond became the first Ashes batsman to tally 900 runs during his remarkable 1928–29 summer, it was a colossal achievement and one most felt would stand for years.

However, just eighteen months later, Don Bradman, then twenty-one and on his first English tour, amassed 974 runs, including a phenomenal 334 at Leeds and 254 at Lord's, the finest innings of his fabled career. He was unstoppable, the player of the hour, the single most potent force any Australian cricket XI had ever paraded.

At a time when the Great Depression was forcing thousands out of work, Bradman's run sprees lifted morale and offered fresh hope to the community. Crowds doubled when the Don was in, teammate Bill Brown telling the story of how Sydney fans would become restless if he and his New South Wales opening partner Jack Fingleton batted too long. 'When one of us did get out, the cheering was amazing and you'd be feeling pretty good about it all, until you realised they were cheering for the man walking in, not the one walking off!'

Bowling attacks simply disintegrated as Bradman amassed centuries, seemingly at will. No one was more ruthless or as focused.

Neil Harvey, one of Bradman's Greats of '48, says the Don after World War II was extraordinarily good, despite seven years out of the game. 'Before the war, he must have simply been out of this world,' he said.

Bradman averaged 56 even in the season of Bodyline when Harold Larwood, Bill Voce and co. were bowling leg theory. His second innings century in Melbourne lifted Australia to its only win of the bloodiest series of all. His performances on three tours of England in the 1930s were superlative. In 1930 he averaged 139, in 1934, 94 and in 1938, 108.

Australia rarely lost when Bradman was in full flow. The Ashes were at stake in 1936–37, England 2–0 up with three Tests to play. Rain interfered early in Melbourne before Bradman led a magnificent fightback, his 270 as valuable as any innings he ever played.

In later years Bradman would deliberately spend periods relaxing at the non-striker's end before re-launching. Before the war he tended to so dominate the strike that teammates often felt they were just out there to run for him.

Technically, the Don regarded his 254 at Lord's as his finest ever knock. 'Practically without exception every ball went where it was intended to go,' he said.[23]

England captain Norman Yardley led three cheers when Bradman arrived at the wicket at The Oval in his final Test match in 1948. The Don needed only a boundary to finish with an average of 100, but was bowled by an Eric Hollies googly, leaving him on 99.94.

Bradman averaged 98 and had a strike-rate of 63 runs per 100 balls in his 33 Tests on Australian soil. His Ashes average in Australia was 78 and in England 102.[24] He was a phenomenon.

Bradman v. England   * not out

Season	Scores	Runs	Ave
1928–29	18, 1, 79, 112, 40, 58, 123, 37*	468	66.85
1930	8, 131, 254, 1, 334, 14, 232	974	139.14
1932–33	0, 103*, 8, 66, 76, 24, 48, 71	396	56.50
1934	29, 25, 36, 13, 30, 304, 244, 77	758	94.75
1936–37	38, 0, 0, 82, 13, 270, 26, 212, 169	810	90.00
1938	51, 144*, 18, 102*, 103, 16	434	108.50
1946–47	187, 234, 79, 49, 0, 56*, 12, 63	680	97.14
1948	138, 0, 38, 89, 7, 30*, 3, 173*, 0	508	72.57

Tests v. England:	37 (52 overall)
Runs:	5,028 (6996)
Average:	89.78 (99.94)
Highest score:	334, Leeds, 1930
100s:	19 (29)

Match of the decade: *Melbourne, 1937*

World-record crowds, including an unprecedented 87 000-plus on Day 3, revelled in one of the great, tactical Tests, England declaring behind on a treacherous, rain-affected wicket and Don Bradman countering by shielding his top-order and sending out tailenders L.O. 'Chuck' Fleetwood-Smith and Bill O'Reilly to open Australia's second innings. Delaying his own entry until No. 7 when the wicket had improved, Bradman, partnered by Jack Fingleton, added a record 346 for the sixth wicket against a most-competitive attack, which include Bodyliner Bill Voce and the celebrated left-arm finger spinner Hedley Verity. His 270 was his sixth century in Melbourne surpassing Jack Hobbs's previous record of five.

Match scores: Australia 200-9 dec. (McCabe 63) and 564 (Fingleton 136, Bradman 270) defeated England 76-9 dec. (Sievers 5-21) and 323 (Leyland 111 not out, Robins 61, Fleetwood-Smith 5-124) by 365 runs

Looking back: *Bill Brown . . . Lord's, 1938*

'Given half a chance, I would have carried the Lord's wicket all around England. I loved it there. I got a 100 the first time I played there [in 1934]. It was only my second Test match and the following tour [1938] I got a double, carrying my bat as well. When I walked in, still not out, Jack Fingleton, one of my great mates, said: "Browny, what have you done!" Funnily enough just two or three overs before the end Eddie Paynter missed me at mid-on. It was a nice, soft catch, too . . .

'I've always thought Lord's tends to bring out whatever you have in you from a cricket point of view because of the atmosphere and all its history and tradition. It was a great for me. I managed to get a few runs there. The wicket was quicker than the average England wicket and played very truly. It was more like an Australian wicket. It suited me better than the slower wickets where you had to force the ball.'

Bill Brown toured England three times, in 1934, 1938 and 1948.
He also captained Australia, for eight hours, in a one-off international against New Zealand, later proclaimed a Test, in 1945–46.

Odd spot: *He died young*

Despite scoring 23, 50 and 80 in his first two Tests as a 22-year-old in 1936–37, Ross Gregory was omitted from Australia's 1938 Ashes touring team, Don Bradman preferring the slick slips catching of 1934 tourist Arthur Chipperfield. Bradman felt Gregory would have future opportunities, but the gifted right-hander was to perish in World War II, aged twenty-six.

One for the statisticians: *An ironical twist*

Only one man featured in both of Australia's two heaviest ever Test defeats, by 675 runs in Brisbane in 1928–29 and by an innings and 579 runs at The Oval in 1938: Don Bradman.

Tests 1930 to 1938

KEY: M Matches **I** Innings **NO** Not out innings **HS** Highest score **BB** Best bowling
5wI 5-wicket innings **10wM** 10-wicket match ***** Not out **#** Second innings **rh** Retired hurt

Series results

	Tests	Aust	Eng	Drawn
1930 (Eng)	5	2	1	2
1932–33 (Aust)	5	1	4	0
1934 (Eng)	5	2	1	2
1936–37 (Aust)	5	3	2	0
1938 (Eng)	4†	1	1	2
Total	**24**	**9**	**9**	**6**
Progressive	143	57	55	31

† The Third Test at Manchester was abandoned without a ball bowled and is excluded.

Summary

	Runs	Wkts	Ave
Australia	13,516	386	35.01
England	13,044	366	35.63

Highest innings totals

Australia		England	
729-6 dec^	Lord's 1930 (2nd Test)	903-7 dec †	The Oval 1938 (5th Test)
701	The Oval 1934 (5th Test)	658-8 dec	Nottingham 1938 (1st Test)
695	The Oval 1930 (5th Test)	627-9 dec	Manchester 1934 (3rd Test)
604	Melbourne 1936–37 (5th Test)	524	Sydney 1932–33 (1st Test)
584	Leeds 1934 (4th Test)	494	Lord's 1938 (2nd Test)
566	Leeds 1930 (3rd Test)	454	Sydney 1932–33 (5th Test)
564	Melbourne (3rd Test) 1936–37#		
491	Manchester 1934 (3rd Test)		

† highest total in Australia versus England Tests
^ highest total by Australia against England

Lowest completed innings totals

Australia		England	
58	Brisbane 1936–37 (1st Test)#	123	Leeds 1938 (4th Test)#
	(one batsman absent)	139	Melbourne 1932–33 (2nd Test)#
80	Sydney 1936–37 (2nd Test)	141	Nottingham 1934 (1st Test)#
	(one batsman absent)	145	The Oval 1934 (5th Test)#
118	Lord's 1934 (2nd Test)#	*Also note:*	
123	The Oval 1938 (5th Test)#	76-9 dec Melbourne 1936–37 (3rd Test)	
	(two batsmen absent)		

Leading run scorers

	M	I	NO	Runs	HS	Ave	100	50
Australia								
D.G. Bradman	23	38	3	3372	334	96.34	13	6
S.J. McCabe	24	43	3	1931	232	48.27	4	10
W.H. Ponsford	11	19	1	1040	266	57.77	3	4
W.A. Brown	11	21	1	907	206*	45.35	3	3
W.M. Woodfull	15	25	2	878	155	38.17	1	7
J.H.W. Fingleton	12	21	0	671	136	31.95	2	2
England								
W.R. Hammond	24	41	2	1779	240	45.61	5	7
M. Leyland	19	32	3	1515	187	52.24	6	2
H. Sutcliffe	13	23	4	1180	194	62.10	2	9
L.E.G. Ames	17	27	2	675	120	27.00	1	4
R.E.S. Wyatt	12	21	2	633	78	33.31	–	5
C.J. Barnett	8	14	0	610	129	43.57	2	2
E. Paynter	7	11	4	591	216*	84.42	1	3

Hundreds

Australia (27)		**England (25)**	
13	D.G. Bradman	6	M. Leyland
4	S.J. McCabe	5	W.R. Hammond
3	W.A. Brown	2	C.J. Barnett
	W.H. Ponsford		L. Hutton
2	J.H.W. Fingleton		H. Sutcliffe
1	C.L. Badcock	1	L.E.G. Ames
	W.M. Woodfull		A.P.F. Chapman
			D.C.S. Compton
			K.S. Duleepsinhji
			J. Hardstaff jnr
			E.H. Hendren
			Nawab of Pataudi
			E. Paynter

Highest individual scores

Australia

334	D. G. Bradman at Leeds 1930 (3rd Test)
	(highest individual score for Australia against England)
304	D. G. Bradman at Leeds 1934 (4th Test)
270	D. G. Bradman at Melbourne 1936–37 (3rd Test)#
266	W. H. Ponsford at The Oval 1934 (5th Test)
254	D. G. Bradman at Lord's 1930 (2nd Test)
244	D. G. Bradman at The Oval 1934 (5th Test)
232	D. G. Bradman at The Oval 1930 (5th Test)
232	S. J. McCabe at Nottingham 1938 (1st Test)
212	D. G. Bradman at Adelaide 1936–37 (4th Test)#
206*	W. A. Brown at Lord's 1938 (2nd Test)
187*	S. J. McCabe at Sydney 1932–33 (1st Test)
181	W. H. Ponsford at Leeds 1934 (4th Test)
169	D. G. Bradman at Melbourne 1936–37 (5th Test)
155	W. M. Woodfull at Lord's 1930 (2nd Test)
144*	D. G. Bradman at Nottingham 1938 (1st Test)#

England

364	L. Hutton at The Oval 1938 (5th Test)
	(highest score for England against all countries)
240	W. R. Hammond at Lord's 1938 (2nd Test)
231*	W. R. Hammond at Sydney 1936–37 (2nd Test)
216*	E. Paynter at Nottingham 1938 (1st Test)
194	H. Sutcliffe at Sydney 1932–33 (1st Test)
187	M. Leyland at The Oval 1938 (5th Test)
173	K. S. Duleepsinhji at Lord's 1930 (2nd Test)
169*	J. Hardstaff jnr at The Oval 1938 (5th Test)
161	H. Sutcliffe at The Oval 1930 (5th Test)
153	M. Leyland at Manchester 1934 (3rd Test)

Carrying bat through completed innings

W. M. Woodfull	73* out of 193 for Australia at Adelaide 1932–33 (3rd Test)#
	(Australia batted one man short)
W. A. Brown	206* out of 422 for Australia at Lord's 1938 (2nd Test)

500 runs in a series

	Season	M	I	NO	Runs	HS	Ave	100	50
Australia									
D. G. Bradman	1930	5	7	0	974	334	139.14	4	–
D. G. Bradman	1936–37	5	9	0	810	270	90.00	3	1
D. G. Bradman	1934	5	8	0	758	304	94.75	2	1
W. H. Ponsford	1934	4	7	1	569	266	94.83	2	1
W. A. Brown	1938	4	8	1	512	206*	73.14	2	1
Also note:									
S. J. McCabe	1936–37	5	9	0	491	112	54.55	1	5
England									
No instance – best:									
M. Leyland	1934	5	8	1	478	153	68.28	3	–

Hundred partnerships

Australia (24)

Partnerships of 150 and over:

451	2nd	W. H. Ponsford and D. G. Bradman at The Oval 1934 (5th Test)
		(Australian 2nd wicket record against all countries)
388	4th	W. H. Ponsford and D. G. Bradman at Leeds 1934 (4th Test)
		(Australian 4th wicket record against all countries)
346	6th	J. H. W. Fingleton and D. G. Bradman at Melbourne 1936–37 (3rd Test)#
		(Australian 6th wicket record against all countries)
249	3rd	D. G. Bradman and S. J. McCabe at Melbourne 1936–37 (5th Test)
243	4th	D. G. Bradman and A. Jackson at The Oval 1930 (5th Test)
231	2nd	W. M. Woodfull and D. G. Bradman at Lord's 1930 (2nd Test)
229	3rd	D. G. Bradman and A. F. Kippax at Leeds 1930 (3rd Test)
196	2nd	W. A. Brown and S. J. McCabe at Manchester 1934 (3rd Test)
192	2nd	W. M. Woodfull and D. G. Bradman at Leeds 1930 (3rd Test)
192	3rd	D. G. Bradman and A. F. Kippax at Lord's 1930 (2nd Test)#
170	2nd	W. A. Brown and D. G. Bradman at Nottingham 1938 (1st Test)#
162	1st	W. M. Woodfull and W. H. Ponsford at Lord's 1930 (2nd Test)
161	5th	C. L. Badcock and R. G. Gregory at Melbourne 1936–37 (5th Test)
159	1st	W. M. Woodfull and W. H. Ponsford at The Oval 1930 (5th Test)
150	3rd	D. G. Bradman and S. J. McCabe at The Oval 1934 (5th Test)#

England (32)

Partnerships of 150 and over:

382	2nd	L. Hutton and M. Leyland at The Oval 1938 (5th Test)
		(English 2nd wicket record against all countries)
222	4th	W. R. Hammond and E. Paynter at Lord's 1938 (2nd Test)
219	1st	C. J. Barnett and L. Hutton at Nottingham 1938 (1st Test)
215	6th	L. Hutton and J. Hardstaff jnr at The Oval 1938 (5th Test)
		(equal English 6th wicket record against Australia)
206	5th	E. Paynter and D. C. S. Compton at Nottingham 1938 (1st Test)
		(English 5th wicket record against Australia)
191	5th	E. H. Hendren and M. Leyland at Manchester 1934 (3rd Test)
188	2nd	H. Sutcliffe and W. R. Hammond at Sydney 1932–33 (1st Test)
186	6th	W. R. Hammond and L. E. G. Ames at Lord's 1938 (2nd Test)
170	6th	H. Sutcliffe and R. E. S. Wyatt at The Oval 1930 (5th Test)
156	5th	M. Leyland and R. E. S. Wyatt at Adelaide 1932–33 (3rd Test)

Leading wicket-takers

	Tests	Balls	Mdns	Runs	Wkts	Ave	BB	5wl	10wM
Australia									
W. J. O'Reilly	19	7,864	439	2,587	102	25.36	7-54	8	3
C. V. Grimmett	13	5,359	267	1,919	59	32.52	6-167	6	1
T. W. Wall	13	3,431	102	1,474	35	42.11	5-72	1	–
L. O. Fleetwood-Smith	7	2,359	54	1,190	33	36.06	6-110	2	1
England									
H. Verity	18	4,930	257	1,656	59	28.06	8-43	3	1
G. O. B. Allen	13	2,783	58	1,603	43	37.27	5-36	1	–
W. Voce	9	2,098	43	967	41	23.58	6-41	1	1
K. Farnes	8	2,153	58	1,065	38	28.02	6-96	3	1
H. Larwood	8	1,928	60	936	37	25.29	5-28	2	1
W. R. Hammond	24	3,248	105	1,325	31	42.74	5-57	1	–
W. E. Bowes	6	1,459	41	741	30	24.70	6-142	3	–

Five wickets in an innings

Australia (20)		**England (17)**	
8	W. J. O'Reilly	3	W. E. Bowes
6	C. V. Grimmett		K. Farnes
2	L. O. Fleetwood-Smith		H. Verity
1	P. M. Hornibrook	1	G. O. B. Allen
	T. W. Wall		E. W. Clark
	F. A. Ward		W. R. Hammond
			I. A. R. Peebles
			M. W. Tate
			W. Voce

Best individual bowling

Australia

7-54	W. J. O'Reilly at Nottingham 1934 (1st Test)#
7-92	P. M. Hornibrook at The Oval 1930 (5th Test)#
7-189	W. J. O'Reilly at Manchester 1934 (3rd Test)
6-102	F. A. Ward at Brisbane 1936–37 (1st Test)#
6-107	C. V. Grimmett at Lord's 1930 (2nd Test)#
6-110	L. O. Fleetwood-Smith at Adelaide 1936–37 (4th Test)#

England

8-43	H. Verity at Lord's 1934 (2nd Test)#
7-61	H. Verity at Lord's 1934 (2nd Test)
6-41	W. Voce at Brisbane 1936–37 (1st Test)
6-96	K. Farnes at Melbourne 1936–37 (5th Test)
6-142	W. E. Bowes at Leeds 1934 (4th Test)
6-204	I. A. R. Peebles at The Oval 1930 (5th Test)

10 wickets in a match

Australia (5)

11-129	W. J. O'Reilly (4-75 and 7-54) at Nottingham 1934 (1st Test)
10-122	W. J. O'Reilly (5-66 and 5-56) at Leeds 1938 (4th Test)
10-129	W. J. O'Reilly (5-63 and 5-66) at Melbourne 1932–33 (2nd Test)
10-201	C. V. Grimmett (5-107 and 5-94) at Nottingham 1930 (1st Test)
10-239	L. O. Fleetwood-Smith (4-129 and 6-110) at Adelaide 1936–37 (4th Test)

England (4)

15-104	H. Verity (7-61 and 8-43) at Lord's 1934 (2nd Test)
10-57	W. Voce (6-41 and 4-16) at Brisbane 1936–37 (1st Test)
10-124	H. Larwood (5-96 and 5-28) at Sydney 1932–33 (1st Test)
10-179	K. Farnes (5-102 and 5-77) at Nottingham 1934 (1st Test)

25 wickets in a series

	Season	Tests	Balls	Mdns	Runs	Wkts	Ave	BB	5wI	10wM
Australia										
C. V. Grimmett	1930	5	2,098	78	925	29	31.89	6-167	4	1
W. J. O'Reilly	1934	5	2,002	128	698	28	24.92	7-54	2	1
W. J. O'Reilly	1932–33	5	2,302	144	724	27	26.81	5-63	2	1
W. J. O'Reilly	1936–37	5	1,982	89	555	25	22.20	5-51	2	–
C. V. Grimmett	1934	5	2,379	148	668	25	26.72	5-64	2	–
England										
H. Larwood	1932–33	5	1,322	42	644	33	19.51	5-28	2	1
W. Voce	1936–37	5	1,297	20	560	26	21.53	6-41	1	1
Also note:										
H. Verity	1934	5	1,628	93	576	24	24.00	8-43	2	1

Leading wicketkeepers

	Tests	Dismissals	Catches	Stumpings
Australia				
W. A. S. Oldfield	19	47	33	14
England				
L. E. G. Ames	17	37	33	4
G. Duckworth	5	12	10	2

Leading fieldsmen

	Tests	Catches		Tests	Catches
Australia			**England**		
S. J. McCabe	24	21	W. R. Hammond	24	36
D. G. Bradman	23	13	G. O. B. Allen	13	15
A. G. Chipperfield	9	13	H. Verity	18	14
V. Y. Richardson	9	11			

Captains

	Tests	Won	Lost	Drawn	Toss won
Australia					
W. M. Woodfull	15	5	6	4	8
D. G. Bradman	9	4	3	2	3
England					
G. O. B. Allen	5	2	3	0	2
D. R. Jardine	5	4	1	0	1
R. E. S. Wyatt	5	1	2	2	4
A. P. F. Chapman	4	1	1	2	2
W. R. Hammond	4	1	1	2	4
C. F. Walters	1	0	1	0	0

Most appearances

Australia (39 players)		England (47 players)	
24	S. J. McCabe	24	W. R. Hammond
23	D. G. Bradman	19	M. Leyland
19	W. A. S. Oldfield	18	H. Verity
	W. J. O'Reilly	17	L. E. G. Ames
15	W. M. Woodfull		

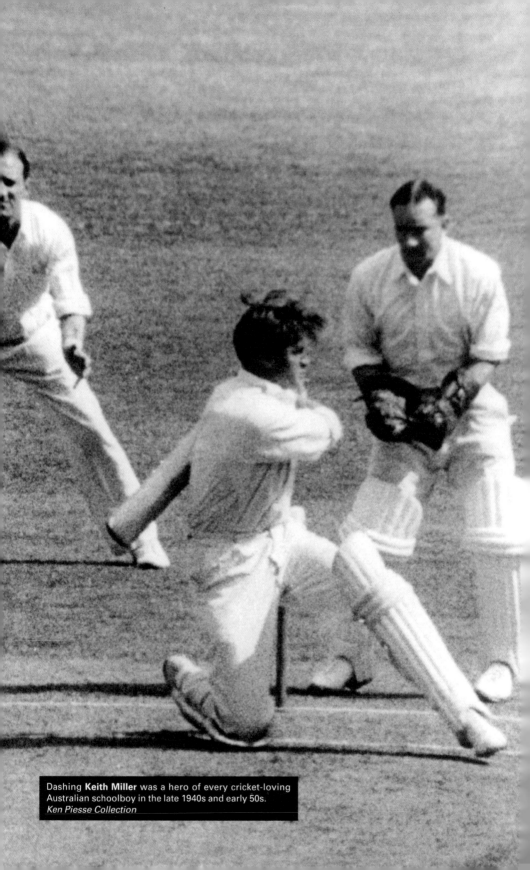

Dashing **Keith Miller** was a hero of every cricket-loving Australian schoolboy in the late 1940s and early 50s. *Ken Piesse Collection*

1940s
NUGGET AND THE ROARING '40S

'After a while they brought [Jim] Laker on to bowl and about the third ball Keith hit him straight back over my head for six. That was pretty good. Two balls later back it came again, over my head and into the crowd for another six. "This can't be such a tough game after all," I thought . . .'

Cricket and everything else was shuffled into the background during the six dark years of the Second World War. The Japanese advances deep into the south-west Pacific saw Manila and Singapore fall. Darwin was bombed and the enemy's midget submarines even made it as far as Sydney Harbour. Never before had Australians felt so threatened.

Among tens of thousands to perish while serving King and Country were some of cricket's most celebrated including Yorkshireman Hedley Verity, England's Ashes strike bowler Ken Farnes and Australian internationals Ross Gregory and Charlie Walker.

Verity was badly wounded and captured in Sicily while leading the Green Howards. Lapsing in and out of consciousness for several days, he spoke of seeing his beloved Headingley again before dying, aged thirty-eight, and having his remains re-interred in Caserta's military cemetery.[1]

Farnes, one of the heroes of G.O. 'Gubby' Allen's 1936–37 campaign, died instantly when he crash-landed during a training drill near the village of Chipping Warden in Northamptonshire. He was thirty.

Gregory died even younger, at twenty-six. The Wellington bomber that he was navigating crashing in a fierce thunderstorm near Ghafargon, Assam, in India. He had been desperately unlucky to miss selection on the 1938 Ashes tour, captain-selector Don Bradman sure that the kid with the widest smile of all would make it another time.

Walker, thirty-three, a two-time tourist to England in the 1930s, was killed in action in an RAAF air battle over Soltau in Germany.

Many from Sheffield Shield ranks also perished, including Victoria Cross recipient, 23-year-old Victorian fast bowler Bill Newton who was beheaded on the beach at Salamaua. In nine months in the Pacific War he'd led more than fifty enemy raids.[2] Few displayed greater bravery in the face of the enemy.

There had been little cricket of consequence since 1940, but the success of the 'Victory Tests' in England in 1945 – the year of Japan's surrender – triggered the relaunching of interstate cricket back home.

An Australian Services XI played an almost full-strength English XI in a series of gloriously carefree matches that provided a much-needed diversion after years of air raids and anguish.

It was during this uplifting summer that the charismatic Melburnian Keith Miller was proclaimed as cricket's budding new champion. He was just a boy when he first represented Victoria and was too young to make the 1938 tour. Back then, too, he was purely a batsman and hardly bowled, even in the nets.

In 1939–40, the final season of Sheffield Shield before the War, Miller made his maiden first-class century against Clarrie Grimmett and South Australia in the Christmas Week fixture in Melbourne. Unlike many of his teammates reluctant to leave the crease against the old spin legend, Miller the Brave advanced yards down the wicket bruising the pickets at long-off.

Itching to be involved in the war, he'd become a bomber pilot flying mainly Beauforts and Mosquitos during thirty hair-raising months based in London and beyond. He always said it was a miracle that he survived. Dozens of others around him, including many of his AIF buddies, weren't as fortunate. Little wonder he was to be nicknamed 'Nugget'.

Then in his mid-20s, Miller wasn't even sure that he wanted to play cricket again after the war. So many of his closest buddies had died. He'd met an American girl he was to marry. Sport seemed unimportant after his wartime experiences. It felt almost surreal donning a pair of creams. Focused he was, but there was a line others crossed, Bradman especially, that had no appeal. It was one of the reasons why the pair clashed so often. Miller admired the Don's sheer cricketing skills, but little else. And he was to remain a bitter critic right up until his death in 2004.

Before the Services' XI had officially formed, Miller had played a diversionary fixture or two, including one for the Dominions' XI at Lord's in 1943 when he bowled for the first time to the gifted Denis Compton.

'What does this chap do, Stan?' said Compton, turning to the team's wicketkeeper Stan Sismey.

'Oh he's not really a bowler,' came the reply. 'Probably just wants some exercise. You might find him a bit quick though.'

After a toss of the head, Miller cantered in from just a dozen strides and sent one whizzing past Compton's shoulder. So fast was the delivery that the hairs on the back of Compton's neck stood to attention. 'It was the fastest ball I'd faced since Ernie McCormick in 1938,' said Compton.[3] In 1945, Miller's first ball at Lord's zeroed into Testman Bob Wyatt's gloves and ballooned to slip for the easiest of catches. He was fast all right.

It was also at Lord's, the cathedral of cricket, that Miller made an epic 185 representing a Dominions XI against England. He always said he never played a finer innings. Included were seven joyful 6s, one soaring hit from leg-spinner Eric Hollies landing on the roof of the broadcasting hut above the England dressing room. Journalist and author E.W. 'Jim' Swanton had never witnessed such hitting and said no ground in the world was big enough for Miller the showman.[4] Imagine how far his hits would have travelled with the bats of today with their ever-so-wide sweet spots!

Warrant officer Lindsay Hassett and Sergeant Cec Pepper, one of the finest never to play Tests, were also leaders among the Australian squad which in all was to play almost fifty games in a prolonged campaign extending back into Australia à la the 1919 AIF boys.

Despite some attempts, the five tests in England were never accorded official status, but their popularity triggered cricket's new dawning with Ashes battles recommencing, home and away, from 1946.

Bradman had spent much of the war convalescing. He'd suffered from fibrosis in his back and complained, too, of a lack of feeling in one hand.

He was to be invalided out of the Army and wasn't well enough to join the first official Australian touring team to New Zealand in the autumn of 1946. But he did help select the side that was chockfull of champions such as Miller, his South Melbourne teammate Ian Johnson, Ray Lindwall, Don Tallon and the great Bill O'Reilly. The team was led by Bill Brown. One international, later proclaimed a Test, was played, which lasted just eight hours.

Bradman returned for 1946–47, under weight and unwell but determined to help cricket revive especially in an Ashes year. Wife Jessie had said it would be a pity if their young son, John, was not to see him play.[5]

The Don's status as cricket's ultimate drawcard was undiminished, 11,560 turning up on a working Monday in October in Adelaide to see his comeback innings, only his fourth in first-class ranks since 1941.

With its food rationing and massive restoration programs, England was affected more than most by the war. Cricket played a vital part in the return to normality.

Walter Hammond had resumed as captain, England hosting India in the summer of 1946 before touring down-under in the winter. While the old master performed modestly in the three home Tests, he amassed four centuries in his first five innings with Gloucestershire on his way to a season average of 108 and was encouraged enough, even at the ripe old age of forty-three, to make his fourth and final tour to Australia.

Star of the northern summer was the Surrey seamer Alec Bedser who took more than 100 county wickets in his first major season, including 11 wickets in his first Test and 11 more in his second despite rib cartilage problems. Tall at 191 cm (6 ft 3 in) and strongly built at 97 kg (15 st 4 lb), Bedser had huge hands and all but made the ball talk. He was to head England's attack for almost a decade on his way to eclipsing Clarrie Grimmett's Test wickets record.

On the resumption of Anglo-Australian rivalries in 1946, the average age of the Australian team was twenty-nine and England thirty-one. The two oldest players to take the field at Brisbane in the first Test were opposing captains Hammond and 38-year-old Bradman. The youngest were Arthur Morris, twenty-four, and Lindwall, twenty-five, less than a year into their Test careers.

Australia's XI for the opening Test in Brisbane included only three who had played before the war: Bradman, Hassett and opening batsman Sid Barnes. Among the rookies were the left-handed Morris, from Bradman's old club St George, where he'd begun as a chinaman bowler who batted in the last four. So rapid was his advance, however, that he was to make twin centuries on debut opening the innings for New South Wales before having to wait another five years to play any more meaningful cricket.

Diminutive George Tribe from Yarraville in Melbourne's west was also part of Australia's first post-war XI, Bradman having vetoed his selection in the Australian XI match against the tourists earlier in the tour so as not to alert the English to his zestful combination of each-way wrist spinners.

With his very first ball at practice at the 'Gabba, Tribe bowled Bradman with his chinaman, the Don immediately starting to bat on off-stump so Tribe couldn't see any of the stumps. 'He was going to make certain if he missed it was going to hit his legs,' Tribe says. 'He wasn't going to be bowled out again.'

Hailstones as big as golf balls dented car roofs on the third night, the centre square resembling a lake with the stumps floating somewhere in the middle. In those days only run-ups could be covered once the game had started. With his first ball of the fourth morning, Miller knocked Cyril Washbrook's cap off with a ball pitched on a half-volley length. Bill Edrich was so bruised and battered in an hour and a half that he came in looking like he'd been in a feature fight at the old Brisbane Stadium.

Bradman's return matches were triumphant. He made 187 in Brisbane and followed with 234 in Sydney as Australia won handsomely, on both occasions with an innings to spare.

There was controversy though, especially at the 'Gabba where Bradman, on 28, appeared to be caught in the gully by Jack Ikin from the bowling of old Bodyliner Bill Voce. To the shock of most, Bradman made no movement to leave and after a moment's hesitation, umpire George Borwick ruled him not out. Hammond was savage. He felt it had been a clear catch and at the change of ends walked past Bradman and said: 'A fine fucking way to start a series'.[6]

In Sydney, having made just 22, the Don appeared to again be caught by Ikin, this time at short-leg from a full-blooded flick at Bedser. He stayed in his crease and again the umpire ruled in his favour. 'Bedser, not a man to dispute any official decision, was dumbfounded and so were three other fieldsmen on the leg-side who had a perfect view of the shot and the catch,' said writer and broadcaster Clif Cary.[7]

From a distance, having eyed both incidents through binoculars, Cary claimed there was no dispute; the Don was out both times. Had the umpire agreed, his aggregate after his first two Test knocks would have been just 50, not 421.

Others, however, including Englishman Bruce Harris felt the ball had 'come off the deck',[8] having been squeezed into the ground before flying to Ikin.

Of Bradman's controversial Brisbane escape, Bedser later wrote that it was the best thing for cricket in the long term. 'He had been far from well and if he had failed, he could easily have retired and not come to England in 1948. His presence on that 1948 Australia tour was an important factor in re-stimulating the game and reawakening public interest after the barren years of the war.'[9]

Hammond may have been miffed but he appreciated the quality of Bradman's batting, which was to bring yet another 600-plus Ashes run aggregate. 'I was forced to admire the cool way Don batted,' he said. 'On one or two occasions when he was well set and when he saw me move a fieldsman he would raise his gloved hand to me in mock salute and then hit the next ball exactly over the place from which the man had been moved!'[10]

Hammond claimed, however, that Bradman injected a 'sense of hostility'[11] into what was meant to be a 'goodwill' series. Writer Cary said Bradman displayed a 'stern, war-like attitude'.[12]

In reply the Don said there were many with long memories from The Oval, 1938, when England, led by Hammond, batted the best part of three days in amassing more than 900 as the Australians were crushed by the biggest ever margin in an Ashes Test.

The third and fourth Tests were to be drawn, ensuring Australia the Ashes. For the first time Tests were limited to six days, with Sunday continuing as the traditional rest day.

Australia's depth was emphasised in Melbourne when No. 7 batsman Colin McCool and the No. 9, Ray Lindwall, both made centuries in a free-scoring Test that almost broke the MCG's match-attendance record from ten years earlier.

The Adelaide wicket was even flatter and there was another draw, both Morris and Compton notching twin centuries and Bradman all but falling for a pair. He later said the inswinging leg-cutter from Bedser that castled him in the first innings was the finest ball he ever faced.[13]

Australia's superiority was confirmed in the final Test in Sydney, but England was unable to pick anywhere near its best side with Hammond's fibrosis forcing him out and first-innings centurion Hutton falling ill mid-match with tonsillitis.

Leg-spinner Douglas Wright enhanced his reputation with 7-105 and 2-93, increasing his series aggregate to 23, the most for the series. He bowled at a bounding medium pace and along with Bedser was world-class.

Such was the strength of the Australian team of the late 1940s that many on the fringes of selection went to England to play – Tribe, Pepper, Bill Alley and star Melburnian all-sportsman Des Fothergill among them.

Bradman announced that he would play one last home season in Sydney against Lala Amarnath's touring Indian team, and representing the Australian XI he motored to his 100th first-class century and received a joyful reception from his old hometown crowd. Later he claimed the moment to be the most moving of his career.[14]

Having initially feared that his business commitments would pre-clude him touring England in 1948, Bradman was to relent and lead the most successful tour of all, his team going undefeated through thirty-four matches and becoming known as the Invincibles. In Lindwall, Miller and the angular left-armer Bill Johnston, he possessed in the same XI three of the finest-ever Australian pacemen. The batting depth was equally formi-dable, led by Morris and Barnes with the youngster Neil Harvey among those to instantly take to Ashes battle as if he'd been on the frontlines all his life. Later, Bradman told fellow selector E.A. 'Chappie' Dwyer: 'The boys really moulded into a great side in the finish and I think if you speak to any of them, they will support me in my view that it would have taken an exceptional team to have beaten us with normal luck'.[15]

The Australians won four Tests and drew the other, the highlight coming at Leeds when they chased down 404 on the last day, the finest win of Bradman's career.

Three weeks later in the final Test at The Oval, Bradman was out for a second–ball duck, having misread Eric Hollies' googly. It signalled the end of the most remarkable career of all. 'Everyone was stunned,' teammate Sam Loxton said. 'Nobody had any idea though what the conclusion was going to be and that he needed only four more runs to average 100 in Test cricket.

'He came in, took off his pads and said: "Fancy doing that!"'

'Funnily enough, back in Leeds, Don had given "Harv" the strike so he could hit the winning 4. We still chip Harv about that. If Don had hit the 4 he would have had an average of an even 100!'

Man of the decade: *Ray Lindwall*

Ray Lindwall has a place in any gallery of the game's elite fast bowlers. In the fifth Test at The Oval in 1948, he produced one of the most electrifying bursts by an Australian in Test cricket in capturing 6-20, including a Barnes-like 5-8 from forty-nine balls as England capitulated for 52.

He was a shining light among Don Bradman's star-studded Invincibles, the first Australian touring team to go unconquered in the UK. Four of Lindwall's victims were bowled and a fifth, Len Hutton, brilliantly caught behind by Tallon as England was dismissed in just two and a half hours. Noted Australian cricket writer Ray Robinson called it the deadliest burst by an Australian fast bowler in Test history. Bill O'Reilly said Lindwall's 'truly inspired' performance set the seal on his reputation as one of the game's finest. 'The [English] batsmen departed with the regularity of the buses from Charing Cross,' he said.[16] His confidence surging, Lindwall took three more wickets, all bowled, in England's second innings to extend his series aggregate to 27, equalling E. A. 'Ted' McDonald's record from 1921. He also made almost 200 runs at 30-plus, superior figures to Miller, a top-order specialist.

'Everything went right for Australia,' said Lindwall of his dynamic spell at The Oval. 'Most of the English batsmen thought that because of the soft state of the turf, the ball would fly from a length. Actually it went through at uniform [stump] height.'[17]

Lindwall, twenty-six, was at the height of his powers and, despite some early injury concerns, was Australia's champion in an elite attack. For the tour he amassed 86 wickets, almost two-thirds of his victims being bowled or lbw. English champion Maurice Tate said Lindwall's bowling had been 'atomic' while the cultured R. C. Robertson-Glasgow described him as 'another Harold Larwood'.[18]

During his illustrious career he was to three times take seven wickets in an innings, including 7-43 against India in Madras in 1956–57, when he was in his mid-thirties.

So admired was Lindwall that he was to play in seventeen of Australia's first eighteen series after World War II. Australia rarely lost when Lindwall was downwind with the new ball.

Bradman said Lindwall 'went from strength to strength' in England in 1948, so often breaking the back of England's top-order that he warranted elite status in any fast-bowling gathering. At 180 cm (5 ft 11 in) he wasn't as tall as his opening partner Miller, but he was consistently quicker and veered the ball away more dangerously. Seeing the stumps cartwheel was a common occurrence when Lindwall was in full rhythm. Often one of his lethal yorkers would be preceded by his skidding bouncer, aimed directly at the throat.

Another former Test teammate, Ken Meuleman, recalled that Lindwall's action was 'as poetic' as any bowler he ever saw:

Ray had a quiet initial approach before accelerating smoothly and reaching top pace just as he came to the popping crease. His pace was in the highest bracket and he was incredibly accurate, too. Until he reverted to medium-pace later in his career with Queensland, he did not have an inswinger but by using the width of the bowling crease he was able to move the ball into the right-handers when he wanted to. Being just under 6ft and with his beautiful side-on action, he could skid the ball off the wicket at a height that constantly caught technically incorrect batsmen lbw or saw them bowled. His outswinger moved late and claimed the best batsmen in the world. He was such an intelligent bowler, too, that when he reverted to medium pace he developed an inswinger as potent as anyone's.

At his quickest, Lindwall's bouncer surprised even seasoned players. In 1954, he knocked out English express Frank Tyson in retaliation at Tyson bouncing him out earlier in the match. With 228 wickets in 61 Tests at a strike-rate of fifty-nine balls per wicket, he was the mainstay of Australia's post-war attack, his durability, stamina and limited international program allowing him to play at the highest level until he was almost forty.

Lindwall v. England

Season	Analysis	Wkts	Ave
1946–47	0-23, 2-64, 1-59, 4-52, 2-60, 7-63, 2-46	18	20.38
1948	1-30, 5-70, 3-61, 4-99, 1-37, 2-79, 2-84, 6-20, 3-50	27	19.62
1950–51	0-1, 2-21, 2-46, 3-29, 2-60, 0-12, 3-51, 0-35, 3-77, 0-12	15	22.93
1953	5-57, 0-37, 5-66, 2-26, 2-30, 5-54, 3-104, 4-70, 0-46	26	18.84
1954–55	3-27, 2-50, 2-47, 3-69, 1-59, 0-52, 3-77	14	27.21
1956	0-43, 3-67, 2-63, 1-36, 1-29	7	34.00
1958–59	1-66, 2-70, 1-36, 3-37	7	29.85

Tests v. England:	29 (61 overall)
Wickets:	114 (228)
Average:	22.44 (23.03)
Best bowling:	7-63, Sydney, 1946–47 (7-38)
5-wicket Innings:	6 (12)
10-wicket Matches:	0
Strike-rate:	59 balls per wkt (59)
Average wkts per Test:	3.9 (3.7)

Match of the decade: *Headingley, 1948*

In running down a fourth-innings target of 404 in just over five hours on a wearing fifth-day wicket at Leeds, Australia achieved the impossible in a Test win Don Bradman claimed to be as memorable as any in his career. A 301-run second-wicket stand between Arthur Morris (182) and Bradman (173 not out) triggered the great escape, Norman Yardley having declared England's second innings closed on the final morning at eight down, believing his team was safe.

> **Match scores:** Australia 458 (Harvey 112, Loxton 93, Lindwall 77, Miller 58) and 404-3 (Morris 182, Bradman 173 not out) defeated England 496 (Washbrook 143, Edrich 111, Bedser 79) and 365-8 (Compton 66, Washbrook 65, Johnston 4-95) by 7 wickets

Odd spot: *A lesser light remembers*

Once asked by a non-cricketing acquaintance if he was present when Don Bradman made his last Test appearance at The Oval in 1948, Arthur Morris said: 'Yes, actually I was.'

'Oh what were you doing there, work, holidays?'

'I was playing.'

'Oh . . . did you make any?'

'Yes, actually I did . . .'

'How many?'

'196!'

As often happened in the Bradman era, few remembered the lesser lights.

Looking back: *Neil Harvey, Headingley, 1948*

'We lost [Lindsay] Hassett and Bradman almost immediately (to Dick Pollard) and we were suddenly 68-3, a frightening thought playing your first Test match against England. Don had just lost his off-stump and I was scared stiff. Fortunately for me I had Keith Miller [at the other end]. He maintained that when we met half way, I said to him: "G'day Nugget. What's happening? Let's get stuck into 'em!" I can't remember if I did or not. But after I'd played and missed two or three times, Keith came down and said: "You get up the bowler's end. I'll take the bowling for a while while you get yourself organised."

'After a while they brought [Jim] Laker on to bowl and about the third ball Keith hit him straight back over my head for six. That was pretty good. Two balls later back it came again, over my head and into the crowd for another six. "This can't be such a tough game after all," I thought to myself.'

Nineteen-year-old Neil Harvey made a century on his Ashes debut and in the early 1950s was regarded as the outstanding batsman in the world. Six of his twenty-one Test centuries were scored against England.

One for the statisticians: *Batting from memory*

In his comeback summer of 1946–47, Don Bradman averaged 97, despite seeming vulnerable at the start of his innings. He scored at just 56 runs per 100 balls, compared with his strike-rate of 61 in 1936–37 and a frenetic 75 in 1932–33. Sid Barnes, who shared an epic stand with the Don in Sydney, scored at 38 runs per 100 balls in 1946–47. Lindsay Hassett was even slower at 34 per 100 balls.[19]

Tests 1946–47 to 1948

KEY: M Matches **I** Innings **NO** Not out innings **HS** Highest score **BB** Best bowling
5wI 5-wicket innings **10wM** 10-wicket match ***** Not out **#** Second innings **rh** Retired hurt

Series results

	Tests	Aust	Eng	Drawn
1946–47 (Aust)	5	3	0	2
1948 (Eng)	5	4	0	1
Total	**10**	**7**	**0**	**3**
Progressive	153	64	55	34

Summary

	Runs	Wkts	Ave
Australia	6355	126	50.43
England	5511	184	29.95

Highest innings totals

Australia		England	
659-8 dec †	Sydney 1946–47 (2nd Test)	496	Leeds 1948 (4th Test)
645	Brisbane 1946–47 (1st Test)	460	Adelaide 1946–47 (4th Test)
536	Melbourne 1946–47 (3rd Test)#	441	Nottingham 1948 (1st Test)#
509	Nottingham 1948 (1st Test)		
487	Adelaide 1946–47 (4th Test)		
460-7 dec	Lord's 1948 (2nd Test)		
458	Leeds 1948 (4th Test)		

† highest total by Australia against England in Australia

Lowest completed innings totals

Australia		England	
221	Manchester 1948 (3rd Test)	52†	The Oval 1948 (5th Test)
	(one batsman retired hurt)	141	Brisbane 1946–47 (1st Test)

† lowest total by England in England

Leading run scorers

	M	I	NO	Runs	HS	Ave	100	50
Australia								
A. R. Morris	10	17	2	1199	196	79.93	6	4
D. G. Bradman	10	17	3	1188	234	84.85	4	4
S. G. Barnes	8	12	2	772	234	77.20	2	4
A. L. Hassett	10	15	1	642	137	45.85	2	1
K. R. Miller	10	14	2	568	141*	47.33	1	3
England								
D. C. S. Compton	10	20	2	1021	184	56.72	4	4
W. J. Edrich	10	20	0	781	119	39.05	2	5
L. Hutton	9	17	1	759	122rh	47.43	1	6
C. Washbrook	9	18	1	719	143	42.29	2	4

Hundreds

Australia (18)		England (9)	
6	A. R. Morris	4	D. C. S. Compton
4	D. G. Bradman	2	W. J. Edrich
2	S. G. Barnes		C. Washbrook
	A. L. Hassett	1	L. Hutton
1	R. N. Harvey		
	R. R. Lindwall		
	C. L. McCool		
	K. R. Miller		

Highest individual scores

Australia

234	S. G. Barnes at Sydney 1946–47 (2nd Test)
234	D. G. Bradman at Sydney 1946–47 (2nd Test)
196	A. R. Morris at The Oval 1948 (5th Test)
187	D. G. Bradman at Brisbane 1946–47 (1st Test)
182	A. R. Morris at Leeds 1948 (4th Test)#
173*	D. G. Bradman at Leeds 1948 (4th Test)#
155	A. R. Morris at Melbourne 1946–47 (3rd Test)#
141	S. G. Barnes at Lord's 1948 (2nd Test)#

England

184	D. C. S. Compton at Nottingham 1948 (1st Test)#
147	D. C. S. Compton at Adelaide 1946–47 (4th Test)
145*	D. C. S. Compton at Manchester 1948 (3rd Test)
143	C. Washbrook at Leeds 1948 (4th Test)

Century in each innings

147 and 103*	D. C. S. Compton (Eng) at Adelaide 1946–47 (4th Test)
122 and 124*	A. R. Morris (Aust) at Adelaide 1946–47 (4th Test)

500 runs in a series

	Season	M	I	NO	Runs	HS	Ave	100	50
Australia									
A. R. Morris	1948	5	9	1	696	196	87.00	3	3
D. G. Bradman	1946–47	5	8	1	680	234	97.14	2	3
D. G. Bradman	1948	5	9	2	508	173*	72.57	2	1
A. R. Morris	1946–47	5	8	1	503	155	71.85	3	1
England									
D. C. S. Compton	1948	5	10	1	562	184	62.44	2	2

Hundred partnerships

Australia (17)

Partnerships of 150 and over:

405	5th	S. G. Barnes and D. G. Bradman at Sydney 1946–47 (2nd Test)
		(Australian 5th wicket record against all countries)
301	2nd	A. R. Morris and D. G. Bradman at Leeds 1948 (4th Test)#
276	3rd	D. G. Bradman and A. L. Hassett at Brisbane 1946–47 (1st Test)
		(Australian 3rd wicket record against England)
189	3rd	A. R. Morris and A. L. Hassett at Adelaide 1946–47 (4th Test)
174	2nd	S. G. Barnes and D. G. Bradman at Lord's 1948 (2nd Test)#
154	8th	D. Tallon and R. R. Lindwall at Melbourne 1946–47 (3rd Test)#
150	5th	K. R. Miller and I. W. G. Johnson at Adelaide 1946–47 (4th Test)

England (15)

Partnerships of 150 and over:

168	1st	L. Hutton and C. Washbrook at Leeds 1948 (4th Test)
150	2nd	L. Hutton and W. J. Edrich at Sydney 1946–47 (5th Test)

Leading wicket-takers

	Tests	Balls	Mdns	Runs	Wkts	Ave	BB	5wI	10wM
Australia									
R. R. Lindwall	9	2,314	77	897	45	19.93	7-63	3	–
K. R. Miller	10	1,808	58	635	29	21.89	7-60	1	–
E. R. H. Toshack	9	2,467	120	801	28	28.60	6-82	2	–
W. A. Johnston	5	1,856	92	630	27	23.33	5-36	1	–
England									
A. V. Bedser	10	3,618	113	1,564	34	46.00	4-81	–	–
D. V. P. Wright	6	2,165	35	1,113	25	44.52	7-105	2	–

Five wickets in an innings

Australia (10)

3	R. R. Lindwall
2	E. R. H. Toshack
	C. L. McCool
1	I. W. G. Johnson
	W. A. Johnston
	K. R. Miller

England (3)

2	D. V. P. Wright
1	W. E. Hollies

Best individual bowling

Australia

7-60	K. R. Miller at Brisbane 1946–47 (1st Test)
7-63	R. R. Lindwall at Sydney 1946–47 (5th Test)
6-20	R. R. Lindwall at The Oval 1948 (5th Test)
6-42	I. W. G. Johnson at Sydney 1946–47 (2nd Test)
6-82	E. R. H. Toshack at Brisbane 1946–47 (1st Test)#

England

7-105	D. V. P. Wright at Sydney 1946–47 (5th Test)

25 wickets in a series

	Season	Tests	Balls	Mdns	Runs	Wkts	Ave	BB	5wI	10wM
Australia										
R. R. Lindwall	1948	5	1,337	57	530	27	19.62	6-20	2	–
W. A. Johnston	1948	5	1,856	92	630	27	23.33	5-36	1	–
England										
No instance – best:										
D. V. P. Wright	1946–47	5	1,922	23	990	23	43.04	7-105	2	–

Leading wicketkeepers

	Tests	Dismissals	Catches	Stumpings
Australia				
D. Tallon	9	32	28	4
England				
T. G. Evans	9	21	17	4

Leading fieldsmen

	Tests	Catches
Australia		
A. L. Hassett	10	11
K. R. Miller	10	11

England

The leading English fieldsmen each caught 6:
D. C. S. Compton (10 Tests), J. F. Crapp (3),
W. J. Edrich (10) and W. R. Hammond (4).

Captains

	Tests	Won	Lost	Drawn	Toss won
Australia					
D. G. Bradman	10	7	0	3	3
England					
N. W. D. Yardley	6	0	5	1	5
W. R. Hammond	4	0	2	2	2

Most appearances

Australia (21 players)		England (27 players)	
10	D. G. Bradman	10	A. V. Bedser
	A. L. Hassett		D. C. S. Compton
	K. R. Miller		W. J. Edrich
	A. R. Morris		N. W. D. Yardley
9	R. R. Lindwall	9	T. G. Evans
	D. Tallon		L. Hutton
	E. R. H. Toshack		C. Washbrook

Peter May (left) and **Richie Benaud** toss the coin in Melbourne, 1958–59. *Gordon Vidler Collection*

TYPHOONED

• •

'... Instinctively turning his back, he was struck a tremendous blow on the back of the skull. As players converged, non-striker Bill Edrich told Lindwall: "My God, Lindy, you've killed him!"'

As Australian cricket lovers pondered life without Don Bradman at No. 3, the emergence of the jaunty Fitzroy left-hander Neil 'Ninna' Harvey re-energised an ageing top-order weakened further by the absence of the mercurial Sid Barnes, who felt cricket wasn't paying him sufficiently well to warrant his continuing attentions.

One of six brothers from Melbourne's most celebrated post-war cricketing family, Harvey learnt to bat in an inner-city laneway with an old molasses tin for a wicket. From his early teens, his sparkling footwork and sense of adventure was compelling. As a 13-year-old in short pants he made twin centuries in a Melbourne third XI Grand Final.

Twice a week at Fitzroy's practice, club coach Joe Plant would place a two-shilling coin yards up the wicket and ask the teenager to skip as quickly as he could down the pitch and play an imaginary drive. They rehearsed for hours, Harvey developing a lightning charge that was to distract spinners around the world. Despite being short-sighted and unable to read scoreboards, Harvey became Australia's outstanding batsman of the 1950s. And only once in 137 Test innings was he ever out stumped.

He was scintillating against South Africa in 1949–50. Harvey averaged 112 including four centuries in five Tests as Australia's winning ways continued, despite the sensational omission of the team's champion Keith Miller from the original touring squad – a direct Bradman reprisal, Miller always believed, for him peppering the Don with bouncers during the Kippax–Oldfield testimonial match weeks earlier in Sydney.

Years later Miller told me that Bradman was jealous of his popularity and profile and he wouldn't have changed a thing, except maybe to have bowled a few more short ones at The Don!

While he was NSW's first choice as captain for years, he was never to be promoted to the Test captaincy, Bradman central in his exclusion.

With his ambassadorial skills and flair, much-loved Lindsay Hassett was the perfect Bradman successor. But, on Hassett's retirement, even Ian Johnson was surprised when he was ordained ahead of Miller in 1954. There was to be one notable blow-up between the two South Melbourne clubmen the following year, during Australia's tour of the Caribbean when Johnson threatened to punch Miller for not following instructions in Barbados.

Hassett had been Bradman's vice-captain during the all-conquering 1948 tour. He'd also led the Australia Services XI during the 'Victory Tests' in England. Not only was he a capital batsman, few were as gregarious – or shared his love of the whimsy. During a civic reception one afternoon in the bush, Hassett was on a podium, thanking the local Lord Mayor for the invitation.

'It is lovely to be here,' he began, surveying the assembled locals. 'But . . . and it should be said . . . never before . . . yes, never before have we ever seen such a motley band of men!' There was a slight tittering and a hush, as Hassett grinned and continued. 'And never before have we ever seen such a gorgeous array of women!'

At an official function in London during the Coronation Ashes tour in 1953, a waiter accidentally spilt a drink over Hassett's trousers. He calmly stood up, removed the soiled trousers, and asked the waiter to have them cleaned, before continuing with his dinner.

From the time he made a century as a Geelong College schoolboy for a Victorian Country XI against the 1930–31 West Indians and was first named, aged twenty, for Victoria, Hassett was a cricketer of infinite possibilities. His defence was sound, strokeplay copybook and twinkling footwork a delight, as good as anyone, Bradman included.

Hassett was also a stickler for the spirit of the game, one time admonishing first-time 12th man Sam Loxton for daring to bring the drinks onto the MCG late one afternoon when Englishman Denis Compton was on 99. 'You never do that son,' he said, 'not when a man is on 99.'

While Australia was re-marshalling its leadership, England was in total rebuild after three home summers where it could win only once in thirteen Tests. Thrashed by both Australia (in 1948) and the West Indies (1950), it played four draws in a row against Test minnows New Zealand. Len Hutton's brilliant form was a saving grace, rekindling the old argument that England's system of amateur captains should be overhauled. Fewer amateurs were proving themselves worthy of a place among the best eleven cricketers in England. No longer could England afford to pick their ten best players *and* a captain.

With Norman Yardley and captain-elect George Mann unavailable to tour down-under in 1950–51, England reverted to one of its old faithfuls to end its years of Ashes disappointments. Freddie Brown, thirty-nine, had made up the numbers during the 1932–33 Bodyline tour and never looked like playing a Test, even with the series decided early. Unlike Arthur Gilligan in 1924–25, Douglas Jardine was never interested in allowing his back-ups a game on sentiment.

Brown had been a purveyor of gentle leg-spin before reverting to medium-pace seamers, which he combined with aggressive middle-order batting. No one doubted his fighting spirit and while the team he was given was too inexperienced to seriously challenge the Australians, their victory in the final Test in Melbourne was the dawn of a new era for English cricket. The pendulum was swinging and Australia would no longer be solely dominant.

Six fledglings were part of Brown's initial seventeen and two more were to reinforce the party from mid-tour. The failure of vice-captain Denis Compton to play anywhere near his best in the Tests was a major factor in Australia's 4–1 win.

Compton also missed the second Test in Melbourne with injury.

Far from being a formality, however, the series was keenly fought, Australia's comfortable winning margin far from a true reflection of the on-field battle. Lion-hearted Alec Bedser with 30 wickets was again feisty and formidable, while Hutton parried and fought tirelessly against Ray Lindwall, Miller and Bill Johnston, amassing more than 500 runs in five

Tests at an average of almost 90. Brown declared the tour as Hutton's 'finest hour'.[1]

In the fourth Test in Adelaide, Hutton carried his bat for 156, batting from 3.50 p.m. on Saturday to 5 p.m. on the Monday in a supreme display of 'technical poise and soundness'.[2]

Australia's unlikely matchwinner was 35-year-old mystery spinner Jack Iverson who overshadowed the strikemen with his each-way spin imparted with an unorthodox flick, similar to a man disposing of a burnt-out cigarette.[3]

During the war years when he was based in New Guinea, Iverson had experimented with a bent finger grip using a table-tennis ball. Like the eccentric 'Chuck' Fleetwood-Smith before him, he enjoyed making the batsmen fan at thin air. He bowled with a leg-spinner's action, yet spun the ball mainly back from the off. Complicating it all, his repertoire also included a leggie, a top-spinner and, for the fun of it, a traditional googly.

Iverson's first season of Sheffield Shield cricket had been a triumph and climaxed in his selection on the 1949–50 Australian tour of New Zealand where he took 75 wickets at an average of seven apiece. At Invercargill, Australia defeated a Southland XI outright in just over a day thanks to 'Big Jake' who took 6-8 and 5-14.

He created similar havoc with the Englishmen, gathering 21 wickets including a remarkable 6-27 to finish the third Test early in Sydney.

While he was to be a shooting star whose Ashes career was limited to twelve short weeks, his influence on the 1950–51 scoreline was as significant as Harold Larwood's wicket sprees in 1932–33 and Sydney Barnes' heroics in 1911–12.

Monsoonal rains in Brisbane saw the first Test finish prematurely in less than ten playing hours, Hassett responding to a brave declaration from Brown by declaring Australia's second innings closed after just an hour. Twenty wickets fell for just 130 balls on the interrupted third day as bowlers from both sides created havoc on the Brisbane 'sticky'. Set less than 200, England was decimated when the first eight wickets fell for 46, including Compton, held back to No. 9, for a first-ball duck. Hutton's 62 not out was a classic solo, reminiscent of the wet-wicket expertise of the Golden Age's Bobby Abel, Jack Hobbs and Herbert Sutcliffe. Bent-finger Iverson claimed 4-43, a confidence-boosting beginning and a forerunner of what was to come.

England had legitimate claims to have been beaten by the Brisbane weather and they pushed the Australians to the hilt again in Melbourne where the scheduling over Christmas included two rest days and a crowd of more than 60,000 on Boxing Day, the first-ever Ashes Test to be contested on what has become the biggest cricketing day of all.

Cracks so widened on the sun-baked wicket over the 48-hour Christmas break that shooters were commonplace from the third day. There were four sub-200 scores, Brown as influential as the higher profiled with 70 runs and five wickets. New cap Trevor Bailey and Bedser each took six wickets. On the first morning when the wicket was at its liveliest, Bedser beat Harvey five or six times outside his off-stump without once inducing a tickle – shades of Tate to Ponsford in Sydney a generation earlier and Ambrose to Steve Waugh in Bridgetown years later.

Set 179 to win, England lost two overnight wickets and played over-cautiously on the crumbling wicket on the fourth day, Brown later declaring he should have promoted himself up the list to spark some momentum. Hutton's 40 in two hours was again a consummate effort, but the pressure was too great for the tail, with Australia's fielding and catching of the highest standard. Brown was certain England would have won had Compton's knee injury not forced his withdrawal.

Australia won the third and fourth Tests comfortably, Miller being at his brilliant best in Sydney, making 145 not out and backing up with four wickets. He also claimed the catch of the season at slip to dismiss Cyril Washbrook, diving full length to his right to intercept a genuine backcut from the bowling of a delighted Ian Johnson. Tom Goodman in the *Sydney Morning Herald* described the stunning catch as worthy of Jack Gregory at his eagle-eyed best.[4] Iverson's remarkable 6-for included four bowled and two caught by wicketkeeper Don Tallon.

With the Ashes safe, the Australians won easily again in Adelaide, Arthur Morris being last out in making his first Test double century and Sydney's Jim Burke joining an elite group to score a century on debut. In the circumstances, however, Hutton's 156 not out was the innings of the match. He gave two chances but it was still an epic in focus and concentration.

Despite the hammerings, Brown remained upbeat that England could take a Test by winning in Melbourne. Thanks to Bedser's 10 wickets and

Reg Simpson's century of a lifetime, England ended Australia's unbeaten run, which had stretched twelve years and twenty-six Tests.

Brown received 400 cables of congratulations after the eight-wicket victory. Fittingly, Hutton was responsible for the winning runs.

In the post-mortems, the omission of experienced Bill Edrich from the touring party was considered critical. He'd averaged almost 50 in a 1,000-run season with Middlesex and his 71 at Manchester had been pivotal in England's only win against the West Indies in 1950. The preference, too, for a teenage fledgling in 19-year-old Brian Close to bowl finger spin ahead of Jim Laker had also bewildered many. Close had taken 7 wickets to Laker's 142 in the 1950 county championship. Laker was angry. 'The emphasis on youth was an unwarranted gamble,' Bedser said, years later.[5]

Bedser's superiority over Morris saw him capture the Australian's wicket five times, the champion left-hander's average slumping to 35 even with his Test-best double century in Adelaide. The wicketkeeping of Godfrey Evans was a revelation. His work standing up to the stumps to Bedser was of a standard rarely seen in years.

'What a wonderful reception we had when we came off the field at the end of the final Test,' said Brown. 'I really believe that the Australian cricketing public wanted us to win that match.'[6]

The Australians hosted the West Indies in the so-called 'Championship of the World' in 1951–52 and South Africa in 1952–53, the Windies being beaten easily but the Springboks playing far beyond expectations to draw the series 2–2.

The objection by the Australian Board of Control to Sid Barnes's recall in December 1951 prompted a bitter libel case, the austere Board members having used a 40-year-old clause to end his international comeback before it had started. Barnes had dropped out of cricket after the Invincibles tour, saying he couldn't afford to play, even though the per-Test wages of £60 represented six times the average weekly wage. He made some powerful enemies during his three years of virtual inactivity, especially over his headlining newspaper column in Sydney's *Daily Telegraph* entitled 'Like it or Lump it'.

Barnes was to win his court battle, which showed the Board to have acted in a high-handed and unjustified manner, but he was never to represent Australia again.

His vitriolic comments continued, too, during the 1953 Ashes tour. He blamed Australia's 1–0 defeat on the excesses of the team, particularly senior pro Miller, who he accused of acting imprudently and outside team rules by being absent from the dressing room when big English race meetings were on. He also questioned the convenience of Miller's perennial sore back flaring at the same time as the running of the English Derby!

Miller always maintained that Barnes was bitter and jealous, a former great cricketer and clown who missed the public's applause. Miller said the youngsters in the Australian touring team idolised captain Hassett and the 1953 tour was the happiest of all.

Their jousting kept cricket in the headlines and after a purely domestic season in 1953–54, there was great anticipation leading up to the arrival of Hutton's Englishmen in 1954, especially as among their ranks was the fastest bowler since Harold Larwood.

The 1953 Australians were at Northants, between Test matches, when they encountered young Frank 'Typhoon' Tyson, twenty-three, playing his first game of the season. Hassett had the game off and stand-in captain Arthur Morris was at the non-striker's end as Tyson, lean and prematurely balding, paced out his run-up, which seemed to start somewhere near the boundary edge.

In he steamed and with his second ball trapped Colin McDonald lbw. Senior batsman Neil Harvey was due to go in at first wicket but was still in his civvies when the appeal went up.

Asking Graeme Hole to go in ahead of him, Harvey was still changing when there was another shout, Hole having been clean bowled second ball! Jimmy de Courcy also fell quickly, the Australians being 10-3 by the time Harvey arrived and was met by a quizzical Morris, who wanted to know where he'd been!

This was the Australians' introduction to England's new express, who in 1954–55 was to unleash the most lethal and intimidating spells of new-ball bowling since Bodyline.

Preferred to emerging Yorkshireman Fred Trueman because of his sheer speed, Tyson headed an armoury of pacemen that also included the veteran Alec Bedser, Brian Statham, Peter Loader and Trevor Bailey. He hadn't even played a Test match when he was chosen. But 70 county wickets in his first full season in 1954 confirmed his promise and he was to be a lynchpin in England's astonishing come-from-behind victory.

Having been humbled in the first Test, England's comeback was truly miraculous, Hutton recovering from the ignominies of Brisbane to pilot a 3–1 series win.

The first professional to lead England in an Ashes clash in seventy years, Hutton's contributions with the bat were relatively modest. Leading into the third Test in Melbourne he all but withdrew, complaining of headaches and fretting about the omission of his champion Bedser. 'Len didn't like hurting people,' said manager Geoffrey Howard.[7]

'In those days the star system was at its height,' said Colin Cowdrey. 'Dropping a celebrity player, which Bedser unquestionably was, required immense tact and careful public relations. In Bedser's case, Hutton showed neither.'[8]

Other than an important 80 in Adelaide when the Ashes were retained, Hutton struggled to exert his normal influence at the head of the order and had become increasingly intense and withdrawn.

England's comeback after being beaten by an innings at the 'Gabba seemed an impossibility. Hutton's gamble to play four pacemen and bowl first backfired amid a plethora of missed catches and some brilliant batting from the left-handers Morris and Harvey. 'At that point,' as Bedser conceded later, 'any odds would have been offered on England taking the series.'[9]

Hutton had so agonised over the toss that he and first-time Australian captain Ian Johnson were almost off the ground when Hutton said: 'Ian?'

'Yes Len?'

'I think you can have strike.'

'Thanks Len.'[10]

It was a tame, easy-paced wicket and Johnson could hardly contain his glee. Shutting the dressing-room door behind him, he yelled: 'He's sent us in!'

The Englishmen were to be thrashed. Tyson, operating from his exaggerated 30-metre run-up, conceded 160 runs for a single wicket. He lacked rhythm and was straining at the crease. Bedser the Lionheart was well short of peak fitness, too. The heat was oppressive and the Englishmen wilted as the Australians batted into a third day, Johnson calling a halt only after the 600-run milestone was reached. According to Hutton the English fielding was 'catastrophic',[11] the withdrawal of Evans, from sunstroke, on the morning of the match being a major handicap even before a ball had been bowled. When Compton broke a bone in his hand running into the wooden palings on the boundary on the first morning, Hutton felt himself truly cursed.

With Lindwall and Miller still hostile with the new ball and the adaptable Johnston starting with mediums before slowing down to orthodox spinners without losing any of his effectiveness, the Australians had balance and options.

During the Brisbane humiliation, Hutton consulted one of Tyson's mentors, ex-Testman and master coach Alf Gover, who was in Australia covering the series for the London *Sunday Mail*. Tyson had bowled off a shortened run indoors. Why not suggest he cut his run-up to help trigger more momentum outdoors? In the game against Victoria immediately afterwards, Tyson took 6-85, the Harvey brothers Neil and Ray among five to be bowled in mid-stroke.

Tyson had operated from a shorter run-up for many years in league cricket ranks and not only re-found the accuracy that had deserted him in Brisbane, his rhythm was improved and his speed unaffected.

Having done the unthinkable by omitting Bedser from his XI in Sydney, Hutton was immediately on the back foot when his side was bowled out for 154, having been sent in on a two-paced, straw-coloured pitch. Tyson grabbed four wickets as Australia's lead was restricted to 74.

During Australia's innings, Tyson aimed a bouncer at Lindwall, who deflected a catch through to Evans. As their local hero walked off, Tyson was roundly booed for defying the unwritten rule refraining fast bowlers from bowling bouncers at each other.[12]

It shook Lindwall up and when England batted a second time, the Australian reciprocated and felled Tyson with a skidding short one, which Tyson claimed to have lost in the background. Instinctively turning his back, he was struck a tremendous blow on the back of the skull. As players converged, non-striker Bill Edrich told Lindwall: 'My God, Lindy, you've killed him!'[13] There was a shocked hush around the ground as a semi-conscious Tyson was walked from the ground with the assistance of two ambulance men. Some thought his Test match over, but returning to the ground, x-rays having cleared him of a skull fracture, Tyson courageously re-took his place at the crease, this time to resounding cheers.

Set 223, Australia seemed well placed at 72-2 before being mown down by Tyson, bowling at a frightening pace, on the fifth morning. Harvey stood supreme, making 92 not out in probably his finest sub-100 performance as Australia was outed for 184, Tyson's ferocity netting him six wickets. Afterwards, in the victorious English dressing rooms, reserve paceman Loader said Tyson had 'bowled like a ding-bat', prompting the nickname 'Dingers' for the rest of the summer.

Just weeks earlier, in his best-selling autobiography *Flying Stumps*, Lindwall said he rarely bowled bumpers at anyone batting below No. 6. 'I take the view if you cannot get them out by bowling straight, they deserve to make any runs they can,' he said.[14]

Tyson had batted more than two hours in Brisbane for seven and 37 not out and coming in at No. 7 was commanding an all-rounder's slot. He conceded in his own book *A Typhoon Called Tyson* that he had been mistaken to have bounced Lindwall, but didn't want Lindwall to repeat his half-century from Brisbane.

Fired-up by the incident and without a semblance of even a headache, Tyson was to bowl one and two yards quicker in the Australian second innings in his most satisfying spell of the tour.

The trend was to continue, too, in Melbourne, where England won again in murderous heat, Tyson's last morning onslaught broadsiding the Australians for the second match running. This was the game where the pitch was saturated illegally by a do-gooding curator worried that the game would finish in three days because of the enormous cracks that had developed from the second day.

Young Cowdrey, on the first of his six visits down-under, made a cultured century to avoid calamity on the first day after Miller took 3-8 in a tremendous solo in the morning session. Miller had thought about bowling only at the eleventh hour after a persistent knee problem. It wasn't until his jockey pal Scobie Breasley suggested he have a friend of his look at his injured knee down at the St Kilda sea baths that Miller considered himself even a half-chance. 'This fella normally tended sick and sore horses,' Miller said, years later. 'I can't remember what he did, but he must have been okay because I was able to run around a bit. Before I hadn't been able to even raise a gallop.'

The day before the match, Miller had told Johnson that he'd only be able to bat, yet on the morning of the game he felt fine and was okay to take the new ball. In an inspirational beginning, Miller took 3-5 from his first five overs. He'd been warned that he should bowl only in short spells, but was feeling so sprightly he operated unchanged for ninety minutes right through until lunch. Eight of his initial nine overs were maidens. Included in his haul was Compton with a rising delivery that the champion could only fend meekly from his bat handle to gully.

England was out for 191, but by stumps on the Saturday night, Australia was 188-8 and sinking.

England's slow over rate had been a heated topic of conversation in Sydney and six- and seven-minute overs were again commonplace as Hutton stopped play and consulted with his bowlers, hoping the regular breaks would conserve the strength of his bowlers and frustrate the Australian top-order into false shotmaking. Sixty-seven eight-ball overs were bowled by the Australians on the first day, but only fifty-six by England on the second. A fortnight earlier in Sydney they'd bowled fifty-one overs on the Saturday.

Of Hutton's captaincy in Melbourne, Cowdrey said he was like a chessmaster, planning and manipulating the plays. 'No captain before or since could have handled his bowlers better or set his fields more effectively.'[15]

So rock-hard was the Melbourne wicket by the second morning that Statham twice skidded and fell in his delivery stride. Batsmen running up the pitch could hear their boot spikes clatter on the surface like they were tap shoes.

Making his debut, Victorian Len Maddocks was relieved to go to stumps on the Saturday night unbeaten on 36. So furious was the English attack that he batted for the first time with a thigh pad, borrowed from Yorkshireman Vic Wilson, a tour reserve. 'Virtually every ball I faced from Tyson, if I'd missed it, it would have drilled me in the throat,' Maddocks recounted later. 'I don't claim him to be the best bowler ever but he could well be the fastest ever. I'd step behind it, hold my bat in front of it and hope that it would hit a bottom edge and go for one. He didn't bowl any half volleys.'

With fierce northerly winds sending the temperature gauge soaring to 105 degrees Fahrenheit, the highest recorded temperatures ever in Melbourne, curator Jack House decided he must do something drastic to prevent the game from finishing early. Ignoring Marylebone regulations forbidding the watering of the wicket once a game had started, House turned on the hose and flooded it.

Percy Beames, a former Victorian captain, covering the match for the Melbourne *Age*, was working in the paper's Collins St office late on Sunday afternoon when he learnt of House's actions. He went to his sports editor Harold Austin and told him of the scandal.

'Is it legal?' asked Austin.

'No.'

'Will it be good for cricket?'

'No.'

'Well, we'll put it aside then – but get all the facts together.'

Alongside Beames's Sunday-night copy, Austin included a paragraph, in highlighted type, about how it was illegal to water wickets. Come the following morning, it was clear that the story had substance, despite the emphatic denials from the Melbourne Cricket Club. Beames made a full exposure in Tuesday morning's *Age*.

'The game wouldn't have lasted,' Beames says. 'The curator [House] was overseeing his first Test. It was illegal but he did it with every good intention to save face. He wanted the game to go the full distance.

'We wrote that it had been watered and they [the Melbourne Cricket Club] threatened to sue us. But you could tell the way the spikes sunk in [that it had happened].'

A groundsman, one of Beames's old football teammates, had alerted him to the story of a lifetime. But so open was the MCG, with the building of the new Olympic Stand, that dozens of people walking in Yarra Park must also have seen it.

On the Monday morning, Maddocks and Johnson, Australia's two not-out batsmen, inspected the wicket and were amazed to find the cracks had all but closed. It was almost like a first-day wicket all over again, only wetter. 'Talk about a transformation,' Maddocks later recalled. 'It was like walking on cheese. Your spikes were making a popping sound. The curator [House] had watered it to try and hold it together. It was virtually a sticky [wicket] before falling apart again.

'Without the extra water the Test would never have lasted five days. It would have been all over in four. By the last day there were cracks going up and down and across the pitch that were literally inches wide. Depending on whether Tyson landed on the offside or the leg side, you'd get a fast, lethal leg or offcutter, or if he landed on the cracks going across, it either hit you on the foot or threatened to take your head off. It was impossible to bat on. Once the cracks opened, we fell apart.'

Had England not enjoyed the best batting conditions on Day 3 of the match, courtesy of House's brain-snap, there could well have been a protest. The Board of Control went into damage control and considered offering MCC a replay had their own team won.

Set 240, Australia tumbled from its overnight 75-2 to be all out for 111, the last eight wickets falling for 34 runs, Tyson taking 6-16 in one of the great Ashes spells. As spectators ate their lunches on early trains back home, Tyson and his MCC teammates celebrated in the bowels of the Grey Smith Stand. And how did the hero of the hour spend his afternoon? He and Northants teammate Keith Andrew went to the pictures![16]

In his autobiography, Tyson said the abnormally hot conditions had panicked House into acting outside the rules. 'It must have seemed logical to water the wicket,' he said.

'He had been brought in to prepare the Test wicket, expressly to prevent the recurrence of the crumbling wicket of the Victorian game (a fortnight previously). Had he not acted there can be little doubt that there would have been hardly any wicket left on the Monday.'[17]

The much-vaunted Australians may have again been humbled, chasing a small fourth-innings target, but the crowds were enormous, more than 300,000 seeing the five days, including 50,483 on the final day, some of whom scampered onto the ground afterwards and secured a souvenir piece of centre wicket turf.

While House may have plunged the game into infamy, the financial benefit was enormous. The gate receipts totalled almost £50,000, despite the loss of reserved seat revenue from the demolished Northern Stand. The tourists' half share of the gate was £23,966, the largest cheque ever paid to a visiting team for a single game. And the Victorian Cricket Association's cut was almost £9,000, just under half its total income for the 1954–55 summer.

Three weeks later, England's climb from the canvas continued when it won a third Test in a row, a thriller in Adelaide, to clinch the Ashes, despite Miller threatening to rout the Englishmen on the final day. Swerving the ball away at speed, Miller took three early wickets as England slumped to 18-3 chasing 94. Hutton, one of the three, was beside himself, saying,

'The booggers have done us' before burying himself in a corner, unable to watch.[18]

Some classic Compton counterpunching helped England home and the Ashes were safe again. Had the rules allowed Miller to bowl from both ends while the shine was on the Kookaburra, it may have been an even closer finish.

In his international farewell, Hutton had emerged a hero, but England's fight back was triggered by Tyson and Statham, whose collective haul was 46 wickets in five Tests, right up there with Bodyline terrors Larwood and Voce who took 48 in 1932–33. The Australians had been well and truly typhooned and the public was far from happy, even Don Bradman being booed by sections of the Sydney crowd when he went out to inspect the wicket during the rain-ruined final match.[19]

Peter May led the twenty-seventh English team to Australia in 1958–59. He'd been the outstanding batsman in the Tests of 1956. In one of the wettest summers on record, England again came from behind to retain the Ashes, off-spinner Jim Laker's 46 wickets being a remarkable new Ashes high. In the most stunning Ashes solo of all, Laker demoralised the Australians with 19 wickets at Old Trafford. All 19 were taken at the Stretford End and while the pitch was sub-standard, Laker bowled brilliantly. Australian captain Johnson conceded that long after the side issues and controversies had been forgotten, memories of Laker's wonderful bowling would remain.

Ear-marked as England's frontline spinner for his maiden trip to Australia, 36-year-old Laker embroiled himself in a dispute with May, also his county captain at Surrey, and in the heat of the moment, withdrew from the tour. May had claimed that Laker hadn't been trying in a county match[20] and it was many weeks before Laker calmed down and agreed to tour.

Bothered by an arthritic spinning finger, Laker's 15 wickets at 21.20 in four Tests was hardly Herculean in what proved to be his international farewell.

Statham shouldered much of the pace-bowling responsibility, but Tyson the hurricane had become a zephyr, being chosen only when the series had been decided. The early-tour breakdown of top-order specialist Raman Subba Row, England's best player of fast bowling, was a cruel blow.

Fellow left-hander Willie Watson, who had made a century on his Ashes debut in 1953, suffered knee lock on the trip out and didn't play until the eve of the opening Test. Instead of being able to stack their top-order with left-handers to counter the angle of the two dominant Australian left-arm bowlers Alan Davidson and Ian Meckiff, the Englishmen floundered against their angle and failed to make even 300 all summer.

In a season of controversy where the actions of its leading fast bowlers all round the country were subject of intense scrutiny, Australia won four of the five Tests so comprehensively that many wondered how England could possibly have held the Ashes since 1953. Victorian Colin McDonald had the season of his career, while young New South Welshman Norman O'Neill was the latest to be tagged as 'the next Bradman'. O'Neill had been in blitzing touch in Sheffield Shield cricket in 1957–58, scoring 1,005 runs and taking 26 wickets with his quickish leg-breaks. Adding to the package was his power-packed throwing arm, which was to attract the attentions of baseball scouts from America.

Davidson and Meckiff collected 41 wickets between them, Davidson's late in-swing in the second Test in Melbourne reducing England to 7-3 in an electrifying start.

Richie Benaud had become Australia's new captain, Neil Harvey's transfer from Melbourne to Sydney costing him his chance at the No. 1 job. Ian Craig had led the touring team to South Africa in 1957–58 and while he captained NSW at the start of the Ashes summer, the after-effects of hepatitis lingered and he stood down after two games and two ducks to concentrate on his pharmaceutical career.

Queensland's prime candidate Ron Archer was also struggling with a knee cartilage injury, which puzzled teams of specialists then but would have been repaired easily now. After the 1956 tour, Archer had been one of the favourites to succeed Johnson, only to break down on the mat at Karachi at the conclusion of the tour, his bowling days over. First chosen in 1953 as a 19-year-old, Archer's career had blossomed in 1956 and at Leeds he claimed frontline trio Cowdrey, Alan Oakman and Peter Richardson for just a single run on his way to 3-68 from 50 overs. Of his day out, he said: 'Rarely did I get the new ball when Ray Lindwall and Keith Miller were in the team. Keith played in that game, but he had some minor injury and the skipper [Ian Johnson] was still trying to get him to bowl. Finally, Miller refused and I was given the ball. I had 3-for from my first six or seven overs but I didn't get any more. There was one lbw [shout] against Cyril Washbrook which was pretty close but it was given not out. If it had gone my way it would have given me four for two. But that's cricket. We weren't able to press on with it.'

Benaud performed remarkably well throughout his first Ashes summer as captain. His ambassadorial and leadership skills were impeccable and he bowled superbly. Seven wickets in the opening Test in Brisbane were followed by one in Melbourne, nine in Sydney and Adelaide and five back in Melbourne, for a total of 33 at an average of under 20 runs apiece.

England was outplayed from the opening Test in Brisbane when debutant O'Neill enlivened proceedings with a majestic 71 not out. Without Subba Row, frontline pair May and Cowdrey lacked top-order support. England had four different sets of openers in the first four Tests and only once did they start with more than 30, when left-handers Richardson and Watson added 89 in the second innings in Adelaide.

On a greentop in Brisbane, Davidson's first ball to Richardson shaved his nose. It had pitched only just short of a good length.[21] England was outed for 134 and remained on the back foot.

In Melbourne, in front of his hometown crowd, Meckiff castled the tourists for 87, his 6-38 making the front page of the Melbourne *Herald* alongside a Soviet rocket launch to the moon. In the first innings he'd bowled May on 113 with his quicker ball and his second-innings heroics prompted an avalanche of criticism from Fleet Street, the just-retired English spinner Johnny Wardle claiming England had been thrown out. Statham's Ashes-best 7-57 in Australia's first innings was soon forgotten in the uproar.

After a dull draw in Sydney, the Australians clinched the Ashes in Adelaide where McDonald, benefiting from some early luck, made 170 and with fellow opener Jimmy Burke added 171 to give the Australians an immediate advantage. Playing his first Test of the tour, Typhoon Tyson took 1-100.

Having triumphed by 10 wickets in Adelaide, the Australians again won comfortably in the final Test in Melbourne, 37-year-old Lindwall passing Clarrie Grimmett's Australian record of 216 wickets when he yorked Trevor Bailey with his fourth ball in England's second innings. Running down the wicket with his arms raised in triumph, Lindwall turned in the direction of the member's stand and waved to his wife Peggy, who had flown down from Brisbane especially for the moment.[22]

For the first time in Australia, Tests were televised but only in the host state.

The general joy at Australia's victory was tempered by the pace of the series, which was funereal. Only one 6 was hit all summer – by Trueman in Sydney. It was almost as if the Ashes had become a lead weight, with captains only going for a win after the draw was assured. Despite the vibrancy of Benaud, it was a malaise that was to blight England–Australia contests into the next decade.

Man of the decade: *Alec Bedser*

England's outstanding bowler in the immediate post-war period, Alec Bedser could make a ball skip sideways off even the flattest of wickets. Behind that warm, gentle smile was a mighty warrior, rated England's finest of all by Don Bradman – surely the ultimate compliment.

Massively built at 191 cm (6 ft 3 in), the genial medium-pacer enjoyed extraordinary success against some of the world's most noted batsmen including the Don, who at one period fell to Bedser five times in five innings, and the left-handed Arthur Morris, who Bedser dismissed so often (eighteen times in twenty Tests) that he became known as 'Bedser's bunny'.

Bradman said a Bedser delivery that bowled him in Adelaide in 1946–47 was the finest ever to take his wicket: 'It must have come three quarters of the way straight on the off stump then suddenly dipped to pitch on the leg stump, only to turn off the pitch and hit the middle and off stumps,' Bradman wrote.[23]

Like the iconic Sydney Barnes, Bedser's leg cutter was unplayable on responsive surfaces, his huge hands allowing him to impart seam others could only wonder at. With his accuracy and stamina from a run-up of no more than six large strides, he was a captain's dream.

In two Ashes summers, in 1950–51 and 1953, the Coronation Year, Bedser amassed almost 70 wickets, including 14 in the opening Test of 1953 at Trent Bridge. On the first day he bowled twenty-five overs and conceded just 26 runs for the wickets of Graeme Hole, Morris and Neil Harvey, beginning his finest summer of all. 'As the much prized wickets came my way, I felt an unashamed exhilaration,' he said.[24]

A newspaper contacted his mother after the match for a comment: 'Well, that's his job [to take wickets],' she said. 'I don't know what the fuss is about.'[25]

Bedser's series haul of 39 surpassed Maurice Tate's longstanding record (of 38) and Fleet Street happily accorded him some spotlight alongside the royals. 'In 1953,' wrote John Woodcock, 'Bedser was the name on everyone's lips. The rubber with Australia yielded him his last great international triumph. England regained the Ashes for the first time since 1938 and Bedser's bowling was the greatest single factor in the victory.'[26]

Bedser thrived, too, on the flatter, harder wickets down-under, his 10 wickets for the match in Melbourne in 1950–51 lifting England to its only victory of an otherwise winless campaign. In four series from 1950–51 to 1953, when he was thirty-six, he took 119 wickets at an average of more than six per Test. He remained a frequent visitor to Australia, too, as a manager and a long-time selector, his identical twin brother, Eric, invariably at his side.

Bedser v. Australia

Season	Analysis	Wkts	Ave
1946–47	2-159, 1-153, 3-99, 3-176, 3-97, 0-68, 2-49, 2-75	16	54.75
1948	3-113, 2-46, 4-100, 1-112, 4-81, 0-27, 3-92, 0-56, 1-61	18	38.22
1950–51	4-45, 3-9, 4-37, 2-43, 4-107, 3-74, 0-62, 5-46, 5-59	30	16.06
1953	7-55, 7-44, 5-105, 3-77, 5-115, 2-14, 6-95, 1-65, 3-88, 0-24	39	17.48
1954–55	1-131	1	131.00

Tests v. Australia:	21 (51 overall)
Wickets:	104 (236)
Average:	27.49 (24.89)
Best bowling:	7-44, Trent Bridge, 1953 (7-44)
5-wicket Innings:	7 (15)
10-wicket Matches:	2 (5)
Strike-rate:	67 balls per wkt (67)
Average wkts per Test:	4.9 (4.6)

Match of the decade: *Sydney, 1954*

Bowled out in just over four hours to concede a 74-run first-innings lead, England marched back into the second Test thanks to Peter May who stroked his way to his first Ashes ton, his century stand in mid-match with rookie Colin Cowdrey, in only his second Test, pivotal in allowing England a sufficiently competitive lead. Frank Tyson, used at first change, demolished the Australians on the fifth morning with sheer pace. He'd been knocked unconscious earlier in the match by a Ray Lindwall bouncer.

Match scores: England 154 and 296 (May 104, Cowdrey 54) defeated Australia 228 (Bailey 4-59, Tyson 4-45) and 184 (Harvey 92 not out, Tyson 6-85) by 38 runs

Odd spot: *The tide turns*

In Brisbane, the Test before he decimated Australia with 10 wickets for the match at the Sydney Cricket Ground in 1954–55, 'Typhoon' Tyson took one for 160 in an inglorious Ashes debut, bowling from an exaggerated 30-metre approach. Australia amassed more than 600 to win by an innings in the first Test match down-under to be contested on a completely covered wicket.

Looking back: *Colin McDonald, Adelaide, 1958–59*

Few were braver than Victoria's Colin McDonald, who wore more bruises than any other Australian opener in history. In those days there were no helmets or thigh guards, most in the top-order going in with nothing more than just a couple of extra hankies stuffed into their pockets. Rated the world's No. 1 batsman in 1959 after amassing 519 runs in five Ashes Tests against Peter May's tourists, McDonald made three 50s in a row, before finishing the series with 170 in Adelaide and 133 and 51 not out in Melbourne.

'It was a thrill of a lifetime,' he said. 'It was the first time I'd made a 100 against England and to make another in the very next Test, too, on my home ground was very satisfying. Funnily enough, in Adelaide, the very first ball I faced from Brian Statham went right through me and only just cleared the middle stump. I could have easily been out for nought and wouldn't have had such a great season. I went on to make 170 and got another 100 in the next Test match too. It ended up being a pretty good year.'

McDonald, then thirty, was rated the world's No. 1 batsman in 1959. He averaged almost 40 in fifteen Ashes Tests.

One for the statisticians: *Drought-breaker*

Neil Harvey's 167 in the second Test at the MCG in 1958–59 was the first century by an Australian against England in four years and eleven Ashes Tests.

Tests 1950–51 to 1958–59

KEY: M Matches **I** Innings **NO** Not out innings **HS** Highest score **BB** Best bowling

5wI 5-wicket innings **10wM** 10-wicket match * Not out # Second innings **rh** Retired hurt

Series results

	Tests	Aust	Eng	Drawn
1950–51 (Aust)	5	4	1	0
1953 (Eng)	5	0	1	4
1954–55 (Aust)	5	1	3	1
1956 (Eng)	5	1	2	2
1958–59 (Aust)	5	4	0	1
Total	25	10	7	8
Progressive	178	74	62	42

Summary

	Runs	Wkts	Ave
Australia	10,303	405	25.43
England	10,203	400	25.50

Highest innings totals

Australia		England	
601-8 dec	Brisbane 1954–55 (1st Test)	459	Manchester 1956 (4th Test)
476	Adelaide 1958–59 (4th Test)		*Next highest:*
426	Sydney 1950–51 (3rd Test)	372	Lord's 1953 (2nd Test)
403-8 dec	Adelaide 1950–51 (4th Test)#		

Lowest completed innings totals

Australia		England	
84	Manchester 1956 (4th Test)	87	Melbourne 1958–59 (2nd Test)#
111	Melbourne 1954–55 (3rd Test)#	122	Brisbane 1950–51 (1st Test)#
111	Adelaide 1954–55 (4th Test)#	123	Sydney 1950–51 (3rd Test)#
123	Nottingham 1953 (1st Test)#		(one batsman absent)

Leading run scorers

	M	I	NO	Runs	HS	Ave	100	50
Australia								
R.N. Harvey	25	47	4	1550	167	36.04	3	8
C.C. McDonald	12	23	1	948	170	43.09	2	4
K.R. Miller	19	35	2	943	145*	28.57	2	3
A.R. Morris	14	26	0	881	206	33.88	2	4
A.L. Hassett	10	19	0	731	115	38.47	2	4
J.W. Burke	14	28	5	676	101*	29.39	1	3
England								
P.B.H. May	17	29	2	1294	113	47.92	3	8
L. Hutton	15	28	5	1196	156*	52.00	2	8
M.C. Cowdrey	15	27	1	954	102	36.69	2	5
T.E. Bailey	23	38	4	875	88	25.73	–	5
T.W. Graveney	14	24	2	622	111	28.27	1	4
D.C.S. Compton	14	25	5	607	94	30.35	–	4

Hundreds

Australia (12)		**England (12)**	
3	R.N. Harvey	3	P.B.H. May
2	A.L. Hassett	2	M.C. Cowdrey
	C.C. McDonald		L. Hutton
	K.R. Miller	1	T.W. Graveney
	A.R. Morris		P.E. Richardson
1	J.W. Burke		Rev. D.S. Sheppard
			R.T. Simpson
			W. Watson

Highest individual scores

Australia

206	A.R. Morris at Adelaide 1950–51 (4th Test)
170	C.C. McDonald at Adelaide 1958–59 (4th Test)
167	R.N. Harvey at Melbourne 1958–59 (2nd Test)
162	R.N. Harvey at Brisbane 1954–55 (1st Test)
153	A.R. Morris at Brisbane 1954–55 (1st Test)
145*	K.R. Miller at Sydney 1950–51 (3rd Test)

England

156*	L. Hutton at Adelaide 1950–51 (4th Test)
156*	R.T. Simpson at Melbourne 1950–51 (5th Test)
145	L. Hutton at Lord's 1953 (2nd Test)

Carrying bat through completed innings

L. Hutton	156* out of 272 for England at Adelaide 1950–51 (4th Test)

500 runs in a series

	Season	M	I	NO	Runs	HS	Ave	100	50
Australia									
C. C. McDonald	1958–59	5	9	1	519	170	64.87	2	1
England									
L. Hutton	1950–51	5	10	4	533	156*	88.83	1	4

Hundred partnerships

Australia (19)

Partnerships of 150 and over:

202	3rd	A. R. Morris and R. N. Harvey at Brisbane 1954–55 (1st Test)
173	4th	R. N. Harvey and G. B. Hole at Manchester 1953 (3rd Test)
171	1st	C. C. McDonald and J. W. Burke at Adelaide 1954–55 (4th Test)
165	2nd	A. R. Morris and K. R. Miller at Lord's 1953 (2nd Test)#
150	7th	K. R. Miller and I. W. G. Johnson at Sydney 1950–51 (3rd Test)

England (16)

Partnerships of 150 and over:

187	4th	P. B. H. May and C. Washbrook at Leeds 1956 (3rd Test)
182	2nd	T. W. Graveney and P. B. H. May at Sydney 1954–55 (5th Test)
182	4th	P. B. H. May and M. C. Cowdrey at Sydney 1958–59 (3rd Test)#
174	1st	P. E. Richardson and M. C. Cowdrey at Manchester 1956 (4th Test)
168	2nd	L. Hutton and T. W. Graveney at Lord's 1953 (2nd Test)
163	5th	W. Watson and T. E. Bailey at Lord's 1953 (2nd Test)#
156	4th	P. B. H. May and D. C. S. Compton at The Oval 1956 (5th Test)
151	1st	P. E. Richardson and M. C. Cowdrey at Nottingham 1956 (1st Test)#

Leading wicket-takers

	Tests	Balls	Mdns	Runs	Wkts	Ave	BB	5wI	10wM
Australia									
R. R. Lindwall	20	4,398	139	1,662	69	24.08	5-54	3	–
K. R. Miller	19	3,909	167	1,314	58	22.65	5-72	2	1
R. Benaud	18	4,133	155	1,465	51	28.72	5-83	2	–
W. A. Johnston	12	3,407	132	1,188	48	24.75	5-35	2	–
A. K. Davidson	15	2,908	105	944	37	25.51	6-64	1	–
R. G. Archer	12	2,443	126	761	35	21.74	5-53	1	–
I. W. G. Johnson	14	2,496	92	857	25	34.28	4-151	–	–
England									
J. C. Laker	12	3,078	162	972	70	13.88	10-53	5	2
A. V. Bedser	11	3,447	96	1,295	70	18.50	7-44	7	1
T. E. Bailey	23	3,303	105	1,373	42	32.69	4-22	–	–
J. B. Statham	13	2,873	75	1,057	39	27.10	7-57	2	–
F. H. Tyson	8	1,724	23	810	32	25.31	7-27	2	1
G. A. R. Lock	10	2,800	161	878	28	31.35	5-45	1	–
J. H. Wardle	8	1,661	81	632	24	26.33	5-79	1	–

Five wickets in an innings

Australia (13)		England (20)	
3	R. R. Lindwall	7	A. V. Bedser
2	R. Benaud	5	J. C. Laker
	W. A. Johnston	2	J. B. Statham
	K. R. Miller		F. H. Tyson
1	R. G. Archer	1	F. R. Brown
	A. K. Davidson		G. A. R. Lock
	J. B. Iverson		F. S. Trueman
	I. Meckiff		J. H. Wardle

Best individual bowling

Australia

6-27	J. B. Iverson at Sydney 1950–51 (3rd Test)#
6-38	I. Meckiff at Melbourne 1958–59 (2nd Test)#
6-64	A. K. Davidson at Melbourne 1958–59 (2nd Test)

England

10-53	J. C. Laker at Manchester 1956 (4th Test)#
	(best innings analysis in all Test cricket)
9-37	J. C. Laker at Manchester 1956 (4th Test)
7-27	F. H. Tyson at Melbourne 1954–55 (3rd Test)#
7-44	A. V. Bedser at Nottingham 1953 (1st Test)#
7-55	A. V. Bedser at Nottingham 1953 (1st Test)
7-57	J. B. Statham at Melbourne 1958–59 (2nd Test)
6-55	J. C. Laker at Leeds 1956 (3rd Test)#
6-85	F. H. Tyson at Sydney 1954–55 (2nd Test)#
6-95	A. V. Bedser at Leeds 1953 (4th Test)

10 wickets in a match

Australia (1)

10-152	K. R. Miller (5-72 and 5-80) at Lord's 1956 (2nd Test)

England (5)

19-90	J. C. Laker (9-37 and 10-53) at Manchester 1956 (4th Test)
	(best match analysis in all first-class cricket)
14-99	A. V. Bedser (7-55 and 7-44) at Nottingham 1953 (1st Test)
11-113	J. C. Laker (5-58 and 6-55) at Leeds 1956 (3rd Test)
10-105	A. V. Bedser (5-46 and 5-59) at Melbourne 1958–59 (5th Test)
10-130	F. H. Tyson (4-45 and 6-85) at Sydney 1954–55 (2nd Test)

25 wickets in a series

	Season	Tests	Balls	Mdns	Runs	Wkts	Ave	BB	5wl	10wM
Australia										
R. Benaud	1958–59	5	1,866	65	584	31	18.83	5-83	2	–
R. R. Lindwall	1953	5	1,444	62	490	26	18.84	5-54	3	–
Also note:										
A. K. Davidson	1958–59	5	1,469	45	456	24	19.00	6-64	1	–
England										
J. C. Laker	1956	5	1,703	127	442	46	9.60	10-53	4	2
A. V. Bedser	1953	5	1,591	58	682	39	17.48	7-44	5	1
A. V. Bedser	1950–51	5	1,560	34	482	30	16.06	5-46	2	1
F. H. Tyson	1954–55	5	1,208	16	583	28	20.82	7-27	2	1

Leading wicketkeepers

	Tests	Dismissals	Catches	Stumpings
Australia				
G. R. A. Langley	9	37	35	2
A. T. W. Grout	5	20	17	3
L. V. Maddocks	5	13	12	1
D. Tallon	6	10	10	0
England				
T. G. Evans	22	55	47	8

Leading fieldsmen

	Tests	Catches		Tests	Catches
Australia			**England**		
A. K. Davidson	15	19	T. E. Bailey	23	16
R. N. Harvey	25	15	L. Hutton	15	15
R. R. Lindwall	20	12	T. W. Graveney	14	14
R. G. Archer	12	11	G. A. R. Lock	10	14
R. Benaud	18	11	M. C. Cowdrey	15	13
G. B. Hole	9	11	P. B. H. May	17	10

Captains

	Tests	Won	Lost	Drawn	Toss won
Australia					
A. L. Hassett	10	4	2	4	9
I. W. G. Johnson	9	2	4	3	3
R. Benaud	5	4	0	1	1
A. R. Morris	1	0	1	0	1
England					
L. Hutton	10	4	1	5	2
P. B. H. May	10	2	5	3	8
F. R. Brown	5	1	4	0	1

Most appearances

Australia (36 players)		England (39 players)	
25	R. N. Harvey	23	T. E. Bailey
20	R. R. Lindwall	22	T. G. Evans
19	K. R. Miller	17	P. B. H. May
18	R. Benaud	15	M. C. Cowdrey
15	A. K. Davidson		L. Hutton
14	J. W. Burke	14	D. C. S. Compton
	I. W. G. Johnson		T. W. Graveney
	A. R. Morris		

Australian opener **Colin McDonald** is stumped by **John Murray** from the bowling of **Tony Lock**, at Leeds in 1961.
McDonald Family Archives

1960s

NOT SO BOLD MESSIAHS

● ●

'Never before have I written to a player to express my regret
at his omission from an Australian Eleven. In your case I am
making an exception because I want you to know how
much my colleagues (Dudley Seddon and Jack Ryder) and
I disliked having to make this move . . .'

A long overdue, bold new era seemed assured after the rollicking
1960–61 West Indian summer, which profiled bright new stars of
the international game in Garry Sobers and Rohan Kanhai and
introduced to Australian cricket audiences the flamboyant giant Wes Hall
from the island of cricket stars Barbados. Even the old-timers couldn't
recall anyone who had run in as far, or bowled as consistently quickly
as Hall, 'Typhoon' Tyson included. One cartoonist had an umpire asking
glamour batsman Norm O'Neill where he'd like the sightscreen posi-
tioned and Norm quipping: 'Halfway up the wicket thanks . . . between
me and Wes!' Included in the exhilarating five-Test Calypso summer was
cricket's first tie. A series of colossal crowds attended, culminating in a new
world record 90,800 on the Saturday of the decider in Melbourne.

From the heart-stopping first Test in Brisbane, Richie Benaud was
hailed as cricket's version of globetrotting American evangelist Billy
Graham. Set 233, Australia was 92-6 at tea on the final day when Sir
Donald Bradman, Australia's selection chairman, joined Benaud and

fellow not-out batsman Alan Davidson during the break. After commenting what a magnificent game it had been, he asked Benaud: 'What are you going for Richie? – a win or a draw?'

'We're going for a win, of course.'

'I'm very pleased to hear it.'[1]

Australia needed more than 120 in even time and thanks to their adventurous strokeplay and between wickets hustle, Benaud and Davidson trailblazed the most famous finish of all. Three wickets fell in the final tumultuous over from Hall, including Australia's No. 10 Ian Meckiff whose despairing dive only just failed to beat Joe Solomon's side-on direct hit. Thinking Australia had lost by a run, Meckiff, known universally as 'The Count', trudged face down for the rooms and it was several minutes before the fog lifted and he was alerted to the fact that the scores were actually all square: 737 runs apiece. He'd just figured in the first-ever tied Test. It was an unforgettable start to a thrilling series unrivalled until 2005 when England ended its years of Ashes desolation.

Benaud's popularity ballooned even more in 1961 with his successful Ashes defence. It was Australia's first series win on British soil since Bradman's Invincibles in 1948. Particularly sweet was the Manchester Test where Benaud went around the wicket in the spell of his life, England plunging from 150-1 to 201 all out. 'We went up on the balcony and looked down and there was no-one there,' O'Neill said later. 'In 1956 when they doctored the wicket, the boys reckoned there were 20,000 people down there and everyone was making speeches. This time they [the English fans] didn't want to know.'

There was particular anticipation approaching the arrival of the 1962–63 Englishmen under the leadership of the glamorous Ted Dexter, England's most attractive batsman and a Cambridge man at ease in any society circle.

Standing Corinthian-like at the crease, he had a magnificent eye and was at his best when attacking, few bowlers in the world being able to restrict his flow of boundaries. Dexter averaged 90 in five home Tests against Pakistan and enhanced his status as one of finest in the world. Included was the most scintillating knock of the northern summer when he took less than four hours to make 172 in the final Test at The Oval.

His resolution, too, to succeed in Australia had been magnified after his modest beginnings when he'd made less than 20 runs in two Tests, having arrived via Paris and totally out of practice in mid-tour four years earlier. The butt of jokes from within and outside a team he hardly knew, the just-engaged Dexter admitted he'd lacked focus in 1958–59 and had his head turned 'by marvellous oyster parties ... [featuring] girls in big hats and short dresses ... it was my first tour abroad and in horse-racing terms I needed a pair of blinkers to keep my mind on the job.'[2] He was slammed unmercifully in the press, the authoritative A. G. 'Johnnie' Moyes rating him the poorest specialist batsman to appear in an Ashes Test in forty years.[3]

His imperious 180 in the opening Test of 1961 at Edgbaston after two early let-offs reminded the Australians of his front-foot ferocity, most of his thirty-one 4s coming straight or through the covers. Dexter loved the big-time and was at his best when truly challenged.

The English selectors, headed by Walter Robins, had been debating for weeks who should lead the MCC on its winter tour. Both Dexter and Colin Cowdrey had captained during the home summer. A third candidate was the Sussex amateur The Rev. David Sheppard, who was having a winter sabbatical from his duties as Warden of the Mayflower Family Centre.[4]

Dexter had led the MCC to India and Pakistan the previous winter. While Pakistan was defeated 1–0, the Englishmen played ultra cautiously against the Indians. Questions were immediately raised as to Dexter's man-management skills after India won the only two Tests decided.

Leading fast bowler Freddie Trueman was among Dexter's critics at the time, saying his rapport with the rank-and-file professionals was non-existent. No one doubted Lord Ted's playing attributes or the power of his personality, but the 1962–63 touring professionals genuinely felt it was an 'us and them' situation, especially when Dexter was flanked by tour manager, the Duke of Norfolk, one of the game's most distinguished patrons and president at Dexter's club Sussex.

Trouble brewed from the first days on board the *Canberra* from Aden to Fremantle when Dexter, having befriended the outstanding British athlete Gordon Pirie, invited Pirie to conduct daily PE classes, as well as making recommendations about diet, including fluids. Trueman was floored when told that nuts and lettuce were a better fuel than his favourite steak and chips. And he really saw red when Pirie dared query the number of beers being consumed. Freddie let it be known that Pirie better be as good a swimmer as he was a runner, as it was highly likely he'd be thrown overboard![5]

The Englishmen won only one lead-up match, the tour opener against Western Australia in Perth. The pre-tour promises of bright, adventurous cricket were ignored as the summer turned pear-shaped, both Dexter and Benaud playing safety-first cricket in a dull, anti-climactic series totally devoid of any of the magic of 1960–61. The widespread boos of the Sydney crowd on the final day were a brickbat to both captains and their teams for a summer devoid of imagination and excitement. Set 241 to win the game and the series, the Australians required little more than three an over for victory, yet settled for a draw, gum-chewing plumber Bill Lawry staying four hours for 49 to widespread derision. In 1961, when he was the find of the tour, Lawry had been dubbed 'William the Conqueror' but after Sydney he was 'The Corpse with Pads On'. Benaud the Brave had been Benaud the Coy, the loss of four frontline wickets on the final afternoon, including two before the interval to off-spinner David Allen, pivotal in his withdrawal. 'Spectators were given no encouragement to ever come again,' said E.M. Wellings in the London *Evening News*.[6]

The Australians needed 170 at tea, but with just 120 minutes left, Benaud felt England could close the game up at any time and Australia would be in genuine danger if any more quick wickets were forfeited. Dexter blamed the existence of the Ashes on triggering the caution evident since the opening international in Brisbane. Had there been a bonus of £1,000 per player to the winning side in the decider, he claimed there would almost certainly have been a result. Even the serious English broadsheets teed off on that one. Lord Ted became Lord Tactless. Lawry was also pilloried in the local press, but he'd only been following instructions to bat and not get out. Benaud went into damage control: 'It would have required one of the greatest entrepreneurs the world has ever seen to turn that fifth Test into an exciting fixture after that sombre ten hours of England batting at the beginning of the match.'[7] It was an unfortunate end to one of the tamest summers of all. 'The derision was loud and long,' said journalist Alan Lee.[8]

The blandness of the wicket had defeated the strokemakers but in making less than 200 from almost ninety eight-ball overs on the opening

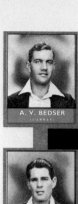

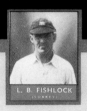

CALENDAR HEROES: Walter Hammond's touring Englishmen are highlighted in a 1947 calendar.

SPORTS IDOL: The charismatic Denis Compton is pictured on the front cover of *Everybody's* magazine. He was one of the few to withstand the bumper attack from Ray Lindwall and Keith Miller in 1948.

Below: Keith Miller (left) mixed easily in any circle. Here he shares a joke with captain Lindsay Hassett and the Duke of Edinburgh at the start of the 1953 Australian tour at East Mosely.

Bottom: Freddie Brown's MCC visitors, 1950–51.

everybody's 3D

PATSY HENDREN ON CRICKET   ENTER DENIS COMPTON
YANGTSE INCIDENT by Lord Vansittart   MUNICH ART TREASURES

J. G. DEWES   D. V. P. WRIGHT   F. R. BROWN (Captain)   D. COMPTON   L. HUTTON   D. B. CLOSE   R. BERRY   R. T. SIMPSON

T. E. BAILEY   A. BEDSER   W. G. A. PARKHOUSE   T. G. EVANS   J. J. WARR   W. E. HOLLIES   A. J. McINTYRE

C. WASHBROOK   D. S. SHEPPARD

ENGLAND'S TEST TEAM 1950 1951

HAPPY SAILORS: The 1948 Australians, undefeated through their entire five-month campaign, became known as Don Bradman's Invincibles. Standing (l–r): Ray Lindwall, Bill Johnston, Doug Ring, Ernie Toshack, Don Tallon, Keith Miller, Sid Barnes (looking down), Colin McCool. Sitting: Sam Loxton, Ian Johnson, Neil Harvey, Lindsay Hassett, Don Bradman (captain), Bill Brown, Arthur Morris, Ron Saggers. Ron Hamence also toured.

INTREPID: Sid Barnes, typically within pickpocket distance of the batsman, all but catches England's Jack Ikin, Melbourne, 1946–47.

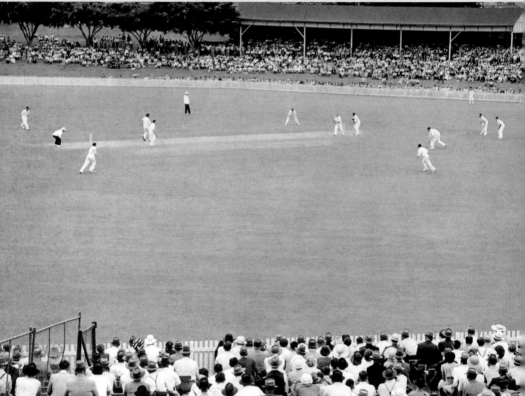

SHINING STAR (top left): Arthur Morris outshone even Don Bradman on the 1948 tour. Eight of his twelve Test centuries were against England.

OLD BULLDOG (top right): Freddie Brown in the nets in Brisbane leading into the first Test. He may have lost the series but he forged many a new friendship with his ready smile and wholehearted attitude.

'GABBA DELIGHTS (above): Australia's Arthur Morris is on strike as the 1950–51 Test series opens in Brisbane, then very much a country ground with its vast expanses of grassy areas and only a grandstand or two.
Cliff Postle

SHOOTING STAR (left): Jack Iverson had a remarkable first summer of Test cricket in 1950–51, capturing 21 wickets at 15 runs apiece before disappearing as quickly as he'd arrived.

HOWZAAT? (below): Gil Langley has hardly appealed, but Ray Lindwall is sure and Peter May has to go, lbw for 44 on the final day of the first Test in Brisbane, 1954–55.

Bruce Postle

TORRENTIAL (bottom): Rarely has a Test match ever been affected more by the weather than the opening Test of the 1950–51 summer in Brisbane. The tropical rains washed out play on the second day and when play did begin late on the third, 20 wickets fell in just four hours.

Jim Fenwick

SPORT MAGAZINE

2/6

FEBRUARY 1951

HOW TO PLAY INDOOR BOWLS

KRAMER WINS AGAIN!

SPECIAL AMATEUR SPORTS COVERAGE

NEIL HARVEY'S BATTING SECRETS

POPULAR (above): Colin Cowdrey averaged 35 in his first Ashes series, in 1954–55, his commanding 102 in heatwave conditions in the third Test in Melbourne helping to set up one of the most memorable English wins of all. *Patrick Eagar*

STARLET: From the time Neil Harvey made a century on his Ashes debut in 1948, he was a darling of the crowds in Australia and England. So short-sighted was he, however, that he could never read a scoreboard and never knew how many he'd made!

INVINCIBLE (right): 'Big Bill' Johnston, one of the heroes of the 1948 tour, was Australia's first truly world-class left-arm paceman, whose ability to slow down and bowl orthodox breaks made him a frontliner even in an attack including Lindwall and Miller.

HUTTON'S CONQUERORS: Thanks to 'the Typhoon', Frank Tyson, England came from behind to retain the Ashes in 1954–55. Back row (l–r): George Duckworth (baggage man), Keith Andrew, Peter Loader, Tom Graveney, Tyson, Mr H. W. Dalton (masseur). Middle: John Wardle, Reg Simpson, Vic Wilson, Bob Appleyard, Jim McConnon, Brian Statham, Colin Cowdrey, Geoffrey Howard (manager). Front: Trevor Bailey, Bill Edrich, Peter May, Len Hutton (captain), Denis Compton, Alec Bedser, Godfrey Evans.

STAND-IN SKIPPER: In his only Ashes appearance as Australia's captain, Arthur Morris saw England snatch a narrow victory in Sydney after a brilliant burst from speedster Frank Tyson on the final day, December 1954. Standing (l–r): Gil Langley, Ron Archer, Graeme Hole, Bill Johnston, Alan Davidson, Les Favell, Billy Watson (12th man). Sitting: Neil Harvey, Richie Benaud, Morris (captain), Ray Lindwall, Jimmy Burke.

YOUNG RICHIE: After a modest beginning, Richie Benaud became Australia's number-one spin bowler on the 1957–58 tour of South Africa and continued with outstanding performances against the English in 1958–59.
Lloyd Holyoak Collection

FAREWELL NUGGET: On the last of his three English tours, Keith 'Nugget' Miller played superbly with bat and ball, increasing his reputation as one of Australia's finest all-rounders. Here he has England's captain Peter May caught behind at Lord's on the final day of the second Test, June 1956.

Your new, bigger SPORT Magazine

68 pages!

2'6

DECEMBER 1958

WHO'LL WIN THE TESTS?

by

JOHN ARLOTT
SID BARNES

•

COACH TALBOT REVEALS KONRADS' TRAINING SECRETS

•

GOLF HINTS by **SAM SNEAD**

TENNIS LESSONS by **DINNY PAILS**

How Good is ◄ NORM O'NEILL? *by Alan Hulls*

SHADES OF THE DON (left): Norman O'Neill was labelled 'another Bradman' when he made 1,000 runs at Sheffield Shield standard and 71 on his Ashes debut in Brisbane in 1958–59.

WELCOME (below): Richie Benaud is featured on the front cover of Roy Webber's 1961 *Cricket Annual*. His six-wicket haul at Old Trafford helped to turn a Test.

MAJESTIC (bottom): Ted Dexter drives Tom Veivers on his way to 174 at Old Trafford in 1964. Bobby Simpson is at slip and Wally Grout is the 'keeper.

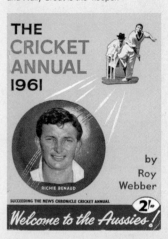

THE CRICKET ANNUAL 1961

RICHIE BENAUD

SUCCEEDING THE NEWS CHRONICLE CRICKET ANNUAL

by Roy Webber

2/-

Welcome to the Aussies!

TIME TO MATURE (above): Bobby Simpson took fifty-two innings to make his first Test century. He promptly turned it into a treble, at Old Trafford in 1964.

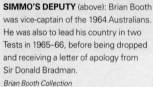

SIMMO'S DEPUTY (above): Brian Booth was vice-captain of the 1964 Australians. He was also to lead his country in two Tests in 1965–66, before being dropped and receiving a letter of apology from Sir Donald Bradman.
Brian Booth Collection

THE OLD FIRM (above right): Bob Simpson and Bill Lawry became one of Australia's most reliable opening partnerships. They are pictured here at Sydney, 1962–63.
Gordon Vidler Collection

TERRIER: Fred Titmus was a real craftsman, his ability to swerve and spin the ball making him a dangerous opponent on the flattest of wickets. Here he traps Wally Grout lbw at Headingley, 1964.

DISAPPOINTING: The 1962–63 Ashes series was anti-climactic, the final Test ending in a disappointing draw and players being booed from the field after Australia refused a last-afternoon chase. Standing (l–r): Brian Booth, Graham McKenzie, Bill Lawry, Alan Barnes (manager), Neil Hawke, Peter Burge, Bobby Simpson. Sitting: Wally Grout, Alan Davidson, Richie Benaud (captain), Neil Harvey, Ken Mackay (12th man), Norm O'Neill.

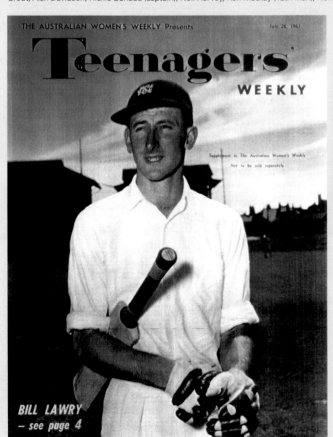

THE AUSTRALIAN WOMEN'S WEEKLY Presents

July 26, 1961

Teenagers'
WEEKLY

Supplement to The Australian Women's Weekly
Not to be sold separately

BILL LAWRY
— see page 4

YOUNG GUN (1): Graham 'Garth' McKenzie leapt to prominence on the 1961 tour as Alan Davidson's new-ball partner.

YOUNG GUN (2) (left): Opening batsman Bill Lawry had a marvellous maiden Ashes tour with a century at Lord's and another at Old Trafford two Tests later.
Women's Weekly, *July, 1961*

TRIPLE-CENTURION (above): Bob Cowper made 307, the highest Test score ever in Melbourne, in front of an appreciative home crowd in 1966.

BUSH PRODIGY (right): Dashing Dougie Walters was in his element from the time he made 155 on his much-remembered Ashes debut in Brisbane in 1965–66.

CHEERS, RAY (below): Australia's captain Ian Chappell (third from left) congratulates Ray Illingworth after England won the decider in Sydney in 1970–71, despite the absence of Geoff Boycott (behind) and, late in the match, John Snow (left).
Bruce Postle

ON THE BEACH (top): Ray Illingworth casts a fatherly glance at his fast bowler John Snow during a rest day in the deciding Test, Sydney, 1970–71.
Bruce Postle

PARTY TIME (above): The Australians celebrate their big win at Lord's in 1972, triggered by the outstanding debut of swing specialist Bob Massie (second from left), who is pictured in an embrace with tour manager Ray Steele and his opening partner Dennis Lillee.

THE FIRST OF 16: Geoff Boycott is bowled by a Bob Massie in-dipper, beginning Massie's extraordinary debut.
Patrick Eagar

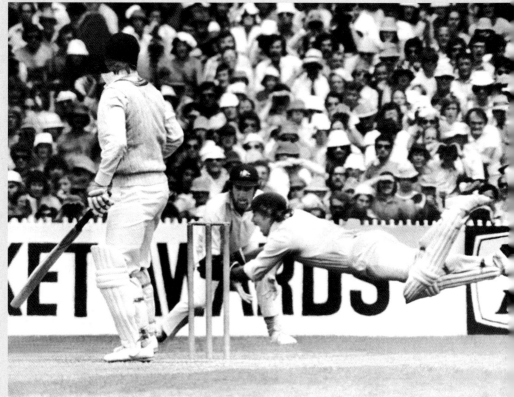

GOT IT: A Rod Marsh special in Melbourne in 1974–75. His reflexes and sure glovework made him Australia's outstanding wicketkeeper before the arrival of Ian Healy.
Patrick Eagar

APPEALING (above): England's Alan Knott would go anywhere for a game, even to a primary school on his day off, Sydney, 1974–75.
Bruce Postle

THOMMO (left): The unique, sling-shot action of tearaway Jeff Thomson is brilliantly captured by the doyen of cricket photographers, Patrick Eagar. Fred Titmus is the batsman, in the third Test, Melbourne, 1974–75.
Patrick Eagar

FRONTLINE FOUR: The opening Tests in Brisbane and Perth in 1974–75 may have been one-sided but there were some outstanding highlights. Tony Greig (above) made a brave century and Bob Willis (top right) took seven wickets in Brisbane. Colin Cowdrey (middle) answered an SOS to bolster the team in Perth, and Greg Chappell (below right) started the summer with three consecutive half-centuries.

Cricketer *magazine*

day, England had played with little fire and imagination. It was an insipid farewell, too, for two of Australia's finest, Neil Harvey and Alan Davidson. Harvey's century in Adelaide was his twenty-first century in Tests and Davidson's 24 series wickets the highest for either side. Harvey's ton was memorable for his early luck – he was dropped three times on a green seamer. 'That's not very good batting, is it Sam?' he said, sauntering down the wicket between overs to his partner Brian 'Sam' Booth. 'Looks like the Poms don't want to get me out today. I'd better get some runs.'[9] He did: 154 of them. To the end he was a little maestro.

'Davo' continually angled the ball across the right-handers, giving his wicketkeeper and slips hope on even the flattest tracks. Even at thirty-three, his control was impeccable and he still swung the new ball both ways, making him a dangerous opponent, even if he wasn't as swift as in his prime.

With so many champions in the two XIs, there were some fine moments in the lead-ups.

Dexter's electric 99 enlivened the final day in Brisbane when the heat was turned up on Benaud's delayed declaration. The Englishmen were amazed at Australia's safety-first attitude. 'Even on the last morning,' said Sheppard, 'there was a long conference between Benaud and [vice-captain] Harvey before a declaration was announced . . . I felt Benaud let us escape in Brisbane. Had he declared [late] on the fourth day and given us a smaller target, we were bound to have chased it all the way . . . it was an ultra-cautious piece of captaincy.'[10]

Dexter enjoyed his finest hour in the second Test in Melbourne when England ran down a fourth-innings target of 234, Trueman's eight wickets and Sheppard's 113 piloting a resounding victory. Trueman was faster than Statham and when he wasn't hooping the ball away from the right-handers, he was jagging it back in with his lethal offcutter. 'Freddie on his day was right up there among the fastest bowlers, too,' said Booth. 'He wasn't necessarily as fast as Hall and Griffith, but no-one was. Griffith had an amazing change up. I didn't have much of a backlift but one tour he sent my stumps spinning twice with deliveries I honestly didn't see. Another grazed my nose. He was the most lethal alright.'

Cowdrey's masterly 113 ensured England a narrow first-innings lead. 'Kipper' loved Melbourne and averaged 50 runs per innings there, well in advance of his career average of 44. 'Cowdrey is an extraordinary player,' said O'Neill. 'Sometimes he will struggle in a curious strokeless mood, as though bereft of confidence as well as shots; other times he will look the best player in the world, making everything look ridiculously easy.'[11]

While the last-day target was modest, England had lost an overnight wicket, Ashes debutant Barry Jarman taking a catch of a lifetime down the leg side to dismiss Geoff Pullar (for five) from a genuine leg-glance against Graham McKenzie. Australia had reason to be confident, having bowled England out for 201 at Manchester during the previous tour. McKenzie, the strapping young giant from Perth, bowled several very fast overs at Dexter, Benaud went around the wicket hoping to bowl into the footmarks only to overpitch and concede four immediately through the covers to Sheppard, one of the few Englishmen prepared to use his feet against the slow bowlers.

Having shared a century stand with Sheppard, Dexter was run out for 52, his dominance important in the accelerating run-rate. 'It was not an innings decorated with flittering boundaries [he hit only four], yet he [Dexter] ranked it as the greatest innings of his life,' said his biographer Lee, 'and the sensation that followed victory as the most satisfying that cricket was ever to give him.'[12]

Dexter had come in himself at No. 3, rather than sending in a nightwatchman on the fourth night. It allowed him to dictate from the opening overs on the fifth morning and England sailed to a handsome seven-wicket win with 75 minutes to spare.

Trueman bowled with gusto all match, revelling in the atmosphere of the huge crowds, which included almost 70,000 on the opening day and 62,000 on the second. In his very first over of the game he appealed for lbw against Lawry to one obviously pitched outside leg-stump. Walking back past first-game umpire Bill Smyth, he smiled and said: 'Just seeing if you were fooking awake!'

Trueman broke Australia's resistance late on the third day when he dismissed Bob Simpson and O'Neill with consecutive deliveries on his way to his first 5-wicket haul on Australian soil. The wicket was flat and, having started brilliantly, he took three of the last four wickets. Booth's 103 was top score in Australia's 248 and his second 100 in as many Tests. Booth's Christian ways had been highlighted in the newspapers, especially when he said God had been on his side during the first of the two 100s. It prompted a headline: 'ENGLAND CAN'T WIN – GOD IS ON BRIAN BOOTH'S SIDE.'[13] He loved that one.

Davidson's double of 4-54 and 5-25 allowed the Australians to square the series in Sydney before the final two Tests were drawn, Ken Barrington's superb back-to-back centuries increasing his series aggregate to almost 600 at a Hobbs-like average of more than 70.

Thanks to Peter Burge, the meaty middle-order batsman from Queensland, the Australians retained the Ashes in England in 1964, Burge's glorious century in the third Test at Leeds changing the game as Ian Botham was to do at the same venue in 1981. In the only result of the five-Test summer, Australia recovered from the precipice of defeat at 178-7 chasing 268 to win by seven wickets. Dexter was held responsible as he had opted to bring back local hero Trueman and arm him with the second new ball, rather than continue with finger spinner Fred Titmus, who was bemusing everyone bar Burge with his drift and subtle turn. From his first 29 overs straight, Titmus had 3-27. 'Ted got things pretty wrong that day I'm afraid,' said Titmus. 'Burge moved from 38 to 160 ... it was the only match of the Test series to produce a conclusive result.'[14]

Trueman was on the verge of 300 Test wickets and felt Burge, a compulsive hooker, could sky a catch at any time. The Tetley beer tents emptied and the fans were treated to some marvellous, aggressive cricket as Burge sailed into the short-pitched bowling in a colossal counter-attack still rated one of the greatest in Ashes annals.

Burge and tailender Neil Hawke added 105 runs in ninety-nine minutes as the match pendulum swung Australia's way. Adopting the tactic Steve Waugh was to use again and again with the Australian tail in the 1990s, Burge marched down to Hawke and said: 'You can hold a bat. I'm not going to hog the strike'.[15]

Thanks to the liberal diet of Trueman bouncers that Burge treated like harmless long-hops, he outscored Hawke two to one. 'Burge was awesome,' said Hawke. 'Trueman tried him with several bouncers which he dispatched with great authority to the square leg and mid-wicket region. Peter was a great hooker ... he went for the bowling and hit it all over the ground.'[16]

Ninety-six of Burge's runs came in boundaries. 'A greedy bear let loose in a honey store could not have been happier or more at home than Burge,' said Alex Bannister in *Playfair Cricket Monthly*. 'He [Trueman] fed Burge's best known shots, the hook and square cut with a series of long hops and short-pitched deliveries.'[17] In his two previous Headingley Tests, Burge had made just nought and one (in 1956) and five and nought (1961).

Bobby Simpson's 311 in the following Test at Old Trafford saw him bat into a third day, Barrington replying with 256 and Dexter 174. Trueman, thirty-three and in his last Ashes tussle, was to take his 300th Test wicket at The Oval, confirming his ranking among England's finest.

Had it not been for the spellbinding authority of teenage debutant Doug Walters, some hijinks at the head of the order by England's Bob Barber and a rare triple century from fellow Australian Bob Cowper in the final, rain-ruined Test, the 1965–66 summer would also have been consigned to mediocrity. The strength of the two batting teams ensured just two results and three draws.

For me, a young schoolboy allowed home early in suburban Melbourne because of the December heat, Walters' knock was transfixing. There was no thought of afternoon tea or a walk around the block with the dogs. The ABC television pictures may only have been black and white but they remain indelible to this day.

Walters was the new face of Australian cricket, just as Neil Harvey had been in the late 1940s, and Benaud and Davidson were in the 1950s; and as Dennis Lillee was to be in the 1970s, the Waugh twins in the 1980s, Warnie in the 1990s and Ricky Ponting in the 2000s. His on-driving against old campaigners Titmus and Allen was daring and added an electric edge to the contest. By making a second century in the following Test in Melbourne, Walters emulated the deeds of Bill Ponsford who had started his Test career with back-to-back centuries in 1924–25.

Captain Simpson was available for only one of the first three Tests because of injury and illness. His replacement was the gentlemanly Booth, who learnt of his promotion via England wicketkeeper Jim Parks at the team motel. 'Congratulations Brian. Well done,' said Parks.[18]

Seeing Booth's puzzled expression, Parks continued: 'The first Test match team for Brisbane has just been announced. I heard it on the radio just now. You're captain.'

The next day a letter arrived from Australia's selection chairman Don Bradman:

Congratulations [Brian] on your appointment as Australian
captain. It is an honour reserved for the very few and I have no
doubt you are proud of it. As one who is privileged to wear the
same tie, I fully appreciate, however, that it brings responsibilities
of a special kind and inevitable criticism. You are well fitted to
accept the former and I'm sure your mature judgement will
enable you to throw off the latter. The Australian Board and the
selection committee have a policy for the coming season which
I would like to discuss with you and probably the team before
the Test . . .[19]

Simpson had been sidelined for eight weeks after having his wrist
broken by pacy Queenslander Peter Allan in the opening Sheffield Shield
fixture of the summer. He missed the first Test, played in the second, and
missed the third because of chicken pox.

After the Englishmen had won the third Test by an innings in Sydney,
Booth was dropped, never to play Test cricket again. After congratulating
counterpart Mike Smith on his team's win as the Englishmen walked into
their dressing rooms, Booth said: 'I think this is it for me, Mike. There'll
have to be changes and I'll be one of them.'[20]

He'd made 16 in Brisbane, 23 and 10 in Melbourne and eight and
27 in Sydney. His place was to be taken by the grandson of Bodyliner
Vic Richardson, emerging South Australian Ian Chappell, who had played
one Test a season earlier against Pakistan. Victoria's batting all-rounder
Keith Stackpole was also included for the first time in Adelaide, while
Allan replaced McKenzie, only to be forced to withdraw at the eleventh
hour with acute shin soreness.[21]

In those days, selectors never had to explain their decisions, but
Bradman again wrote to Booth, this time with an apology:

Never before have I written to a player to express my regret
at his omission from an Australian Eleven. In your case I am
making an exception because I want you to know how much
my colleagues (Dudley Seddon and Jack Ryder) and I disliked
having to make this move. Captain one match and out of the
side the next looks like ingratitude but you understand the
circumstances and will be the first to admit that your form has
not been good. I sincerely hope that your form will return
quickly and in good measure and in any event assure you of the

high personal regard in which you are held by us all and our appreciation of the way you have always tried to do everything in your power to uphold the good name and prestige of Australia.[22]

Even years after his retirement, Bradman was the most dominant personality in Australian cricket, his stamina for meetings rivalling his appetite for runs. Instrumental in helping to stamp out throwing, his experience and guidance was welcomed by cricket administrators around the world. Bradman the selector tended to favour younger players. Years earlier he'd ended Clarrie Grimmett's Test career when Frank Ward was chosen for the 1938 tour. When queried years later, he wrote: 'Grimmett [in 1938] was finished.' On the same tour, his selection of the seasoned Arthur Chipperfield over the ill-fated youngster Ross Gregory provided a rare exception to his tendency towards youth.

The Don oversaw a transformation of Australia's middle-order in the final Tests of 1965–66. The teenage Walters was just one of the debutants. In Adelaide, he was joined by Ian Chappell, in at No. 7, and Stackpole at No. 8. The left-handed Bob Cowper, too, was just twenty-five and a relative tyro.

By rights, England should have won the series, but were hamstrung by fast bowler David Larter's ongoing injury problems, which robbed the attack of its potential No. 1 striker. The 200 cm (6 ft 7 in) Larter, from Northamptonshire, Tyson's old club, had taken 71 championship wickets in the 1965 season. In a wicket spree in June, he took 24 wickets in two matches. He'd toured down-under in 1962–63 without playing a Test. But in the 1965 home summer, he'd taken 13 wickets in three Tests, including a 5-for against the touring South Africans at Trent Bridge. David Brown and the left-armer Jeff Jones made useful contributions, but they were no Trueman and Statham and with Titmus also lacking the menace of 1962–63, the attack was pedestrian. Wicketkeeper Jim Parks, too, struggled throughout, maintaining his place only because of his considerable batting ability.

Touring captain Smith was a double international, having, a decade earlier, also represented England as a rugby fly. Following the forgettable summer of 1962–63, his orders were to play bright cricket and after a drawn first Test in Brisbane he could easily have won at Melbourne, but for Parks on the final morning missing a simple stumping against Burge down the offside from the occasional wrist-spinner Bob Barber.

Burge had made just 34 and Australia was fighting for survival before he and Walters ensured the draw with a purposeful near double-century stand.

In Brisbane, England had followed-on in a rain-ruined draw but were angered when Lawry, on nought, didn't walk after appearing to be caught at the wicket third ball of the series. He was to make 166 in seven hours. 'Those of us near the wicket were convinced there was a touch of the glove as the ball flew through to Jim Parks,' said John Edrich.[23]

One English writer accused Lawry of cheating[24] but Lawry said the English press were merely grasping for copy on a slow news day. 'I always have and always will wait for the umpire's decision,' said Lawry in his auto-biography, released soon afterwards.[25] 'During my career I have been the victim of bad decisions and have also enjoyed my share of good fortune with lucky decisions . . . some people maintain it is not good sportsman-ship to remain at the crease when you know you should have been given out. I disagree.'[26]

In the drawn second Test in Melbourne, the Englishmen dominated most of the match, Cowdrey's MCG century habit continuing and the gritty left-hander Edrich topscoring with 109 in a score of 558, England's highest Test score down-under since 1928–29. He couldn't pick the second of Simpson's two wrong-uns and constantly played and missed to the anguish of wicketkeeper Wally Grout. His cousin, Bill, had been an English Test star before and after World War II and Edrich was just as brave and determined. He'd made a century on his Ashes debut at Lord's in 1964 and his broad bat and focus was to frustrate many a bowler around the world in the next decade. He was England's permanent No. 3 all summer, behind the new pairing of the left-handed Barber and 25-year-old first-time tourist Geoff Boycott.

England's touring highpoint came in Sydney where they won by an innings well inside four days, a rollicking 234-run opening stand between Barber and Boycott providing a matchwinning launch-pad. Barber's 185 was the innings of the summer. He'd played at Lancashire as a teenager before blossoming at Warwickshire and winning back his Test place as an adventurous and entertaining strokemaker. For the first time in the sum-mer, Australia had both frontline new-ball strikers McKenzie and Neil Hawke available, adding to their pre-match confidence. Hawke claimed a Test-best 7-105, with most taken from around the wicket. He was rewarded with a shower of coins by appreciative fans as he did the bound-ary riding between overs.[27] Few new-ball pacemen transferred their line so dramatically; Hawke's ability to swing the ball back in, even from wide of the return crease, integral in his planning.

The rest of the attack, however, was spanked, McKenzie included. Ashes newcomer David Sincock dropped an important early catch, con-ceded overthrows and bowled an expansive width, one nervous beginning delivery being taken chest-high on the full by wicketkeeper Wally Grout.

'It was the beginning of an unhappy day for David who bowled as many full tosses as you would see in a game of two-up,' said ex-Testman Ken Mackay in his book of the summer.[28]

When the intimidating Barber wasn't driving through the covers, he was playing audacious sweeps, some to deliveries pitched wide of off-stump.

Sincock, a matchwinner in domestic cricket, was punished unmerci-fully. He was even denied a late wicket when Peter Philpott at slip dived forward for a brilliant reflex catch off the edge of David Allen's bat only for umpire Lou Rowan to rule not out. 'Apparently he [Lou] thought I had signalled "no catch" and when he realised his error it was too late,' said Philpott.[29] England's last wicket stand was to be worth 55, Allen scoring 50 not out.

Cowper, in at No. 3 showed sterling resolve in lasting 250 minutes for 60, but Grahame Thomas was the only other to make a half-century, the Australians going down by an innings, Allen and Titmus proving to be irre-sistible in tandem. They each took four wickets in the Australian second innings. England captain Smith rarely made the headlines for his batting but his fielding in the leg trap was outstanding and he claimed three catches as the Australians collapsed.

Stand-in captain Booth and the two wrist spinners were never to play Test cricket again, the selectors being immediately rewarded for their youth policy with the Australians hitting back emphatically in Adelaide.

With 6-48, McKenzie bowled with much of his old fire, Allan having dropped out of the team at the eleventh hour with injury.

McKenzie had bowled without luck earlier in the series and his dis-missal created a torrent of headlines, especially in his home town Perth. Bowling with effortless rhythm, he rifled Barber's defences with a late inswinger and at last enjoyed some good fortune with a series of superb catches being taken behind the wicket, including a blinder by Chappell at third slip to dismiss Boycott. It was as good as any taken all season. Only Barrington among the English top-order reached 50.

In reply, reunited openers Simpson and Lawry started with an Ashes record 244, passing England's score themselves. They scampered between the wickets for what seemed like suicidal singles and made them with ease. 'We scored 95 singles,' said Simpson, 'statistical evidence of the success of our run-for-everything policy.'[30]

Like Wilfred Rhodes years before, who once said when he was coming for a run he'd say 'yaaas' and when he wasn't he'd say 'nooo', Simpson and Lawry's method was simple: whoever was on strike would call and the other would immediately respond.

Just as Barber had decimated the field placings in Sydney, Simpson and Lawry did the same in Adelaide, Smith unable to exert any inner-ring pressure. The pitch was as flat and true as any prepared all summer and Simpson and Lawry were also able to hit with impunity over the in-field.

Simpson finished with 225 and Lawry 119. Thomas, with 52, also launched an exciting array of front-foot shots and at one stage the Australians were 331-1. Hawke's five wickets and run out of Parks from side-on helped Australia to win by an innings. It was the first time in Ashes history Australia had lost and then won by an innings in consecutive Tests.

The decider back in Melbourne was anti-climactic, despite a whirlwind 100 from Barrington, which included a 6 over the sightboard against the off-spin of Veivers. He'd faced just 122 balls, an extraordinarily fast century for the time.

With rain intervening, the entire fourth day being lost, Australia was satisfied to settle with an Ashes-retaining draw, Cowper's extraordinary triple-century seeing him bat on days two, three and five. The soggy conditions made it impossible for off-spinner Titmus to grip the ball and he even resorted to a few overs of medium pace as the Australians reached 500, guaranteeing the draw they wanted. Cowper batted for more than twelve hours before being castled by an in-dipping beauty by Barry Knight. The water-logged outfield saw him hit twenty 4s and twenty-six 3s, a record that is unlikely ever to be beaten, especially with roped-off boundaries now a standard safety feature at almost all the Test grounds around the world.

Having defeated India 4–0, Australia was to retain the Ashes under the captaincy of Lawry in 1968, the series set up by Australia's first Test win at Old Trafford, a match in which England included only three specialist bowlers. In a wet summer that dramatically cut into the playing hours, Alan Connolly was outstanding for the Australians with 23 wickets, his mastery of a slower ball and a shorter run-up allowing him to be both strike and stock bowler. England used twenty players to Australia's sixteen, former captain Ted Dexter among those to win a recall. Sussex speedster John Snow was also promoted and with his pace, in-slant and attitude was an immediate menace. On his Ashes debut at Old Trafford he dismissed Ian Redpath and Cowper in three balls on his way to 4-97 in the most promising of beginnings. Basil D'Oliveira's 158 at The Oval was also to have a dramatic effect on the world of cricket.

Lawry had first assumed the captaincy midway through the 1967–68 home summer against the Indians, Simpson standing down in mid-series having advised Bradman and co. of his unavailability for England. Like his predecessor Richie Benaud, Simpson said the Don was a driving force throughout his leadership reign. 'He was always particularly helpful,' he said.

> He always came into the dressing room when Richie was captain or I was captain. If you wanted to have a talk, fine. If not he'd wander off and have his lunch. Whenever you spoke to him he'd always give you a detailed explanation and if you wrote to him you'd get a long letter giving all the points. How many people in life have answered every letter they've ever got? And he got tens of thousands more than anyone else. It says a lot about a man who cared so much for the game and the people who followed it.

Man of the decade: *Ken Barrington*

England's top-order was never more formidable than in the 1960s when Ken Barrington was in occupation. Unflustered by the sharpest bowling and devastating against the slow bowlers, Barrington's record was unequalled in the decade.

Few were braver, more defiant or responsible for saving as many matches. K. F. Barrington was a quality foot soldier, determined, resolute and loyal. His two-eyed stance, impregnable defence and simple, uncomplicated technique made his wicket a prize for opposing bowlers every time he went into battle. Contemporary John Edrich was the only one who seemed to possess as wide a bat and only two Englishmen in the first 130 years of Anglo-Australian Test cricket have superior averages – Eddie Paynter (84) and Herbert Sutcliffe (66) – and neither played anywhere near as often.

Barrington's Test-best 256 may have come in a meaningless draw on the friendliest of surfaces at Old Trafford in 1964, but he scored four other Ashes tons, all in Australia, including one from just 122 balls on his Melbourne farewell in 1966, which earned him a £250 bonus and the Lawrence Trophy for the fastest 100 of the Test year. Having seen Barrington lift a Keith Stackpole straight break into the stands like a tracer bullet, Australia's wicketkeeper Wally Grout turned to Barrington and said: 'You drunk or something mate?'[31]

E.W. Swanton, the doyen of England's post-war cricket writers, said Barrington seemed capable of batting forever, especially at renowned batting venues such as Adelaide.

Barrington was the one most would have trusted with their life. No one of his time was more enduring or built as fine a record, the best by any visiting Englishman since Walter Hammond. 'He had the widest set of pads I ever saw. They completely covered the stumps,' said Australian opponent Alan Connolly. 'I happened to bowl him one day [Leeds, 1968] and only knew it because of the crowd roar. I certainly didn't see any stumps fly!'

Barrington had been dropped for slow scoring after making a century in the first Test against the 1965 New Zealanders at Edgbaston. Barrington was so bitter he all but retired on the spot.[32]

On return, however, he made a century, re-launching one of the great careers. Always powerful through point and cover, he was to extend his repertoire in later years to include shots all around the wicket. He had a penchant for six-hits and four times reached Test centuries with 6s, twice in Ashes contests, in Adelaide in 1962–63 and in Melbourne in 1965–66, when the ovation was as long and lasting as even the Australians could recall. Coming in afterwards, having made 115 out of 178, he was congratulated by the legendary Denis Compton and quipped: 'That was almost a Compo job, wasn't it!'[33]

An outstanding slips fieldsman, Barrington also bowled handy leg-breaks, numbering among his victims leading Australians Bob Cowper and Doug Walters. He also kept wickets occasionally and loved it when asked.

In retirement, he toured many times as England's assistant-manager, his trademark grin and gregarious ways essential in team-bonding and morale.

Long-time Australian opponent Bill Lawry said Barrington would have become an even finer contributor had the selectors made him captain. 'I only wish I could have been as good a cricketer,' he said.[34]

Barrington v. Australia

* not out

Season	Scores	Runs	Ave
1961	21, 48*, 4, 66, 6, 78, 5, 53, 83	364	45.50
1962–63	78, 23, 35, 0*, 35, 21, 63, 132*, 101, 94	582	72.75
1964	22, 33, 5, 29, 85, 256, 47, 54*	531	73.85
1965–66	53, 38, 63, 1,60, 102, 115, 32*	464	66.28
1968	75, 0, 49, 46*	170	56.66

Tests v. Australia:	23 (82 overall)
Runs:	2,111 (6,806)
Average:	63.96 (58.67)
Highest score:	256, Old Trafford, 1964 (256)
100s:	5 (20)

Match of the decade: *Old Trafford, 1961*

Richie Benaud enjoyed his finest moments in cricket in piloting the massive comeback crucial to Australia's Ashes' defence. England had made the running for most of the game and, thanks to Ted Dexter, looked set to run down a fifth-day target of 256 before Benaud went around the wicket and claimed 5-12 (and six for the innings) bowling into footmarks, a tactic mirrored, many times, years later by Shane Warne.

> **Match scores:** Australia 190 (Lawry 74, Statham 5-53) and 432 (Lawry 102, Simpson 51, O'Neill 67, Davidson 77 not out, Allen 4-58) defeated England 367 (Pullar 63, May 95, Barrington 78, Simpson 4-23) and 201 (Dexter 76, Benaud 6-70) by 54 runs

Odd spot: *Thanks but no thanks*

Australian captain Bobby Simpson gave the selectors notice in 1967 of his intention to stand down from the following winter's tour to England. Despite back-to-back centuries in the opening two Tests of the summer against the touring Indians, he was immediately dropped!

Looking back: *Tom Veivers, Old Trafford, 1964*

'I bowled all (the fifth) day from the one end apart from the last twenty minutes when England eventually was dismissed. John Price took a big swing at a full toss and was bowled, much to the disappointment of everyone – me, the Australian players, the Englishman and the crowd who were all waiting for me to break the world record (of 98 overs in an innings, held by West Indian Sonny Ramadhin).

'It was cool and a huge wind was blowing, making it hard for fast bowlers. "Simmo" (Bob Simpson) said: "I think you'd better bowl the first over today". First ball Ken Barrington edged between the 'keeper Wally Grout and Simmo at slip. It was about the only half chance he gave all day on his way to a big double. Simmo came up and said: "I think you'd better continue from that end". And that was it. He kept me going.'

> Veivers, twenty-seven, bowled fifty-one overs straight and a near-record 95.1 for the innings on the final two days of the high-scoring fourth Test. His eventual figures were 3-155, Australia scoring 656-8 dec and 4-0, England 611.

One for the statisticians: *A run crawl*

Australia's run-rate slumped to just 36 runs per 100 balls in the 1968 Ashes series, its lowest rate since 1956 when they were Lakered and scored at under 30 runs per 100.

Tests 1961 to 1968

KEY: M Matches   **I** Innings   **NO** Not out innings   **HS** Highest score   **BB** Best bowling
5wI 5-wicket innings   **10wM** 10-wicket match   * Not out   # Second innings   **rh** Retired hurt

Series results

	Tests	Aust	Eng	Drawn
1961 (Eng)	5	2	1	2
1962–63 (Aust)	5	1	1	3
1964 (Eng)	5	1	0	4
1965–66 (Aust)	5	1	1	3
1968 (Eng)	5	1	1	3
Total	25	6	4	15
Progressive	203	80	66	57

Summary

	Runs	Wkts	Ave
Australia	12,223	358	34.14
England	12,751	378	33.73

Highest innings totals

Australia		England	
656-8 dec	Manchester 1964 (4th Test)	611	Manchester 1964 (4th Test)
543-8 dec	Melbourne 1965–66 (5th Test)	558	Melbourne 1965–66 (2nd Test)
516-9 dec	Birmingham 1961 (1st Test)	494	The Oval 1968 (5th Test)
516	Adelaide 1965–66 (4th Test)	488	Sydney 1965–66 (3rd Test)
494	The Oval 1961 (5th Test)	485-9 dec	Melbourne 1965–66 (5th Test)

Lowest completed innings totals

Australia		England	
78	Lord's 1968 (2nd Test)	104	Sydney 1962–63 (3rd Test)#
	(one batsman retired hurt)		*Next lowest:*
120	Leeds 1961 (3rd Test)#	165	Manchester 1968 (1st Test)
125	The Oval 1968 (5th Test)#		

Leading run scorers

	M	I	NO	Runs	HS	Ave	100	50
Australia								
W. M. Lawry	24	41	3	1,909	166	50.23	7	10
R. B. Simpson	18	30	3	1,405	311	52.03	2	9
P. J. P. Burge	17	28	4	1,058	181	44.08	4	2
B. C. Booth	15	26	5	824	112	39.23	2	4
N. C. O'Neill	14	23	1	790	117	35.90	2	4
K. D. Walters	10	16	1	753	155	50.20	2	4
R. N. Harvey	10	18	0	733	154	40.72	2	4
R. M. Cowper	9	15	1	686	307	49.00	1	3
England								
K. F. Barrington	23	39	6	2,111	256	63.96	5	13
E. R. Dexter	17	31	0	1,340	180	43.22	2	8
M. C. Cowdrey	20	35	3	1,232	113	38.50	3	6
J. H. Edrich	13	21	0	1,090	164	51.90	4	5
G. Boycott	12	20	2	753	113	41.83	1	4

Hundreds

Australia (22)		England (20)	
7	W. M. Lawry	5	K. F. Barrington
4	P. J. P. Burge	4	J. H. Edrich
2	B. C. Booth	3	M. C. Cowdrey
	R. N. Harvey	2	E. R. Dexter
	N. C. O'Neill		R. Subba Row
	R. B. Simpson	1	R. W. Barber
	K. D. Walters		G. Boycott
1	R. M. Cowper		B. L. D'Oliveira
			Rev. D. S. Sheppard

Highest individual scores

Australia

311	R. B. Simpson at Manchester 1964 (4th Test)
307	R. M. Cowper at Melbourne 1965–66 (5th Test)
	(highest individual Test score in Australia)
225	R. B. Simpson at Adelaide 1965–66 (4th Test)
181	P. J. P. Burge at The Oval 1961 (5th Test)
166	W. M. Lawry at Brisbane 1965–66 (1st Test)
160	P. J. P. Burge at Leeds 1964 (3rd Test)
155	K. D. Walters at Brisbane 1965–66 (1st Test)
154	R. N. Harvey at Adelaide 1962–63 (4th Test)

England

256	K. F. Barrington at Manchester 1964 (4th Test)
185	R. W. Barber at Sydney 1965–66 (3rd Test)
180	E. R. Dexter at Birmingham 1961 (1st Test)#
174	E. R. Dexter at Manchester 1964 (4th Test)
164	J. H. Edrich at The Oval 1968 (5th Test)
158	B. L. D'Oliveira at The Oval 1968 (5th Test)

500 runs in a series

	Season	M	I	NO	Runs	HS	Ave	100	50
Australia									
W. M. Lawry	1965–66	5	7	0	592	166	84.57	3	2
Also note:									
R. M. Cowper	1965–66	4	6	0	493	307	82.16	1	2
England									
J. H. Edrich	1968	5	9	0	554	164	61.55	1	4

Hundred partnerships

Australia (25)

Partnerships of 150 and over:

244	1st	R. B. Simpson and W. M. Lawry at Adelaide 1965–66 (4th Test)
219	5th	R. B. Simpson and B. C. Booth at Manchester 1964 (4th Test)
212	3rd	W. M. Lawry and R. M. Cowper at Melbourne 1965–66 (5th Test)
201	1st	W. M. Lawry and R. B. Simpson at Manchester 1964 (4th Test)
198	5th	P. J. P. Burge and K. D. Walters at Melbourne 1965–66 (2nd Test)#
194	4th	R. N. Harvey and N. C. O'Neill at Adelaide 1962–63 (4th Test)
187	5th	W. M. Lawry and K. D. Walters at Brisbane 1965–66 (1st Test)
185	5th	P. J. P. Burge and B. C. Booth at The Oval 1961 (5th Test)
172	4th	R. M. Cowper and K. D. Walters at Melbourne 1965–66 (5th Test)
160	2nd	R. B. Simpson and R. N. Harvey at Sydney 1962–63 (3rd Test)
152	5th	A. P. Sheahan and I. M. Chappell at Manchester 1968 (1st Test)

Hundred partnerships

England (16)

Partnerships of 150 and over:

246	3rd	E. R. Dexter and K. F. Barrington at Manchester 1964 (4th Test)
234	1st	G. Boycott and R. W. Barber at Sydney 1965–66 (3rd Test)
178	3rd	J. H. Edrich and K. F. Barrington at Melbourne 1965–66 (5th Test)
175	3rd	E. R. Dexter and M. C. Cowdrey at Melbourne 1962–63 (2nd Test)
172	5th	R. Subba Row and K. F. Barrington at The Oval 1961 (5th Test)#
161	4th	E. R. Dexter and K. F. Barrington at Birmingham 1961 (1st Test)#
156	4th	P. B. H. May and D. C. S. Compton at The Oval 1956 (5th Test)

Leading wicket-takers

	Tests	Balls	Mdns	Runs	Wkts	Ave	BB	5wI	10wM
Australia									
G. D. McKenzie	22	6,570	219	2,658	89	29.86	7-153	6	–
A. K. Davidson	10	3,092	116	1,052	47	22.38	6-75	4	–
N. J. N. Hawke	12	3,176	128	1,119	37	30.24	7-105	4	–
R. Benaud	9	3,151	134	1,176	32	36.75	6-70	2	–
England									
F. S. Trueman	13	3,056	55	1,449	57	25.42	6-30	4	1
F. J. Titmus	15	4,786	198	1,434	40	35.85	7-79	2	–
J. B. Statham	9	2,532	57	1,081	30	36.03	5-53	1	–
D. A. Allen	10	2,492	120	892	28	31.85	4-47	–	–

Five wickets in an innings

Australia (20)		England (13)	
6	G. D. McKenzie	4	F. S. Trueman
4	A. K. Davidson	2	D. J. Brown
	N. J. N. Hawke		F. J. Titmus
2	R. Benaud	1	R. Illingworth
1	A. N. Connolly		I. J. Jones
	K. D. Mackay		P. I. Pocock
	P. I. Philpott		J. B. Statham
	R. B. Simpson		D. L. Underwood

Best individual bowling

Australia

7-105	N. J. N. Hawke at Sydney 1965–66 (3rd Test)
7-153	G. D. McKenzie at Manchester 1964 (4th Test)
6-47	N. J. N. Hawke at The Oval 1964 (5th Test)
6-48	G. D. McKenzie at Adelaide 1965–66 (4th Test)
6-70	R. Benaud at Manchester 1961 (4th Test)#
6-75	A. K. Davidson at Melbourne 1962–63 (2nd Test)
6-115	R. Benaud at Brisbane 1962–63 (1st Test)

England

7-50	D. L. Underwood at The Oval 1968 (5th Test)#
7-79	F. J. Titmus at Sydney 1962–63 (3rd Test)
6-30	F. S. Trueman at Leeds 1961 (3rd Test)#
6-79	P. I. Pocock at Manchester 1968 (1st Test)
6-87	R. Illingworth at Leeds 1968 (4th Test)#
6-118	I. J. Jones at Adelaide 1965–66 (4th Test)

10 wickets in a match

Australia

No instance

England (1)

11-88	F. S. Trueman (5-58 and 6-30) at Leeds 1961 (3rd Test)

25 wickets in a series

	Season	Tests	Balls	Mdns	Runs	Wkts	Ave	BB	5wI	10wI
Australia										
G. D. McKenzie	1964	5	1,506	61	654	29	22.55	7-153	2	–
Also note:										
A. K. Davidson	1962–63	5	1,410	30	480	24	20.00	6-75	2	–
England										
No instance – best:										
F. J. Titmus	1962–63	5	1,891	54	616	21	29.33	7-79	2	–

Leading wicketkeepers

	Tests	Dismissals	Catches	Stumpings
Australia				
A. T. W. Grout	17	56	52	4
B. N. Jarman	7	18	18	0
England				
J. M. Parks	10	21	17	4
J. T. Murray	6	19	18	1
A. P. E. Knott	5	15	11	4
A. C. Smith	4	13	13	0

Leading fieldsmen

Australia	Tests	Catches	England	Tests	Catches
R. B. Simpson	18	30	M. C. Cowdrey	20	21
R. Benaud	9	13	K. F. Barrington	23	19
W. M. Lawry	24	13	F. S. Trueman	13	12
I. R. Redpath	11	12	E. R. Dexter	17	10
R. M. Cowper	9	11	T. W. Graveney	8	10
G. D. McKenzie	22	10			

Captains

	Tests	Won	Lost	Drawn	Toss won
Australia					
R. Benaud	10	3	2	5	5
R. B. Simpson	8	2	0	6	2
W. M. Lawry	4	1	1	2	1
B. C. Booth	2	0	1	1	1
B. N. Jarman	1	0	0	1	1
England					
E. R. Dexter	10	1	2	7	6
M. C. Cowdrey	6	1	2	3	5
M. J. K. Smith	5	1	1	3	3
P. B. H. May	3	1	1	1	1
T. W. Graveney	1	0	0	1	0

Most appearances

Australia (36 players)		England (47 players)	
24	W. M. Lawry	23	K. F. Barrington
22	G. D. McKenzie	20	M. C. Cowdrey
18	R. B. Simpson	17	E. R. Dexter
17	P. J. P. Burge	15	F. J. Titmus
	A. T. W. Grout		
15	B. C. Booth		
14	N. C. O'Neill		

Terry Jenner is downed by a bouncer from **John Snow**, Sydney, 1970–71.
Bruce Postle

1970s

CHOSEN ON A HUNCH

....

'Snow went wide on the crease and again pitched it in short. This time with the brand new ball, it came onto me a lot quicker. I'd stepped across to cover my stumps and in the split second saw the ball coming at my head. There was time only to turn my head and half duck. It was like a car accident. Unavoidable.'

So furious was John Snow's onslaught in the opening weeks of the 1970–71 summer that Australia sacked its best batsman and captain and trialled a swag of newcomers from 21-year-old West Australian tearaway Dennis Lillee to 35-year-old Victorian Ken Eastwood.

While Eastwood and others were soon to disappear, Lillee became Australia's most noted fast bowler of all, ahead of Fred Spofforth, Jack Gregory and even the great Ray Lindwall.

The enigmatic Snow had bullied the Australians all summer, taking 26 wickets in the first five Tests including a match-settling 7-for in Sydney. With just two Tests to play, England led 1–0 and had one hand on the Ashes.

The Australians were rebuilding after a 4–0 thumping in South Africa. Six new to the cauldron of Test cricket were included in the first seven weeks of the international summer, but only one, the South Australian virtuoso Greg Chappell, was an unqualified success. In Melbourne, newcomers Alan 'Froggie' Thomson and Ross Duncan were labelled the most insipid new-ball pairing in Ashes history.

In his last season as Australia's selection chairman, Sir Donald Bradman met with fellow selectors Neil Harvey and Sam Loxton. It was Australia Day 1971 and the Australians had just toiled for half a day against Geoff Boycott and John Edrich without looking like breaking through.

'Gentlemen, we need to find a fast bowler,' began the Don. 'Have you seen anyone?'

'As a matter of fact we have.'

'Who?'

'A kid from Perth . . . his name is Lillee. Dennis Lillee.'

'Is he fast?'

'Yes, very fast.'

'Does he know where it's going?'

'No, but if he doesn't know, the batsman certainly doesn't!'

'Pencil him in!'

'Dennis still doesn't believe us,' Loxton recounts. 'But it was true . . . he was chosen on a hunch. Don hadn't seen him bowl. There was very little television, especially of [Sheffield] Shield games back then and no one had heard of the Internet. Dennis had knocked Geoff Boycott's hat off in a state match, so he was quick alright. We didn't get them all right that summer, but you'd have to agree . . . Dennis proved to be a good 'un, didn't he!'

Also among the debutants was the roly-poly West Australian wicketkeeper Rodney Marsh who overcame an inglorious beginning in Brisbane to become one of Australia's most celebrated.

In what proved to be Bill Lawry's last summer as captain, three of the first five Tests were drawn and another abandoned without a ball being bowled. The first-ever official one-day international was also contested, as an afterthought, to give holidaying Melburnians some cricket after unseasonable January rains ruined their Test match.

The touring Englishmen had a formidable frontline and played decisively from the start, the experienced Boycott and Edrich joined at the head of the order by assured Kent right-hander Brian Luckhurst who just months earlier had been included in the five 'Tests' against the Rest of the World with immediate success. With an energetic and highly skilled wicketkeeper in Alan Knott, a shrewd captain in Ray Illingworth and the fastest and most intimidating bowler on the two sides in Snow, the tourists were tough and talented.

The Australians were flattered by their 400-plus beginning in Brisbane, television replays showing that their well-padded opener Keith Stackpole had clearly been run out at 18. Instead of being 32-2 on the first morning, Australia finished at 308-2 and Stackpole hooked and cut his way to a Test-best 207. Before play, Stackpole had broken his favourite bat in the warm-ups and had been forced to use a brand-new one, straight from its plastic wrappers. It proved to be the sweetest possible replacement, Stackpole making more than 100 runs in boundary hits. The tension was extreme and in mid-afternoon when Ken Shuttleworth queried Stackpole's luck after one of his up-and-under cut shots flew harmlessly to the third-man fence, he received a sharp return volley from the Australian, Stackpole querying Shuttleworth's right to take the new ball as he was bowling 'half rat power'.[1]

Snow was fast and venomous from the start, rarely allowing a drive. Stackpole scored most of his runs square and behind the wicket. He took 49 overs for his first 100 and just 42 for his second. From 418-3, however, Australia was dismissed for 433, the last seven wickets falling for 15 runs, Paul Sheahan, debutant Terry Jenner and John Gleeson collecting ducks. Left-armer Derek Underwood improved his figures dramatically by dismissing Ian Redpath, Sheahan and centurion Doug Walters in seven balls without conceding a run. After England established a narrow lead on the first innings, only Lawry's steely 84 was to save the Australians from total collapse, Shuttleworth proving his detractors wrong with 5-47. The game was drawn very much in England's favour and new-boy Marsh dubbed 'Iron-gloves' by some of the more caustic among the English press corp.

The next Test in Perth was also a high-scoring draw, more than 80,000 attending the first Test ever at the picturesque old ground built years before on an old swamp. Greg Chappell's unforgettable 108 on debut was studded by brilliant leg-side drives. To their chagrin, ABC cricket fans in the east were denied the opportunity to see him join the elite because of the seven o'clock news! Replying to England's 397, Australia was 17-3, including Lawry for a duck, before Redpath and Chappell led a revival, Redpath shielding Chappell from a rampant Snow.

Chosen as Australia's seventh specialist batsman, 22-year-old soft-drink salesman Chappell says it was the culmination of his dreams and a chance to stand up in his own right, just like his brother and cricket hero Ian.

Having taken forty minutes to score his first run, Chappell's last 60 runs came in just seventy minutes. 'I'd dreamed about playing Test cricket all through my childhood but didn't really believe it would happen,' he recalls. 'It was more of a pipe dream than anything else. I'd played against most of the English bowlers for a couple of seasons with Somerset and had seen them all before. And as the seventh specialist batsman in that team, there weren't as many expectations on me. We were 107-5 when I went in. They concentrated their efforts on "Redder" who was the more senior player. I don't think I faced John Snow even once in the first hour I was at the crease. Redder soaked up Snowy through that entire period. You'd never find a better team man than Red.'

Eighty-five per cent of Chappell's runs came on the onside, including all ten of his 4s. Writing in the *Times*, John Woodcock ranked Chappell's virtuoso as 'the most irrepressive ever made by a young batsman in his first Test match'.[2]

Redpath said the quality of Chappell's innings was staggeringly good for one so young.

Ian Chappell, too, gained inspiration from the doings of his young brother. 'I started to play my best when Greg came into the side,' he said. 'I had this little bloke I used to beat up in the backyard and suddenly he's playing better than I can and I'd better get off my backside. He gave me the needle.'

Set 245 to win in 145 minutes, Stackpole was out immediately to Snow. Ian Chappell followed quickly and Lawry laboured sixty-eight minutes over his first six to ensure the draw.

The third Test was abandoned due to rain, but after a toss was made, ensuring the game counted towards Melbourne's first 100 Tests. England won the fourth in Sydney, which included Snow's Tyson-like 7-40. McKenzie was struck in the face and forced to retire hurt, an inglorious end to a mighty career. Only Lawry could withstand Snow's fury. He became only the second Australian after 'the unbowlable' Bill Woodfull to carry his bat in an Ashes Test. England's 299-run winning margin was emphatic evidence of the withering advantage provided by Snow, who seamed the ball both ways and made it bounce disconcertingly from just short of a good length. Illingworth, too, was proving to be an inspired choice as captain. On the third morning, having seen his No. 5 batsman and handy change bowler Basil d'Oliveira swing the ball around in the nets, Illingworth threw 'Dolly' the ball first-up: 'Are you kidding, man?' said D'Oliveira. 'Snowy's got to bowl from this end . . .'

'Ray simply told me to get on with it and I got [Ian] Redpath with my second ball and Johnny Gleeson shortly afterwards.'[3] The unflappable Redpath, in at No. 3, had topscored and from an overnight 189-4, Australia cost its last six wickets for less than 50 runs and never recovered.

The return Test in Melbourne was drawn, 39-year-old d'Oliveira's 117 the top score in another run-fest.

In Adelaide, West Australian Dennis Lillee made a memorable debut with five wickets, but the reunited openers Boycott and Edrich notched century stands in each innings, providing the starts denied the Australians all summer.

Lawry was sacked as Australia's captain and lost his place, too, in the XI, a ridiculous call given his 40-plus average against one of the most potent English new-ball attacks since the war. After a decade of loyal service, he learnt of his dismissal via the radio. 'The selectors blundered for sure,' said Stackpole. 'If they had been frantic to win the series, they should have played Lawry, because with him we would have won the last Test in Sydney . . . Eastwood in his mid-thirties was too old to be playing his first Test against England.'[4]

Never was Illingworth's leadership more valuable than in the hastily arranged seventh Test when he orchestrated a series-deciding victory. It was the fifth Test in six weeks and proved to be the most momentous in years.

Ian Chappell was Lawry's successor and, immediately showing his appetite for adventure, inserted England on a greentop, the visitors tumbling for 184. It had rained virtually non-stop for two days and the outfield was still water-logged, making a boundary hit a genuine feat. Six of the wickets were taken by the wrist spinners Jenner and blond Sydneysider Kerry O'Keeffe.

The second day's play was the most tumultuous since Adelaide, 1933, Snow felling tailender Jenner with an in-slanting bouncer that thudded into Jenner's unprotected skull and sent him reeling from the wicket *à la* Bertie Oldfield in 1933. Other than a cut just above his ear, however, he was basically unhurt, the ball rebounding all the way to cover point.

'Snow had taken the (second) new ball and given our scoreline (180-7), the stakes could not have been higher,' Jenner said. 'The field was closing in around me, looking for a catch. Snow went wide on the crease and again pitched it in short. This time with the brand new ball, it came onto me a lot quicker. I'd stepped across to cover my stumps and in the split second saw the ball coming at my head. There was time only to turn my head and half duck. It was like a car accident. Unavoidable.'[5]

As a bleeding and groggy Jenner was being assisted from the field, Snow and Illingworth were in a spirited argument with umpire Lou Rowan after his censuring of Snow for bowling an excessive number of short-pitched deliveries.

Illingworth waved his finger at Rowan and said Jenner had ducked in to the ball. Had he stood up he would have played it at chest height.[6]

'By warning Snowy for no reason, the umpire whipped up the crowd, who became very hostile,' said Illingworth. 'When John went down to field on the boundary, some of the crowd threw cans and bottles in his direction, so I called the players into the middle and we sat down while the missiles were cleared off the outfield. But when Snowy returned to the boundary, more cans and bottles were hurled, some of them full, and a spectator leaned over the fence and grabbed Snowy, who'd have got in real trouble if he'd bobbed him one back. One of the bottles hit the sight-screen attendant and he was carted off to hospital. That could easily have been a player, so I said to the umpires: "If you're not going to do anything to stop this, I'm not prepared to have my players on the field".'[7]

To a torrent of boos and jeers, Illingworth led his team from the field, risking the forfeiture of the match. A few in the Australian team declared: 'We've won, we've won!'[8]

Australia's not-out batsmen Greg Chappell and Lillee stayed in the centre throughout the short break before the Englishmen returned to fresh volleys of jeers. The pressure was electric for the rest of the match and the Australians, set 223, were to be dismissed for 160, giving England the Ashes 2–0. Top-scorer Stackpole made 67 of the first 95 runs before being bowled by Illingworth. When Chappell missed Illingworth's arm ball and was stumped on the fifth morning, England's joy was complete. It was a tremendous come-from-behind win, especially as the striker Snow was only able to bowl two overs, having dislocated a finger of his bowling hand crashing into a fence attempting to catch a skied shot from Stackpole.

'It was the greatest match I ever played in,' said d'Oliveira. 'The tension throughout was unbelievable on every day.'[9]

Illingworth had been criticised for under bowling himself earlier in the series, but with only three lbw appeals upheld all summer and the Australians fielding an array of right-handers, he felt England would have more success with bowlers taking the ball *away* rather than zeroing back *into* the batsmen.

On the final day, however, with Australia 123-5 and needing just 100 more to square the series and retain the Ashes, Illingworth produced his most important spell of the summer, taking 3-39 overs from 20 overs as the Aussies succumbed. Illingworth was carried off shoulder-high, the first visiting MCC captain since Douglas Jardine to regain the Ashes.

Lawry's replacement, the left-handed Eastwood, hadn't even been in Victoria's best XI at the season-start, and after making seven and nought was never picked again.

Twenty-four of Snow's 31 wickets in six Tests were in the top-order. It was an inspirational effort, one of the finest in Ashes chronicles. Knott said while Snow and Boycott were standouts, the team had been as unified as any he was to be involved in and Illingworth had consistently been able to get the best out of his players. 'He gave me the feeling that we could win under his leadership in any situation. He was always prepared to fight on, convinced that you had to give everything until the game was won or lost,' said Knott.[10]

The Australians may have forfeited the Ashes but the emergence of champions-to-be in Chappell, Lillee and Marsh had added an exciting new edge to the team, and having defeated England twice in 1972 and the West Indies twice in 1973, England's next visit in 1974–75 shaped as a world championship showdown.

The reintroduction, too, of Jeff Thomson into Australia's XI to partner Lillee provided the ammunition for an extraordinary series. Thomson had match figures of 0-110 in his only Test, two years previously against Pakistan in Melbourne. Later it was diagnosed he had played with a broken bone in his foot. The miffed selectors had been slow to forgive and others had been preferred even at state level before his sensational comeback game, the last of the 1973–74 summer for New South Wales against Queensland. He took nine wickets, including 7-for in the Queensland first innings.

Greg Chappell, newly based in Brisbane, thought him the fastest bowler he'd ever faced. A shift north and further headlining publicity in the off-season guaranteed his profile. In a famous interview with leading Australian cricket writer Phil 'Redcap' Wilkins in *Cricketer* magazine, he ignored convention and any niceties with a full-frontal verbal onslaught. In it, he claimed:

- 'I enjoy hitting a batsman more than getting him out';
- 'It doesn't worry me to see a batsman hurt, rolling around screaming and blood on the pitch';
- 'If I want to hit a bloke, I'll hit him'; and
- 'When they dropped me it just made me bowl faster. It was just like a fellow smacking me for four ... I went off my brain.'[11]

No Australian had ever bowled faster – or been as quotable – and with Lillee returning to big cricket after twelve months on the sidelines, Ian Chappell had the most potent new-ball attack since Lindwall and Miller.

Thanks to its bold newcomer, the South African-born Tony Greig, who had taken 13 wickets in the deciding Test in Trinidad, England had forced a draw in the West Indies in 1973–74 and trounced India on home wickets in 1974, Mike Denness averaging 96, Dennis Amiss 92, John Edrich 101, Keith Fletcher 189 and left-handed opener David Lloyd 260. So emphatic was England's superiority that even Boycott's self-imposed step into the wilderness[12] was temporarily forgotten.

Within days of being wiped out in Brisbane, however, England was calling for top-order reinforcements, portly Colin Cowdrey, rising forty-two, answering an SOS for a record-equalling sixth tour down-under. Why the tough Yorkshire-born opener Barry Wood was again overlooked was a mystery. On debut against the Australians at The Oval in 1972, he'd impressed with 26 and 90 and seemed a star in the making. Cowdrey had played his first Test in Australia twenty years earlier. He was past it.

Rather than dominate against a diet of non-stop spin, as had been on show in their home summer, the Englishmen were confronted by blister-ing pace from both ends on a set of fast, uneven wickets and capitulated 4–1. So dispirited did captain Denness become that he stood down in mid-tour. Others were injured; all were glad when the demolition was over. 'Never in my career have I witnessed so much protective gear applied to individuals before they went out to bat,' said Denness. 'On the plane flying back from Australia to New Zealand the players were clearly more relieved that they had left Australia intact without fatal injury.'[13]

Thomson's opening salvo in Brisbane was electrifying. Bowling into a stiff breeze with his athletic, slingshot action, he broke Amiss's thumb with a vicious lifter. Denness was greeted with one that zeroed straight at his jaw and ended up thumping into his shoulder. Welcome to Australia, skipper. If it wasn't for Tony Greig's magnificent counter-punching and Edrich's bravery in lasting almost four hours for 48 despite a broken finger, England would have been severely embarrassed. Thomson's memorable Ashes debut netted him nine wickets. 'He even frightened me sitting 200 yards away in the press box,' said Keith Miller.[14]

Wicketkeeper Rod Marsh was standing a cricket pitch and more behind the wicket and was still taking the ball at shoulder height. 'Hell that hurt,' he said after one Thomson steepler thumped into his gloves, 'but I love it!'[15]

Chappell had initially planned to use Thomson at first change, with the wind after Lillee, but changed his mind and instead threw the ball to Thomson with a 'good luck mate'.[16]

Thomson's first deliveries were express. Watching from first slip Chappell said he was simply 'in awe'. He had never seen anyone bowl faster.[17] 'I don't think the Englishmen knew what had hit them,' he said.[18]

It was the fastest and most intimidating new-ball onslaught witnessed in Australia since 1954–55, Thomson establishing an immediate psychological superiority unbroken for the remainder of the tour. 'I was a man on a mission,' said Thomson. 'It wouldn't have mattered who I was playing against. I was just going to give them a work over.'[19]

English opener Amiss, on the verge of establishing a new record for most runs in a calendar year, said Thomson was as quick as the famed West Indian Michael Holding and even more lethal with his low, slinging action, which reminded him of watching Frank Tyson years before on television. 'Thommo bowled in that corridor of uncertainty and was always asking questions,' he said. 'He had the aggression, determination and energy to make him a great fast bowler. Dennis could be [as fast]. He could really let them go. He was the best I ever faced.'

Having been beaten up in Brisbane, the prospect of an even faster wicket in Perth saw the upper-order adapt a range of extra protective gear from forearm shields to chest and rib protectors.

Chappell's standard fields for the opening volleys included eight fieldsmen behind the wicket and only one in front, Ross Edwards at cover point. England tried to wear the Australians down but both Lillee, twenty-five, and Thomson, twenty-four, were at the height of their pace and power, Lillee's exhaustive training regime under former world sprint champion Austin Robertson snr paying handsome dividends. His action, too, was more streamlined and he was still genuinely quick.

Throughout the summer, the Australian bowlers were backed by some brilliant fielding, the catching close to the wicket being as good as in any Ashes series ever contested. Off-spinner Ashley Mallett wasn't as sharp as some on his feet but he loved the gully and took some blinding catches. 'I could cut down the angles there,' he said. 'With Thommo and Lillee bowling, we got lots of opportunities, too.'

Thomson grabbed seven more wickets in Perth but the feature was Doug Walters reaching a century in a session with a hooked six from the very last ball of the second day's play from Bob Willis. Seventy of the runs came in the first hour of the last session. It was exhilarating strokeplay of a Trumper-like standard and he was given a hero's reception walking in, by everyone bar his own teammates who as a joke hid in the showers!

In his first Test match in three years, Cowdrey made 22 and 41. He came in at No. 3 in the first innings and opened in the second. 'I certainly admired Cowdrey for accepting the challenge,' said Chappell. 'If the same challenge was given to me, I'd turn it down.'[20] As the well-rounded man from Kent wandered past Thomson on the first day, he said a courteous 'Good morning'.[21] Thommo's reaction bordered on the blue, but was something like: 'Get ready to duck!' Having just got his head out of the way of a first-ball bouncer, Cowdrey sauntered down the wicket to David Lloyd and said: 'This is good fun, isn't it?'[22]

Lloyd made 49 and back in the rooms, having survived the ordeal of his life, started shaking uncontrollably – such was his reaction after having to dodge and duck for three hours on the bounciest track in the world. 'They were an awesome pairing,' he said. 'Get through an over from one of them and there was not a moment of respite with the other one pawing the ground. We were still playing by the old Australian regulation of eight-ball overs and there were times when five of the eight were flying past nose or chest.'[23]

The third Test in Melbourne was a low-scoring draw, Australia's conservative approach on the final day when they needed less than 250 drawing rounds of boos and slow handclapping. Despite 61 from Greg Chappell and 40 from Marsh, they finished eight runs short, at 238-8. Greig took 4-56 and the veteran Freddie Titmus 2-64. 'Australia's tactics puzzled me,' said Denness. 'I do not believe any England side would have played it that way during the last fifteen overs (in the hour). I would have wanted to go all out to take a three-nil lead.'[24]

Having made just eight and two in Melbourne and 65 runs for the Test series, Denness elected to drop himself in favour of Keith Fletcher from the New Year Test in Sydney. Suggestions that Snow be returned to the side had been raised in Melbourne. He was in Australia commentating on the series, but Denness felt the batting and not its bowling had been letting England down.

More than 52,000 attended on the opening day and rejoiced in new-boy Rick McCosker, a leg-side specialist, making 80 on debut, having opened the innings alongside Ian Redpath. The wicket was as fast as even the great Bill O'Reilly could remember and Thomson several times sent bouncers rearing over the head of wicketkeeper Marsh.

Lillee broke acting captain Edrich's ribs but the little streetfighter still returned late in the innings and made a gallant contribution. The noise emanating from the Hill area was enormous. They chanted 'LILL-LEEE, LILL-LEEE, LILL-LEEE' and then 'KILL, KILL, KILL', their roars building to a crescendo just as Lillee delivered. It was very disconcerting for the English batsmen and only three reached half-centuries, Edrich and wicketkeeper Alan Knott in the first innings and Greig in the second. Australia had reclaimed the Ashes and only a few of the Englishmen were prepared to cross the members' bar into the Australian dressing room to share a celebratory glass of beer. 'Some players, in the light of the aggravation there had been on the field, found it difficult to offer congratulations,' said Denness. 'Instead they thought it better to disappear and return to the hotel. I would not criticise a player for taking that attitude. Everyone was very sad that we had lost the series after only four matches, none more so than myself.'[25]

Lloyd tried to relieve the tension by writing a letter home to his mother: 'Dear Mum', he began. 'Today I received a half volley . . . in the nets.'[26]

Knott said even Thomson's pitched up deliveries would take off. 'On that tour, as a pair, Lillee and Thomson were the fastest two I have ever seen . . . They were probably at their quickest by the fourth Test in Sydney. Their [fast bowler] Geoff Arnold received a ball from Lillee that missed his head by a whisker and he never moved. It went high over Rodney Marsh, first bounce into the sightscreen. Even Lillee looked relieved that it had not hit the batsman.'[27] Never again in his 96-match career was Marsh to concede as many as 28 byes in a game.

Underwood's 11 wickets and an unbeaten century from the in-form Knott in Adelaide weren't enough to save the Englishmen from further disappointment, Denness, back in the side, borrowing some of Chappell's adventure and sending the Australians into bat on a damp one. He watched with delight as Underwood took the first seven wickets before Jenner made a Test-best 74 from No. 7. Set 405, the Englishmen lost all chance going to stumps at 94-5 before Knott's timely, against-the-tide century showed his upper-order teammates what could be achieved.

Despite averaging less than 20, Cowdrey played every Test from Perth. Adelaide was his record forty-second Ashes appearance, breaking the long-time record held by Jack Hobbs and Wilfred Rhodes. Soon into the tour he'd turned to Tony Greig and said: 'You can't play them off, can you? They keep on roaring in.'[28]

Thomson was to miss the final Test in Melbourne, having injured shoulder tendons playing social tennis in the Adelaide hills on the rest day. Lillee also broke down with an ankle injury in Melbourne and England made 529 after the Australians had earlier succumbed to Peter Lever. Denness's 188 was top score. Fletcher made 146. Shouldering fresh new-ball responsibility, Max Walker took 8-143 to the joy of his home town supporters in the expansive MCG outer. While England won by an innings, it was a hollow victory, the Ashes having been decided five weeks earlier.

The Australians built an aura of formidability in the mid-1970s, Chappell's strong leadership and team ethos prompting a rare unity. Not only did he have a team of champions, but a champion team. 'Chappelli didn't rant or rave,' says long-time teammate Mallett. 'Sometimes it was just a look. If you misfielded a ball he'd give you a look which made you think: "Geez, I'm not going to stuff up next time". He'd also empower you. He'd never talk about how badly or how well you were bowling. But he'd give you the confidence just from his conversations. "We're going to try this or this," he'd say.'

Chappell won fifteen and lost only five of his thirty Tests as captain. His combative style was wearying, however, and he was to step down after the 1975 series in England, complaining of being 'stale and tired'.

The Australians figured in a four-Test series following the inaugural World Cup in 1975. After winning for the first time ever at Edgbaston, they drew the last three Tests before returning home to thrash the West Indies 5–1, the captaincy having been handed from one Chappell to another. 'Had there been a five or six month break in between the two series, I probably would have continued,' said Ian.[29]

Had the players enjoyed, too, a more rightful split of the lucrative monies in the game, his decision may have been delayed. Chappell was to formally announce his retirement at the end of the 1975–76 summer, only to return to international cricket just twelve months later as one of the lynchpins in the breakaways, Kerry Packer's World Series Cricket movement.

The relationships between the Australian Cricket Board and the leading players went into free fall in the mid-1970s, Lillee and Ian Chappell leading a wall of resentment. Despite unprecedented profits at the gate and the growing opportunity to maximise television rights, there was little financial security for even the elite cricketers. Testmen like Bob Cowper and Paul Sheahan had backed away from the game to pursue outside careers when they were at the height of their powers. The Board had more money at their disposal than in any period in history, but were typically tunnel-visioned on how it should be spent – and the players weren't even on the whiteboard. 'There are 500,000 cricketers who would love to play for Australia for nothing,' Board secretary Alan Barnes said in *The Australian*.[30]

The Australians were fuming and Barnes made the mistake of visiting the dressing rooms and was promptly pinned against a wall by an enraged Ian Redpath. 'You bloody idiot,' said Redpath. 'Of course 500,000 would play for nothing but how bloody good would they be.'[31]

Almost one million fans saw the six Ashes Tests in 1974–75 and another 750,000 the following West Indian summer. The gate takings were enormous and while there were player concessions and bonuses, they were piecemeal.

By the time of the Centenary Test in Melbourne in March 1977, virtually the entire Australian XI had secretly signed with World Series Cricket on guaranteed contracts worth three or four times the money on offer in traditional ranks. The rebellion was on and as the brilliant South Australian youngster David Hookes was charming more than 50,000 with five consecutive 4s from the bowling of England's captain Greig, Packer's chief recruiter Austin Robertson jnr was sorting hefty sign-on advances for distribution. In the Australian rooms that night he brazenly handed one of the envelopes to Doug Walters: 'Here's your theatre tickets, Dougie!'[32]

In the first of three English visits in four seasons, the 1976–77 tourists had been on a full-scale tour to India, winning 3–1 and unearthing a rising champion in Derek Randall. Never before had an English team won back-to-back Tests in India and in Greig, Underwood, Willis, Amiss and Knott, it had a formidable nucleus of experience to stand up beside the emerging youngsters.

In what proved to be cricket's ultimate birthday party, more than 200 former English Testmen accepted invitations to attend the match, the likes of Harold Larwood and Bill Voce being reunited and enjoying their re-meetings, too, with some of Australia's between-the-wars icons such as Don Bradman, Jack Ryder and Clarrie Grimmett. Also present was a near-blind Percy Fender, at eighty-four, the oldest Englishman to attend. He'd played in 1920–21. At his side was his grandson Nicholas to act as his eyes.

Bradman may have been sixty-eight and in semi-retirement but his opinions still carried weight. The Don wanted Hookes to be promoted into Australia's top six for the Centenary Test. He'd seen Hookes make five exhilarating 100s in six innings for South Australia and in a letter to selector Sam Loxton, he said he was totally out of line to even make the suggestion, 'but please Sam, I implore you,' he wrote. 'Pick Hookes for the Centenary Test . . . I've seen him bat over here . . . he is just the player the game needs.'

The emerging 22-year-old had celebrated his maiden first-class century against Victoria by smashing leg-spinner Colin Thwaites for four 6s in five balls. Even if Australia's best were on tour in NZ, weakening the ranks of the state teams, he was clearly a young player in a hurry.

In a memorable, see-sawing game that was to last five days despite both teams being bowled out cheaply in their first innings, Australia clinched a 45-run win, remarkably mirroring the result of the inaugural Test at the

MCG, 100 years earlier. Lillee's 11 wickets cemented his standing as one of Australia's greatest-ever, while Ashes debutant and man-of-the-match Randall, with 164, led a spirited revival that all but saw the Englishmen chase down a 450-run target. Far from being unnerved by Lillee's bouncers – one crowned him and another saw him complete a somersault as he backed away – he smiled and even doffed his cap at the Australian.

Underwood claimed his 250th Test wicket and Marsh surpassed Wally Grout's Australian record of 187 dismissals. But far and above the statistics was the bravery of Rick McCosker who had his jaw broken by a Willis bouncer in the first innings before insisting on batting in the second. When the crowd saw him emerge from the members' gate, his jaw wired and encased in a large white bandage, they started singing 'Waltzing McCosker, Waltzing McCosker ...'

It was a magnificent match and marked the dawning of a new era of professionalism that was to dramatically increase the wages of the cricketers and enhance the profile of the game like never before.

It was in May 1977, just six weeks after the Centenary Test, that news broke of Packer's intentions. The business magnate, unhappy at being shunted behind the ABC in the race for cricket's television rights, confirmed he was setting up a rival set of Supertests involving the finest players in Australia and overseas and at some of the major grounds.

All but four of Greg Chappell's 1977 Australian tourists had signed, including the major box-office attractions the Chappell brothers, Lillee (who was unavailable for the English tour), Marsh and the game's newest star Hookes, who was to receive two-thirds of his first $25 000 WSC contract upfront.

When the news leaked via broadsheet journalists Peter McFarline and Alan Shiell, the Australians had played just four games of a thirty-two-match program and some wondered why the Australian Cricket Board didn't immediately recall them and name a replacement squad. 'It was a pretty ordinary, unpleasant tour,' said Hookes years later. 'We thirteen players who had signed with WSC should have been sent home ... nothing was achieved by us staying in England.'[33]

The Australians lost the Tests 3–0. Geoff Boycott agreed to his first Tests in three years and topped the averages, scoring back-to-back centuries at Trent Bridge and Headingley.

Greg Chappell, twenty-nine, genuinely felt he'd played his last Test match. The prospect of being well paid, at last, by the game he loved was too alluring. He signed on the spot.

While the World Series publicists talked-up their exhibitions and started to win more space in even the non-Packer press, Australians recalled Bobby Simpson to lead the Test team against the 1977–78 Indians. He was forty-one and still a top-line club player in Sydney. In an exciting series, the second-string Australians won 3–2. Simpson averaged 53 and led the team to the West Indies, too, the following autumn. He was preparing to captain again at home in 1978–79 against the visiting Englishmen, only for the Victorian left-hander Graham Yallop to be selected instead. Yallop, twenty-five, had played just eight Tests and as a captain was a greenhorn. Only two had been younger, Billy Murdoch and Ian Craig.

While his contributions with the bat were far superior to English counterpart Mike Brearley, he was widely castigated for his leadership skills and admitted by late in the summer that he simply felt overpowered by the responsibilities.[34]

From the opening seventy-five minutes in Brisbane when Yallop elected to bat on a green seamer and watched in horror as the first six wickets crumbled for 26, the young Australians were outplayed. Even the extraordinary debut of Victorian-born journeyman Rodney Hogg, who took 41 wickets, failed to avert a humiliating 5–1 series reverse. It was Australia's worst performance of the twentieth century and proof that the talent pool down-under was far from infinite.

The warring with World Series was bitter and costly and Yallop was a pawn in the muddying waters. Encouraged at every turn to slam 'the mercenaries', his sole focus should have been on bonding with his new teammates. But he'd only just been appointed Richmond and Victoria's captain and lacked the man-management skills and experience of others. He headed a team of virtual no-names, most of whom were unknown to him and the bonhomie notable under Simpson the previous summer was missing throughout his nightmarish reign.

In Adelaide, during an on-field confrontation with the fiery Hogg, Yallop was invited behind the grandstand. 'And I don't think he had a tennis match on his mind,' the young captain said.[35]

Australia's cricketing chiefs were too embroiled in their war with Kerry Packer to offer Yallop the support staff now integral in every Australian campaign, home and away. The wet-behind-the-ears skipper found himself not only having to organise field placings and batting orders, but taxis to and from the grounds. 'We were on our own and we simply sunk,' he said.

No visiting captain had ever won five Tests in Australia and while Brearley the batsman proved easy pickings for Hogg and new-ball partner Alan Hurst, he led with his customary acumen in the field. The presence of first-timers David Gower and Ian Botham added flair and skill, alongside Centenary Test hero Randall and the complicated, much-misunderstood Boycott, who toured again after years in exile.

In Brisbane, Australia's entire XI had played just sixty-six matches between them, vice-captain Gary Cosier the most experienced with seventeen. By comparison, England's players had figured in 267 Tests, and Boycott, with seventy-five, was hailed as a returning hero. Only once, however, was the famed Yorkshireman to pass 50. His pre-tour dismissal as Yorkshire's captain and the loss of his mother provided distractions even he could not overcome, not to mention Hogg's full-frontal new-ball assaults. In Perth he made 77 but it took him more than seven hours. In retrospect it would have been better if he had stayed home.

Having lost by seven wickets in Brisbane, the Australians were bowled out in less than fifty overs to go down by 166 runs in Perth, Gower's majestic strokeplay providing unforgettable memories. Fewer than 40,000 had bothered to attend in Brisbane and fewer still came to Perth, providing worrying indications that the Australian public's allegiances were as mottled and confused as those in organisation.

Hogg increased his personal tally to 27 in three Tests courtesy of five wickets in each innings in Melbourne as England suffered its only loss of the summer. He'd been fast-tracked into the Test team with Jeff Thomson's abdication to World Series and immediately thrived. He and his captain were poles apart, however, in background and philosophy. Yallop had been a champion batsman at Carey Grammar, one of Melbourne's blueblood private schools. Hogg had attended Thornbury Tech. They rarely spoke, even in the dressing room, and Yallop soon lost patience with Hogg's insistence on being rested every three or four overs. 'I was the shock bowler, not the stock bowler,' Hogg says. 'He'd always be at me to have one more, one more. But I'd put so much effort into the first overs, that often I couldn't. I had asthma attacks and couldn't breathe on some days. It was hot and they were eight-ball overs that summer. I wasn't putting it on.'

The roar from the Melbourne outer when Hogg castled Boycott with an off-cutter midway through his second over could be heard in South Yarra. 'Peter McFarline writing in the old *Sunday Press* said it was amazing the roof of the Southern Stand didn't lift off,' Hogg recounts. 'Funnily enough I didn't hear a thing. The adrenalin was rushing, everything was spinning. It was a blessing lunch was only just around the corner. I was out on my feet.'

A young left-hander from Sydney, Allan Border, played for the first time in Australia's middle-order, making 29 and nought in an unpretentious start to one of the great careers. He'd followed a debut century for New South Wales in Perth with another against the Victorians in Sydney and was one of the form players in the country.

In Sydney he made 60 and 45, both times not out, but Australia, set just 205 in four and a half hours to square the series, was bowled out for 111, again in under fifty overs. Openers Graeme Wood and the helter-skelter Rick Darling had started with 38, only for the final nine wickets to fall for 73, with off-spinners John Emburey and Geoff Miller being dominant. The run out of Wood, who had hit and run to cover and ended up at the same end as non-striker Kim Hughes, was the beginning of the end. 'That pathetic dismissal,' said Yallop, 'took the wind out of our sails and gave the Englishmen every reason to think that we would panic in the run-chase and capitulate, which is exactly what happened.'[36]

Instead of being 2–2 with two Tests to play, Yallop's Australians were 3–1 down. The Ashes had been retained.

In Adelaide the feud between Hogg and Yallop bubbled into the public arena after Hogg walked off the ground after four overs. 'I told him to hang on and asked why he had to leave the field,' said Yallop. 'He didn't explain and just repeated more forcibly that he was going off. I insisted and he told me to get lost (or words to that effect) and headed for the pavilion.'[37]

So upset was Yallop that soon afterwards he asked permission from the umpires to go off, too. Inside he was told by the team's physiotherapist that his star fast bowler was stiff and sore in the legs but would be okay to bowl again after the break. Had the two shared more of a rapport, Australia may well have won the Test, but were to be beaten by more than 200 runs, after an unlikely 135-run stand between perky wicketkeeper Bob Taylor and Miller.

With seven wickets for the game, Hogg passed Clarrie Grimmett as Australia's leading wicket-taker in an Ashes series. He may have been hard to handle, but this was the summer of his life. Few had ever bowled with such unrelenting ferocity or return.

The Adelaide Oval wicket was a greentop and England lost 27-5 before reviving. Darling was struck such a blow by Bob Willis just below the ribs that he momentarily stopped breathing, only some quick remedial action from Englishman John Emburey averting a calamitous situation. 'I thought it had hit him in the box,' said Taylor, 'but when we got to him his eyes were open and he didn't seem to be breathing. There was no emotion on his face and "Embers" turned him over and thumped his chest to get him breathing. Their physio came on, pulled his tongue out and extracted the chewing gum from his mouth to stop him from choking on it . . . it scared the life out of me.'[38]

Bob Taylor's 97 was to be top score, the popular little 'keeper having batted six hours in the innings of his life. A direct hit from mid-on by Boycott to dismiss Wood was the start of another Australian collapse, the underrated Mike Hendrick and Willis sharing 6 wickets between them. Afterwards Phil Ridings, Australia's selection chairman, commented at the presentation ceremony how close the series had been, his gaffe bringing howls of laughter.

In Sydney, 4–1 soon became 5–1, Australia's start of 198, dominated by Yallop's 121, never enough on a true batting wicket. Yallop had come in at 19-2 and left at 198-9 before becoming one of Botham's four victims. Botham had impressed as one of the leading young all-rounders in the world, bowling at brisk pace and hitting boldly from No. 6. Just two years earlier, he'd spent a winter in Melbourne, creating more headlines off the field than on. His rapid improvement had been a huge bonus for the Englishmen who had not had an all-rounder of such quality in years.

Hogg, however, was the champion of the summer. 'He bowled very, very fast that year,' Gower recalls. 'From over the wicket he'd be angling it across. When he went around it came straight at you. He was a handful alright.'

Just 22,617 bothered to attend the sixth Test, the poorest attendance in any Test at the SCG since 1888. Weeks earlier, more than 50,000 had attended a World Series day-night game at the ground. Traditional cricket was losing its grip and the Australian Cricket Board knew it.

As England was charging towards victory in Sydney, Kerry Packer was flying to Adelaide for a meeting that would finally deliver the television rights to Channel Nine. He'd arranged to meet with 70-year-old Sir Donald Bradman at his home in Adelaide. The morning newspaper headlines were proclaiming further World Series tours with a full-strength Pakistan team to visit in 1979–80, but, as Packer told the Don, he had no interest in running cricket long-term or continuing to promote unsanctioned tours flying in the face of the traditionalist game. He may have lost millions on his venture, but if the Don could convince Bob Parish and his Board to allow Channel Nine the exclusive television rights, he would close his rival all-star troupe then and there.

It was Tuesday, 13 February 1979, just twenty-four hours before England completed its 5–1 trouncing of Yallop's shell-shocked Aussies. Within two months of the unreported meeting, the two parties announced to the world that cricket was once again in traditional hands, albeit at a cost of millions to both parties. Channel Nine had been granted the rights it had sought years earlier. To celebrate the new union, a full-strength Australia would join England and the West Indies in two mini-Test series and a one-day triangular.

Six Tests were scheduled, three between Australia and the Windies and three between Australia and England, the proviso being that the Ashes would *not* be at stake given the exceptional, shorter-than-normal series.

While the Australians were beaten 2–0 by the West Indies, they defeated England 3–0. The return of the World Series stars, including both Chappell brothers, Lillee and Thomson, ensured a far more competitive Australia.

Only three from traditional ranks – Border, Hogg and Hughes – made the first Australian squads of the compromise summer. Only Border and Hughes played every Test.

While the summer was disjointed and totally lacked scheduling rhythm, the sheer talent of Greg Chappell and Lillee shone throughout, Lillee's tantrums in Perth after being barred from using his aluminium bat ensuring front-page headlines, which had been a rarity for the game in the two previous seasons of division.

Boycott's effort in Perth, where he carried his bat for 99 not out, was a particularly illustrious performance against a crack attack including Lillee, Thomson and an unlikely destroyer, Queensland's Geoff Dymock, who took 6–34 and nine wickets for the match.

In Sydney, Gower's classic 98 not out was a gem of a knock, a taste of what was to come. Botham's 4–29 in the Australian first innings showed that he, too, was truly world-class.

The biggest crowds of the Test summer came in the third Test in Melbourne, almost 40,000 attending Sunday's play when Greg Chappell finished at 99 not out on his way to 114. Lillee's 11-wicket haul continued his love affair with Melbourne but never again was an English touring team forced to contend with a shortened series. And never again were the Ashes to be withheld.

Man of the decade: *Dennis Lillee*

So swift and spectacular was Dennis Lillee's rise in Sheffield Shield ranks that Australia's selection chairman Sir Donald Bradman hadn't even seen him bowl when he named him for his Ashes debut in early 1971. Replacing Queenslander Ross Duncan in the sixth Test of a summer dominated by England's John Snow, 21-year-old Lillee grabbed five wickets on debut, his fire, hostility and outswing immediately on show.

His captain Bill Lawry started him into the wind, preferring fellow Victorian Alan 'Froggie' Thomson with it. So wild was his beginning that his overnight figures of 1-41 from fourteen eight-ball overs flattered him. But the following morning, given the breeze, he bowled with rhythm and pace taking four wickets for just 43 runs, including England captain Ray Illingworth with a giant break-back.

His run-up may have been overly long and all over the place, but he bowled fast and hooped it away from the right-handers. Three more wickets at the SCG in the final Test confirmed Bradman's hunch. He'd helped unearth a champion.

Lillee was to become the first Australian to 300 Test wickets and many believe but for two seasons spent with World Series Cricket he would have taken more than 400. Pound for pound, he is in the Bradman class as Australia's finest and most destructive fast bowler, ahead of everyone else, including Jack Gregory, Ray Lindwall and Glenn McGrath.

The Lillee philosophy was to go flat out at all times. He said once he'd gladly die on the pitch if it meant Australia winning.

Lillee tormented batsmen like no Australian before or since, his controversial, headlining career seeing him average almost six wickets per Ashes Test at a stunning strike-rate of 50 balls per wicket.

Included was more than 90 wickets on three Test tours to England; he missed a fourth through injury.

Carried shoulder high from the MCG after taking 11 wickets for the match in the 1977 Centenary Test, Lillee demanded first use of the new ball. Once when captain Greg Chappell felt he was bowling well within himself on a placid wicket, he instructed wicketkeeper Rod Marsh to stand over the stumps. Lillee responded with a furious bouncer that all but broke his mate's hand.

He enjoyed most success in Melbourne, well before the age of drop-in wickets, which encouraged extra pace. There was an extra challenge in gaining life out of a batsmen-friendly wicket. He also loved the crowds: 'Lill-eee, Lill-eee, Lill-eee'.

'I knew if I got wickets in Melbourne I had worked bloody hard to get 'em,' he said. 'While I loved bowling at the pacier venues like the WACA [his home ground], my success rate was better in Melbourne than anywhere else. The crowds had a lot to do with it, too. They really are amazing and in my time, so supportive of me every time I went out.'

Lillee v. England

Season	Analysis	Wkts	Ave
1970–71	5-84, 0-40, 1-32, 2-43	8	24.87
1972	2-40, 6-66, 2-90, 2-50, 4-35, 2-40, 2-39, 1-7, 5-58, 5-123	31	17.67
1974–75	2-73, 2-25, 2-48, 2-59, 2-70, 2-55, 2-66, 2-65, 4-49, 4-69, 1-17	25	23.84
1975	5-15, 2-45, 4-84, 1-80, 1-53, 2-48, 2-44, 4-91	21	21.90
1976–77	6-26, 5-139	11	15.00
1979–80	4-73, 2-74, 4-40, 2-63, 6-60, 5-78	23	16.86
1980	4-43, 1-53	5	19.20
1981	3-34, 5-46, 0-102, 3-82, 4-49, 3-94, 2-61, 2-51, 4-55, 2-137, 7-89, 4-70	39	22.20
1982–83	3-96, 1-89	4	46.25

Tests:	29 (70)
Wickets:	167 (355)
Average:	21.00 (23.92)
Best bowling:	7-89, The Oval, 1989 (7-83)
5-wicket Innings:	11 (23)
10-wicket Matches:	4 (7)
Strike-rate:	50 balls per wkt (52)
Average wkts per Test:	5.7 (5)

Match of the decade: *Lord's, 1972*

After losing the opening Test at Old Trafford, Australia hit back to win the second at Lord's in three and a half days thanks to the banana-like swing of 25-year-old debutant Bob Massie who took 16 wickets in the match of his life. Massie took full advantage of a low cloud cover and swung the ball prodigiously. Greg Chappell's century against John Snow and co. on the Friday was a classic, Australia's win ending an unprecedented eleven-match run without an Ashes victory.

> **Match scores:** Australia 308 (G. Chappell 131, Marsh 50, Snow 5-57) and 81-2 defeated England 272 (Greig 54, Massie 8-84) and 116 (Massie 8-53) by 8 wickets

Odd spot: *A historic streak*

Cricket's first streaker, Michael Angelow, a cook in the Merchant Navy, became the first streaker in Ashes history when he hurdled both sets of stumps at 3.20 p.m. on the fourth day of the drawn Lord's Test in 1975.

Looking back: *Basil D'Oliveira, Perth, 1970–71*

'I was too old to tour Australia when I did [at the age of thirty-nine]. The large grounds found me wanting. I had to struggle to get around . . . the Press called us "Dad's Army" and with three players pushing forty and a few others in their thirties, we weren't exactly spring lambs. But Ray [Illingworth] nursed us along, with an uncanny ability to make use of all his resources, slender or otherwise. A classic example of this came on the last day of the final Test at Sydney – we were without our best batsman, [Geoff] Boycott, and our best bowler, [John] Snow, but Ray pulled the strings at the right time and we snatched a magnificent win.'[39]

In his one and only tour of Australia, Cape-coloured d'Oliveira played every Test, averaging 36 and taking some handy wickets, too. Just a few years earlier, he'd been at the centre of one of the greatest storms of all which was to trigger the isolation of apartheid-driven South Africa.

One for the statisticians: *No lbws*

England didn't have even one lbw given in its favour in the 1970–71 summer of seven Tests.

Tests 1970–71 to 1979–80

KEY: M Matches **I** Innings **NO** Not out innings **HS** Highest score **BB** Best bowling
5wl 5-wicket innings **10wM** 10-wicket match ***** Not out **#** Second innings **rh** Retired hurt

Series results

	Tests	Aust	Eng	Drawn
1970–71 (Aust)	6†	0	2	4
1972 (Eng)	5	2	2	1
1974–75 (Aust)	6	4	1	1
1975 (Eng)	4	1	0	3
1976–77 (Aust)	1	1	0	0
1977 (Eng)	5	0	3	2
1978–79 (Aust)	6	1	5	0
1979–80 (Aust)	1††	1	0	0
Total	**34**	**10**	**13**	**11**
Progressive	237	90	79	68

† The Third Test at Melbourne was abandoned without a ball bowled and is excluded.
†† The other two Tests in the 1979–80 series were played in January and February 1980 and are included in records for the following decade.

Summary

	Runs	Wkts	Ave
Australia	16,443	564	29.15
England	16,990	568	29.91

Highest innings totals

Australia		England	
532-9 dec	The Oval 1975 (4th Test)	538	The Oval 1975 (4th Test)#
493-9 dec	Melbourne 1970–71 (5th Test)	529	Melbourne 1974–75 (6th Test)
481	Perth 1974–75 (2nd Test)	470	Adelaide 1970–71 (6th Test)
		464	Brisbane 1970–71 (1st Test)

Lowest completed innings totals

Australia		England	
103	Leeds 1977 (4th Test)	95	Melbourne 1976–77 (Cent Test)
111	Sydney 1978–79 (4th Test)#	101	Birmingham 1975 (1st Test)
116	Sydney 1970–71 (4th Test)	116	Lord's 1972 (2nd Test)#
	(one batsman retired hurt)		
116	Brisbane 1978–79 (1st Test)		

Leading run scorers

	M	I	NO	Runs	HS	Ave	100	50
Australia								
G. S. Chappell	27	49	4	1,869	144	41.53	6	9
I. M. Chappell	21	40	1	1,602	192	41.07	4	11
R. W. Marsh	28	47	7	1,253	110*	31.32	1	7
K. D. Walters	26	46	5	1,228	112	29.95	2	9
K. R. Stackpole	11	22	1	1,112	207	52.95	3	7
I. R. Redpath	12	24	3	969	171	46.14	2	6
R. B. McCosker	13	23	2	900	127	42.85	2	6
R. Edwards	13	22	3	805	170*	42.36	2	5
England								
J. H. Edrich	19	36	3	1,554	175	47.09	3	8
G. Boycott	17	33	6	1,533	191	56.77	4	8
A. P. E. Knott	27	45	4	1,388	135	33.85	2	9
A. W. Greig	21	37	1	1,303	110	36.19	1	10
D. W. Randall	13	24	4	771	174	38.55	2	4
B. W. Luckhurst	11	21	2	677	131	35.63	2	3
K. W. R. Fletcher	14	25	0	638	146	25.52	1	3
B. L. D'Oliveira	11	19	1	602	117	33.44	1	3

Hundreds

Australia (27)		England (21)	
6	G. S. Chappell	4	G. Boycott
4	I. M. Chappell	3	J. H. Edrich
3	K. R. Stackpole		R. A. Woolmer
2	R. Edwards	2	A. P. E. Knott
	R. B. McCosker		B. W. Luckhurst
	I. R. Redpath		D. W. Randall
	K. D. Walters	1	M. H. Denness
	G. N. Yallop		B. L. D'Oliveira
1	A. R. Border		K. W. R. Fletcher
	K. J. Hughes		D. I. Gower
	R. W. Marsh		A. W. Greig
	G. M. Wood		

Highest individual scores

Australia

207	K. R. Stackpole at Brisbane 1970–71 (1st Test)
192	I. M. Chappell at The Oval 1975 (4th Test)
171	I. R. Redpath at Perth 1970–71 (2nd Test)
170*	R. Edwards at Nottingham 1972 (3rd Test)
144	G. S. Chappell at Sydney 1974–75 (4th Test)#

Highest individual scores

England

191	G. Boycott at Leeds 1977 (4th Test)
188	M. H. Denness at Melbourne 1974–75 (6th Test)
175	J. H. Edrich at Lord's 1975 (2nd Test)#
174	D. W. Randall at Melbourne 1976–77 (Cent Test)
150	D. W. Randall at Sydney 1978–79 (4th Test)#
149	R. A. Woolmer at The Oval 1975 (4th Test)#
146	K. W. R. Fletcher at Melbourne 1974–75 (6th Test)
142*	G. Boycott at Sydney 1970–71 (4th Test)#

500 runs in a series

	Season	M	I	NO	Runs	HS	Ave	100	50
Australia									
K. R. Stackpole	1970–71	6	12	0	627	207	52.25	2	2
G. S. Chappell	1974–75	6	11	0	608	144	55.27	2	5
Also note:									
I. R. Redpath	1970–71	6	12	2	497	171	49.70	1	3
England									
G. Boycott	1970–71	5	10	3	657	142*	93.85	2	5
J. H. Edrich	1970–71	6	11	2	648	130	72.00	2	4

Hundred partnerships

Australia (25)

Partnerships of 150 and over:

277	2nd	R. B. McCosker and I. M. Chappell at The Oval 1975 (4th Test)
220	2nd	I. R. Redpath and I. M. Chappell at Sydney 1974–75 (2nd Test)
219	6th	I. R. Redpath and G. S. Chappell at Perth 1970–71 (2nd Test)
209	3rd	K. R. Stackpole and K. D. Walters at Brisbane 1970–71 (1st Test)
202	2nd	K. R. Stackpole and I. M. Chappell at Adelaide 1970–71 (6th Test)#
201	3rd	I. M. Chappell and G. S. Chappell at The Oval 1972 (5th Test)
180†	2nd	I. M. Chappell and I. R. Redpath at Melbourne 1970–71 (5th Test)
170	4th	G. N. Yallop and K. J. Hughes at Brisbane 1978–79 (1st Test)#
170	5th	R. Edwards and K. D. Walters at Perth 1974–75 (2nd Test)
151	2nd	K. R. Stackpole and I. M. Chappell at Brisbane 1970–71 (1st Test)

† *202 runs were added for this wicket; W. M. Lawry retired hurt after 22 runs had been scored and was replaced by Redpath.*

England (16)

Partnerships of 150 and over:

215	6th	G. Boycott and A. P. E. Knott at Nottingham 1977 (3rd Test)
		(equal English 6th wicket record against Australia)
192	4th	M. H. Denness and K. W. R. Fletcher at Melbourne 1974–75 (6th Test)
171	1st	G. Boycott and B. W. Luckhurst at Perth 1970–71 (2nd Test)
169	2nd	J. H. Edrich and K. W. R. Fletcher at Adelaide 1970–71 (6th Test)
166	3rd	D. W. Randall and D. L. Amiss (Melbourne) 1976–77 (Cent Test)#
161*	1st	G. Boycott and J. H. Edrich at Melbourne 1970–71 (5th Test)#
160	4th	R. A. Woolmer and A. W. Greig at Manchester 1977 (2nd Test)
158	4th	G. Boycott and D. I. Gower at Perth 1978–79 (2nd Test)
154	1st	J. M. Brearley and G. Boycott at Nottingham 1977 (3rd Test)#
151	6th	R. A. Woolmer and A. P. E. Knott at The Oval 1975 (4th Test)#

Leading wicket-takers

	Tests	Balls	Mdns	Runs	Wkts	Ave	BB	5wI	10wM
Australia									
D. K. Lillee	19	5,391	221	2,115	102	20.73	6-26	7	2
J. R. Thomson	15	3,849	140	1,732	75	23.09	6-46	3	–
M. H. N. Walker	16	4,912	200	1,858	56	33.17	8-143	2	–
A. A. Mallett	13	3,165	144	1,182	42	28.14	5-114	1	–
R. M. Hogg	6	1,740	60	527	41	12.85	6-74	5	2
A. G. Hurst	6	1,634	44	577	25	23.08	5-28	1	–
England									
R. G. D. Willis	22	4,485	104	2,069	79	26.18	7-78	5	–
D. L. Underwood	23	6,133	275	2,178	76	28.65	7-113	3	2
J. A. Snow	15	3,855	124	1,618	66	24.51	7-40	4	–
I. T. Botham	9	2,191	64	945	44	21.47	6-78	4	1
A. W. Greig	21	3,472	114	1,663	44	37.79	4-53	–	–
M. Hendrick	10	2,210	69	708	35	20.22	4-41	–	–
G. G. Arnold	8	1,992	51	898	30	29.93	5-86	1	–
C. M. Old	9	1,955	48	919	29	31.68	4-104	–	–
G. Miller	9	1,687	63	459	26	17.65	5-44	1	–
P. Lever	9	2,117	49	928	25	37.12	6-38	1	–

Five wickets in an innings

Australia (25)		England (21)	
7	D. K. Lillee	5	R. G. D. Willis
5	R. M. Hogg	4	I. T. Botham
3	J. R. Thomson		J. A. Snow
2	R. A. L. Massie	3	D. L. Underwood
	M. H. N. Walker	1	G. G. Arnold
1	G. Dymock		P. H. Edmonds
	G. J. Gilmour		P. Lever
	J. D. Higgs		G. Miller
	A. G. Hurst		K. Shuttleworth
	A. A. Mallett		
	M. F. Malone		

Best individual bowling

Australia

8-53	R. A. L. Massie at Lord's 1972 (2nd Test)#
8-84	R. A. L. Massie at Lord's 1972 (2nd Test)
8-143	M. H. N. Walker at Melbourne 1974–75 (6th Test)
6-26	D. K. Lillee at Melbourne 1976–77 (Cent Test)
6-34	G. Dymock at Perth 1979–80 (1st Test)
6-46	J. R. Thomson at Brisbane 1974–75 (1st Test)#
6-66	D. K. Lillee at Manchester 1972 (1st Test)#
6-74	R. M. Hogg at Brisbane 1978–79 (1st Test)
6-85	G. J. Gilmour at Leeds 1975 (3rd Test)

England

7-40	J. A. Snow at Sydney 1970–71 (4th Test)#
7-78	R. G. D. Willis at Lord's 1977 (1st Test)
7-113	D. L. Underwood at Adelaide 1974–75 (5th Test)
6-38	P. Lever at Melbourne 1974–75 (6th Test)
6-45	D. L. Underwood at Leeds 1972 (4th Test)#
6-66	D. L. Underwood at Manchester 1977 (2nd Test)#
6-78	I. T. Botham at Perth 1979–80 (1st Test)
6-114	J. A. Snow at Brisbane 1970–71 (1st Test)

10 wickets in a match

Australia (5)

16-137	R. A. L. Massie (8-84 and 8-53) at Lord's 1972 (2nd Test)
	(best match analysis for Australia in all Tests)
11-165	D. K. Lillee (6-26 and 5-139) at Melbourne 1976–77 (Cent Test)
10-66	R. M. Hogg (5-30 and 5-36) at Melbourne 1978–79 (3rd Test)
10-122	R. M. Hogg (5-65 and 5-57) at Perth 1978–79 (2nd Test)
10-181	D. K. Lillee (5-58 and 5-123) at The Oval 1972 (5th Test)

England (3)

11-176	I. T. Botham (6-78 and 5-98) at Perth 1979–80 (1st Test)
11-215	D. L. Underwood (7-113 and 4-102) at Adelaide 1974–75 (5th Test)
10-82	D. L. Underwood (4-37 and 6-45) at Leeds 1972 (4th Test)

25 wickets in a series

	Season	Tests	Balls	Mdns	Runs	Wkts	Ave	BB	5wl	10wM
Australia										
R. M. Hogg	1978–79	6	1,306	60	527	41	12.85	6-74	5	2
J. R. Thomson	1974–75	5	1,401	34	592	33	17.93	6-46	2	–
D. K. Lillee	1972	5	1,499	83	548	31	17.67	6-66	3	1
A. G. Hurst	1978–79	6	1,226	44	577	25	23.08	5-28	1	–
D. K. Lillee	1974–75	6	1,462	36	596	25	23.84	4-49	–	–
England										
J. A. Snow	1970–71	6	1,805	47	708	31	22.83	7-40	2	–
R. G. D. Willis	1977	5	1,000	36	534	27	19.77	7-78	3	–
Also note:										
J. A. Snow	1972	5	1,235	46	555	24	23.12	5-57	2	–

Leading wicketkeepers

	Tests	Dismissals	Catches	Stumpings
Australia				
R. W. Marsh	28	90	83	7
J. A. Maclean	4	18	18	0
England				
A. P. E. Knott	27	84	80	4
R. W. Taylor	7	27	24	3

Leading fieldsmen

Australia	Tests	Catches	England	Tests	Catches
G. S. Chappell	27	46	A. W. Greig	21	37
I. M. Chappell	21	26	J. M. Brearley	13	14
K. D. Walters	26	21	G. A. Gooch	8	11
I. R. Redpath	12	16	K. W. R. Fletcher	13	10
A. A. Mallett	13	14	M. Hendrick	10	10
K. R. Stackpole	11	13	R. Illingworth	11	10
			R. G. D. Willis	22	10

Captains

	Tests	Won	Lost	Drawn	Toss won
Australia					
I. M. Chappell	16	7	4	5	8
G. S. Chappell	7	2	3	2	3
G. N. Yallop	6	1	5	0	5
W. M. Lawry	5	0	1	4	3
England					
J. M. Brearley	12	8	2	2	4
R. Illingworth	11	4	2	5	6
M. H. Denness	6	1	4	1	2
A. W. Greig	4	0	1	3	3
J. H. Edrich	1	0	1	0	0

Most appearances

Australia (57 players)		England (43 players)	
28	R. W. Marsh	27	A. P. E. Knott
27	G. S. Chappell	23	D. L. Underwood
26	K. D. Walters	22	R. G. D. Willis
21	I. M. Chappell	21	A. W. Greig
19	D. K. Lillee	19	J. H. Edrich
16	M. H. N. Walker	17	G. Boycott
15	J. R. Thomson	15	J. A. Snow

John Emburey and **Mike Gatting** celebrate England's Ashes victory, Melbourne, 1986–87. *Cricketer magazine*

1980s

CAPTAIN GRUMPY'S ROCKY RIDE

• •

'Basically, as "AB" told us, we were sick of losing. We didn't want to make it a tea party for them out there. We wanted to isolate them, make them feel uncomfortable. And we did.'

A sense of belonging is everything for a cricketer. Allan Border was to build one of the most illustrious of all Test reputations, yet midway through the Ashes Centenary summer, he was agonising over his future, fully expecting to be dropped. Then twenty-seven, he'd batted five times without even once making 35. When he was dismissed for two in the first innings in the 1982 Christmas Test in Melbourne, he knew he was on the brink. And so low was his confidence level, he wondered if he could return.

After being run over by Ian Botham and co. in England in 1981, Australia had steadied under the reinstated Greg Chappell. A high-scoring draw in Perth preceded back-to-back wins in Brisbane and Adelaide, triggered by New South Wales paceman Geoff Lawson who in a rare purple patch claimed 20 wickets in two Tests. He'd toured Pakistan months earlier as a freshman and returned as Australia's player-of-the-series. An enlightening mid-tour chat with Pakistani pace great Imran Khan had accelerated his improvement, Lawson being particularly taken by Imran's comments on how he 'switched on' every time he was thrown the ball. Aggression, Imran said, was as important a part of a fast bowler's psyche as consistently hitting the top of off. From underling status, Lawson proved himself to be the quickest of learners and soon became Australia's new No. 1 striker.

Border, however, was in free fall. In Melbourne, having gone in No. 5 in the first innings, he found himself at No. 6 and scrambling around to borrow a bat in the second, with Australia 171-4 chasing 292 to win the Ashes.

'I wanted to get Australia over the line and make sure I scored enough runs to keep my Test career going,' Border says. 'It was touch and go there for a while.'

David Hookes was out almost immediately, victim of a miscued pull shot against the Jamaican-born Norman Cowans, his 68 from 87 balls a glimpse of his alluring talent.

With two wickets in his first six overs and three in his first twelve, Cowans was threatening to run through the middle-order and Border watched on helplessly from the non-striker's end as Cowans mowed down Rod Marsh, Rodney Hogg and Bruce Yardley. In an astonishing revival, Cowans was eyeing a Test 7-for, having failed to take a wicket in either of the first two Tests before being dropped for the third.

At 218-9 the game was all but over, and as No. 11 Jeff Thomson strolled to the wicket several of the Australians headed downstairs to dress for an early exit. 'It was unlikely that we were going to win the game,' Border says, 'especially given Jeff's previous batting history'.

Umpires Tony Crafter and Rex Whitehead also figured the game would finish that night and extended play a further half an hour, but the ball was soft and had lost almost all its shine and Cowans was spent. While Thomson defended to the cheers of almost 40,000, Border began to bat with growing authority, forcing play into a fifth day.

By stumps, the Australians were still 37 short of an improbable victory. As Border and Thomson walked onto the arena the following morning, there was a roar of approval and a sense of expectation that caught them both by surprise. Admission was free and even before 11 a.m. the crowd had swelled to almost 10,000. It was to double during one of the most dramatic morning sessions of all. 'When Thommo first joined me, we were something like 200-1 to win,' Border recounts. 'Eighteen thousand people came on the final morning but out there it seemed like there were 40,000 or 50,000. Their support was incredible and made us all the more determined to, at worst, lose gloriously.'

Cowans delivered the first over from the member's end and Thomson defended with the poise of a top-order player. There was widespread applause even when he let the ball go. Cowans' second over, too, was a maiden and again Thomson seemed in little bother.

Border, meantime, was scoring ones and twos, England captain Bob Willis having spread the field wide to protect the boundaries and stop Border from dominating the strike.

Cowans took the second new ball at 11.29 a.m. Only five runs had come in the first half an hour, a hush preceding every delivery before excited chatter and applause as it was either let go or safely negotiated.

As the two Australians settled and news of their partnership spread, thousands sprinted for vantage spots and there was a roar like a Grand Final crowd when Allan Lamb and substitute fieldsman Ian Gould collided as Border stole a daredevil single to reduce the target to under 20.

'Every time a single was scored or Jeff played out an over, the crowd went berserk,' Border says. 'The pressure built up. You could see the Englishmen succumbing. It was a couple of great hours of Test cricket. Extraordinarily, 18,000 people turned up to see what possibly could have been one ball. They were the smart people that morning.'

Border snicked Willis to where second slip would normally have been, but for the safety-first spreading of the field.

Less than a dozen were needed and Willis conferred with his deputies for three minutes before deciding who was to bowl the next over. 'It was an incredible situation,' Border says. 'Here was the No. 11 bloke trying very hard and [together] we were pulling something special out.'

Border's clever manipulation of the strike had seen the partnership balloon to 70. Only four was needed and Thomson on strike when Botham was again entrusted with the ball. With his first delivery of his twenty-sixth over he induced a thick edge from a Thomson flail that flew comfortably at shoulder height to Chris Tavare at second slip. Border had the clearest of views from the opposing end and initially thought the snick may clear Tavare only for it to loop virtually into his hands. Somehow, however, he misjudged it and the ball ballooned from his hands over his shoulder, only for quick-thinking Geoff Miller at slip to turn and take the ball on the rebound. England had won by three runs. Miller and Botham embraced and sprinted for the pavilion, ahead of hundreds of invaders. England's winning margin was the narrowest since the Old Trafford Test of 1902. Technically, the four all-out scores of 284, 287, 294 and 288 made it the closest match of all.

'Thommo had tears in his eyes when he and Border returned to the room,' said Hookes.[1] 'He took the defeat badly having fought so hard for so long only to get pipped by three lousy runs. The atmosphere in our room was suitably sombre. Then Marshy sang out: "Don't worry about it. We'll get 'em in Sydney". But for once Greg Chappell was not impressed with Marsh's timing and snapped: "Rodney, just shut up and let the batsmen sit down and console themselves".'[2]

With 62 not out, Border had cemented his place once and for all. The 1980s were to be tough years for Australia, especially after the retirements in 1984 of champion trio Chappell, Dennis Lillee and Rod Marsh within weeks of each other, but never again was Border's place to be questioned as he built one of the most illustrious records of all. 'We'd gone within a whisker of pinching the Test,' he says. 'It was another defeat, but it captured people's imagination and brought the series back to life. We had been 2–0 up coming to Melbourne. Now the Poms were back in the series.'

Botham, worried by a back complaint all tour, joked the result was never in doubt, but he was relieved to have taken the last wicket as he'd lent Border his Duncan Fearnley bat with which he so nearly won the match.[3] Had he been able to steal a single late in the penultimate over from Willis, the Aussies may well have recorded a historic victory, but Willis finished with two yorkers that Border could only dig out.

The deciding Test in Sydney was drawn, the reborn Border top-scoring for the game with 89 and 83 and Thomson taking 5-50 and 2-30 and producing some serious bounce reminiscent of his violent Ashes beginnings. Before his infamous Christmas Eve collision with Alan Turner on the Adelaide Oval in 1976, he was rated even ahead of West Indian Michael Holding as the fastest bowler of the generation. He'd missed the Centenary Test and rarely again bowled with the same intimidating gusto as had characterised his blistering Ashes beginning in 1974–75. But he was in fine rhythm in front of his old home crowd and nice and cranky, too, after Chappell opened the bowling with Lawson and Hogg.

With 18 wickets for the series, Willis had averaged a wicket every fifty-five balls. While Botham also took 18, they cost 40 apiece, and he admitted later that he hadn't been able to deliver despite the faith shown in him by Willis. Kim Hughes was the heaviest-scoring Australian, his 137 in the final Test guaranteeing the Ashes when John Dyson and Chappell had been dismissed cheaply.

More than 500,000 fans witnessed the Tests, a figure unequalled until 2002–03. However, the over rates continued to decline, a factor soon to be spotlighted with the world champion West Indies deliberately bowling as few as twelve and thirteen overs in an hour without penalty.

Having said farewell to its three champions and seen Kim Hughes resign the captaincy in tears after the 1984–85 Brisbane Test, Australia's 1985 Ashes campaign was to be complicated by the withdrawal of many of its prime candidates who had signed to tour South Africa for the first of two unsanctioned tours in the mid-1980s. England's 3–1 home win was emphatic, Australia's solitary victory coming at Lord's where Border made 196 and 41 not out and mature-age Newcastle leg-spinner Bob Holland claimed five second-innings wickets.

For the rest of the tour, Australia was consistently outplayed, England captain David Gower making more than 700 runs including 166 at Trent Bridge and 215 at Edgbaston. Few rivalled Gower for his effortless ease or the splendour of his majestic cover driving which was worth the price of admission alone. Mike Gatting was almost as prolific with 527 runs while Botham's 31-wicket haul was the best for either side.

Gatting, twenty-nine, was to lead the Ashes defence in 1986–87 and while he was one of ten on their first tour down-under, the experience of three seasons in Sydney grade ranks enabled him to better cope with flat wickets and the unremitting heat – as well as the on-field chat and the sledging by the London tabloids. After one of the first preliminary games, it was suggested by one newspaper that England had only three problems: 'They can't bat, they can't bowl and they can't field.'[4]

But by winning in Brisbane and Melbourne, the tourists skipped to an unassailable 2–0 lead approaching the final Test in Sydney. 'Without a doubt that [series] was the Ashes highpoint for me,' Botham recalls. 'We won everything that summer, the Tests, the one-dayers and the America's Cup. We had a great bunch. It was the happiest of tours.'

Unpretentious Gloucester opener Chris Broad scored three centuries in a row and by the end of the summer of his life was being called

'Who-da' by Gatting – as in 'who'da thought it of you, Broady?'[5] Only Jack Hobbs, Herbert Sutcliffe and Walter Hammond had previously made three tons on end. Broad was in a rare stratosphere.

Botham, so often Australia's nemesis, cornered the headlines from the opening Test in Brisbane when he made a cavalier 138, including thirteen 4s and four 6s. The shorter paceman Merv Hughes bowled, the further Botham lifted him, far and beyond the old dog track, prompting Ian Chappell in the Channel Nine commentary box to say: 'The trouble with Merv Hughes is that he thinks he's a fast bowler.'

At the height of his pummelling, an exasperated Hughes sought the advice of David Boon at mid-off and was told to try pitching it up. When Botham dispatched it high and handsome back over his head for another boundary, Merv snarled: 'Good philosophy, Boonie'[6], as his figures ballooned to 3-134.

The young Australians followed on, before losing by seven wickets, paceman Graham Dilley taking five wickets in the first innings and off-spinner John Emburey five in the second. The three rookie Australian pacemen – Bruce Reid in his ninth Test, Chris Matthews in his first and Hughes in his second – took 10 expensive wickets between them.

After two high-scoring draws in Perth and Adelaide, England confirmed its superiority in the Christmas Test in Melbourne with a stunning innings victory in just three days, ever-smiling paceman Gladstone Small exploiting favourable conditions to take 5-48 in the signature performance of his career. Born in Barbados, he had shifted to England as a 15-year-old and played his first Tests with only moderate reward earlier in the calendar year against the visiting New Zealanders. Dilley had been forced to withdraw on the morning of the match and Small responded with the immediate wicket of Boon. His nervous initial spell also included a wide, pitched outside the cut part of the wicket, but he soon settled and after lunch took four more wickets for just 23 in thirteen unchanged overs. 'There was plenty of juice in the wicket. Ideal bowling conditions really,' Small says. 'The support from everyone in the field was marvellous, too. It was one of those days where we could do nothing wrong.'

Botham, operating from a restricted run-up, was equally destructive, with five wickets. The Australians lasted just two sessions, forfeiting any chance of squaring the series and highlighting the gap between the two teams. Several acrobatic early catches by Jack Richards were world-class, opener Geoff Marsh falling to a goalkeeping-like leap and Border being caught at the wicket with Richards diving to his left in front of first slip Emburey before clasping the ball just centimetres from the ground. 'His dismissal simply knocked all the heart out of them,' said Gatting.[7]

Australia hadn't made a lower starting score in Melbourne since its 138 on the opening day of the Centenary Test but this time there was no Dennis Lillee or Max Walker to launch a counter attack, although young Queensland express Craig McDermott was whole-hearted and pacy and the 203 cm (6 ft 8 in) Reid tough to play with his extra bounce.

Leading by 208 on the first innings, thanks to Broad's steady 112, the Englishmen settled the spoils by late afternoon on the third day, Australia's last seven wickets crumbling for 41, left-armer Phil Edmonds and spinning sidekick Emburey taking five wickets. English rock star Elton John was among the well-wishers in the rooms spraying champagne around and enjoying the return of the Ashes. He'd been at the game every day. 'I don't think there will ever be another day in my cricketing life to match today,' said Gatting in his diary of the tour.[8] 'It was some time before we cleared the England dressing room but that did not put a stop to the celebrations. Ian [Botham] threw a victory party in his hotel room along with Elton acting as disc jockey on the tape deck...What a night! What a day! Victory over Australia inside three days, the first time they had lost an Ashes game in Australia inside three days since 1901–02. Remarkable!'[9]

The Englishmen dubbed their celebrity supporter and rock icon 'EJ the DJ'. He was friendly with the entire team, particularly Botham and his wife Kathy and on one night even acted as babysitter so they could have a meal away from their kids. 'On our return,' said Botham, 'we found he had been feeding them jelly and ice-cream, reading them stories and had even tucked them into bed. Elton was magic. He had plenty of problems of his own, yet he still found time to help me'.[10]

Gatting was only the fourth English captain since 1928–29 to successfully defend the Ashes.

Having included only four batting specialists alongside all-rounders Steve Waugh, Greg Matthews and Peter Sleep in Melbourne, the Australian selectors surprised again approaching the final Test in Sydney by failing to pick a second specialist opener and calling in obscure off-spinner Peter Taylor. Taylor, thirty, had played only once for NSW all season and six games in total. His inclusion was savaged even by the Sydney press, who labelled him 'Peter Who?' Some thought the wrong Taylor may have been chosen, given 22-year-old Mark Taylor's sterling efforts at the head of the order for NSW.

Peter Taylor, however, was ready and was the right choice, particularly on the spin-friendly Sydney Cricket Ground. 'I was aware that some interest was being shown in my performances,' he said of his selection, 'although I didn't really think I'd be playing for Australia, I must confess. But in many ways it wasn't a surprise to me and I guess to the people who were in the know. They knew a little more about it than a lot of people.'[11]

Taylor was to take eight wickets and make 53 runs for the game to win the man-of-the-match award as Australia clinched its only win of the summer with one over to spare. Set 320, England was bowled out for 264. Among Taylor's haul was Botham in both innings, including a first-baller in the second innings, courtesy of a magnificent running catch from Dirk Wellham, a turning point on the final afternoon. Leg-spinner Sleep cashed in later with the final wickets. The Englishmen had needed 90 from the last twenty overs but stumbled with the dismissal of Gatting who was caught and bowled by Steve Waugh just four runs short of a much-deserved 100. 'Dirk's catch probably won the Test match,' said Taylor. 'I don't think anyone else in Australia could have caught the ball. He moved so fast over about thirty yards and more or less picked it up with his fingernails on the grass. It was a fantastic catch.'[12]

Dean Jones with 184 not out and 30 also made a timely contribution on his way to a series-high 511 runs. He'd been distraught to have been overlooked from English tour selection in 1985, but rather than sign with the South African rebels he determined to re-win his place, and after a magnificent double century in Madras in 1986 he was on a roll.

A one-off Test marking the Bicentennial celebrations was also played the following summer, in Sydney in January 1988, when Australia was forced to follow-on before saving the game comfortably thanks to an unbeaten 184 from David Boon, who had been discarded from the corresponding match twelve months earlier. Taylor was again included and took four wickets. England's star, again, was Broad, who made 139 before thumping his stumps down in frustration after being bowled by Steve Waugh.

Boon batted eight hours to ensure the draw and rejuvenate his career. 'I tried to be as positive as I could,' said Boon. 'As often as I could, I hit

(John) Emburey over the top of mid-on until he'd put the fieldsman back. Then I'd push ones into the gap I'd created until the field was brought in. Then I'd go over the top again.'[13] At one stage Boon was charging Eddie Hemmings before he'd bowled. Hemmings withheld the ball and threatened to run him out. Had frontline pacemen Dilley and Neil Foster not been inconvenienced by injury, England may well have won.

The fallout after the simultaneous retirement of Lillee, Chappell and Marsh had seen the Australians lose regularly, even to New Zealand at home. But slowly and surely, the rebuilding continued and eventually a new band of champions emerged, Mark Taylor, Boon and Steve Waugh at the head of the order and Hughes, Bruce Reid and Craig McDermott with the new ball. Wicketkeeper Ian Healy was another most promising inclusion and, in England in 1989, Border gained some revenge for previous defeats by piloting a 4–0 series win. It had been a torrid ride for Border, who had all but resigned in a grump after an infamous tour of New Zealand years earlier. The string of defeats had hardened his attitude and, taking the advice of ex-players such as Ian Chappell, who had claimed him to be 'too chummy'[14] in 1985, Border had little time or interaction with the English in 1989, especially between the hours of eleven and six. 'Basically, as "AB" told us, we were sick of losing,' Hughes says. 'We didn't want to make it a tea party for them out there. We wanted to isolate them, make them feel uncomfortable. And we did.'

Man of the decade: *Ian Botham*

Buccaneering Ian Botham was a favourite with crowds around the world. Thrilling to the challenge of Ashes battle, Botham displayed the flair and bravado of a Miller and a Constantine, entertaining with the bat, seaming and swinging the new ball and catching with poise and alacrity.

So astonishing were his headlining solos that England made him captain, but after failing to win any of his twelve games and angered by the refusal of the hierarchy to appoint him on more than a Test-by-Test basis, he stood down early into the memorable 1981 summer. Responsibility-free, he immediately recaptured his thrilling best, stamping himself as an undeniably classy all-rounder. With 34 wickets and almost 400 runs, Botham stole the Ashes single-handedly like Jim Laker in 1956 and Don Bradman in 1930.

Despite a Boys' Own arrival into international ranks against Greg Chappell's 1977 Australians, many had initially doubted his credentials. But his happy knack of performing when it counted made him England's 'go-to' player and a sporting hero with the warts the tabloids loved.

Tallish at 185 cm (6 ft 1 in) and with the broad shoulders of an axeman, his six-hitting exploits were wondrous. Only West Indian pair Viv Richards and Clive Lloyd boasted more 6s in the first 125 years of Test cricket. And Botham's sixty-seven 6s more than doubled the six-hitting feats of the next best Englishman, Ken Barrington with twenty-seven.

Botham won the momentous Melbourne Christmas Test of 1982–83 when he dismissed Australia's last man Jeff Thomson after a 70-run last-wicket stand had all but lifted Australia to a glorious victory. Only three Ashes Test finishes have been as gripping: Old Trafford 1902, Melbourne 1907–08 and Edgbaston 2005. Botham's captain Bob Willis affectionately dubbed his new-ball partner 'Golden Bollocks' and whenever tested would always turn to his larger-than-life champion.

At the height of his headlining career, Botham played sixty-five successive Tests, equalling Alan Knott's English record.

At his best in English conditions, 79 of Botham's record 148 Ashes wickets came on home soil, including 34 in the never-to-be-forgotten summer of 1981 and 31 in 1985. However, it was in Australia in 1979–80 that he produced his most outstanding innings figures of 6-78 in the opening Test in Perth. He followed with five wickets in the second innings, bowling with a Trueman-like ferocity from an extended run-up.

As world cricket's biggest name throughout the 1980s, Botham would have been the first chosen in almost any team in the world.

In 1986, he surpassed Dennis Lillee's mark of 355 wickets to become Test cricket's new leading wicket-taker. In the same game, at The Oval, he struck New Zealand's Derek Stirling for a record-equalling 24 from an over on his way to a blazing half-century. When in the mood, no cricketer was as feared or as unstoppable. He may have been a man of excesses, but he was a helluva player.

Botham v. Australia

* not out

Batting

Season	Scores	Runs	Ave
1977	25, 0	25	12.50
1978–79	49, 11, 30, 22, 10, 59, 6, 74, 7, 23	291	29.10
1979–80	15, 18, 27, 0, 8, 119	187	37.40
1980	0	0	–

Season	Scores	Runs	Ave
1981	1, 33, 0, 0, 50, 149*, 26, 3, 0, 118, 3, 16	399	36.27
1982–83	12, 0, 40, 15, 35, 58, 27, 46, 5, 32	270	27.00
1985	60, 12, 5, 85, 38, 20, 18, 12	250	31.25
1986–87	138, 0, 6, 29, 16, 0	189	31.50
1989	46, 0, 4, 12	62	15.50

Tests v. Australia:	36 (102)
Runs:	1.673 (5200)
Average:	29.35 (33.54)
Highest score:	149 not out, Leeds, 1981 (208)
100s:	4 (14)

Bowling

Season	Analysis	Wkts	Ave
1977	5-74, 0-60, 5-21, 0-47	10	20.20
1978–79	3-40, 3-95, 0-46, 0-54, 3-68, 3-41, 2-87, 4-42, 1-37, 4-57	23	24.65
1979–80	6-78, 5-98, 4-29, 0-43, 3-105, 1-18	19	19.52
1980	0-89, 1-43	1	132.00
1981	2-34, 1-34, 2-71, 1-10, 6-95, 1-14, 1-64, 5-11, 3-28, 2-86, 6-125, 4-128	34	20.58
1982–83	2-121, 0-17, 3-105, 0-70, 4-112, 1-45, 1-69, 2-80, 4-75, 1-35	18	40.50
1985	3-86, 4-107, 5-109, 2-49, 3-107, 4-79, 0-50, 1-108, 3-52, 3-64, 3-44	31	27.58
1986–87	2-58, 1-34, 1-72, 0-13, 5-41, 0-19, 0-42, 0-17	9	32.88
1989	1-75, 2-63, 0-103	3	80.33

Wickets:	148 (383)
Average:	27.65 (28.40)
Best bowling:	6-78, Perth, 1979–80 (8-34)
5-wicket Innings:	9 (27)
10-wicket Matches:	2 (4)
Strike-rate:	57 balls per wkt (56)
Average wkts per Test:	4.1 (3.75)

Match of the decade: *Leeds, 1981*

No Test match of the twentieth century had previously been won by the team following on, England's remarkable comeback being triggered by deposed captain Ian Botham and bouncy paceman Bob Willis who returned career-best figures. The cricket world was spellbound by Botham's heroics, England averting an innings defeat and forcing Australia to chase 130. At 56-1, a comfortable victory loomed before Willis tore through the top-order, star Aussies Kim Hughes, Allan Border and Graham Yallop all out for ducks as England snatched a miraculous win.

Match scores: England 174 (Botham 50, Lillee 4-49) and 356 (Botham 149 not out, Dilley 56, Alderman 6-135) defeated Australia 401-9 dec. (Dyson 102, Hughes 89, Yallop 58, Botham 6-95) and 111 (Willis 8-43) by 18 runs

Odd spot: *Rags to riches*

The 1981 English summer was unforgettable for gregarious 22-year-old Michael Whitney from the Sydney beaches. Agreeing to ever-so-modest terms with Fleetwood in the northern Lancashire league, he found himself co-opted into Gloucestershire's first XI and into Australia's fifth Test team of 1981 after injuries to frontliners Geoff Lawson and Rodney Hogg. Bowling from first-change on debut at Old Trafford, he took 2-50 and 2-74, the first of fifty appearances he was to make in Australian colours.

Looking back: *Ian Botham, Leeds, 1981*

'It was one of those crazy, glorious one-off flukes . . . "Brears" (captain Mike Brearley) had given up the ghost. He had actually changed out of his cricket gear, showered and packed up his kit. Diplomatically he chose to put on a clean cricket shirt so that if anyone looked up at the England balcony, his defeatism would not be too obvious. As far as they (Australia) was concerned, the match was all but over (and) the Ashes were in the bag.'[15]

Botham's whirlwind 149, his first Ashes century, set up one of the greatest comebacks in Test history. In mid-match, bookmakers Ladbrokes laid 500–1 against an English victory.

One for the statisticians: *The Snail*

Kent's Chris Tavare took an hour to score in both the first and second innings in Perth in 1982–83. His 89 and 9 came in almost ten hours at an average of just 10 runs per hour . . . shades of Trevor 'The Boil' Bailey in 1958–59.

LETHAL: Rodney Hogg careered to a new Australian Ashes record of 41 wickets in 1978–79. Less than two years earlier he'd been an Adelaide milkman, wondering if his big break would ever come.
Australian Cricket *magazine*

COMEBACK (left): Ian Chappell's short-lived comeback in the first reconciliation season in 1979–80 included a farewell double of 75 and 26 not out against the Englishmen in Melbourne.

MASTER (above): Having been reinstated as Australia's captain, Greg Chappell played with flair and majesty and scored two centuries, including 114 against England in the Melbourne Test, the sixth of the summer.

PANIC (below): Englishmen Ian Gould (a substitute fieldsman) and Allan Lamb (centre) collide as Jeff Thomson steals a short single during the gripping final morning in Melbourne, 1982–83.

Jason Childs (The Age)/Cricketer *magazine*

YALUMBA (top): Dennis Lillee (left) and Ian Botham (centre) relax during an Adelaide rest day, a long-lost Ashes tradition.

Patrick Eagar

UNSTOPPABLE (above): Allan Border during his triumphant 1989 summer when Australia won 4–0.

Patrick Eagar

LEGEND (right): In taking 355 Test wickets, Dennis Lillee retired in 1984 as the most prolific Test bowler in history. A generation later, Shane Warne all but doubled his mark.

Ken Rainsbury/Cricketer magazine

A ONE-OFF: Charismatic Greg Matthews celebrates a wicket with Merv Hughes, who was to take more than 200 Test wickets despite being written off early in his career.
Bruce Postle

FANCY DRESS (below): Christmas Day in Melbourne in 1990 for Graham Gooch (centre) and his Englishmen, their families and friends.
Jason Childs (The Age)/Cricketer *magazine*

PARTY TIME (left): Fans celebrate England's only win of the 1994–95 Test summer, by 106 runs in Adelaide.
Bruce Postle

DESTRUCTIVE (below left): Bruce Reid on his way to 13 wickets for the match in Melbourne in 1990–91. Australia won easily.

BEST EVER (below): Glenn McGrath is applauded into the Lord's pavilion after taking a Test-best 8/38, 1997.
David Munden/Sportsline Photographic

TALENTED (above): David Hookes.

Stephen Laffer

INDESTRUCTIBLE (right): Steve Waugh.

Stephen Laffer

THE BEST (below left): Shane Warne.

Bruce Postle

HOSTILE (below right): Jason Gillespie.

Jack Atley

UNCONQUERED: Mark Taylor (left) and Geoff Marsh batted through the entire first day's play of the fifth Test on their way to a record stand of 329, as England was beaten by an innings at Trent Bridge, 1989.

Patrick Eager

The Sunday Telegraph

Fearsome Freddie flays the Aussies

Flintoff triumphs with bat and ball to put England on brink of historic Test victory

SPORT, PAGES 1-4

304   AUGUST 7 2005   £1.40

WIN A LUXURY HEALTH BREAK

TRAVEL, PAGE 4

SUPERMAN (above): Andrew Flintoff's performances throughout 2005 were among the greatest ever in Ashes combat. He won the inaugural Compton-Miller Medal for being the player of the series.

Sunday Telegraph, *London*

Edgbaston **2005**

npower Test Series
ENGLAND v AUSTRALIA
Thursday 4th August 2005
Stanley Barnes Stand   Block 18
Row O   Seat 10
Adult   50.00

Warwickshire County Cricket Club
0870 062 1902   www.edgbaston.com

BEST SEAT IN THE HOUSE (left): Those lucky enough to gain admittance to Edgbaston on the deciding day of the second Test saw one of the great finishes, Australia falling just three runs short of an amazing win.

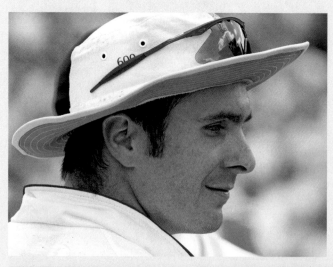

MASTERMIND (left): Michael Vaughan led England to one of the great series victories.
Patrick Eagar

ATHLETIC (below): Adam Gilchrist takes a superb leg-side catch from the bowling of Brett Lee, Lord's, 2005.
Richard Hicks

TRUE GRIT (left): In what proved to be his farewell Ashes tour, Justin Langer (left) was the only Australian to average 40 in 2005. He is pictured with captain Ricky Ponting.
Patrick Eagar

CHAMPION PAIR (above): Glenn McGrath and Shane Warne walk off The Oval arm-in-arm, 2005. The Ashes may have been lost but their reputations had only been enhanced as two of the greatest strike bowlers in history.
Patrick Eagar

CELEBRATION (below): Shane Warne indulges in a little pre-partying with the English press corps, 2005.
Patrick Eagar

MAGNIFICENT: Andrew Flintoff was the difference between the two teams
with some marvellous performances, from Edgbaston on, 2005.

Patrick Eagar

HISTORIC (top): Shane Warne holds
court after taking his 700th Test wicket, in
Melbourne, 2006–07.
Patrick Eagar

BLOCKBUSTER (above): Adam Gilchrist
hooks Steve Harmison during his
whirlwind century in Perth, the fastest
in Ashes history, 2006–07.
Patrick Eagar

LATE BLOOMER: Michael Hussey celebrated his promotion to No.4 with a century in Perth, where Australia regained the Ashes, 2006–07.

Patrick Eagar

THE BEST SINCE BRADMAN: Ricky Ponting's masterly displays ensured him the Compton-Miller Medal for the outstanding player of the 2006–07 summer. His centuries in the opening two Tests were marvellously assured.

FIND OF THE SUMMER (left): Stuart Clark was the find of the 2006–07 summer, taking 26 wickets in his maiden Ashes series.
Patrick Eagar

FOUR IN A ROW (below): The Australians win by an innings in three days in Melbourne, 2006, with Brett Lee the centre of attention. Captain Ricky Ponting pulls Lee's shirt, celebrating with (l–r) Hayden, Hussey, Warne and Gilchrist.

WINNERS ARE GRINNERS: Ask Andrew Symonds after he reached his maiden Test century with a six down the ground into the Melbourne members, fourth Test, 2006–07.

Patrick Eagar

THE ASHES RETURN: And aren't Ricky Ponting and his
Australians triumphant! Perth, 2006.

Patrick Eagar

Tests 1979–80 to 1989

KEY: M Matches **I** Innings **NO** Not out innings **HS** Highest score **BB** Best bowling

5wI 5-wicket innings **10wM** 10-wicket match ***** Not out **#** Second innings **rh** Retired hurt

Series results

	Tests	Aust	Eng	Drawn
1979–80 (Aust)	2†	2	0	0
1980 (Eng)	1	0	0	1
1981 (Eng)	6	1	3	2
1982–83 (Aust)	5	2	1	2
1985 (Eng)	6	1	3	2
1986–87 (Aust)	5	1	2	2
1987–88 (Aust)	1	0	0	1
1989 (Eng)	6	4	0	2
Total	**32**	**11**	**9**	**12**
Progressive	269	101	88	80

† *The first Test in the 1979–80 series was played in December 1979 and is included in records for the previous decade.*

Summary

	Runs	Wkts	Ave
Australia	17,584	481	36.55
England	16,781	521	32.20

Highest innings totals

Australia		England	
602-6 dec	Nottingham 1989 (5th Test)	595-5 dec	Birmingham 1985 (5th Test)
601-7 dec	Leeds 1989 (1st Test)	592-8 dec	Perth 1986–87 (2nd Test)
539	Nottingham 1985 (3rd Test)	533	Leeds 1985 (1st Test)
528	Lord's 1989 (2nd Test)	482-9 dec	Manchester 1985 (4th Test)
514-5 dec	Adelaide 1986–87 (3rd Test)	464	The Oval 1985 (6th Test)
477	Melbourne 1979–80 (3rd Test)	456	Nottingham 1985 (3rd Test)
468	The Oval 1989 (6th Test)	456	Brisbane 1986–87 (1st Test)
		455	Adelaide 1986–87 (3rd Test)

Lowest completed innings totals

Australia		England	
111	Leeds 1981 (3rd Test)#	123	Sydney 1979–80 (2nd Test)
121	Birmingham 1981 (4th Test)#	125	Nottingham 1981 (1st Test)#
129	The Oval 1985 (6th Test)#		
130	Manchester 1981 (5th Test)		

Leading run scorers

	M	I	NO	Runs	HS	Ave	100	50
Australia								
A. R. Border	32	58	15	2,569	196	59.74	6	16
D. M. Jones	12	21	2	1,157	184*	60.89	3	7
K. J. Hughes	14	25	1	1,050	137	43.75	2	5
D. C. Boon	15	28	4	906	184*	37.75	2	4
S. R. Waugh	12	17	5	843	177*	70.25	2	4
M. A. Taylor	6	11	1	839	219	83.90	2	5
G. R. Marsh	12	23	0	837	138	36.39	2	3
K. C. Wessels	10	19	0	754	162	39.68	1	4
G. S. Chappell	8	16	4	750	117	62.50	3	3
G. M. Wood	13	25	1	719	172	29.95	2	2
G. M. Ritchie	10	19	3	666	146	41.62	1	2
England								
D. I. Gower	30	54	2	2,402	215	46.19	6	10
M. W. Gatting	20	35	4	1,388	160	44.77	3	11
I. T. Botham	27	45	2	1,324	149*	30.79	4	4
G. A. Gooch	19	34	0	1,005	196	29.55	1	6
A. J. Lamb	17	29	2	943	125	34.92	1	5
B. C. Broad	8	14	2	708	162	59.00	4	–
G. Boycott	9	18	1	659	137	38.76	2	2
J. E. Emburey	20	27	7	600	69	30.00	–	3

Hundreds

Australia (30)		**England (28)**	
6	A. R. Border	6	D. I. Gower
3	G. S. Chappell	4	I. T. Botham
	D. M. Jones		B. C. Broad
2	D. C. Boon	3	M. W. Gatting
	K. J. Hughes	2	G. Boycott
	G. R. Marsh		R. T. Robinson
	M. A. Taylor		R. A. Smith
	S. R. Waugh	1	G. A. Gooch
	G. M. Wood		A. J. Lamb
1	J. Dyson		D. W. Randall
	A. M. J. Hilditch		C. J. Richards
	G. M. Ritchie		R. C. Russell
	D. M. Wellham		
	K. C. Wessels		
	G. N. Yallop		

Highest individual scores

Australia

219	M. A. Taylor at Nottingham 1989 (5th Test)
196	A. R. Border at Lord's 1985 (2nd Test)
184*	D. M. Jones at Sydney 1986–87 (5th Test)
184*	D. C. Boon at Sydney 1987–88 (Bic Test)#
177*	S. R. Waugh at Leeds 1989 (1st Test)
172	G. M. Wood at Nottingham 1985 (3rd Test)
162	K. C. Wessels at Brisbane 1982–83 (2nd Test)
157	D. M. Jones at Birmingham 1989 (3rd Test)
152*	S. R. Waugh at Lord's 1989 (2nd Test)
146*	A. R. Border at Manchester 1985 (4th Test)#
146	G. M. Ritchie at Nottingham 1985 (3rd Test)

England

215	D. I. Gower at Birmingham 1985 (5th Test)
196	G. A. Gooch at The Oval 1985 (6th Test)
175	R. T. Robinson at Leeds 1985 (1st Test)
166	D. I. Gower at Nottingham 1985 (3rd Test)
162	B. C. Broad at Perth 1986–87 (2nd Test)
160	M. W. Gatting at Manchester 1985 (4th Test)
157	D. I. Gower at The Oval 1985 (6th Test)
149*	I. T. Botham at Leeds 1981 (3rd Test)#
148	R. T. Robinson at Birmingham 1985 (5th Test)
143	R. A. Smith at Manchester 1989 (4th Test)

500 runs in a series

	Season	M	I	NO	Runs	HS	Ave	100	50
Australia									
M. A. Taylor	1989	6	11	1	839	219	83.90	2	5
A. R. Border	1985	6	11	2	597	196	66.33	2	1
D. M. Jones	1989	6	9	1	566	157	70.75	2	3
A. R. Border	1981	6	12	3	533	123*	59.22	2	3
D. M. Jones	1986–87	5	10	1	511	184*	56.77	1	3
S. R. Waugh	1989	6	8	4	506	177*	126.50	2	1
England									
D. I. Gower	1985	6	9	0	732	215	81.33	3	1
R. A. Smith	1989	5	10	1	553	143	61.44	2	3
M. W. Gatting	1985	6	9	3	527	160	87.83	2	3
Also note:									
R. T. Robinson	1985	6	9	1	490	175	61.25	2	1

Hundred partnerships

Australia (37)

Partnerships of 150 and over:

329	1st	G. R. Marsh and M. A. Taylor at Nottingham 1989 (4th Test)
		(Australia 1st wicket record against England)
216	5th	A. R. Border and G. M. Ritchie at Lord's 1985 (2nd Test)
196	4th	A. R. Border and D. M. Jones at The Oval 1989 (5th Test)
162	1st	D. C. Boon and G. R. Marsh at Sydney 1987–88 (Bic Test)#
161	6th	G. M. Wood and G. M. Ritchie at Nottingham 1985 (3rd Test)

England (31)

Partnerships of 150 and over:

351	2nd	G. A. Gooch and D. I. Gower at The Oval 1985 (6th Test)
331	2nd	R. T. Robinson and D. I. Gower at Birmingham 1985 (5th Test)
223	1st	B. C. Broad and C. W. J. Athey at Perth 1986–87 (2nd Test)
207	6th	D. I. Gower and C. J. Richards at Perth 1986–87 (2nd Test)
187	3rd	D. I. Gower and M. W. Gatting at Nottingham 1985 (3rd Test)
161	2nd	B. C. Broad and M. W. Gatting at Adelaide 1986–87 (3rd Test)
161	4th	C. J. Tavaré and A. J. Lamb at Melbourne 1982–83 (4th Test)
156	4th	M. W. Gatting and A. J. Lamb at Manchester 1985 (4th Test)

Leading wicket-takers

	Tests	Balls	Mdns	Runs	Wkts	Ave	BB	5wl	10wM
Australia									
G. F. Lawson	21	5,460	196	2,763	97	28.48	7-81	7	1
T. M. Alderman	13	3,824	159	1,689	84	20.10	6-128	10	1
D. K. Lillee	10	3,126	140	1,392	65	21.41	7-89	4	1
C. J. McDermott	8	1,777	33	1,049	34	30.85	8-141	2	–
M. G. Hughes	10	1,955	68	1,059	29	36.51	4-71	–	–
J. R. Thomson	6	1,108	26	686	25	27.44	5-50	2	–
England									
I. T. Botham	27	6,288	233	3,148	104	30.26	6-95	5	1
J. E. Emburey	20	6,152	282	2,242	59	38.00	7-78	3	–
R. G. D. Willis	13	2,809	96	1,277	49	26.06	8-43	2	–
G. R. Dilley	11	2,456	80	1,252	38	32.94	5-68	1	–
P. H. Edmonds	10	2,925	137	1,087	30	36.23	4-40	–	–

Five wickets in an innings

Australia (32)		England (16)	
10	T. M. Alderman	5	I. T. Botham
7	G. F. Lawson	3	J. E. Emburey
4	D. K. Lillee	2	R. M. Ellison
2	C. J. McDermott		G. C. Small
	J. R. Thomson		R. G. D. Willis
1	R. J. Bright	1	N. G. Cowans
	R. G. Holland		G. R. Dilley
	C. J. McDermott		
	P. R. Sleep		
	P. L. Taylor		
	S. R. Waugh		
	B. Yardley		

Best individual bowling

Australia

8-141	C. J. McDermott at Manchester 1985 (4th Test)
7-81	G. F. Lawson at Lord's 1981 (2nd Test)
7-89	D. K. Lillee at The Oval 1981 (6th Test)
6-47	G. F. Lawson at Brisbane 1982–83 (2nd Test)
6-60	D. K. Lillee at Melbourne 1979–80 (3rd Test)
6-70	C. J. McDermott at Lord's 1985 (2nd Test)
6-72	G. F. Lawson at Manchester 1989 (4th Test)
6-78	P. L. Taylor at Sydney 1986–87 (5th Test)
6-128	T. M. Alderman at Lord's 1989 (2nd Test)
6-135	T. M. Alderman at Leeds 1981 (3rd Test)

England

8-43	R. G. D. Willis at Leeds 1981 (3rd Test)#
7-78	J. E. Emburey at Sydney 1986–87 (5th Test)#
6-77	N. G. Cowans at Melbourne 1982–83 (4th Test)#
6-77	R. M. Ellison at Birmingham 1985 (5th Test)
6-95	I. T. Botham at Leeds 1981 (3rd Test)
6-125	I. T. Botham at The Oval 1981 (5th Test)

10 wickets in a match

Australia (4)

11-134	G. F. Lawson (6-47 and 5-87) at Brisbane 1982–83 (2nd Test)
11-138	D. K. Lillee (6-60 and 5-78) at Melbourne 1979–80 (3rd Test)
11-159	D. K. Lillee (7-89 and 4-70) at The Oval 1981 (6th Test)
10-151	T. M. Alderman (5-107 and 5-44) at Leeds 1989 (1st Test)

England (2)

10-104	R. M. Ellison (6-77 and 4-27) at Birmingham 1985 (5th Test)
10-253	I. T. Botham (6-125 and 4-128) at The Oval 1981 (5th Test)

25 wickets in a series

	Season	Tests	Balls	Mdns	Runs	Wkts	Ave	BB	5wI	10wM
Australia										
T. M. Alderman	1981	6	1,950	76	893	42	21.26	6-135	4	–
T. M. Alderman	1989	6	1,616	68	712	41	17.36	6-128	6	1
D. K. Lillee	1981	6	1,870	81	870	39	22.30	7-89	2	1
G. F. Lawson	1982–83	5	1,384	51	687	34	20.20	6-47	4	1
C. J. McDermott	1985	6	1,406	21	901	30	30.03	8-141	2	–
G. F. Lawson	1989	6	1,663	68	791	29	27.27	6-72	1	–
England										
I. T. Botham	1981	6	1,635	81	700	34	20.58	6-95	3	1
I. T. Botham	1985	6	1,510	36	855	31	27.58	5-109	1	–
R. G. D. Willis	1981	6	1,516	56	666	29	22.96	8-43	1	–

Leading wicketkeepers

	Tests	Dismissals	Catches	Stumpings
Australia				
R. W. Marsh	14	58	58	0
I. A. Healy	6	14	14	0
T. J. Zoehrer	4	10	10	0
England				
R. W. Taylor	10	30	30	0
P. R. Downton	7	22	21	1
R. C. Russell	6	18	14	4
C. J. Richards	5	16	15	1

Leading fieldsmen

	Tests	Catches		Tests	Catches
Australia			**England**		
A. R. Border	32	42	I. T. Botham	27	45
G. S. Chappell	8	15	D. I. Gower	30	20
D. C. Boon	15	14	A. J. Lamb	17	18
S. R. Waugh	12	12	M. W. Gatting	20	14
K. C. Wessels	10	11	P. H. Edmonds	10	10
T. M. Alderman	13	10	G. A. Gooch	19	10
G. R. Marsh	12	10			

Captains

	Tests	Won	Lost	Drawn	Toss won
Australia					
A. R. Border	18	6	5	7	8
G. S. Chappell	8	4	1	3	6
K. J. Hughes	6	1	3	2	3
England					
D. I. Gower	12	3	5	4	7
J. M. Brearley	6	3	2	1	4
M. W. Gatting	6	2	1	3	3
R. G. D. Willis	5	1	2	2	1
I. T. Botham	3	0	1	2	0

Most appearances

Australia (55 players)		England (59 players)	
32	A. R. Border	30	D. I. Gower
21	G. F. Lawson	27	I. T. Botham
15	D. C. Boon	20	J. E. Emburey
14	K. J. Hughes		M. W. Gatting
	R. W. Marsh	19	G. A. Gooch
		17	A. J. Lamb

Shane Warne on his way to a Test-best 8-71 against England, Brisbane, 1994–95.
Cricketer magazine

1990s
THE COMING OF WARNE

· ·

'They all must have been in panic, especially the way "Gatt" hung around at the wicket shaking his head. Warnie had them scarred psychologically and he'd bowled only one ball!'

A fter years of West Indian domination, the 1990s ushered unprecedented prosperity for Australian cricket and its leading players, a threat of strike action forcing the staid Australian Cricket Board to broker a more meaningful agreement and a more equitable split of the lucrative monies pouring into the game via sponsorships, television and media rights, and snowballing takings at the gate.

Having decimated the Englishmen in the northern summer of 1989, Australia launched an unprecedented run of series success, unbroken until 2005 in the greatest Ashes summer of them all. They played gloriously attractive cricket and with the arrival of Shane Warne and Glenn McGrath possessed matchwinners of rare quality.

England, too, fielded some fine players, but the Australians were more vibrant and athletic and developed an enviable depth of ready-to-go replacements courtesy of their elite feeder systems. Warne and McGrath were among the first to leap-frog into Test cricket via the Cricket Academy run by legendary Rod Marsh in Adelaide.

The captaincy baton passed from Allan Border to Mark Taylor, the retirement of other frontliners such as Craig McDermott, David Boon,

Geoff Marsh and Bruce Reid soon covered with barely a blimp on Australia's winning radar.

Never before were Ashes results so one-sided:

- 1990–91: Australia won 3–0
- 1993: Australia 4–1
- 1994–95: Australia 3–1
- 1997: Australia 3–2
- 1998–99: Australia 3–1.

The majority of England's wins came at the end of campaigns when the series had already been decided. Their tours down-under developed a depressingly familiar theme with frequent changes of leadership, key players injured and others well short of their best form.

In 1990–91, England's appointed captain Graham Gooch missed a month's cricket, including the first Test, with a poisoned hand. His deputy Allan Lamb injured a calf jogging back to the team hotel in Ballarat and was even accused by management of partying too hard. Fast bowler Chris Lewis flew home after the first Test with stress fractures of the back while ex-captain David Gower was treated like a schoolboy despite being one of the most consistent runmakers.

Rarely could England string more than a winning session or two together and while first-innings leads were established in both the opening Tests in Brisbane and Melbourne, Australia careered to comfortable wins.

Having taken five wickets in Australia's 10-wicket win in the opening Test, Reid captured 13 in the second, triggering the most monumental Ashes collapse of all. High-quality left-arm bowlers tend to emerge only once a generation and Reid exerted a Lillee-like influence over the English in each of the four Tests he played. 'Only Dennis in my time had bowled better [than Reid],' captain Border says. 'Being 6 ft 8 in and left-handed obviously gives him an advantage but his sustained effort in the conditions just couldn't be better.'

Following his 6-97 in the first innings, Reid proved even more menacing in the second. England was comfortably placed at 78-1 at lunch on the fourth day, an overall lead of more than 120 with five sessions to play. Reid had an early wicket when opener Mike Atherton edged one behind. Another angled delivery to Gooch steepled and cut so sharply that wicketkeeper Ian Healy took it in front of second slip.

Bowling in tandem with off-spinner Greg Matthews, Reid changed the game immediately after the break by dismissing Gooch and No. 4 Robin Smith. Matthews claimed first-innings centurion Gower for a rare duck and the slide was on. From 147-4 and an overall lead of 193 at tea-time, England caved in. In twelve overs, the tourists lost 6 for 3, including 4-0 to Reid from his last six overs. 'It was one of the most spectacular collapses in Ashes history,' said Gower. 'It was almost beyond belief.'[1]

Aiming at a little green patch just short of a length on the off-stump line, Reid took 7-51 from 22 overs. 'I always loved bowling at the MCG with its history and atmosphere,' Reid says. 'It's so flat and level. Unlike other grounds, you never felt like you were running up a hill. You'd always get yourself up for the Boxing Day Test. The MCG always has a buzz about it. Everyone is in a good mood and for me things just seemed to flow nicely. Once I had a bit of success there, I was ready to come out and do it again. I never felt under pressure. The crowds were so big and knowledgeable.'

The only Englishman to look like matching Reid in Melbourne was giant seamer and first-time tourist Gus Fraser whose ability to obtain zip on the flattest of wickets saw him take 6-82. The Australians said batting against him was like facing a bowling machine. Rarely would anything be sprayed wide of the stumps, all his wickets coming either bowled, lbw or to catches behind by lively Jack Russell. When he succumbed to a hip injury, Gooch was deprived of his most reliable trundler.

Another first-timer Phil Tufnell all but grabbed a hat-trick in the next Test in Sydney, Gower at silly point just failing to take a sharp catch from Steve Waugh to the first ball he faced. It would have been one of the most high-profile hat-tricks of all, too, with Border and Dean Jones having fallen to the previous two balls. It had taken Tufnell three Tests and 440 balls to take a wicket and he celebrated by taking a 5-for which gave England a slim chance of a shock win. Set 255 runs at nine an over, Gooch and Gower started with 81 from eleven overs, before Matthews, a first-innings centurion, dismissed them both to ensure an Ashes-retaining draw. Earlier, Atherton's 105 was the slowest ever century in Ashes annals.

Steve Waugh lost his place in the final Tests to his twin brother Mark, who celebrated with a classic century on debut on a belter in Adelaide. Ninety-five of his runs came in the last session on the opening day. For years he'd been overshadowed by his brother's all-round feats, so much so that he was dubbed 'Afghanistan' – the forgotten Waugh. But given the opportunity mid-summer, he proved to be a batting aristocrat on the same halcyon level as a Harvey, McCabe and Trumper. As he was taking his guard, his Essex county teammate Robin Smith, fielding in close, whispered: 'Now's the time to release the handbrake, champ.'[2]

Within moments Waugh had sweetly driven Phil DeFreitas straight back past his outstretched right hand for three, and was away.

Technically, it remained one of the finest innings of his illustrious 100-plus Test career. It also confirmed his father Rodger's high opinion and belief that Mark, twenty-five, could match the feats of his higher-profiled twin. 'Everything I hit went for 4,' said Waugh. 'I can't remember mishitting even one ball. Naturally I was disappointed for Stephen [to be dropped] . . . it took a bit of gloss off it at the time . . . it would have been great if we'd both made it, but at least one of us was there. If my brother was dropped it was best that I took his place.'[3]

Waugh was the fifteenth Australian to score a hundred on debut and only the eighth to do so in the first innings of a Test against England. The game was to be drawn, a double-century stand between Gooch and Atherton on the final day a belated show of defiance. In the rooms, though, morale was low, the fallout after a Gold Coast joy flight by Gower and John Morris in two Tiger Moths having cost the pair £1,000 fines. Gower was furious at the treatment and made only 11 and 16 in Adelaide, his careless first-innings dismissal prompting a huge backlash from Gooch. 'I was made to feel that I had not scored a run for years,' said Gower, in his 113th Test.[4]

In Perth, McDermott's 11-wicket match haul included the first seven wickets in a row. After Allan Lamb's 91 and Robin Smith's 58, no one else made 30 and Australia won in ten sessions. Boon, with 530 runs, and Reid, 27 wickets, were primary in Australia's supremacy.

For the first time since 1958–59, England had failed to win a Test during a five-match rubber against Australia and the gap between the two teams was to widen, too, with the fast-tracking of a chubby, uncomplicated young leg-spinner from the Melbourne bayside in Shane Warne.

Warne won the 1992 Christmas Test on his home ground, Melbourne, with a flipper that snaked past West Indian maestro Richie Richardson's defences and scuttled into his off-stump. Hours later in the dressing rooms, he was still modestly shaking his head about that one. From 143-1, chasing 359, the long-time world champions were humbled for 219, Warne's share being a remarkable 7-52. The Windies hit back to win the last two Tests and the series 2–1, but the wind of change was apparent and during the following fourteen seasons of Warne's reign as the game's out-standing spin bowler, Australia wasn't to lose even once at home.

If England had initially underrated Warne as Border's frontline spin-ner in the team of 1993, they soon reassessed as with his first famous delivery at Old Trafford: Warne bowled Mike Gatting with an unplayable leg-break that curved in the air before spinning back and hitting the top of Gatting's off-stump. A disbelieving Gatting lingered at the wicket. He'd never seen a ball spin so far. 'I would have liked to have been a fly on the wall in the English rooms that day,' Australian Paul Reiffel says. 'They all must have been in panic, especially the way "Gatt" hung around at the wicket shaking his head. Warnie had them scarred psychologically and he'd bowled only one ball!'

Warne's bag of eight wickets heralded the arrival of a new Ashes champion and the Australians completed a runaway 4–1 series win.

Having taken 72 wickets in the 1993 Test calendar year, Warne was to help himself to 70 more in 1994, his zest for the game and passion for representing Australia unquenchable. His control was remarkable, helped by the Englishmen who remained crease-bound and unsure, the selection backfiring of champions-in-decline Gooch, 41, and Gatting, 37. No fewer than six reinforcements were called for, five of the original squad forced to return home prematurely with injury. Colourful Phil Tufnell trashed a hotel room in Perth but after a visit to a psychiatric unit, discharged him-self and reported back to the team's hotel, ready for duty.

England ran a poor second from Brisbane when Warne all but finished the Test with a hat-trick, his googly just shaving an unprepared Tufnell's off-stump. Atherton was unable to hide his veterans in the field and, despite the impressive input of bubbly newcomer Darren Gough, lacked the overall arsenal to truly test the Australians. 'There are times as a captain when you feel like Canute, totally overwhelmed and powerless,' said Atherton. 'Brisbane was one of those occasions.'[5]

With opening find Michael Slater blazing his way to 176 and Warne finishing with a career-best 8-71, England was humbled and there was a repeat dose in Melbourne, where England, set 388, was bowled out for 91, McDermott finishing with 5-42 and Warne taking his first hat-trick even going back to his junior days at East Sandringham. With 20 wickets in two Tests, Warne was on target to emulate the feats of Jim Laker from 1956. The Englishmen had failed to fathom his irresistible combo of biting leg-breaks, flippers and an ever-so-occasional wrong-'un, thrown in just for the fun of it. As England's No. 11 Devon Malcolm was ambling to the crease to face Warne's hat-trick ball, non-striker Alec Stewart turned to the Melburnian and said he'd never have a better chance of taking three in three. Malcolm duly gloved a top-spinning leg-break, which was brilliantly snatched one-handed by Boon at short leg. 'I should have tried to swat it,' said big Dev.[6]

The third Test in Sydney was drawn, ensuring Australia the Ashes. But Gough was a revelation with 6-49 and a belligerent half-century in near even time. Atherton's belated second-innings declaration with Graeme Hick on 98 triggered immediate team ructions. 'At the time we were almost 450 runs on and tea was approaching. I sent word (out to the middle) that I wanted to have two goes with the new ball, one before the break and one after, so I needed to declare at least half an hour before the interval . . . in purely cricketing terms the move was justified. Hick was becalmed in the 90s. However, it had a disheartening effect on the team . . . Hick did not talk to me for the rest of the day . . . and barely spoke to me for the rest of the tour.'[7]

Malcolm didn't even have his bowling boots on when Atherton called Hick and Graham Thorpe in. 'That's a bit harsh, isn't it?' Malcolm said. 'The crowd was stunned, so was our dressing room and when poor Graeme came in, he threw his bat across the dressing room, his face deathly white.'[8]

Had Atherton declared an hour earlier, it's doubtful that Australia would have been able to save the game. A double-century opening stand between Mark Taylor and Slater and some spirited resistance from tail-enders Tim May and Warne ensured the draw, despite continuing big-hearted contributions from Fraser, who bowled just about all afternoon to finish with 5-73.

England finally broke through in Adelaide, Malcolm taking 4-39 and bowling with intimidating gusto. Set 263, Australia lost 4-23 and finished with 156, wicketkeeper Ian Healy outscoring everyone with an unbeaten 51.

Only months earlier at The Oval, Malcolm had ripped through the

South Africans with 9-57, only to miss the first Ashes Test with illness. He was seriously fast and in the middle session tore through the top-order, his dismissal first ball of Steve Waugh pivotal. 'I was torn between pitching it up or bowling a bouncer,' said Malcolm, 'and I still wasn't sure as I ran in. So I stopped halfway and as I walked back, I decided to pitch it up. The ball came into Waugh and knocked back his off-stump.'[9]

After England's day out in Adelaide, Australia hit back in Perth with a massive victory, rookie Greg Blewett making his second century in as many Tests and McDermott, bowling outswingers at near-express pace, decimating the English top-order with 6-38 on his way to 32 wickets for the series. Thorpe and Atherton were among the few to defy the Australians, Stewart starting promisingly before re-breaking his finger and being one of those forced home early. Other than in Adelaide, where he made a responsible century, Gatting was out of his depth. Like Gooch, he was batting from memory.

Having amassed 416 runs in his maiden Ashes summer in 1993, Slater had followed with 623, the most for either side. Like Ashes celebrities of yesteryear Victor Trumper and Charlie Macartney, Slater rarely allowed maidens, playing his shots from the opening overs with blissful freedom, his habit of kissing the coat of arms on his helmet on reaching three figures central in his joyful celebrations. With the Waugh twins entrenched in the top-order, Australia had developed batting depth that was to soon carry it to the world championship.

Australia's defeat of the West Indies in the decider at Sabina Park in 1995 confirmed cricket's new order. Centuries by Steve and Mark Waugh saw them rated for the first time as the top batsmen in the world.

Losses were rare home and away and a strong team came from behind in England in 1997 to retain the Ashes 3–2. Having lost at Edgbaston, Taylor's side was robbed of victory by rain at Lord's before winning the next three Tests on end. Ashes newcomers such as tall opening batsman Matthew Elliott and Ricky Ponting added flair to the top-order, while McGrath's eight wickets at Lord's was a magnificent feat that deserved more than a draw. Joined by South Australian express Jason Gillespie, McGrath took 36 wickets in the finest Ashes series of his career. What he may have lacked in intimidating pace was countered by the pressure he built with his accuracy. Having been dropped after each of his first three

Tests when he tried to emulate the outswing of McDermott, he found that his disciplined line and signature off-cutter were enough to quieten most batsmen and in time he was to surpass the deeds even of Lillee, one of his long-time key mentors at the Cricket Academy.

The measure of McGrath's importance to Australia came in 1998–99 when a shoulder operation allowed Warne to play only in the final Test, in Sydney. England under Stewart were an experienced, talented unit, yet they lost the Ashes in just thirteen days, McGrath taking 16 wickets in the first three Tests, confirming his status among the finest fast bowlers in the world. He'd had an injury-plagued 1997–98 but worked harder than ever before during the off-season in Sydney with personal trainer Kevin Chevall, known as the 'King of Pain', aiming for the tour of Pakistan and England's visit from November.

Taylor had also worked with Chevall, losing ten kilograms in the process and reaching his hundredth Test milestone in Brisbane in what was to prove to be his last Test series.

Like his predecessor Border, Taylor placed a real onus on starting the series well, and centuries to Steve Waugh and Ian Healy, as well as 71 not out from fast bowler Damien Fleming, allowed the Australians an immediate ascendancy. In the second innings, Slater motored to a 129-ball century.

With 6-85 and 1-30, McGrath also helped set the agenda, Mike Atherton falling in both innings, continuing McGrath's amazing dominance over one of England's finest. Only a fierce thunderstorm and spectacular tropical rains, which within minutes covered the 'Gabba in sheets of water, saved the English on the final day.

Before the deluge, Warne's understudy Stuart MacGill claimed three of the six wickets, including Nasser Hussain to a beautiful googly, which he totally misread. MacGill had shifted from Perth to the more spin-friendly wickets of the east and had been an immediate headliner – not always for his considerable on-field skill. 'MacGill was a real threat,' said Hussain. 'He turned the ball more than Warne and his googly was much trickier, but he still was only about three quarters the bowler Warne was, as much in character as anything else.'[10]

On a bouncy wicket assisting the bowlers in Perth, Jason Gillespie picked up seven wickets for the match including four in six balls in the English second innings: Dominic Cork (16), Alex Tudor (0), Gough (0) and last man Alan Mullally (0). Earlier he had conceded 23 runs to

Graeme Hick and Mark Ramprakash from his seventh over. Hick's 68 was the highest score in the game, but having lost six wickets in the first two hours on the opening day, England's 112 was never going to be enough to truly extend the Australians.

Justin Langer's unbeaten 179 was the highlight of the third Test in Sydney, and for the first time the Ashes were decided by Christmas.

The Melbourne Test continued the trend until the final day when Australia, set 175, collapsed for 162 to be beaten inside three days, no play being possible on Boxing Day because of persistent rain. Steve Waugh, a centurion in the first innings, was marooned on 30 not out as Dean Headley mowed through the Australian middle-order. Others in the English touring party had more ability than Headley, but only Gough possessed the courage to also bowl long spells in 100-degree heat. With 6-60 from seventeen overs, Headley outbowled even Gough and helped England to 2–1 down with a Test to play.

Warne returned for his only Test of the summer in Sydney, clearly short of match practice. MacGill, with 12 wickets, ensured Australia a comfortable win after Slater's dominant 123 out of 180 runs scored while he was at the crease. He should have been out, run out at 35, but for Peter Such inadvertently clouding the third umpire's view. Slater's rapid-fire century, his third of the summer, saw him lift his series aggregate to 460, ahead of everyone bar Steve Waugh, with almost 500.

Had England's tailenders been able to contribute more, the series may have been closer. On average the last four wickets added just 41 and they were to bat for less than an hour, figures easily surpassed by the Australian tail.

Having averaged only 22 for the series, Taylor stood down for Steve Waugh, the Australians embarking on a rare run of success that saw them win sixteen Tests on end, surpassing the deeds even of the best West Indian teams under the leadership of Clive Lloyd. They were also champions at one-day level and won the 1999 World Cup in the UK, Warne again the catalyst after the team's patchy start. The gap between Australia and the rest was widening and England seemed incapable of arresting the momentum.

Man of the decade: *Shane Warne*

The first Australian to amass 700 Test wickets, Shane Warne was named with Australia's batting colossus Don Bradman among the five *Wisden* Cricketers of the Twentieth Century. Warne's self-belief, personality and wondrous skill made him the ultimate matchwinner and central in the majority of Australia's ninety-one Test wins recorded during his 144 Tests, an extraordinary strike-rate of two wins every three matches, unequalled even by Bradman in the first 130 years of Test cricket.

From the time his fairytale first ball in Ashes cricket, a curving, fizzing leg-break darting sideways to hit Mike Gatting's off bail at Old Trafford in 1993, Warne weaved a theatrical web of mystique, spinning the ball sharply from all angles, varying his pace and trajectory, intimidating leaden-footed batsmen and even an umpire or two with a flamboyance and ferocity some felt had no place in the gentleman's game.

A headliner from the time he was expelled, aged twenty, from the Australian Cricket Academy after some boyish pranks around a pool in Darwin, Warne reigned for more than a decade, defying injury setbacks, a marriage break-up and even a twelve-month suspension for taking a banned drug, to revive an ailing art.

His passion for the game and ability to impose himself in high-pressure situations saw him slice through even premier line-ups like they were tenderfoots.

When Warne and the almost-as-celebrated Glenn McGrath were working in tandem Australia was rarely beaten, and in an unprecedented run of success amassed sixteen Test wins in a row from 1999 to 2001. On his retirement in 2007, Australia had won twelve more on end.

Warne's massive workload triggered finger and shoulder breakdowns, but back he'd bob, ready for more, immediately landing the ball on a dinner plate and encouraging the strokemakers to come at him.

Throughout his many golden years, he strutted and cavorted, spinning and ripping the ball, cornering the headlines, polarising opinions and revelling in a profile higher than any Australian cricketer of the generation. While he was a soloist supreme, Warne also embraced the toughest team situations, bowling some incredibly long and brave spells for Australia on shirtfront wickets in difficult conditions, his accuracy as prominent as his biting breaks.

The Gatting ball – dubbed 'the ball from hell' – was rated the finest of the Ashes century, alongside a Chuck Fleetwood-Smith chinaman in Adelaide in 1936–37, which dismissed the celebrated Walter Hammond, and a Syd Barnes' bender, which skittled Clem Hill during his fabled first-morning onslaught in Melbourne in 1911–12.

Warne loved the theatre of Ashes battle, claiming a career-best 8-71 in Brisbane in 1994, and a hat-trick in the very next Test, in home town Melbourne.

A decade later, on his fourth tour of England, his 40-wicket haul saw him surpass Dennis Lillee as the most prolific wicket-taker in the history of Anglo-Australian Test cricket. Coupled with almost 250 runs, it was an all-round performance of monumental proportions and kept the Australians in the contest until the very last day of the series.

Warne had intended to retire had Australia retained the Ashes in 2005, but delayed an announcement until after the Ashes had been regained, in Perth in 2006. He led the Australians onto the field in his farewell Test in Melbourne, and again in Sydney alongside McGrath and Justin Langer, also making the New Year Test their last. Warne farewelled the game with a spectacular 71 and some key wickets, including England's captain Andrew Flintoff.

Warne v. England

Season	Analysis	Wkts	Ave
1993	4-51, 4-86, 4-57, 4-102, 3-74, 3-108, 1-43, 0-63, 1-63, 5-82, 2-70, 3-78	34	25.79
1994–95	3-39, 8-71, 6-64, 3-16, 1-88, 0-48, 2-72, 2-82, 2-58, 0-11	27	20.33
1997	1-110, 0-27, 0-9, 2-47, 6-48, 3-63, 0-2, 1-53, 4-86, 3-43, 2-32, 2-57	24	24.04
1998–99	1-67, 1-43	2	55.00
2001	5-71, 3-29, 2-16, 1-58, 2-37, 6-33, 0-49, 1-58, 7-165, 4-64	31	18.70
2002–03	1-87, 3-29, 4-93, 3-36, 1-32, 2-70	14	24.78
2005	2-19, 4-64, 4-116, 6-46, 4-99, 0-74, 4-102, 4-31, 6-122, 6-124	40	19.92
2006–07	0-25, 4-124, 1-167, 4-49, 1-41, 4-115, 5-39, 2-46, 1-69, 1-23	23	30.34

Tests v. England:	36 (144 overall*)
Wickets:	195 (702)
Average:	23.25 (25.47)
Best bowling:	8-71, Brisbane, 1994–95 (8-71)
5-wicket Innings:	11 (37)
10-wicket Matches:	4 (10)
Strike-rate:	55 balls per wicket (57)
Average wkts per Test:	5.41 (4.87)

Overall statistics do not include the one-off exhibition Test between Australia and a World XI, in Sydney 2005–06.

Match of the decade: *Melbourne, 1998*

With another Ashes challenge in tatters, England miraculously won a three-day Test match by 12 runs after Australia faltered in a run chase from 130-3 to be all out for 162. Play extended past 7.30 p.m. on the final day, the tea-to-stumps session lasting three drinks' breaks and almost four hours as Dean Headley, bowling reverse swing at high pace, claimed 4-4, leaving Australia's master craftsman Steve Waugh, in at No. 5, marooned on 30 not out.

> **Match scores:** England 270 (Stewart 107, Ramprakash 63, MacGill 4-61) and 244 (Stewart 52, Hussain 50, Hick 60) defeated Australia 340 (Waugh 122 not out, Gough 5-96) and 162 (Headley 6-60) by 12 runs

Odd spot: *A duck-free zone*

David Gower enjoyed a record sequence of 119 Test innings without a duck before being dismissed by Greg Matthews without scoring in the second innings of the Christmas Test in Melbourne in 1990–91.

Looking back: *Shane Warne, on childhood days*

'Like most kids down at East Sandringham I wanted to be another Dennis Lillee and would run in as fast as I could. I didn't bowl leggies until I was eleven or twelve and struggled to land them or hit the wicket. I'd bowl a few, get smashed and revert to mediums. Luckily I stuck at it. As I got older the club captain Kim Pitt told me to be very patient with my bowling and just persist because it would be worthwhile in the end.'

> Shane Warne was to revitalise the art of leg-spin bowling. Along the way he was the key bowler in six successful Ashes defences in a row.

One for the statisticians: *A rare six*

In 190 Test innings, including 57 against England, chunky David Boon only ever hit one 6: a deliberate up-and-under cut from England's Devon Malcolm that sailed over the third-man ropes and into the crowd at The Oval in 1993.[11]

Tests 1990–91 to 1998–99

KEY: M Matches **I** Innings **NO** Not out innings **HS** Highest score **BB** Best bowling
5wI 5-wicket innings **10wM** 10-wicket match ***** Not out **#** Second innings **rh** Retired hurt

Series results

	Tests	Aust	Eng	Drawn
1990–91 (Aust)	5	3	0	2
1993 (Eng)	6	4	1	1
1994–95 (Aust)	5	3	1	1
1997 (Eng)	6	3	2	1
1998–99 (Aust)	5	3	1	1
Total	**27**	**16**	**5**	**6**
Progressive	296	117	93	86

Summary

	Runs	Wkts	Ave
Australia	15,087	405	37.25
England	13,246	495	26.75

Highest innings totals

Australia		England	
653-4 dec	Leeds 1993 (4th Test)	478-9 dec	Birmingham 1997 (1st Test)
632-4 dec	Lord's 1993 (2nd Test)	469-8 dec	Sydney 1990–91 (3rd Test)
518	Sydney 1990–91 (3rd Test)		
501-9 dec	Leeds 1997 (4th Test)		
485	Brisbane 1998–99 (1st Test)		
477	Birmingham 1997 (1st Test)#		

Lowest completed innings totals

Australia		England	
104	The Oval 1997 (6th Test)#	77	Lord's 1997 (2nd Test)
116	Sydney 1994–95 (3rd Test)	92	Melbourne 1994–95 (2nd Test)#
118	Birmingham 1997 (1st Test)	112	Perth 1998–99 (2nd Test)
		113	Brisbane 1990–91 (1st Test)#
		123	Perth 1994–95 (5th Test)#

Leading run scorers

	M	I	NO	Runs	HS	Ave	100	50
Australia								
M. E. Waugh	24	43	4	1,774	140	45.48	4	10
S. R. Waugh	25	43	11	1,731	157*	54.09	5	8
M. A. Taylor	27	50	1	1,657	129	33.81	4	10
M. J. Slater	16	30	0	1,499	176	49.96	7	3
D. C. Boon	16	29	4	1,331	164*	53.24	5	4
I. A. Healy	27	42	7	1,166	134	33.31	2	6
A. R. Border	11	16	2	714	200*	51.00	1	4
G. S. Blewett	8	14	1	630	125	48.46	3	2
England								
M. A. Atherton	26	52	2	1,606	105	32.12	1	13
G. A. Gooch	15	32	0	1,344	133	42.00	3	9
A. J. Stewart	24	48	5	1,259	107	29.27	1	8
G. P. Thorpe	15	29	4	1,213	138	48.52	3	8
N. Hussain	15	29	3	1,022	207	39.30	2	5
G. A. Hick	10	20	1	669	98*	35.21	–	6
M. R. Ramprakash	8	16	2	615	72	43.92	–	6

Hundreds

Australia (36)		England (14)	
7	M. J. Slater	3	G. A. Gooch
5	D. C. Boon		G. P. Thorpe
	S. R. Waugh	2	D. I. Gower
4	M. A. Taylor		N. Hussain
	M. E. Waugh	1	M. A. Atherton
3	G. S. Blewett		M. A. Butcher
2	M. T. G. Elliott		M. W. Gatting
	I. A. Healy		A. J. Stewart
1	A. R. Border		
	J. L. Langer		
	G. R. J. Matthews		
	R. T. Ponting		

Highest individual scores

Australia

200*	A. R. Border at Leeds 1993 (4th Test)
199	M. T. G. Elliott at Leeds 1997 (4th Test)
179*	J. L. Langer at Adelaide 1998–99 (3rd Test)
176	M. J. Slater at Brisbane 1994–95 (1st Test)
164*	D. C. Boon at Lord's 1993 (2nd Test)
157*	S. R. Waugh at Leeds 1993 (4th Test)
152	M. J. Slater at Lord's 1993 (2nd Test)

England

207	N. Hussain at Birmingham 1997 (1st Test)
138	G. P. Thorpe at Birmingham 1997 (1st Test)

Century in each innings

108 and 116	S. R. Waugh (Aust) at Manchester 1997 (3rd Test)

500 runs in a series

	Season	M	I	NO	Runs	HS	Ave	100	50
Australia									
M. J. Slater	1994–95	5	10	0	623	176	62.30	3	1
M. T. G. Elliott	1997	6	10	0	556	199	55.60	2	2
D. C. Boon	1993	6	10	2	555	164*	69.37	3	1
M. E. Waugh	1993	6	10	1	550	137	61.11	1	5
D. C. Boon	1990–91	5	9	2	530	121	75.71	1	3
Also note:									
S. R. Waugh	1998–99	5	10	4	498	122*	83.00	2	2
England									
G. A. Gooch	1993	6	12	0	673	133	56.08	2	4
M. A. Atherton	1993	6	12	0	533	99	46.08	–	6

Hundred partnerships

Australia (38)

Partnerships of 150 and over:

332*	5th	A. R. Border and S. R. Waugh at Leeds 1993 (4th Test)
268	5th	M. T. G. Elliott and R. T. Ponting at Leeds 1997 (4th Test)
260	1st	M. A. Taylor and M. J. Slater at Lord's 1993 (2nd Test)
208	1st	M. A. Taylor and M. J. Slater at Sydney 1994–95 (3rd Test)#
203	6th	S. R. Waugh and G. S. Blewett at Perth 1994–95 (5th Test)#
194	2nd	M. A. Taylor and G. S. Blewett at Birmingham 1997 (1st Test)#
190	4th	M. E. Waugh and S. R. Waugh at Sydney 1998–99 (5th Test)
187*	3rd	G. R. Marsh and D. C. Boon at Melbourne 1990–91 (2nd Test)#
187	6th	S. R. Waugh and I. A. Healy at Brisbane 1998–99 (1st Test)
183	3rd	M. J. Slater and M. E. Waugh at Perth 1994–95 (5th Test)
182	3rd	M. J. Slater and M. E. Waugh at Brisbane 1994–95 (1st Test)
180*	6th	S. R. Waugh and I. A. Healy at Manchester 1993 (1st Test)#
175	3rd	D. C. Boon and M. E. Waugh at Lord's 1993 (2nd Test)
174	6th	G. S. Blewett and I. A. Healy at Adelaide 1994–95 (4th Test)
171	6th	M. E. Waugh and G. R. J. Matthews at Adelaide 1990–91 (4th Test)
162	2nd	M. J. Slater and J. L. Langer at Brisbane 1998–99 (1st Test)#
157*	1st	G. R. Marsh and M. A. Taylor at Brisbane 1990–91 (1st Test)#
153	6th	M. E. Waugh and S. R. Waugh at Birmingham 1993 (5th Test)

England (21)

Partnerships of 150 and over:

288	4th	N. Hussain and G. P. Thorpe at Birmingham 1997 (1st Test)
203	1st	G. A. Gooch and M. A. Atherton at Adelaide 1990–91 (4th Test)#
174	4th	M. A. Atherton and J. P. Crawley at Sydney 1994–95 (3rd Test)
162	1st	M. A. Butcher and M. A. Atherton at Lord's 1997 (2nd Test)#
160	3rd	G. A. Hick and G. P. Thorpe at Brisbane 1994–95 (1st Test)#
158	5th	G. P. Thorpe and M. R. Ramprakash at Perth 1994–95 (5th Test)#
150	6th	G. A. Gooch and G. P. Thorpe at Nottingham 1993 (3rd Test)

Leading wicket-takers

	Tests	Balls	Mdns	Runs	Wkts	Ave	BB	5wI	10wM
Australia									
S. K. Warne	18	5,833	338	2,113	87	24.28	8-71	4	1
G. D. McGrath	13	3,081	136	1,422	66	21.54	8-38	3	–
C. J. McDermott	9	2,271	79	1,161	50	23.22	8-97	6	1
M. G. Hughes	10	2,631	116	1,210	46	26.30	5-92	1	–
P. R. Reiffel	7	1,517	59	689	30	22.96	6-71	3	–
B. A. Reid	4	1,081	49	432	27	16.00	7-52	2	1
S. C. G. MacGill	4	1,112	33	478	27	17.70	7-50	2	1
D. W. Fleming	7	1,423	59	666	26	25.61	5-46	1	–
England									
D. Gough	12	2,978	101	1,623	57	28.47	6-49	3	–
D. E. Malcolm	14	3,204	101	1,730	41	42.19	4-39	–	–
A. R. C. Fraser	9	2,326	63	1,060	37	28.64	6-82	3	–
P. C. R. Tufnell	11	2,996	124	1,199	35	34.25	7-66	2	1
A. R. Caddick	9	1,997	55	1,122	29	38.68	5-42	2	–
P. M. Such	7	2,140	88	864	27	32.00	6-67	2	–
P. A. J. DeFreitas	8	2,067	70	1002	25	40.08	4-56	–	–

Five wickets in an innings

Australia (28)		England (14)	
6	C. J. McDermott	3	A. R. C. Fraser
4	S. K. Warne		D. Gough
3	G. D. McGrath	2	A. R. Caddick
	P. R. Reiffel		P. M. Such
2	J. N. Gillespie		P. C. R. Tufnell
	S. C. G. MacGill	1	D. W. Headley
	B. A. Reid		A. D. Mullally
1	T. M. Alderman		
	D. W. Fleming		
	M. G. Hughes		
	M. S. Kasprowicz		
	T. B. A. May		
	M. E. Waugh		

Best individual bowling

Australia

8-38	G. D. McGrath at Lord's 1997 (2nd Test)
8-71	S. K. Warne at Brisbane 1994–95 (1st Test)#
8-97	C. J. McDermott at Sydney 1990–91 (5th Test)
7-36	M. S. Kasprowicz at The Oval 1997 (6th Test)#
7-37	J. N. Gillespie at Leeds 1997 (4th Test)
7-50	S. C. G. MacGill at Sydney 1998–99 (5th Test)#
7-51	B. A. Reid at Melbourne 1990–91 (2nd Test)#
7-76	G. D. McGrath at The Oval 1997 (6th Test)
6-38	C. J. McDermott at Perth 1994–95 (5th Test)
6-47	T. M. Alderman at Brisbane 1990–91 (1st Test)
6-48	S. K. Warne at Manchester 1997 (3rd Test)
6-53	C. J. McDermott at Brisbane 1994–95 (1st Test)
6-64	S. K. Warne at Melbourne 1994–95 (2nd Test)
6-71	P. R. Reiffel at Birmingham 1993 (5th Test)
6-85	G. D. McGrath at Brisbane 1998–99 (1st Test)
6-97	B. A. Reid at Melbourne 1990–91 (2nd Test)

England

7-66	P. C. R. Tufnell at The Oval 1997 (6th Test)
6-49	D. Gough at Sydney 1994–95 (3rd Test)
6-60	D. W. Headley at Melbourne 1998–99 (4th Test)#
6-67	P. M. Such at Manchester 1993 (1st Test)
6-82	A. R. C. Fraser at Melbourne 1990–91 (2nd Test)

10 wickets in a match

Australia (4)

13-148	B. A. Reid (6-97 and 7-51) at Melbourne 1990–91 (2nd Test)
12-107	S. C. G. MacGill (5-57 and 7-50) at Sydney 1998–99 (5th Test)
11-110	S. K. Warne (3-39 and 8-71) at Brisbane 1994–95 (1st Test)
11-157	C. J. McDermott (8-97 and 3-60) at Sydney 1990–91 (5th Test)

England (1)

11-93	P. C. R. Tufnell (7-66 and 4-27) at The Oval 1997 (6th Test)

Hat-tricks

S. K. Warne (Aust) at Melbourne 1994–95 (2nd Test)#
    (P. A. J. DeFreitas lbw, D. Gough c I. A. Healy, D. E. Malcolm c D. C. Boon)

D. Gough (Eng) at Sydney 1998–99 (5th Test)
    (I. A. Healy c W. K. Hegg, S. C. G. MacGill b, C. R. Miller b)

25 wickets in a series

	Season	Tests	Balls	Mdns	Runs	Wkts	Ave	BB	5wl	10wM
Australia										
G.D. McGrath	1997	6	1,499	67	701	36	19.47	8-38	2	–
S.K. Warne	1993	6	2,639	178	877	34	25.79	5-82	1	–
C.J. McDermott	1994–95	5	1,397	56	675	32	21.09	6-38	4	–
M.G. Hughes	1993	6	1,778	78	845	31	27.25	5-92	1	–
B.A. Reid	1990–91	4	1,081	49	432	27	16.00	7-52	2	1
S.C.G. MacGill	1998–99	4	1,094	33	478	27	17.70	7-50	2	1
S.K. Warne	1994–95	5	1,537	84	549	27	20.33	8-71	2	1
Also note:										
G.D. McGrath	1998–99	5	1,180	53	492	24	20.50	6-85	1	–
S.K. Warne	1997	6	1,423	69	577	24	24.04	6-48	1	–
England										
No instance – best:										
A.R. Caddick	1997	5	1,079	27	634	24	26.51	5-42	2	–

Leading wicketkeepers

	Tests	Dismissals	Catches	Stumpings
Australia				
I.A. Healy	27	121	109	12
England				
A.J. Stewart†	17	54	52	2
S.J. Rhodes	5	21	20	1
R.C. Russell	3	10	9	1

† A.J. Stewart held another four catches in five Tests in which he did not keep wicket.

Leading fieldsmen

	Tests	Catches		Tests	Catches
Australia			**England**		
M.A. Taylor	27	41	G.A. Hick	10	20
M.E. Waugh	24	34	G.P. Thorpe	15	18
S.K. Warne	18	13	M.A. Atherton	26	14
S.R. Waugh	25	13	N. Hussain	15	14
G.S. Blewett	8	12	M.A. Butcher	10	13
A.R. Border	11	12			
D.C. Boon	16	11			

Captains

	Tests	Won	Lost	Drawn	Toss won
Australia					
M. A. Taylor	16	9	4	3	12
A. R. Border	11	8	1	2	5
England					
M. A. Atherton	13	4	7	2	6
G. A. Gooch	8	0	6	2	4
A. J. Stewart	5	1	3	1	0
A. J. Lamb	1	0	1	0	0

Most appearances

Australia (35 players)		England (46 players)	
27	I. A. Healy	26	M. A. Atherton
	M. A. Taylor	24	A. J. Stewart
25	S. R. Waugh	15	G. A. Gooch
24	M. E. Waugh		N. Hussain
18	S. K. Warne		G. P. Thorpe
16	D. C. Boon	14	D. E. Malcolm
	M. J. Slater		

Matthew Hayden made five centuries in six Tests in Melbourne from 2001. *Clive Mackinnon*

2000s
A HEAVENLY FAREWELL

•••

'Whoever is writing my scripts is doing a great job. It was a special day in my life . . . one of the best days I have ever had.'

Just as Shane Warne made it trendy to again bowl wrist spinners, Adam Gilchrist forever refashioned the role of the wicketkeeper with his explosive middle-order batting skills complementing glovework of the highest calibre.

Choosing to shift from one side of Australia to the other to gain more recognition, Gilchrist was pivotal in Australia's eighth consecutive Ashes victory in 2001.

Starting the first Ashes summer of the new Millennium with an exhilarating 152 at Edgbaston and 90 at Lord's, Gilchrist's 54 in the following Test at Trent Bridge was priceless in the context of a low-scoring game. Having bowled England out cheaply on the opening day, the Australians also collapsed and faced a sizeable first-innings deficit. 'We were in trouble,' recalls Gilchrist. '(Andy) Caddick and (Alex) Tudor got a real roll on (Australia tumbling from 48-0 to 94-5). We'd been going along nicely, too, before all of a sudden bang, bang, bang. We also lost "Marto" (Damien Martyn) and "Warnie" that night and Brett (Lee) soon afterwards at the start of the second day.'

For the first time all summer, England had the edge before Jason

Gillespie, in at No. 10, and Gilchrist added 66 to ensure the Australians a narrow lead. 'I couldn't believe how positively "Dizzy" (Gillespie) strode out to the wicket and took control of the situation,' Gilchrist says. 'It was if he was the senior member of the partnership. We sorted out our goals into 10-run lots and snatched the lead.'

Just over a day later, the Australians had bowled England out a second time for just 162 and recorded a seven-wicket win on their way to a 4–1 series victory, continuing their unprecedented run of success against the old enemy.

'People looking back at the series scoreline would think it was one-sided,' Gilchrist says. 'But it wasn't. England had very good form coming into the series and at times played very well. It's just that we played better.'

In the opening Test, noted for Gilchrist's spectacular 22-run assault from one Mark Butcher over, the Australian left-hander added 63 for the last wicket with Glenn McGrath, McGrath's share being a single run. Gilchrist finished with a Test-best 152 after centuries from captain Steve Waugh and Martyn. For the summer, Gilchrist was to amass 340 runs at an average of 68, his runs coming at almost a run a ball. He also claimed twenty-four catches and two stumpings, confirming his status as one of cricket's elite all-rounders.

Gilchrist had a lengthy apprenticeship, Ian Healy's bulldog determination and sheer class for years repelling all suitors. Gilchrist was bordering twenty-eight when finally selected. With 81 on debut against Pakistan at the 'Gabba followed by 149 not out in his second Test, in Hobart, Gilchrist began one of the great careers, including his first ninety Tests uninterrupted. When once a wicketkeeper was chosen purely for his skill with the gloves, Gilchrist ensured that Test wicketkeepers also had to be accomplished batsmen.

With Glenn McGrath and Warne weaving their usual Ashes web, each taking more than 30 wickets, and the Waugh twins and the enigmatic Martyn tallying six 100s between them, the Australians played aggressively with the bat and went out of their way to isolate the batting team and make it a hostile mid-pitch environment. Under the Waugh blueprint, it was always eleven against two. Waugh dubbed it 'mental disintegration' and his two trumps Warne and McGrath were masters of the confrontational, invariably targeting the opposition's leading player. England's Nasser Hussain may have been one of the world's quality batsmen and one of the few to score a double hundred against the Australians, but he was known for over-complicating his own game and becoming introspective, frailties quickly seized upon by the Australians. Standing at slip, Warne would lead the chorus. 'C'mon lads,' he'd say, 'let's get Mr Popular out' or 'let's get dodgy technique out.'[1]

Indian champion Sachin Tendulkar was about the only frontliner in the world who commanded total respect from the Australians. All chirping tended to cease when The King was in.

The Australians won sixteen Tests in a row before an epic Rahul Dravid–V.V.S. Laxman partnership at Kolkata changed the series fortunes in 2001, ending Waugh's dream of a hoodoo-breaking victory in India. It was the only hiccup as Australia thrashed everyone else, home and away, including the Englishmen yet again.

In 2002–03, Hussain was in charge of England's wintertime Ashes campaign but injuries and withdrawals conspired against him from the start, the losses of Darren Gough, Graeme Thorpe and Andrew Flintoff proving insurmountable. 'They just kept pulling away from us when the pressure was on,' said veteran tourist Alec Stewart. 'It was still no consolation to be beaten by such a fantastic side . . . I could only hope that in time the empty feeling would pass.'[2]

Flintoff had played through pain as the English forced a draw with India in a four-Test home series preceding their winter away and, after delaying a hernia operation, missed all the 2002–03 Ashes Tests and played only in the last of the one-day internationals.

Expressman Simon Jones, a genuine matchwinner with his ability to bend the ball late at pace, badly injured his knee in Brisbane. After Hussain won the toss and bowled, English fans watched in horror as Australia began with 364-2. 'I was never involved in a close series against Australia,' Hussain said. 'And I went into each one almost with a feeling of "here we go again." '[3]

Australia was to retain the Ashes in eleven days, an unprecedented domination. In 1990–91 and 1998–99, the Australians had re-won the Ashes in just thirteen days, and it took fifteen in 1994–95. Even Stewart conceded that England had won only three sessions during the first three Tests.[4] The gulf between the sides was widening. 'We turned up for Brisbane for the first Test under-prepared,' said Hussain. 'I was getting very sceptical about our chances of ever bowling Australia out on their pitches but there was a good covering of grass on the 'Gabba pitch and the nets did a bit, so maybe I thought, just maybe, there might be some hope of getting early wickets. In the game before against Queensland, they had batted first and got 500 for three on a flat wicket. Those figures terrified me, so that green grass seemed like a lifeline. Without my frontline bowlers, I was clutching at straws. The day before the Test I was looking at the wicket and bumped into (ex-player and writer) Derek Pringle who, as if he was reading my mind, told me not to get suckered into bowling first and that I had to bat if I won the toss. What did he know?'[5]

Last time Australia had been sent in by England at the 'Gabba, they'd made 600. Hussain duly won the toss – and bowled. There was a deathly silence as he told his players of his decision. 'I could see Andrew Caddick's face drop straight away at the prospect of being thrust into the spotlight,' said Hussain. 'By the fifth or sixth over nothing was happening and I could feel the world closing in on me. I thought to myself: "Oh God, Nass, what have you done?"'[6] Australia made almost 500 on their way to a 4–1 series victory. Hardly a bouncer was bowled in the first session as the Australians continued to bully and intimidate. It wasn't until the Ashes had been decided that England forced a Test into a fifth day.

In the circumstances, Hussain's opening 51 at the 'Gabba was commendable, the Australians quick to remind him, however, of his faux pas at the toss and how it had been a good one to win! The Englishmen were outed for 325 and 79. Their campaign was in tatters and there were still four Tests to go.

Without Michael Vaughan, who was to make three centuries in the next four Tests, the tourists could easily have lost every match. So authoritative was the 28-year-old Yorkshireman that by Melbourne, Hussain reckoned he 'was playing like God'.

The Australians had to bat only once in Adelaide and Perth on their way to emphatic victories. In Perth, a skidding bouncer from expressman Brett Lee cannoned into Alex Tudor's visor and gashed him just above his eye. Lee saw the blood and turned deathly pale and kept asking Tudor: 'Are you okay, mate?'[7] Lee almost cleaned up Steve Harmison, too, second ball with a bouncer on his way to five wickets for the match. He'd been 12th man behind Queenslander Andy Bichel in the opening two Tests and was itching to make an impression. 'Brett was seriously quick that day,' said Stewart, 'reminiscent of Wasim and Waqar at Old Trafford in '92 and Allan Donald at Johannesburg in '95. He had the Fremantle doctor [Perth's afternoon breeze] behind him as he roared in. It was the quickest, bounciest wicket I had batted on'.[8]

Ricky Ponting had begun with back-to-back centuries, continuing his brilliant calendar year form which had also carried him to 100s in Cape Town, Colombo and Sharjah. Years earlier when he was a first-timer at the Cricket Academy in Adelaide, Rod Marsh soon identified him as the most talented teenage batsman he'd ever seen. Fast bowler Paul Wilson, who later played for Australia, was new and keen to impress and bowled a bouncer with all the energy he could muster. Rather than being intimidated, 15-year-old Ponting rocked onto the back foot and played a pull shot right out of the screws, convincing Marsh that he was watching a champion in the making.

The kid from working-class Mowbray, just outside Launceston, was so good he had secured his first bat sponsorship with Kookaburra as a 13-year-old and played for Tasmania at an even younger age than the celebrated David Boon. After being dropped from Australia's Ashes team in mid-summer in 1998–99, he was hungry to succeed, and throughout 2002–03 displayed rare poise and purpose.

Matthew Hayden, too, had begun with twin centuries in Brisbane and was to make another century in Melbourne, beginning a run of five 100s in six Boxing Day Tests. He'd also taken a remarkable catch at short gully in Brisbane when he turned his back on a full-blooded Stewart cut shot and caught the rebound! Waugh had been one of the most instrumental in Hayden's rebirth as an elite player and after his opening double of 197 and 103 claimed him to 'be batting better than anyone in the history of the game.'

About the only top-line Australian struggling to assert himself was Waugh himself. His brother Mark had been dropped at the start of the summer and with Steve making only modest contributions in each of the first three Tests, the pressure was mounting. He was becoming growingly tetchy, too, about continually having to discuss his future plans.

Two days before the Christmas Test in Melbourne, where it had all begun for Waugh seventeen seasons earlier, he marched into the on-ground nets to standing applause. Justin Langer was marking his guard in an adjoining net and with an impish grin said: 'Is that [applause] for you or for me, mate?'

Waugh had steeled himself to be strong, positive and assertive[9] and on the recall of Harmison, England's quickest bowler, he was amazed to see Hussain giving Langer an easy single to a spread-eagled field to get Waugh back on strike. 'You smart-arse prick!'[10] Waugh said, before backing away to the first steepling Harmison delivery and lifting it flamboyantly over the top of point, beginning a rollicking innings and a memorable Christmas–New Year period that forever stamped him as one of the greats of Australian cricket. 'If their plan was to humiliate me, then I wanted to counterpunch as quickly as possible,' said Waugh,[11] who raced to 50 at a run a ball.

Equally commanding was Langer, who amassed a Test-best 250 including centuries on each of the first and second days. He lifted Richard Dawson into the bleachers over long-on to reach his first century and without bothering to run, stood in mid-pitch with his arms raised in triumph to the acclaim of almost 65 000 first-day fans.

Vaughan's second-innings century was outstanding before he was neatly caught at slip by debutant Martin Love. It was one of four catches taken by Love, including three from MacGill, who once again was a prolific wicket-taker in the absence of the injured Warne.

With the game all but settled, Harmison and Caddick led a late revival, Australia losing five wickets in the pursuit of 107. Had anyone bothered to appeal, Waugh would have been out almost immediately, caught behind, adding an extra edge to the tense finish.

England was to finally breakthrough in Sydney, Waugh saying goodbye to Ashes cricket in fairytale fashion with a century from the very last ball of the opening day, from Dawson. Some explosive hitting from Gilchrist was totally overshadowed as Waugh struck eighteen 4s in an unforgettable three hours, including the last past cover from the very last ball of the day. Waugh's bat speed had always been a key to his game and he rifled this one through the in-field before being hugged by an equally delighted Gilchrist. The reception was phenomenal. 'It had been a boyhood dream to hit the last ball for 6 ever since the 1974–75 season, when on television I saw Doug Walters hit Bob Willis for 6 at the WACA [ground],' Waugh said. 'To do something like that, passing 10,000 Test runs and equalling the Don on twenty-nine Test match centuries added up to the perfect day in cricket terms.'[12]

Afterwards, Waugh appeared at the press conference at the SCG's indoor nets with his baggy green cap still on, to be greeted with applause from dozens of English and Australian media representatives, who were as thrilled as the 45,000 fans present to be part of history. It was the ideal time to retire, but Waugh was insistent he wanted to keep touring and playing – even if it was to be only for one more year.

Hussain, Stewart and Caddick were finished as Ashes participants as England went into a rebuilding phase and looked to young lions such as Flintoff and the fit-again Jones to launch a revival.

Those querying Shane Warne's inclusion alongside Don Bradman among *Wisden's* Five Cricketers of the Century were silenced forever in 2005 as the charismatic leg-spinner enjoyed his finest moments in the game.

Warne amassed 40 wickets in what proved to be his last English tour – yet played on the losing side!

Having held the Ashes for a record sixteen years, the Australians began brilliantly at Lord's, only to be outplayed for the rest of the summer. The English crowds were overjoyed to see their team victorious at last. Some, to their discredit, misbehaved, Warne-bashing high on the agenda, especially at Edgbaston where many in the crowd wore fancy dress, watched little of the game and delivered stinging salvos and taunts at a rapidity matched only by their intake of pints.

After his most-public split from his wife, Simone, father-of-three Warne was a prime target for a vociferous, out-of-control Barmy Army. From apparently harmless ditties such as 'You All Live in a Convict Colony' (sung to the tune of 'Yellow Submarine'), the Army slipped into the gutter with their particularly tasteless 'Where's your Missus Gone? – Far, Far, Away' (to 'Chirpy Chirpy Cheep Cheep').

No matter what one's stance was on Warne's *joie de vivre*, he didn't deserve the abuse that at times was venomous, leaving a most regrettable black mark on what proved to be the greatest summer of all.

With Australia all but out of the second Test, Warne launched a stunning counter-attack of his own, hitting the English where it counted most: on the scoreboard. In taking 6-46 from 23.1 overs in England's second innings, Warne stood taller than ever before, in his own unsinkable zone, using the taunts as motivation. Far from being demoralised by the rowdies, he strutted and cavorted, spinning and ripping his leg-breaks and enjoying the theatre, as bizarre as it was. As he ran through the English middle-order one by one, he'd eye the rowdies in the Eric Hollies Stand and doff his hat. Even under the most intense personal fire, he was still cricket's magnetic man, the showman supreme.

Even as a rookie unsure of his status within Australia's XI, he'd wanted to take the wicket that turned the game. At Edgbaston he grabbed 10 and backed it up with a gallant cameo with the bat the following morning, which all but snatched an incredible victory in one of the closest Ashes Tests of them all.

Throughout 2005, Warne imposed his will on the series like no one before, not even the Don. While he had some mates – most notably Glenn McGrath at Lord's, Brett Lee at Edgbaston and Ricky Ponting at Old Trafford – no one since Steve Waugh in the Windies in 1995 had been so important to Australia's bottom line. Single-handedly Warne lifted Australia, forcing the grandfather of all Ashes finishes at Edgbaston, stunning England at Trent Bridge and giving Test cricket a rare run, even in the soccer-crazy tabloids.

With McGrath struggling with his fitness, Warne was Australia's go-to man and while the English frontliners such as Flintoff and flamboyant newcomer Kevin Pietersen had their moments against him, none conquered. In surpassing his fabulous figures from his dreamy debut tour in 1993, Warne substituted science for spin and turned back the clock with his batting to be Australia's outstanding player. It was an extraordinary effort from one of the game's all-time greats and ensured he would, in the short term, remain ahead of Sri Lanka's Muthiah Muralidaran in the race for most Test wickets.

In winning the Ashes 2–1, England was superb, the Aussies flattered by the scoreline. A fit-again Jones struck at a rate of a wicket every thirty-three balls while Flintoff was similarly unstoppable with 402 runs and 24 wickets. Both swerved the ball at high speed while Harmison was menacing with his bounce and in-slant. The South African-born Pietersen survived the ignominy of three dropped catches at Lord's to amass more runs than anybody, including a belligerent 158 at The Oval that ended any chance the Australians had of squaring the series. It was an extraordinary, rejuvenating summer, the best in more than 100 years.

Just eighteen months later, the teams met again, the expectations for a classic confrontation between the two elite elevens in the world prompting incredible interest. More than twenty thousand visitors from Britain joined thousands on holidays from around Australia, their tickets having been paid for many months in advance.

Instead of a contest, however, they witnessed a walk-over, the 2006–07 Englishmen under a stand-in captain in Flintoff outgunned from the first Test in Brisbane. Their gloom was complete in the last Test in Sydney where they became only the second English touring team in more than eighty years to lose 5–0.

Injuries to key players may have conspired against England even before the first toss, but the planning and selection was mediocre and the drive and desire of the Australians underrated.

The pre-tour withdrawals of Vaughan and Jones and Marcus Trescothick's illness robbed the tourists of three of their finest. Harmison was so rusty that his first ball of the series was taken by Flintoff at second slip. It wasn't until the third Test in Perth that he bowled with any consistency or zip. Inexplicably, Ashley Giles was preferred to exciting newcomer Monty Panesar, despite not having played a first-class game for a year, and rookies Alastair Cook, Ian Bell and Paul Collingwood saddled with senior top-four responsibility against the most intimidating attack in the world.

England rarely won two sessions in a row, let alone three, but the public's appetite for the contest remained at a record level, the pre-selling of tickets leading to sell-outs at every venue. In Melbourne, an Ashes record 89,155 jammed the Melbourne Cricket Ground on Boxing Day, the prospect of witnessing local hero Shane Warne's 700th Test wicket particularly enticing. Only days before, Warne and his long-time sidekick Glenn McGrath had announced their intention to retire at the conclusion of the series, Warne saying he would have retired twelve months earlier had Australia still held the Ashes.

Justin Langer was another to farewell Test cricket in Sydney, having achieved more, he said, than he could have ever hoped. It was fitting that he began so productively in Brisbane with 82 and 100 not out, ensuring his place for the entire campaign. Ponting, too, was in ominous early form and was to be named man-of-the-match in both the first and second Tests with 256 runs in Brisbane and 191 in Adelaide.

Having agreed to just one first-class game and a two-day fourteen-a-side match as preparation, England conceded 600 runs in the Australian first innings and only just managed to force the game into a fifth day.

In Adelaide, however, on a heavenly wicket for batsmen, the tourists started with 551-6 declared, Collingwood making 206 and Pietersen 158 in a record stand. 'K.P.' had been likened to a runaway train by the Australians in 2005 and they still hadn't found the secret of restricting his strokeplay.

The Australians replied with 513 and the game seemed certain to be drawn, especially with England 59-1 in their second innings and leading by almost 100 with just a day to play. However, once opener Andrew Strauss was unluckily given out caught at the wicket in the first forty minutes, the Englishmen froze, scoring just 30 runs in the first session for the loss of 4 frontline wickets. A revived Warne triggered havoc, bowling around the wicket direct into footmarks at the river end, the dismissal of Pietersen, bowled around his legs sweeping, as important a wicket as any in the series.

Set 168 from a maximum of 36 overs, Australia won with three overs to spare, an ecstatic Ponting proclaiming the match as the best Test he'd ever been involved in. Warne's menace had been diluted early by the lifeless pitch, yet three days after taking one for 1-67, he again proved to be Australia's trump, his figures on the final day a remarkable 4-29 from twenty-seven unchanged overs, from the northern end. When Mike Hussey made the winning hit through the covers, the Australians charged down the members' steps onto the ground in wild celebrations normally seen only at the end of a summer. Ponting had his arms raised in triumph and spoke about 'the remarkable cricket' Australia had played. The sudden retirement of the enigmatic Damien Martyn was the only low point for the Aussies, but they won in Perth anyway to reclaim the Ashes, Hussey's double of 74 not out and 103 increasing his Test average to almost 80. Playing in his first Ashes Test series at the age of thirty-one, Hussey replaced Martyn at No. 4 and, following some early fortune, played with calm assuredness. Gilchrist's 57-ball century was the fastest by an Australian in Test cricket, his 162-run stand with fellow centurion Michael Clarke coming from just twenty-one overs. Even Panesar, who had taken five wickets in the first innings, was unable to rein in the out-of-control Gilchrist.

A major problem all summer for the English was the failure of their bottom five to make the important late-order runs the Australians took for granted. In Perth, Pietersen defied the trend, batting brilliantly with the tail to make 70 and helping the last five to add 108. He was to be marooned, however, in the second innings, on 60, as the last five wickets tumbled for just 14.

Set 557 to win and remain in the fight for the Ashes, England was outed for 350, Cook topscoring with his first century in Ashes cricket and fourth overall. At twenty-one, no Englishman had made more Test tons at a younger age. His partner Strauss, so dominant in 2005, struggled without the depressed Trescothick, who had gone home within the first fortnight. Strauss reached his only half-century in Melbourne on Boxing Day. Having battled for almost 200 minutes for 50, he became Warne's 700th Test victim when he was bowled hitting across a leg-break, the Australian responding by running off towards mid-off with his arm in the air before being engulfed by overjoyed teammates.

Statisticians had been squabbling for two summers whether to include the exhibition Test in October 2005 between Australia and Rest of the World XI in Sydney in their records. The International Cricket Council, looking to raise their credibility after years of maladministration, said yes but Bill Frindall, Charlie Wat and others, with a lifetime in the game, disagreed, saying that the Rest of the World team was multinational and true Tests should only be considered as those contested between two countries. Adding to the statistician's ire was that the Rest of the World XI was not representative of the best available players, having been chosen many months earlier – and on reputation, rather than form. While Australia played its No. 1 side, the game barely lasted over three days and was a monumental mismatch.[13]

Warne had taken six wickets in this game, and if these were ignored, Strauss's wicket was only his 694th and *not* his 700th. In a remarkable opening to his farewell Melbourne Test, Warne was to take four more wickets, to finish with 5-39. Afterwards, he admitted he had been worried that he'd even get a bowl. 'The wicket was seaming around a bit. I was hoping to bowl a few overs at the tail,' he said in a press conference. 'Whoever is writing my scripts is doing a great job. It was a special day in my life ... one of the best days I have ever had.'

England's 159 was its lowest starting score in a Test at the MCG since 1894–95[14] and while batting was tough, the Englishmen failed the examination. For once the Australian top-order also floundered, and at 5-84 the game was evenly poised before Matthew Hayden and Andrew Symonds went on a run-a-minute spree, adding 279 for the sixth wicket to wrest control again. The beneficiary of Shane Watson's continued fitness problems, Symonds hadn't expected to play any of the Ashes Tests. Sledged by Pietersen as being little more than 'a specialist fieldsman', Symonds benefited from some nonsensical field placings to score singles at will and settle himself for a late-afternoon onslaught. He reached his maiden Test 100 with a huge 6 down the ground, twelve rows back into the members. Having entered the 90s, Symonds wondered if he should get the remaining runs for his 100 in singles, 'or give him [Paul Collingwood] some Larry Dooley'.[15]

'I went with Larry Dooley,' he said. 'I knew I'd got it. I didn't see it go for 6 or 4, but I knew I'd got it.'

Hayden provided the backbone of the innings, and while less than a year younger than Langer, said he had no plans just yet of following the other veterans into retirement, especially with the prospect of a World Cup recall on offer.

Australia's lead was 260 and England collapsed again to be beaten by an innings in just three days. Brett Lee, Stuart Clark and Warne shared the wickets, Warne taking out two tailenders with his flipper and leaving the MCG arm-in-arm with McGrath to a tumultuous reception.

Flintoff spoke passionately between the Tests, saying England had no intention of returning home 5–0 losers. But all the momentum was with Australia, the withdrawal of big-hearted Matthew Hoggard with a side strain a huge blow given his prominence in England's Ashes triumph of 2005.

More than 40,000 attended each of the four days in Sydney, including 46,000 on the first day, as Ponting stepped aside to allow McGrath, Warne and Langer to lead the team onto the field.

England's 291 was competitive, highlighted by Flintoff's 89, but the Australian tail again showed its mettle, 190-5 becoming 393 all out with Warne making an enterprising 71 from just 65 balls including a 4 and a 6 from the first two balls of his innings. When a gloved catch behind was missed later in the Panesar over by umpire Aleem Dar, Warne continued his assault, revelling in a high-octane, mid-pitch argy-bargy with aggrieved slipsman Collingwood. Warne questioned Collingwood's right to have received an MBE in 2005, after he'd been selected in only the last of the five Tests and failed in both innings. 'It's embarrassing you getting an MBE for getting seven,' he said, comments picked up word-for-word by the television microphones.

With Clark also hitting lustily, Australia opened a 102-run lead and bowled England out a second time for 147 to win early on the fourth day, Ponting insisting afterwards that it was the send-off that Warne, McGrath and Langer deserved given their dedication to the team over the previous fifteen years. 'It has been the best six weeks of my life,' Ponting told reporters, as he became the first Australian to win the Compton-Miller Medal, named after two of the Ashes' most celebrated post-war champions. 'It's a special time for us. No one has done this for eighty-odd years. You've seen the hunger in everyone's eyes over the last few weeks.'

Asked about Warne's heavenly farewell and overall contribution to Australian cricket, he paused and said: 'He's probably the greatest cricketer who has ever been.'

Man of the decade: *Ricky Ponting*

A week before the first Test of 2006–07, Ricky Ponting was in full battle mode, practising morning and night at the Melbourne Cricket Ground, even after fielding all day for his state team Tasmania. His focus on the Ashes summer had been burning for months and it was little wonder he started with back-to-back centuries in Brisbane and Adelaide on his way to player-of-the-series honours.

Few Ashes captains had ever played as well or been as driven, and he was to increase his Ashes average from the low 40s to almost 50.

In 2005, he'd played with equal resolution but lacked support against Steve Harmison, Andrew Flintoff, Simon Jones and co. At Old Trafford, however, his rallying 156 saved Australia from defeat, his near-chanceless display the finest of his first thirty Test centuries and his most satisfying as captain.

Ever since his majestic century on his Ashes debut in difficult circumstances at Leeds in 1997, Ponting's wicket had been considered a prize for English bowlers. While he'd been discarded after the third Test in 1998–99, his sheer talent was impossible to ignore and on return he played some supreme knocks to cement his place in a world championship XI once and for all.

At Leeds in 2001, he made 144 from just 154 balls, playing with 'a rare panache'.[16] Two further centuries to start the 2002–03 summer in Brisbane and Adelaide were assured displays from a player totally comfortable with his promotion to No. 3.

Like Charlie Macartney, cricket's 'Governor-General', the 178 cm (5 ft 10 in) Ponting looked to score from every ball, bowlers being congratulated warmly if they happened to bowl a maiden against him. If the faster bowlers pitched even a fraction off-line, they were punished unmercifully. Ponting's pull shot remained his signature as he passed his fifty-century milestone for Australia at Test and ODI level – and he was still only thirty-two! He was murderous, too, against the spinners, delighting in hitting them straight back down the ground.

England paid dearly for Ponting's failures in 1998–99 and soon learnt that once Ponting was set, he was as dominant and formidable as anyone in the world, Brian Lara and Sachin Tendulkar included.

His ruthless approach against the 2006–07 Englishmen saw him make almost 600 runs at an average of 82 as the Ashes were re-won 5–0. And not for the first time, he was being ranked as Australia's greatest since the Don.

Ponting v. England   * not out

Season	Scores	Runs	Ave
1997	127, 9, 45, 40, 20	241	48.20
1998–99	21, 11, 5, 10	47	11.75
2001	11, 14, 4, 14, 17, 144, 72, 62	338	42.25
2002–03	123, 3, 154, 68, 21, 30, 7, 11	417	52.12
2005	9, 42, 61, 0, 7, 156, 1, 48, 35	359	39.88
2006–07	196, 60*, 142, 49, 2, 75, 7, 45	576	82.26

Tests v. England:	26 (109 overall)
Runs:	1,978 (9268)
Average:	48.24 (59.41)
Highest score:	196, Brisbane, 2006–07 (257)
100s:	7 (33)

Match of the decade: *Edgbaston, 2005*

One of the great Test matches of all ended when Australian No. 11 Michael Kasprowicz was caught down the leg-side by England's much-maligned 'Aussie' wicketkeeper Geraint Jones, squaring the series at 1–1.

Australia's exciting Sunday comeback came after the world champions were 175-8 chasing 282. All-rounder Andrew Flintoff had a Botham-like influence on the matches with 141 bullying runs, nine 6s, seven wickets and two catches.

Match scores: England 407 (Trescothick 90, Pietersen 71, Flintoff 68, Warne 4-116) and 182 (Flintoff 73, Lee 4-82, Warne 6-46) defeated Australia 308 (Langer 82, Ponting 61) and 279 by 2 runs

Odd spot: *Instant stardom*

Gary Pratt, twenty-three, had lost his place even at county level when called into England's squad to act as a specialist fielder in 2005. Substituting for an injured Simon Jones in the fourth Test at Trent Bridge, Pratt's direct-hit run out of Ricky Ponting on 48 in the Australian second innings was the decisive moment in the match and ensured Pratt instant cult hero status as England stormed to a 2–1 Ashes lead.

Looking back: *Stephen Waugh, Melbourne, 2002–03*

'England came at us hard on that last morning and bowled very well. It's never easy to win any Test match (no matter the fourth-innings target). I was feeling dizzy out there (with a migraine headache). Coming away with the win was what counted.'

Had Waugh shared teammate Adam Gilchrist's penchant for 'walking' when he believed himself out, Australia may well have caved in. Waugh admitted he'd tickled a catch behind from expressman Steve Harmison, but the appeal was belated and umpire Dave Orchard ruled not out. 'As long as I have played,' said Waugh in explanation, 'they've never walked either.'

> Waugh made only 14 but it was decisive as the Australians chased 107, losing 90-5 before Gilchrist and Test debutant Martin Love shared the matchwinning stand, Gilchrist's uppercut against Harmison to third man the winning hit.

One for the statisticians: *Oh brother*

Brothers-in-law Darren Lehmann and Craig White were on opposing sides for the first three Ashes Tests of 2002–03. Lehmann married White's sister, Andrea, in 1999.

Tests 2001 to 2006–07

KEY: M Matches **I** Innings **NO** Not out innings **HS** Highest score **BB** Best bowling
5wI 5-wicket innings **10wM** 10-wicket match ***** Not out **#** Second innings **rh** Retired hurt

Series results

	Tests	Aust	Eng	Drawn
2001 (Eng)	5	4	1	0
2002–03 (Aust)	5	4	1	0
2005 (Eng)	5	1	2	2
2006–07 (Aust)	5	5	0	0
Total	**20**	**14**	**4**	**2**
Progressive	316	131	97	88

Summary

	Runs	Wkts	Ave
Australia	11,570	266	43.49
England	10,735	377	28.47

Highest innings totals

Australia		England	
641-4 dec	The Oval 2001 (5th Test)	551-6 dec	Adelaide 2006–07 (2nd Test)
602-9 dec	Brisbane 2006–07 (1st Test)	477	Nottingham 2005 (4th Test)
576	Birmingham 2001 (1st Test)	452-9 dec	Sydney 2002–03 (5th Test)#
552-9 dec	Adelaide 2002–03 (2nd Test)	444	Manchester 2005 (3rd Test)
551-6 dec	Melbourne 2002–03 (4th Test)		
527-5 dec	Perth 2006–07 (3rd Test)#		
513	Adelaide 2006–07 (2nd Test)		
492	Brisbane 2002–03 (1st Test)		
456	Perth 2002–03 (3rd Test)		

Lowest completed innings totals

Australia		England	
190	Lord's 2005 (1st Test)	129	Adelaide 2006–07 (2nd Test)#
		147	Sydney 2006–07 (5th Test)#

Leading run scorers

	M	I	NO	Runs	HS	Ave	100	50
Australia								
R. T. Ponting	20	33	1	1,690	196	52.81	6	6
M. L. Hayden	20	35	3	1,461	197	45.65	5	2
J. L. Langer	16	28	4	1,222	250	50.91	4	3
A. C. Gilchrist	20	28	4	1,083	152	45.12	3	6
D. R. Martyn	17	27	2	925	118	37.00	2	6
M. J. Clarke	10	16	2	724	135*	51.71	2	3
S. R. Waugh	9	13	2	626	157*	56.90	3	2

England								
M. E. Trescothick	15	30	0	1,013	90	33.76	–	7
K. P. Pietersen	10	20	2	963	158	53.50	2	6
M. P. Vaughan	10	20	0	959	183	47.95	4	1
M. A. Butcher	10	20	1	774	173*	40.73	2	2
A. Flintoff	10	20	1	656	102	34.52	1	5
A. J. Strauss	10	20	0	640	129	32.00	2	1

Hundreds

Australia (29)		England (14)	
6	R. T. Ponting	4	M. P. Vaughan
5	M. L. Hayden	2	M. A. Butcher
4	J. L. Langer		K. P. Pietersen
3	A. C. Gilchrist		A. J. Strauss
	S. R. Waugh	1	P. D. Collingwood
2	M. J. Clarke		A. N. Cook
	D. R. Martyn		A. Flintoff
	M. E. Waugh		M. R. Ramprakash
1	M. E. K. Hussey		
	A. Symonds		

Highest individual scores

Australia

250	J. L. Langer at Melbourne 2002–03 (4th Test)
197	M. L. Hayden at Brisbane 2002–03 (1st Test)
196	R. T. Ponting at Brisbane 2006–07 (1st Test)
157*	S. R. Waugh at The Oval 2001 (5th Test)
156	R. T. Ponting at Manchester 2005 (3rd Test)#
156	A. Symonds at Melbourne 2006–07 (4th Test)
154	R. T. Ponting at Adelaide 2002–03 (2nd Test)
153	M. L. Hayden at Melbourne 2006–07 (4th Test)
144	R. T. Ponting at Leeds 2001 (4th Test)
142	R. T. Ponting at Adelaide 2006–07 (2nd Test)

England

206	P. D. Collingwood at Adelaide 2006–07 (2nd Test)
183	M. P. Vaughan at Sydney 2002–03 (5th Test)#
177	M. P. Vaughan at Adelaide 2002–03 (2nd Test)
173*	M. A. Butcher at Leeds 2001 (4th Test)#
166	M. P. Vaughan at Manchester 2005 (3rd Test)
158	K. P. Pietersen at The Oval 2005 (5th Test)#
158	K. P. Pietersen at Adelaide 2006–07 (2nd Test)
145	M. P. Vaughan at Melbourne 2002–03 (4th Test)#

Century in each innings

197 and 103	M. L. Hayden (Aust) at Brisbane 2002–03 (1st Test)

500 runs in a series

	Season	M	I	NO	Runs	HS	Ave	100	50
Australia									
R.T. Ponting	2006–07	5	8	1	576	196	82.28	2	2
Also note:									
M.L. Hayden	2002–03	5	8	0	496	197	62.00	3	–
England									
M.P. Vaughan	2002–03	5	10	0	633	183	63.30	3	–
Also note:									
K.P. Pietersen	2006–07	5	10	1	490	158	54.44	1	3

Hundred partnerships

Australia (26)

Partnerships of 150 and over:

279	6th	M.L. Hayden and A. Symonds at Melbourne 2006–07 (4th Test)
272	2nd	M.L. Hayden and R.T. Ponting at Brisbane 2002–03 (1st Test)
242	3rd	R.T. Ponting and D.R. Martyn at Adelaide 2002–03 (2nd Test)
221	3rd	R.T. Ponting and M.E. Waugh at Leeds 2001 (4th Test)
209	4th	R.T. Ponting and M.E.K. Hussey at Brisbane 2006–07 (1st Test)
197	3rd	M.E. Waugh and S.R. Waugh at The Oval 2001 (5th Test)
195	1st	J.L. Langer and M.L. Hayden at Melbourne 2002–03 (4th Test)
192	4th	R.T. Ponting and M.E.K. Hussey at Adelaide 2006–07 (2nd Test)
185	1st	J.L. Langer and M.L. Hayden at The Oval 2005 (5th Test)
162*	6th	M.J. Clarke and A.C. Gilchrist at Perth 2006–07 (3rd Test)#
160	6th	D.R. Martyn and A.C. Gilchrist at Birmingham 2001 (1st Test)
158	1st	M.L. Hayden and J.L. Langer at The Oval 2001 (5th Test)
155	4th	D.R. Martyn and M.J. Clarke at Lord's 2005 (1st Test)#
153	3rd	M.L. Hayden and D.R. Martyn at Brisbane (1st Test)#
151	4th	M.E.K. Hussey and M.J. Clarke at Perth 2006–07 (3rd Test)#
151	5th	J.L. Langer and M.L. Love at Melbourne 2002–03 (4th Test)

England (19)

Partnerships of 150 and over:

310	4th	P.D. Collingwood and K.P. Pietersen at Adelaide 2006–07 (2nd Test)
		(English 4th wicket record against Australia)
189	3rd	M.P. Vaughan and N. Hussain at Sydney 2002–03 (5th Test)#
177	6th	A. Flintoff and G.O. Jones at Nottingham 2005 (4th Test)
170	2nd	A.N. Cook and I.R. Bell at Perth 2006–07 (3rd Test)#
166	3rd	M.A. Butcher and N. Hussain at Sydney 2002–03 (5th Test)
153	4th	P.D. Collingwood and K.P. Pietersen at Brisbane 2006–07 (1st Test)#

Leading wicket-takers

	Tests	Balls	Mdns	Runs	Wkts	Ave	BB	5wI	10wM
Australia									
S.K. Warne	18	4,924	150	2,422	108	22.42	7-165	7	3
G.D. McGrath	17	4,199	196	1,864	91	20.48	7-76	7	–
B. Lee	18	3,921	101	2,518	62	40.61	4-47	–	–
J.N. Gillespie	13	2,537	101	1,444	42	34.38	5-53	1	–
S.R. Clark	5	1,166	53	443	26	17.03	4-72	–	–
England									
S.J. Harmison	14	2,783	79	1,618	36	44.94	5-43	1	–
A. Flintoff	10	1,986	50	1,136	35	32.45	5-78	1	–
M.J. Hoggard	12	2,200	57	1,334	35	38.11	7-109	1	–
A.R. Caddick	9	2,092	52	1,438	35	41.08	7-94	2	1

Five wickets in an innings

Australia (16)		England (11)	
7	S.K. Warne	2	A.R. Caddick
	G.D. McGrath		S.P. Jones
1	J.N. Gillespie	1	A. Flintoff
	S.C.G. MacGill		D. Gough
			S.J. Harmison
			M.J. Hoggard
			M.S. Panesar
			A.J. Tudor
			C. White

Best individual bowling

Australia

7-76	G.D. McGrath at Leeds 2001 (4th Test)
7-165	S.K. Warne at The Oval 2001 (5th Test)
6-33	S.K. Warne at Nottingham 2001 (3rd Test)#
6-46	S.K. Warne at Birmingham 2005 (2nd Test)#
6-50	G.D. McGrath at Brisbane 2006–07 (1st Test)
6-122	S.K. Warne at The Oval 2005 (5th Test)
6-124	S.K. Warne at The Oval 2005 (5th Test)#

England

7-94	A.R. Caddick at Sydney 2002–03 (5th Test)#
7-109	M.J. Hoggard at Adelaide 2006–07 (2nd Test)
6-53	S.P. Jones at Manchester 2005 (3rd Test)

10 wickets in a match

Australia (3)

12-246	S.K. Warne (6-122 and 6-124) at The Oval 2005 (5th Test)
11-229	S.K. Warne (7-165 and 4-64) at The Oval 2001 (5th Test)
10-162	S.K. Warne (4-116 and 6-46) at Birmingham 2005 (2nd Test)

England (1)

10-215	A.R. Caddick (3-121 and 7-94) at Sydney 2002–03 (5th Test)

25 wickets in a series

	Season	Tests	Balls	Mdns	Runs	Wkts	Ave	BB	5wI	10wM
Australia										
S.K. Warne	2005	5	1,517	37	797	40	19.92	6-46	3	2
G.D. McGrath	2001	5	1,166	56	542	32	16.93	7-76	4	–
S.K. Warne	2001	5	1,172	41	580	31	18.70	7-165	3	1
S.R. Clark	2006–07	5	1,166	53	443	26	17.03	4-72	–	–
England										
No instance – best:										
A. Flintoff	2005	5	1,164	32	655	24	27.29	5-78	1	–

Leading wicketkeepers

	Tests	Dismissals	Catches	Stumpings
Australia				
A.C. Gilchrist	20	96	89	7
England				
G.O. Jones	8	25	24	1
A.J. Stewart	9	24	24	0
C.M.W. Read	2	12	11	1

Leading fieldsmen

	Tests	Catches		Tests	Catches
Australia			**England**		
M.L. Hayden	20	29	I.R. Bell	10	13
R.T. Ponting	20	21	M.E. Trescothick	15	12
S.K. Warne	18	18	M.A. Butcher	10	10
J.L. Langer	16	10			

Captains

	Tests	Won	Lost	Drawn	Toss won
Australia					
R.T. Ponting	10	6	2	2	4
S.R. Waugh	9	8	1	0	4
A.C. Gilchrist	1	0	1	0	1
England					
N. Hussain	8	2	6	0	4
A. Flintoff	5	0	5	0	3
M.P. Vaughan	5	2	1	2	3
M.A. Atherton	2	0	2	0	1

Most appearances

Australia (23 players)		England (39 players)	
20	A. C. Gilchrist	15	M. E. Trescothick
	M. L. Hayden	14	S. J. Harmison
	R. T. Ponting		
18	B. Lee		
	S. K. Warne		
17	G. D. McGrath		
	D. R. Martyn		
16	J. L. Langer		

SUMMARY STATISTICS

Results on each ground

	Tests	Aust	Eng	Drawn
In Australia				
Adelaide	29	16	8	5
Brisbane				
Woollongabba	18	10	4	4
Exhibition Ground	1	0	1	0
Melbourne	53	27	19	7
Perth	11	7	1	3
Sydney	53	25	21	7
Total in Australia	165	85	54	26
In England				
Birmingham	12	3	5	4
Leeds	23	8	7	8
London				
Lord's	33	14	5	14
The Oval	34	6	15	13
Manchester	28	7	7	14
Nottingham	20	7	4	9
Sheffield	1	1	0	0
Total in England	151	46	43	62
Overall Total	316	131	97	88

Summary

	Runs	Wkts	Ave
Australia	154 645	4978	31.06
England	152 186	5194	29.30
Total	306 831	10 172	30.16

Highest innings totals

Australia		**England**	
729-6 dec	Lord's 1930 (2nd Test)	903-7 dec	The Oval 1938 (5th Test)
701	The Oval 1934 (5th Test)	658-8 dec	Nottingham 1938 (1st Test)
695	The Oval 1930 (5th Test)		
659-8 dec	Sydney 1946–47 (2nd Test)		
656-8 dec	Manchester 1964 (4th Test)		
653-4 dec	Leeds 1993 (4th Test)		

Lowest completed innings totals

Australia		**England**	
36	Birmingham 1902 (1st Test)	45	Sydney 1886–87 (1st Test)
42	Sydney 1887–88 (Only Test)	52	The Oval 1948 (5th Test)
44	The Oval 1896 (3rd Test)#	53	Lord's 1888 (1st Test)
53	Lord's 1896 (1st Test)		
58	Brisbane 1936–37 (1st Test)#		
	(one batsman absent)		

Leading run scorers

	M	I	NO	Runs	HS	Ave	100	50
Australia								
D. G. Bradman	37	63	7	5028	334	89.78	19	12
A. R. Border	47	82	19	3548	200*	56.31	8	21
S. R. Waugh	46	73	18	3200	177*	58.18	10	14
C. Hill	41	76	1	2660	188	35.46	4	16
G. S. Chappell	35	65	8	2619	144	45.94	9	12
M. A. Taylor	33	61	2	2496	219	42.30	6	15
R. N. Harvey	37	68	5	2416	167	38.34	6	12
V. T. Trumper	40	74	5	2263	185*	32.79	6	9
D. C. Boon	31	57	8	2237	184*	45.65	7	8
W. M. Lawry	29	51	5	2233	166	48.54	7	13
M. E. Waugh	29	51	7	2204	140	50.09	6	11
S. E. Gregory	52	92	7	2193	201	25.80	4	8
W. W. Armstrong	42	71	9	2172	158	35.03	4	6
I. M. Chappell	30	56	4	2138	192	41.11	4	15
A. R. Morris	24	43	2	2080	206	50.73	8	8

Leading run scorers

	M	I	NO	Runs	HS	Ave	100	50
England								
J. B. Hobbs	41	71	4	3636	187	54.26	12	15
D. I. Gower	42	77	4	3269	215	44.78	9	12
G. Boycott	38	71	9	2945	191	47.50	7	14
W. R. Hammond	33	58	3	2852	251	51.85	9	7
H. Sutcliffe	27	46	5	2741	194	66.85	8	16
J. H. Edrich	32	57	3	2644	175	48.96	7	13
G. A. Gooch	42	79	0	2632	196	33.31	4	16
M. C. Cowdrey	43	75	4	2433	113	34.26	5	11
L. Hutton	27	49	6	2428	364	56.46	5	14
K. F. Barrington	23	39	6	2111	256	63.96	5	13

Most hundreds

Australia		**England**	
19	D. G. Bradman	12	J. B. Hobbs
10	S. R. Waugh	9	D. I. Gower
9	G. S. Chappell		W. R. Hammond
8	A. R. Border	8	H. Sutcliffe
	A. R. Morris	7	G. Boycott
7	D. C. Boon		J. H. Edrich
	W. M. Lawry		M. Leyland
	R. T. Ponting		
	M. J. Slater		

Highest individual scores

Australia

334	D. G. Bradman at Leeds 1930 (3rd Test)
311	R. B. Simpson at Manchester 1964 (4th Test)
307	R. M. Cowper at Melbourne 1965–66 (1st Test)
304	D. G. Bradman at Leeds 1934 (4th Test)
270	D. G. Bradman at Melbourne 1936–37 (3rd Test)#
266	W. H. Ponsford at The Oval 1934 (5th Test)
254	D. G. Bradman at Lord's 1930 (2nd Test)
250	J. L. Langer at Melbourne 2002–03 (4th Test)

England

364	L. Hutton at The Oval 1938 (5th Test)
287	R. E. Foster at Sydney 1903–04 (1st Test)
256	K. F. Barrington at Manchester 1964 (4th Test)
251	W. R. Hammond at Sydney 1928–29 (2nd Test)

600 runs in a series

	Season	M	I	NO	Runs	HS	Ave	100	50
Australia									
D. G. Bradman	1930	5	7	0	974	334	139.14	4	–
M. A. Taylor	1989	6	11	1	839	219	83.90	2	5
D. G. Bradman	1936–37	5	9	0	810	270	90.00	3	1
D. G. Bradman	1934	5	8	0	758	304	94.75	2	1
A. R. Morris	1948	5	9	1	696	196	87.00	3	3
D. G. Bradman	1946–47	5	8	1	680	234	97.14	2	3
K. R. Stackpole	1970–71	6	12	0	627	207	52.25	2	2
M. J. Slater	1994–95	5	10	0	623	176	62.30	3	1
G. S. Chappell	1974–75	6	11	0	608	144	55.27	2	5
England									
W. R. Hammond	1928–29	5	9	1	905	251	113.12	4	–
H. Sutcliffe	1924–25	5	9	0	734	176	81.55	4	2
D. I. Gower	1985	6	9	0	732	215	81.33	3	1
G. A. Gooch	1993	6	12	0	673	133	56.08	2	4
J. B. Hobbs	1911–12	5	9	1	662	187	82.75	3	1
G. Boycott	1970–71	5	10	3	657	142*	93.85	2	5
J. H. Edrich	1970–71	6	11	2	648	130	72.00	2	4
M. P. Vaughan	2002–03	5	10	0	633	183	63.30	3	–

Partnerships of 250 and over

Australia

451	2nd	W. H. Ponsford and D. G. Bradman at The Oval 1934 (5th Test)
405	5th	S. G. Barnes and D. G. Bradman at Sydney 1946–47 (2nd Test)
388	4th	W. H. Ponsford and D. G. Bradman at Leeds 1934 (4th Test)
346	6th	J. H. W. Fingleton and D. G. Bradman at Melbourne 1936–37 (3rd Test)#
332*	5th	A. R. Border and S. R. Waugh at Leeds 1993 (4th Test)
329	1st	G. R. Marsh and M. A. Taylor at Nottingham 1989 (4th Test)
301	2nd	A. R. Morris and D. G. Bradman at Leeds 1948 (4th Test)#
279	6th	M. L. Hayden and A. Symonds at Melbourne 2006–07 (4th Test)
277	2nd	R. B. McCosker and I. M. Chappell at The Oval 1975 (4th Test)
276	3rd	D. G. Bradman and A. L. Hassett at Brisbane 1946–47 (1st Test)
272	2nd	M. L. Hayden and R. T. Ponting at Brisbane 2002–03 (1st Test)
268	5th	M. T. G. Elliott and R. T. Ponting at Leeds 1997 (4th Test)
260	1st	M. A. Taylor and M. J. Slater at Lord's 1993 (2nd Test)

England

382	2nd	L. Hutton and M. Leyland at The Oval 1938 (5th Test)
351	2nd	G. A. Gooch and D. I. Gower at The Oval 1985 (6th Test)
331	2nd	R. T. Robinson and D. I. Gower at Birmingham 1985 (5th Test)
323	1st	J. B. Hobbs and W. Rhodes at Melbourne 1911–12 (4th Test)
310	4th	P. D. Collingwood and K. P. Pietersen at Adelaide 2006–07 (2nd Test)
288	4th	N. Hussain and G. P. Thorpe at Birmingham 1997 (1st Test)
283	1st	J. B. Hobbs and H. Sutcliffe at Melbourne 1924–25 (2nd Test)
262	3rd	W. R. Hammond and D. R. Jardine at Adelaide 1928–29 (4th Test)#

Leading wicket-takers

	Tests	Balls	Mdns	Runs	Wkts	Ave	BB	5wl	10wM
Australia									
S.K. Warne	36	10,757	488	4,535	195	23.25	8-71	11	4
D.K. Lillee	29	8,516	361	3,507	167	21.00	7-89	11	4
G.D. McGrath	30	7,280	332	3,286	157	20.92	8-38	10	–
H. Trumble	31	7,895	448	2,945	141	20.88	8-65	9	3
M.A. Noble	39	6,845	353	2,860	115	24.86	7-17	9	2
R.R. Lindwall	29	6,728	216	2,559	114	22.44	6-20	6	–
C.V. Grimmett	22	9,224	426	3,439	106	32.44	6-37	11	2
G. Giffen	31	6,391	434	2,791	103	27.09	7-117	7	1
W.J. O'Reilly	19	7,864	439	2,587	102	25.36	7-54	8	3
C.T.B. Turner	17	5,195	457	1,670	101	16.53	6-15	11	2
T.M. Alderman	17	4,717	192	2,117	100	21.17	6-47	11	1
J.R. Thomson	21	4,951	166	2,418	100	24.18	6-46	5	–
England									
I.T. Botham	36	8,479	297	4,093	148	27.65	6-78	9	2
R.G.D. Willis	35	7,294	200	3,346	128	26.14	8-43	7	–
W. Rhodes	41	5,791	233	2,616	109	24.00	8-68	6	1
S.F. Barnes	20	5,749	264	2,288	106	21.58	7-60	12	1
D.L. Underwood	29	8,000	410	2,770	105	26.38	7-50	4	2
A.V. Bedser	21	7,065	209	2,859	104	27.49	7-44	7	2
R. Peel	20	5,216	444	1,715	101	16.98	7-31	5	1

Eight or more wickets in an innings

Australia

9-121	A.A. Mailey at Melbourne 1920–21 (4th Test)
8-31	F.J. Laver at Manchester 1909 (4th Test)
8-38	G.D. McGrath at Lord's 1997 (2nd Test)
8-43	A.E. Trott at Adelaide 1894–95 (3rd Test)#
8-53	R.A.L. Massie at Lord's 1972 (2nd Test)#
8-65	H. Trumble at The Oval 1902 (5th Test)
8-71	S.K. Warne at Brisbane 1994–95 (1st Test)#
8-84	R.A.L. Massie at Lord's 1972 (2nd Test)
8-97	C.J. McDermott at Sydney 1990–91 (5th Test)
8-141	C.J. McDermott at Manchester 1985 (4th Test)
8-143	M.H.N. Walker at Melbourne 1974–75 (6th Test)

England

10-53	J.C. Laker at Manchester 1956 (4th Test)#
9-37	J.C. Laker at Manchester 1956 (4th Test)
8-35	G.A. Lohmann at Sydney 1886–87 (2nd Test)
8-43	H. Verity at Lord's 1934 (2nd Test)#
8-43	R.G.D. Willis at Leeds 1981 (3rd Test)#
8-58	G.A. Lohmann at Sydney 1891–92 (2nd Test)
8-68	W. Rhodes at Melbourne 1903–04 (2nd Test)#
8-81	L.C. Braund at Melbourne 1903–04 (5th Test)
8-94	T. Richardson at Sydney 1897–98 (5th Test)
8-107	B.J.T. Bosanquet at Nottingham 1905 (1st Test)#
8-126	J.C. White at Adelaide 1928–29 (4th Test)#

13 wickets in a match

Australia

16-137	R. A. L. Massie (8-84 and 8-53) at Lord's 1972 (2nd Test)
14-90	F. R. Spofforth (7-46 and 7-44) at The Oval 1882 (Only Test)
13-77	M. A. Noble (7-17 and 6-60) at Melbourne 1901–02 (2nd Test)
13-110	F. R. Spofforth (6-48 and 7-62) at Melbourne 1878–79 (Only Test)
13-148	B. A. Reid (6-97 and 7-51) at Melbourne 1990–91 (2nd Test)
13-236	A. A. Mailey (4-115 and 9-121) at Melbourne 1920–21 (4th Test)

England

19-90	J. C. Laker (9-37 and 10-53) at Manchester 1956 (4th Test)
15-104	H. Verity (7-61 and 8-43) at Lord's 1934 (2nd Test)
15-124	W. Rhodes (7-56 and 8-68) at Melbourne 1903–04 (2nd Test)
14-99	A. V. Bedser (7-55 and 7-44) at Nottingham 1953 (1st Test)
14-102	W. Bates (7-28 and 7-74) at Melbourne 1882–83 (2nd Test)
13-163	S. F. Barnes (6-42 and 7-121) at Melbourne 1901–02 (2nd Test)
13-244	T. Richardson (7-168 and 6-76) at Manchester 1896 (2nd Test)
13-256	J. C. White (5-130 and 8-126) at Adelaide 1928–29 (4th Test)

Most wickets in a series

	Season	Tests	Balls	Mdns	Runs	Wkts	Ave	BB	5wI	10wM
Australia										
T. M. Alderman	1981	6	1,950	76	893	42	21.26	6-135	4	–
R. M. Hogg	1978–79	6	1,306	60	527	41	12.85	6-74	5	2
T. M. Alderman	1989	6	1,616	68	712	41	17.36	6-128	6	1
S. K. Warne	2005	5	1,517	37	797	40	19.92	6-46	3	2
D. K. Lillee	1981	6	1,870	81	870	39	22.30	7-89	2	1
A. A. Mailey	1920–21	5	1,465	27	946	36	26.27	9-121	4	2
G. D. McGrath	1997	6	1,499	67	701	36	19.47	8-38	2	–
England										
J. C. Laker	1956	5	1,703	127	442	46	9.60	10-53	4	2
A. V. Bedser	1953	5	1,591	58	682	39	17.48	7-44	5	1
M. W. Tate	1924–25	5	2,528	62	881	38	23.18	6-99	5	1

Leading wicketkeepers

	Tests	Dismissals	Catches	Stumpings
Australia				
R. W. Marsh	42	148	141	7
I. A. Healy	33	135	123	12
A. C. Gilchrist	20	96	89	7
W. A. S. Oldfield	38	90	59	31
A. T. W. Grout	22	76	69	7
England				
A. P. E. Knott	34	105	97	8
A. A. Lilley	32	84	65	19
A J. Stewart^	26	78	76	2
T. G. Evans	31	76	64	12

^ *A. J. Stewart held another six catches in seven Tests in which he did not keep wicket.*

Leading fieldsmen

	Tests	Catches		Tests	Catches
Australia			**England**		
G.S. Chappell	35	61	I.T. Botham	36	48
M.A. Taylor	33	46	W.R. Hammond	33	43
A.R. Border	47	45	M.C. Cowdrey	43	40
H. Trumble	31	45	W.G. Grace	22	39
W.W. Armstrong	42	37	A.W. Greig	21	37
			L.C. Braund	20	35

Most captaincies

	Tests	Won	Lost	Drawn	Toss won
Australia					
A.R. Border	29	14	6	9	13
J. Darling	18	5	4	9	5
I.M. Chappell	16	7	4	5	8
W.L. Murdoch	16	5	7	4	7
M.A. Taylor	16	9	4	3	12
R. Benaud	15	7	2	6	6
G.S. Chappell	15	6	4	5	9
M.A. Noble	15	8	5	2	11
W.M. Woodfull	15	5	6	4	8
England					
A.C. MacLaren	22	4	11	7	11
J.M. Brearley	18	11	4	3	8
M.A. Atherton	15	4	9	2	7

Most appearances

Australia		**England**	
52	S.E. Gregory	43	M.C. Cowdrey
47	A.R. Border	42	G.A. Gooch
46	S.R. Waugh		D.I. Gower
42	W.W. Armstrong	41	J.B. Hobbs
	R.W. Marsh	38	W. Rhodes
41	C. Hill		G. Boycott
40	V.T. Trumper	36	I.T. Botham
39	M.A. Noble	35	A.C. MacLaren
38	W.A.S. Oldfield		R.G.D. Willis
37	D.G. Bradman		
	R.N. Harvey		
36	K.D. Walters		
	S.K. Warne		
35	J.M. Blackham		
	G.S. Chappell		

ASHES ROLL OF HONOUR

Leading batsmen: series by series

Summer	Player/country	Most runs	Ave
1876–77	C. Bannerman (A)	209	69.7
1878–79	A.C. Bannerman (A)	73	73.0
1880	W.G. Grace (E)	161	161.0
1881–82	G. Ulyett (E)	438	54.8
1882	H.H. Massie (A)	56	28.0

The Ashes

Summer	Player/country	Most runs	Ave
1882–83	A.G. Steel (E)	274	45.7
1884	H.J.H. Scott (A)	220	73.3
1884–85	W. Barnes (E)	369	52.7
1886	A. Shrewsbury (E)	243	60.7
1886–87	H. Moses (A)	116	29.0
1887–88	A. Shrewsbury (E)	45	22.5
1888	W. Barnes (E)	90	27.5
1890	J.J. Lyons (A)	122	30.5
1891–92	J.J. Lyons (A)	187	47.8
1893	A. Shrewsbury (E)	284	71.0
1894–95	G. Giffen (A)	475	52.8
1896	K.S. Ranjitsinhji (E)	235	78.3
1897–98	J. Darling (A)	537	67.1
1899	T. Hayward (E)	413	68.8
1901–02	C. Hill (A)	521	52.1
1902	F.S. Jackson (E)	311	44.4
1903–04	V.T. Trumper (A)	574	63.7
1905	F.S. Jackson (E)	492	70.2
1907–08	G. Gunn (E)	462	51.3
1909	W. Bardsley (A)	396	39.6

Summer	Player/country	Most runs	Ave
1911–12	J.B. Hobbs (E)	662	82.7
1912	J.B. Hobbs (E)	224	56.0
1920–21	J.B. Hobbs (E)	505	50.5
1921	F.E. Woolley (E)	343	42.8
1924–25	H. Sutcliffe (E)	734	81.5
1926	J.B. Hobbs (E)	486	81.00
1928–29	W.R. Hammond (E)	905	113.1
1930	D.G. Bradman (A)	974	139.1
1932–33	H. Sutcliffe (E)	440	55
	W.R. Hammond (E)	440	55.0
1934	D.G. Bradman (A)	758	94.7
1936–37	D.G. Bradman (A)	810	90.0
1938	W.A. Brown (A)	512	73.1
1946–47	D.G. Bradman (A)	680	97.1
1948	A.R. Morris (A)	696	87.0
1950–51	L. Hutton (E)	533	88.8
1953	L. Hutton (E)	443	55.3
1954–55	R.N. Harvey (A)	354	44.2
1956	P.B.H. May (E)	453	90.9
1958–59	C.C. McDonald (A)	520	65.0
1961	R. Subba Row (E)	468	46.8
1962–63	K.F. Barrington (E)	582	72.7
1964	K.F. Barrington (E)	531	75.8
1965–66	W.M. Lawry (A)	592	84.5
1968	J.H. Edrich (E)	554	61.5
1970–71	G. Boycott (E)	657	93.9
1972	K.R. Stackpole (A)	485	53.8
1974–75	G.S. Chappell (A)	608	55.5
1975	I.M. Chappell (A)	429	75.5
1976–77	D.W. Randall (E)	178	89.0
1977	G. Boycott (E)	442	147.3
1978–79	D.I. Gower (E)	420	42.0
1979–80	G.S. Chappell (A)	317	79.3
1980	K.J. Hughes (A)	201	201.0
1981	A.R. Border (A)	533	59.3
1982–83	K.J. Hughes (A)	469	67.0
1985	D.I. Gower (E)	732	81.3
1986–87	D.M. Jones (A)	511	56.8
1987–88	D.C. Boon (A)	196	196.0
1989	M.A. Taylor (A)	839	83.9
1990–91	D.C. Boon (A)	530	75.7
1993	G.A. Gooch (E)	673	56.0
1994–95	M.J. Slater (A)	623	62.3
1997	M.T.G. Elliott (A)	556	55.6
1998–99	S.R. Waugh (A)	498	83.0
2001	M.A. Butcher (E)	456	50.6

Summer	Player/country	Most runs	Ave
2002–03	M.P.Vaughan (E)	633	63.3
2005	K.P.Pietersen (E)	473	52.5
2006–07	R.P.Ponting (A)	576	82.2

Leading bowlers: series by series

Summer	Player/country	Most wkts	Ave
1876–77	T.K.Kendall (A)	14	15.4
1878–79	F.R.Spofforth (A)	13	8.4
1880	F.Morley (E)	8	18.2
1881–82	G.E.Palmer (A)	24	21.8
1882	F.R.Spofforth (A)	14	6.4

The Ashes

Summer	Player/country	Most wkts	Ave
1882–83	G.E.Palmer (A)	21	18.9
1884	G.E.Palmer (A)	14	18.57
1884–85	R.Peel (E)	21	21.5
1886	J.Briggs (E)	17	7.7
1886–87	J.J.Ferris (A)	18	13.5
1887–88	C.T.B.Turner	12	7.25
1888	R.Peel (E)	24	7.54
1890	J.J.Ferris (E)	13	13.1
1891–92	J.Briggs (E)	17	15.8
1893	G.Giffen (A)	16	21.3
	J.Briggs (E)	16	18.3
1894–95	G.Giffen (A)	34	24.1
1896	T.Richardson (E)	24	18.2
1897–98	T.Richardson (E)	22	35.2
1897–98	E.Jones (A)	22	25.1
1899	E.Jones (A)	26	25.2
1901–02	M.A.Noble (A)	32	19.0
1902	H.Trumble (A)	26	14.2
1903–04	W.Rhodes (E)	31	15.7
1905	F.Laver (A)	16	31.8
	W.W.Armstrong (A)	16	33.6
1907–08	J.V.Saunders (A)	31	23.0
1909	C.Blythe (E)	18	13.4
1911–12	H.V.Hordern (A)	32	24.3
	F.R.Foster (E)	32	21.6
1912	G.R.Hazlitt (A)	12	18.16
	W.J.Whitty (A)	12	21.0
1920–21	A.A.Mailey (A)	36	26.2
1921	E.A.McDonald (A)	27	24.7
1924–25	M.W.Tate (E)	38	23.18
1926	A.A.Mailey (A)	14	42.2
1928–29	J.C.White (E)	25	30.4

Summer	Player/country	Most wkts	Ave
1930	C.V. Grimmett (A)	29	31.8
1932–33	H. Larwood (E)	33	19.51
1934	W.J. O'Reilly (A)	28	24.9
1936–37	W.Voce (E)	26	21.5
1938	W.J. O'Reilly (A)	22	27.7
1946–47	D.V.P. Wright (E)	23	43.0
1948	R.R. Lindwall (A)	27	19.6
	W.A. Johnston (A)	27	23.3
1950–51	A.V. Bedser (E)	30	16.0
1953	A.V. Bedser (E)	39	17.4
1954–55	F.H. Tyson (E)	28	20.82
1956	J.C. Laker (E)	46	9.6
1958–59	R. Benaud (A)	31	18.8
1961	A.K. Davidson (A)	23	24.8
1962–63	A.K. Davidson (A)	24	20.0
1964	G.D. McKenzie (A)	29	22.5
1965–66	N.J.N. Hawke (A)	16	26.1
	G.D. McKenzie (A)	16	29.1
1968	A.N. Connolly (A)	23	25.6
1970–71	J.A. Snow (E)	31	22.8
1972	D.K. Lillee (A)	31	17.6
1974–75	J.R. Thomson (A)	33	17.9
1975	D.K. Lillee (A)	21	21.9
1976–77	D.K. Lillee (A)	11	15.0
1977	R.G.D. Willis (E)	27	19.7
1978–79	R.M. Hogg (A)	41	12.75
1979–80	D.K. Lillee (A)	23	16.9
1980	L.S. Pascoe (A)	6	22.0
	C.M. Old (E)	6	23.0
1981	T.M. Alderman (A)	42	21.2
1982–83	G.F. Lawson (A)	34	20.2
1985	I.T. Botham (E)	31	27.5
1986–87	B.A. Reid (A)	20	26.4
1987–88	P.L. Taylor (A)	4	21.0
1989	T.M. Alderman (A)	41	17.3
1990–91	B.A. Reid (A)	27	16.0
1993	S.K. Warne (A)	34	25.7
1994–95	C.J. McDermott (A)	32	21.1
1997	G.D. McGrath (A)	36	19.4
1998–99	S.C.G. MacGill (A)	27	17.7
2001	G.D. McGrath (A)	32	16.9
2002–03	J.N. Gillespie (A)	20	24.6
	A.R. Caddick (E)	20	34.5
2005	S.K. Warne (A)	40	19.9
2006–07	S.R. Clark (A)	26	17.0

NOTES

■ **1 1860s: THE PIONEERS**

1   David Frith, *The Trailblazers: The First English Cricket Tour of Australia: 1861–62*, Boundary Books, Cheshire, England, 1999, p. 58.

2   Tom Melville, *The Tented Field: A History of Cricket in America*, Bowling Green State University Press, Ohio, 1998, p. 44.

3   Harry Altham & E.W. 'Jim' Swanton, *History of Cricket*, George Allen and Unwin Ltd, London, 1962 edition, p. 131.

4   Ken Piesse & Jim Main, *Duel for Glory: English Cricket Tours to Australia from 1862*, Wedneil Publications, Melbourne, 1982, p. 84.

5   Altham & Swanton, p. 131.

6   Frith, *The Trailblazers*, p. 60.

7   Richard Christen, *Some Grounds to Appeal*, self-published, Parramatta, 1995, p. 59.

8   Keith Dunstan, *The Paddock That Grew*, Cassell & Company Ltd, Melbourne, 1962, p. 23.

9   William Caffyn, *Seventy-One Not Out: The Reminiscences of William Caffyn*, edited by 'Mid-On', William Blackwood and Sons, London, 1899, p. 176–7.

10 Frith, *The Trailblazers*, p. 151.

11 Geoff Amey, *Julius Caesar: The Ill-fated Cricketer*, Bodyline Books, London, 2000, p. 73.

12 Amey, p. 74.

■ **2 1870s: A MIGHTY OCCASION**

1   Stanley Brogden, *The First Test*, The Hawthorn Press, Melbourne, 1946, p. 7.

2   Max Bonnell, *Currency Lads: The Life and Cricket of T. W. Garrett, R. C. Allen, S. P. Jones & R. J. Pope*, The Cricket Publishing Company, Cherrybrook, Sydney, 2001, p. 29.

3   Piesse & Main, p. 88.

4   Melville, p. 83.

5   Bill Frindall, *England Test Cricketers: The Complete Record from 1877*, Willow Books Collins, London, 1989, p. 194.

6   James Lillywhite (ed.), *John and James Lillywhite's Cricketers' Companion, 1880*, John & James Lillywhite & Co., London, 1880, p. 41.

7   James D. Coldham, *Lord Harris*, George Allen & Unwin (Publishers) Ltd, London, 1983, p. 45.

8   Coldham, p. 45.

9   Coldham, p. 46.

10   Ray Webster, *First-class Cricket in Australia, Vol. 1 1850–51 to 1941–42*, edited by Alan Miller, self-published, Melbourne, 1991, p. 26.

11   James Lillywhite (ed.), *James Lillywhite's Cricketers' Annual 1879*, Frowd & Co., London, 1879, p. 17.

12   A.W. Pullin (Old Ebor), *Alfred Shaw, Cricketer: His Career and Reminiscences*, Cassell and Company, London, 1902, p. 59.

■ 3 1880s: REBUILDING BRIDGES

1   Coldham, p. 49.

2   Peter Wynne-Thomas, *The Complete History of Cricket Tours Home & Abroad*, Hamlyn Publishing, London, 1989, p. 212.

3   Pullin, p. 71.

4   'Looker-On', *Bringing Back the Ashes: The MCC Tour of Australia 1903–04*, Sheffield Telegraph Ltd, Sheffield, p. 81.

5   Norman Grubb, *C. T. Studd Cricketer and Pioneer*, The Religious Tract Society, London, 1934, p. 29.

6   R.D. Beeston, *St. Ivo and the Ashes*, Australian Press Agency, Melbourne, 1883, p. 1.

7   Joy Munns, *Beyond Reasonable Doubt: The Birthplace of the Ashes*, self-published, Sunbury, 1994, p. 7.

8   Munns, p. 17.

9   Ralph Barker, writing in *The Cricketer 1972*, Spring Annual, p. 18.

10   Six runs were first given for over-the-fence hits in Australian cricket in 1905.

11   A.G. Steel and The Hon. R.H. Lyttelton, *The Badminton Library of Sports and Pastimes: Cricket*, Longmans, Green & Co., London, 1888, p. 209.

12   Ken Piesse, *Cricket's Colosseum*, Hardie Grant Books, Prahran, 2002, p. 27.

13   Piesse, *Cricket's Colosseum*, p. 28.

14   Bernard Whimpress and Nigel Hart, *Adelaide Oval Test Cricket 1884–1984*, Wakefield Press, Adelaide, 1984, p. 3.

15   Richard Cashman, *The 'Demon' Spofforth*, NSW University Press, Sydney, 1990, p. 166.

16   Cashman, p. 171.

17   Lillywhite, *Cricketers' Annual, 1886*.

18   *Wisden Cricketers' Almanack, 1887*, John Wisden & Co., London, p. 1.

19   Piesse & Main, p. 92.

20   Pullin, p. 101.

21   *Wisden Cricketers' Almanack, 1889*, John Wisden & Co., London, p. 302.

22   Cashman, p. 125.

23   Altham & Swanton, p. 168.

24   Altham & Swanton, p. 170.

25   Cashman, p. 211.

26   Peter Wynne-Thomas, *'Give me Arthur': A Biography of Arthur Shrewsbury*, Arthur Barker Ltd, London, 1985, p. 66.

■ 4 1890s: FORWARD TO FEDERATION

1   Piesse, *Cricket's Colosseum*, p. 42.

2   Lillywhite, *James Lillywhite's Cricketers' Annual, 1892*.

3   David Frith, *My Dear Victorious Stod: A Biography of A. E. Stoddart*, privately published, Surrey, 1970, p. 53.

4   David Kynaston, *Bobby Abel: Professional Batsman*, Secker & Warburg, London, 1982, p. 63.

5   M.A. 'Monty' Noble, *The Game's the Thing: A Record of Cricket Experience*, Cassell & Co., Sydney, 1926.

6   Richard Binns, *Cricket in Firelight*, Selwyn & Blount Ltd, London, 1935, p. 160.

7   Frith, *My Dear Victorious Stod*, p. 97.

8   F.S. Ashley-Cooper (ed.), *MCC Scores & Biographies, Vol. XV*, Marleygone Cricket Club, London, p. 249.

9   Piesse & Main, p. 97.

10 Piesse & Main, p. 98.

11 Roland Wild, *The Biography of Colonel His Highness Shri Sir Ranjitsinhji*, Rich & Cowan, London, 1934, p. 39.

12 *Wisden Cricketers' Almanack, 1897*, John Wisden & Co., London, p. 239.

13 Wild, p. 40.

14 Clem Hill, 'Great Leaders' Tactics On and Off the Field' (Feature No. 3), *The Sporting Globe*, Melbourne, March 1933.

15 Hill, *The Sporting Globe*.

16 Hill, *The Sporting Globe*.

■ 5 1900s: GOLDEN TIMES

1   Noble, *The Game's The Thing*, p. 163.

2   Noble, *The Game's The Thing*, p. 169.

3   Christopher Scoble, *Colin Blythe: Lament for a Legend*, Sports Books, Cheltenham (UK), 2005, p. 39.

4   P.F. 'Plum' Warner, *How We Recovered the Ashes*, Chapman & Hall, London, 1904, p. 262.

5   Warner, *How We Recovered the Ashes*, p. 126.

6   Warner, *How We Recovered the Ashes*, p. 127.

7   Warner, *How We Recovered the Ashes*, p. 133.

8   Jack Hobbs, *My Cricket Memories*, Heinemann, London, 1924, p. 74.

9   Whimpress & Hart, p. 39.

10 Whimpress & Hart, p. 39.

11 Leslie Duckworth, *S. F. Barnes: Master Bowler*, The Cricketer– Hutchinson, London, 1967, p. 93.

12 Patrick Morrah, *The Golden Age of Cricket*, Eyre and Spottiswoode, London, 1967, p. 141.

13 Jack Fingleton, *The Immortal Victor Trumper*, Collins, Sydney, 1978, p. 21.

14 Fingleton, p. 20.

15 Duckworth, p. 73.

16 Charles Macartney, *My Cricketing Days*, William Heinemann Ltd, London, 1930, p. 40.

■ 6 1910s: AN UNHOLY ROW

1   Gideon Haigh, *The Big Ship: Warwick Armstrong and the Making of Modern Cricket*, Text Publishing, Melbourne, 2001, p. 220.

2   P.F. 'Plum' Warner, *Long Innings: The Autobiography of Sir Pelham Warner*, George G. Harrap and Co., London, 1951, p. 87.

3   Warner, *Long Innings*, p. 87.

4   Duckworth, p. 160.

5   Duckworth, p. 92.

6   *The Sporting Globe*, Melbourne, February–March 1933.

7   Duckworth, p. 202.

8   Duckworth, p. 43.

9   *Wisden Cricketers' Almanack, 1913*, John Wisden & Co., London, (second section), pp. 16–17.

10   Gerald Brodribb, *Next Man In: A Survey of Cricket Laws and Customs*, Putnam & Co., London, 1952, p. 142.

11   Jack Hobbs, *My Life Story*, The Star Publications Dept, London, 1935, p. 140.

12   Cecil Parkin, *Parkin on Cricket*, Hodder & Stoughton, London, 1923, p. 41.

13   David Lemmon, *Johnny Won't Hit Today*, Allen & Unwin, London, 1983, p. 15.

14   C.B. Fry, *Life Worth Living*, Eyre & Spottiswoode, London, 1939, p. 247.

■   **7   1920s: GELIGNITE JACK ARRIVES**

1   From Norm Sowden's unpublished work *Sydney Grade Cricketer Index, from 1893–94 to date* (1987). Gregory's first-grade debut was delayed until 1920–21 when he played the first of three seasons with Sydney District CC. Sydney was the first of five grade clubs he was to represent.

2   Ronald Cardwell, *The A.I.F. Cricket Team*, privately printed, Sydney, 1980, p. 33.

3   Hobbs, *My Cricket Memories*, p. 213.

4   Arthur Mailey, *10 for 66 and All That*, Phoenix House, Sydney, 1958, p. 75.

5   Mailey, p. 76.

6   Hobbs, *My Cricket Memories*, p. 215.

7   Altham & Swanton, p. 319.

8   R.H. Campbell, *Cricket Casualties*, ABC, Sydney, 1933, p. 27.

9   Piesse & Main, p. 104.

10   Webster, p. 564.

11   Percy Fender, *Defending the Ashes*, Chapman and Hall Ltd, London, 1921, p. 118.

12   Fender, p. 162.

13   Herbert Strudwick, *Twenty-five years Behind the Stumps*, Hutchinson & Co., London, 1926, p. 220.

14   Maurice Tate, *My Cricket Reminiscences*, Stanley Paul & Co., London, 1934, p. 66.

15   Jack Fingleton, *Masters of Cricket*, William Heinemann Limited, London, 1958, p. 129.

16   Ashley Mallett, *Clarrie Grimmett: The Bradman of Spin*, University of Queensland Press, Brisbane, 1993, p. 44.

17   A grinning Bradman is pictured walking off the SCG in 1929 in *Pavilion 2007*, official journal of the Australian Cricket Society Inc, edited by Ken Piesse, p. 8.

18   Don Bradman, *Farewell to Cricket*, Hodder & Stoughton, London, 1950, p. 28.

19   Alan Hill, *Herbert Sutcliffe: Cricket Maestro*, Simon & Schuster, London, 1991, p. 113.

20   Bradman, p. 29.

21   Basil Ashton Tinkler, *A Somerset Hero Who Beat the Aussies: The Life and Times of J. C. 'Farmer' White*, The Parrs Wood Press, Manchester, 2000, p. 102.

22   R.S. Whitington and George Hele, *Bodyline Umpire: An Eyewitness Account of a Dramatic Era in Test Cricket*, Rigby Limited, Adelaide, 1974, p. 61.

23   Whitington & Hele, p. 61.

24   David Frith, *The Archie Jackson Story*, The Cricketer, Beech Hanger, Kent, 1974, p. 15.

25   Irving Rosenwater, *Sir Donald Bradman: A Biography*, BT Batsford Ltd, London, 1978, p. 59.

26   Rosenwater, p. 59.

27   M.A. Noble, *Gilligan's Men*, Chapman & Hall, London, 1925, p. 121.

28   John Arlott, *Cricket: The Great Ones*, Pelham Books, London, 1967.

29 Arlott, p. 64.

30 Ken Piesse, *All Out for One and Other Cricket Anecdotes*, Viking Books, Melbourne, 2003, p. 63.

31 Bradman, p. 12.

■ **8 1930s: HUNTING THE DON**

1 *Bodyline: A Great Australian Story* (television series), Kennedy-Miller, 1984.

2 David Frith, *Bodyline Autopsy: The Full Story of the Most Sensational Test Cricket Series: Australia v England 1932–33*, ABC Books, Sydney, 2002, p. 44.

3 Charles Davis, *Test Cricket in Australia 1877–2002*, self-published, Melbourne, 2002.

4 Whitington & Hele, p. 103.

5 Whitington & Hele, p. 101.

6 Jack McHarg, *Stan McCabe: The Man and His Cricket*, Collins Australia, Sydney, 1987, p. 36.

7 Frith, *Bodyline Autopsy*, p. 153.

8 Ken Piesse, *Down at the Junction, There's a Cricket Ground*, St Kilda Cricket Club, 2005, p. 253.

9 Frith, *Bodyline Autopsy*, p. 185.

10 Jack Pollard (ed.), *Six and Out*, Penguin Books, Melbourne, 1990 edition, p. 208.

11 Ken Piesse, *Cricket's Greatest Scandals*, Viking, Melbourne, 2000, p. 136.

12 Frith, *Bodyline Autopsy*, p. 137.

13 Frith, *Bodyline Autopsy*, p. 355.

14 E.W. Swanton, *Gubby Allen: Man of Cricket*, Hutchinson/Stanley Paul, London, 1985, p. 109.

15 Walter Hammond, *Cricket: My Destiny*, Stanley Paul & Co., London, 1946, p. 128.

16 Greg Growden, *A Wayward Genius: The Fleetwood-Smith Story*, ABC Books, Sydney, 1991, p. 121.

17 Growden, p. 121.

18 Ken Farnes, *Tours & Tests*, R.T.S. – Lutterworth Press, London, 1940, p. 150.

19 Swanton, p. 125.

20 E.A. 'Ned' Wallish, *The Great Laurie Nash*, Ryan Publishing, Melbourne, 1998, pp. 146–7.

21 Swanton, p. 150.

22 Swanton, p. 199.

23 Bradman, pp. 37–8.

24 Davis, *Test Cricket in Australia 1877–2002*.

■ **9 1940s: NUGGET AND THE ROARING '40s**

1 David Frith, *The Ross Gregory Story*, Lothian Books, Melbourne, 2003, p. 80.

2 Piesse, *Down at the Junction There's a Cricket Ground*, pp. 88–9.

3 R.S. Whitington, *The Quiet Australian: The Lindsay Hassett Story*, William Heinemann Ltd, Melbourne, 1969, pp. 96–7.

4 Terry Smith, *Bedside Book of Cricket Centuries*, Angus & Robertson, Sydney, 1991, p. 13.

5 Charles Williams, *Bradman*, Little, Brown & Company, London, 1996, p. 206.

6 Rosenwater, p. 308.

7 Clif Cary, *Cricket Controversy: Test Matches in Australia 1946–1947*, T. Werner Laurie Ltd., London, 1948, p. 19.

8 Bruce Harris, *With England in Australia: The Truth About the Tests*, Hutchinson, London, 1947, p. 91.

9 Alec Bedser, *Twin Ambitions: An Autobiography*, Stanley Paul, London, 1986, p. 44.

10 Walter Hammond, *Cricket's Secret History*, Stanley Paul & Co., London, 1952, p. 65.

11   Hammond, *Cricket's Secret History*, p. 65.

12   Cary, p. 17.

13   Bedser, p. 43.

14   Williams, p. 219.

15   A letter from Don Bradman to Chappie Dwyer, November 1948.

16   *Sydney Morning Herald*, 14 August 1948.

17   Ray Lindwall, *Flying Stumps*, Stanley Paul & Co., London, 1954, p. 74.

18   John Ringwood, *Ray Lindwall: Cricket Legend*, Kangaroo Press, Sydney, 1995, p. 64.

19   Davis, 1946–47 section.

■   10   1950s: TYPHOONED

1   Freddie Brown, *Cricket Musketeer*, Nicholas Kaye, London, 1954, p. 56.

2   *Sydney Morning Herald*, 6 February 1951.

3   David Frith, *The Slow Men*, Richard Smart Publishing, Sydney, 1984, p. 137.

4   *Sydney Morning Herald*, 5 January 1951.

5   Bedser, p. 48.

6   Brown, p. 15.

7   Stephen Chalke, *At the Heart of English Cricket: The Life and Memories of Geoffrey Howard*, Fairfield Books, Bath, 2001, p. 87.

8   Colin Cowdrey, *MCC: The Autobiography of a Cricketer*, Hodder and Stoughton, London, 1976, p. 67.

9   Bedser, p. 51.

10   Gideon Haigh, *The Summer Game*, ABC Books, Sydney, 2006 edition, p. 85.

11   Len Hutton, *Fifty Years in Cricket*, Stanley Paul & Co., London, 1984, p. 122.

12   The bouncer-free 'zone' remained in vogue until the advent of winner-take-all World Series Cricket from 1977, when even the bowlers donned crash helmets to avoid being injured by bounce-happy opposing speedsters.

13   Frank Tyson, *In the Eye of the Typhoon*, The Parrs Wood Press, Manchester, 2004, p. 131.

14   Lindwall, p. 210.

15   Cowdrey, p. 69.

16   Tyson, p. 156.

17   Frank Tyson, *A Typhoon Called Tyson*, William Heinemann Ltd, London, 1961, p. 114.

18   Gerald Howat, *Len Hutton: The Biography*, Heinemann Kingswood, London, 1988, p. 160.

19   Hutton, p. 134.

20   Jim Laker, *Over to Me*, Frederick Muller Limited, London, 1960, pp. 12–13.

21   Laker, p. 45.

22   Ringwood, p. 124.

23   Bradman, p. 139.

24   Bedser, p. 75.

25   Bedser, p. 75.

26   John Arlott (ed.), *Cricket: The Great Bowlers*, Pelham Books, London, 1968, p. 133.

■   11   1960s: NOT SO BOLD MESSIAHS

1   Richie Benaud, *A Tale of Two Tests*, Hodder & Stoughton, London, 1962, p. 32.

2   Ted Dexter, *Ted Dexter Declares*, Stanley Paul & Co., London, 1966, p. 44.

3   Alan Lee, *Lord Ted: The Dexter Enigma*, Gollancz Witherby, London, 1995, p. 55.

4   Bill Frindall, *England Test Cricketers: The Complete Record Since 1877*, Willow Books, London, 1989, p. 393.

5   Fred Trueman, *As It Was: The Memoirs of Fred*, Pan Macmillan Ltd, London, 2004, pp. 276–7.

6   E.M. Wellings, *Dexter v Benaud, MCC Tour Australia 1962–3*, Bailey Bros & Swinfen, London, 1963, p. 152.

7   Richie Benaud, *Spin Me a Spinner*, Hodder & Stoughton, London, 1963, p. 151.

8   Lee, p. 117.

9   Brian Booth, *Booth to Bat: An Autobiography*, Anzea Publishers, Homebush, 1983, p. 163.

10   David Sheppard, *Parson's Pitch*, Hodder & Stoughton, London, 1964, pp. 211–12.

11   Norm O'Neill, *Ins & Outs*, Pelham Books, London, 1964, p. 130.

12   Lee, p. 112.

13   Booth, p. 105.

14   Fred Titmus, *My Life in Cricket*, John Blake Publishing, London, 2005, p. 149.

15   Neil Hawke, *Bowled Over*, Rigby Publishers, Adelaide, 1982, p. 72.

16   Hawke, p. 72.

17   *Playfair Cricket Monthly*, August 1964, p. 7.

18   Booth, p. 149.

19   Booth, pp. 149–50.

20   Booth, p. 159.

21   Webster, p. 595.

22   Booth, pp. 151–2.

23   John Edrich, *Runs in the Family*, Stanley Paul & Co., London, 1969, p. 66.

24   Bill Lawry, *Run-Digger: Bill Lawry's Own Story*, Souvenir Press, London, p. 14.

25   Lawry, p. 15.

26   Lawry, p. 15.

27   Hawke, p. 111.

28   Ken 'Slasher' Mackay, *Quest for the Ashes*, Pelham Books, London, 1966, p. 112.

29   Peter Philpott, *A Spinner's Yarn*, ABC, Sydney, 1990, p. 114.

30   Bobby Simpson, *Captain's Story*, Stanley Paul & Co., London, 1966, p. 128.

31   Ken Barrington, *Playing it Straight*, Stanley Paul & Co., London, 1968, p. 130.

32   Barrington, p. 95.

33   Mark Peel, *England Expects: A Biography of Ken Barrington*, The Kingswood Press, London, 1992, p. 107.

34   Lawry, p. 90.

■   12   1970s: CHOSEN ON A HUNCH

1   Keith Stackpole, *Not Just for Openers*, Stockwell Press, Melbourne, 1974, p. 93.

2   *The Times*, London, 16 December 1970.

3   Basil d'Oliveira, *Time to Declare: An Autobiography*, J. M. Dent & Son., London, p. 97.

4   Stackpole, pp. 105–6

5   Terry Jenner, *T. J. Over The Top: Cricket, Prison & Warnie*, Information Australia, Melbourne, 1999, p. 74.

6   Sam Pilger and Rob Wightman (eds), *Match of My Life: The Ashes*, Gary Allen Pty Ltd, Sydney, 2006, p. 31.

7   Pilger & Wightman, p. 31.

8   Jenner, p. 75.

9.   d'Oliveira, p. 100.

10   Alan Knott, *It's Knott Cricket*, Macmillan London Ltd., 1985, p. 44.

11   *Cricketer* magazine, Newspress Pty Ltd, Melbourne, June 1974, pp. 5–7.

12   Boycott was to miss 30 Tests home and abroad from 11 June 1974 to 28 July 1977.

13   Mike Denness, *I Declare*, Arthur Barker Ltd, London, 1977, pp. 129–30.

14   Writing in *Truth* newspaper, reproduced by Ken Piesse in *Magic Moments: Glory Days in Australian Cricket 1902–2002*, Emap Australia, Sydney, 2002, p. 40.

15   Ashley Mallet with Ian Chappell, *Chappelli Speaks Out*, Allen & Unwin, Sydney, 2005, p. 99.

16   Ian Chappell, *Chappelli*, Hutchinson Group (Australia), Richmond, Melbourne, 1976, p. 106.

17   Mallet with Chappell, p. 98.

18   Mallet with Chappell, p. 98.

19   Mallet with Chappell, p. 98.

20   Chappell, p. 107.

21   David Lloyd, *David Lloyd: The Autobiography*, Collins Willow, London, 2001, p. 91.

22   Lloyd, p. 91.

23   Lloyd, p. 90.

24   Denness, p. 113.

25   Denness, p. 121.

26   Knott, p. 72.

27   Knott, p. 72.

28   Knott, p. 73.

29   Chappell, p. 120.

30   *The Australian*, 4 January 1975.

31   Mallett with Chappell, p. 108.

32   Piesse, *Cricket's Greatest Scandals*, p. 82.

33   David Hookes, *Hookesy*, ABC, Sydney, 1993, p. 38.

34   Graham Yallop, *Lambs to the Slaughter*, Outback Press, Melbourne, 1979, p. 3.

35   Yallop, p. 82.

36   Yallop, p. 80.

37   Yallop, p. 85.

38   Bob Taylor & David Gower, *Anyone for Cricket*, Pelham Books, London, 1979, p. 109.

39   d'Oliveira, p. 93.

■   **13 1980s: CAPTAIN GRUMPY'S ROCKY RIDE**

1   Hookes, pp. 88–9.

2   Hookes, p. 89.

3   Allan Lamb, *Allan Lamb: My Autobiography*, Collins Willow, London, 1996, p. 108.

4   Allan Border, *Beyond Ten Thousand*, Swan Publishing, Nedlands, WA, 1993, p. 106.

5   Chris Broad, *Home Truths from Abroad*, George Weidenfeld & Nicolson Ltd, London, 1987, p. 86.

6   David Boon, *Boon in the Firing Line: An Autobiography*, Sun Books, Sydney, 1993, p. 92.

7   Mike Gatting, *Triumph in Australia*, Queen Anne Press, London, 1987, p. 104.

8   Gatting, p. 107.

9   Gatting, p. 115.

10   Ian Botham, *Botham: My Autobiography*, Collins Willow, London, 1994, p. 270.

11   Frank Crook, *Talking Cricket*, ABC Books, Sydney, 1989, pp. 74–5.

12   Crook, p. 75.

13   David Boon, *Under the Southern Cross*, HarperSports, Sydney, 1996, p. 96.

14   Border, p. 134.

15   Botham, p. 130.

■   **14   1990s: THE COMING OF WARNE**

1   David Gower with Martin Johnson, *Gower: The Autobiography*, Fontana Books, London, 1992, p. 203.

2   Piesse, *Magic Moments*, p. 24.

3   Mark Gately, *Waugh Declared: The Story of Australia's Famous Cricketing Twins*, Ironbark Press, Sydney, 1992, p. 135.

4   Gower with Johnson, p. 219.

5   Mike Atherton, *Opening Up*, Hodder and Stoughton, London, 2002, p. 132.

6   Devon Malcolm, *You Guys Are History!*, Collins Willow, London, 1998, p. 125.

7   Atherton, pp. 136–7.

8   Malcolm, p. 126.

9   Malcolm, p. 128.

10   Nasser Hussain, *Playing with Fire: The Autobiography*, Michael Joseph, London, 2004, p. 214.

11   Ross Smith, *Test Match Sixes*, self-published, Launceston, 1998, p. 102.

■   **15   2000s: A HEAVENLY FAREWELL**

1   Hussain, p. 407.

2   Alec Stewart, *Playing for Keeps*, BBC Books, London, 2003, p. 219.

3   Hussain, p. 347.

4   Stewart, p. 219.

5   Hussain, p. 376.

6   Hussain, p. 377.

7   Steve Waugh, *Out Of My Comfort Zone: The Autobiography*, Penguin Group (Australia), Melbourne, 2005, p. 665.

8   Stewart, p. 224.

9   Waugh, p. 675.

10   Waugh, p. 675.

11   Waugh, p. 676.

12   Waugh, p. 682.

13   The Melbourne Cricket Club was a most influential body which also went against the ICC by declaring its 2006–07 Ashes Test as the hundredth at the ground. They included the washed-out Test from 1970–71 in their records; a toss had been made and the team lists exchanged. The ICC didn't include the game among its official lists, however, as a ball was not bowled.

14   When England was bowled out for 75.

15   Larry Dooley was a famous early Australian boxer renowned for throwing flurries of punches from the opening bell.

16   *Wisden Cricketers' Almanack*, John Wisden & Co., London, 2002, p. 445.

BIBLIOGRAPHY

Books

Altham, Harry & E.W. 'Jim' Swanton, *A History of Cricket*, George Allen & Unwin Ltd, London, 1948 edition

Amey, Geoff, *Julius Caesar: The Ill-fated Cricketer*, Bodyline Books, London, 2000

Arlott, John (ed.), *Cricket: The Great Bowlers*, Pelham Books, London, 1968

Arlott, John (ed.), *Cricket: The Great Ones*, Pelham Books, London, 1967

Atherton, Mike, *Opening Up*, Hodder and Stoughton, London, 2002

Barrington, Ken, *Playing it Straight*, Stanley Paul, London, 1968

Bedser, Alec, *Twin Ambitions: An Autobiography*, Stanley Paul & Co., London, 1986

Beeston, R.D., *St. Ivo and the Ashes*, Australian Press Agency, Melbourne, 1883

Benaud, Richie, *A Tale of Two Tests*, Hodder & Stoughton, London, 1962

Benaud, Richie, *Spin Me a Spinner*, Hodder & Stoughton, London, 1963

Binns, Richard, *Cricket in Firelight*, Selwyn & Blount, London, 1935

Bonnell, Max, *Currency Lads: The Life and Cricket of T.W. Garrett, R.C. Allen, S.P. Jones & R.J. Pope*, The Cricket Publishing Company, Cherrybrook, Sydney, 2001

Boon, David, *Boon in the Firing Line: An Autobiography*, Sun Books, Sydney, 1993

Boon, David, *Under the Southern Cross*, HarperSports, Sydney, 1996

Booth, Brian, *Booth to Bat*, Anzea Publishers, Homebush, 1983

Border, Allan, *Beyond Ten Thousand*, Swan Publishing, Nedlands, 1993

Botham, Ian, *Botham: My Autobiography*, Collins Willow, London, 1994

Bradman, Don, *Farewell to Cricket*, Hodder & Stoughton, London, 1949

Broad, Chris, *Home Truths from Abroad*, George Weidenfeld & Nicolson Ltd, London, 1987

Brodribb, Gerald, *Next Man In: A Survey of Cricket Laws and Customs*, Putnam & Co., London, 1952

Brogden, Stanley, *The First Test*, The Hawthorn Press, Melbourne, 1946

Brown, Freddie, *Cricket Musketeer*, Nicholas Kaye, London, 1954

Caffyn, William, edited by 'Mid-On', *Seventy-One Not Out: The Reminiscences of William Caffyn*, William Blackwood and Sons, London, 1899

Campbell, R.H., *Cricket Casualties*, ABC, Sydney, 1933

Cardwell, Ronald, *The AIF Cricket Team*, privately printed, Sydney, 1980

Cary, Clif, *Cricket Controversy: Test Matches in Australia 1946–1947*, T. Werner Laurie Ltd, London, 1948

Cashman, Richard, *The 'Demon' Spofforth*, NSW University Press, Sydney, 1990

Chalke, Stephen, *At the Heart of English Cricket: The Life and Memories of Geoffrey Howard*, Fairfield Books, Bath, 2001

Chappell, Ian, *Chappelli*, Hutchinson Group (Australia), Richmond, Melbourne, 1976

Christen, Richard, *Some Grounds to Appeal*, self-published, Parramatta, 1995

Coldham, James D., *Lord Harris*, George Allen & Unwin (Publishers) Ltd, London, 1983

Cowdrey, Colin, *MCC: The Autobiography of a Cricketer*, Hodder and Stoughton, 1976

Crook, Frank, *Talking Cricket*, ABC Books, Sydney, 1989

Davis, Charles, *Test Cricket in Australia, 1877–2002*, self-published, Melbourne, 2002

Denness, Mike, *I Declare*, Arthur Barker Ltd, London, 1977

Dexter, Ted, *Ted Dexter Declares*, Stanley Paul & Co., London, 1966

D'Oliveira, Basil, *Time to Declare: An Autobiography*, J. M. Dent & Sons, London, 1980

Duckworth, Leslie, *S.F. Barnes: Master Bowler*, The Cricketer–Hutchinson, London, 1967

Dunstan, Keith, *The Paddock That Grew*, Cassell & Company Ltd, Melbourne, 1962

Edrich, John, *Runs in the Family*, Stanley Paul & Co., London, 1969

Farnes, Ken, *Tours & Tests*, RTS – Lutterworth Press, London, 1940

Fender, Percy, *Defending the Ashes*, Chapman and Hall Ltd, London, 1921

Fingleton, Jack, *Masters of Cricket*, William Heinemann Limited, Sydney, 1958

Fingleton, Jack, *The Immortal Victor Trumper*, Collins, Sydney, 1978

Frindall, Bill, *England Test Cricketers: The Complete Record Since 1877*, Willow Books, London, 1989

Frindall, Bill, *The Wisden Book of Test Cricket*, various volumes, Headline Books, London

Frith, David, *Bodyline Autopsy: The Full Story of the Most Sensational Test Cricket Series: Australia v England 1932–33*, ABC Books, Sydney, 2002

Frith, David, *My Dear Victorious Stod: A Biography of A.E. Stoddart*, privately published, Surrey, 1970

Frith, David, *The Archie Jackson Story*, The Cricketer, Beech Hanger, Kent, 1974

Frith, David, *The Ross Gregory Story*, Lothian Books, Melbourne, 2003

Frith, David, *The Slow Men*, Richard Smart Publishing, Sydney, 1984

Frith, David, *The Trailblazers: The First English Cricket Tour of Australia: 1861–62*, Boundary Books, Cheshire, 1999

Fry, C.B., *Life Worth Living*, Eyre & Spottiswoode, London, 1939

Gately, Mark, *Waugh Declared: The Story of Australia's Famous Cricketing Twins*, Ironbark Press, Sydney, 1992

Gatting, Mike, *Triumph in Australia*, Queen Anne Press, London, 1987

Gower, David with Martin Johnson, *Gower: The Autobiography*, Fontana Books, London, 1992

Growden, Greg, *A Wayward Genius: The Fleetwood-Smith Story*, ABC Books, Sydney, 1991

Grubb, Norman, *C.T. Studd Cricketer and Pioneer*, The Religious Tract Society, London, 1934

Haigh, Gideon, *The Big Ship: Warwick Armstrong and the Making of Modern Cricket,* Text Publishing, Melbourne, 2001

Haigh, Gideon, *The Summer Game*, ABC Books, Sydney, 2006 edition

Hammond, Walter, *Cricket: My Destiny*, Stanley Paul & Co., London, 1946

Hammond, Walter, *Cricket's Secret History*, Stanley Paul & Co., London, 1952

Harris, Bruce, *With England in Australia: The Truth About the Tests*, Hutchinson, London, 1947

Hawke, Neil, *Bowled Over*, Rigby Publishers, Adelaide, 1982

Haygarth, Arthur, *Cricket Scores and Biographies, Vol. 14*, Longmans and Company, London, 1895

Hill, Alan, *Herbert Sutcliffe: Cricket Maestro*, Simon & Schuster, London, 1991

Hobbs, Jack, *My Life Story*, The Star Publications Dept., London, 1935

Hobbs, Jack, *My Cricket Memories*, Heinemann, London, 1924

Hookes, David, *Hookesy*, ABC Books, Sydney, 1993

Howat, Gerald, *Len Hutton: The Biography*, Heinemann Kingswood, London, 1988

Hussain, Nasser, *Playing with Fire: The Autobiography*, Michael Joseph, London, 2004

Hutton, Len, *Fifty Years in Cricket*, Stanley Paul & Co., London, 1984

Jenner, Terry *T.J. Over The Top: Cricket, Prison & Warnie*, Information Australia, Melbourne, 1999

Keenan, Terry, *A Triumvirate of Test Cricketers*, Port Melbourne Cricket Club, Melbourne, 1994

Knott, Alan, *It's Knott Cricket*, Macmillan London Ltd, 1985

Kynaston, David, *Bobby Abel: Professional Batsman*, Secker & Warburg, London, 1982

Laker, Jim, *Over To Me*, Frederick Muller Limited, London, 1960

Lamb, Allan, *Allan Lamb: My Autobiography*, Collins Willow, London, 1996

Lawry, Bill, *Run-Digger: Bill Lawry's Own Story*, Souvenir Press, London, 1966

Lee, Alan, *Lord Ted: The Dexter Enigma*, Gollancz Witherby, London, 1995

Lemmon, David, *Johnny Won't Hit Today*, Allen & Unwin, London, 1983

Lindwall, Ray, *Flying Stumps*, Stanley Paul and Co., Sydney, 1954

Lloyd, David, *David Lloyd: The Autobiography*, Collins Willow, London, 2001

'Looker-On', *Bringing Back the Ashes, the MCC Tour of Australia 1903–04,* Sheffield Telegraph Ltd, Sheffield, 1904

Macartney, Charles, *My Cricketing Days*, William Heinemann Ltd, London, 1930

Mackay, Ken 'Slasher', *Quest for the Ashes*, Pelham Books, London, 1966

Mailey, Arthur, *10 for 66 and All That*, Phoenix House, 1958

Malcolm, Devon, *You Guys Are History!*, Collins Willow, London, 1998

Mallett, Ashley, *Clarrie Grimmett: The Bradman of Spin*, University of Queensland Press, Brisbane, 1993

Mallet, Ashley with Ian Chappell, *Chappelli Speaks Out*, Allen & Unwin, Sydney, 2005

Mason, Ronald, *Jack Hobbs*, Hollis & Carter, London, 1960

McHarg, Jack, *Stan McCabe: The Man and His Cricket*, Collins Australia, Sydney, 1987

Melville, Tom, *The Tented Field: A History of Cricket in America*, Bowling Green State University Press, Ohio, 1998

Morrah, Patrick, *The Golden Age of Cricket*, Eyre and Spottiswoode, London, 1967

Moyes, A.G. 'Johnnie', *A Century of Cricketers*, Angus & Robertson, Sydney, 1950

Munns, Joy, *Beyond Reasonable Doubt: The Birthplace of the Ashes*, self-published, Sunbury, 1994

Noble, M.A. 'Monty', *The Game's the Thing: A Record of Cricket Experience,* Cassell & Co., Sydney, 1926

Noble, M.A., *Gilligan's Men*, Chapman & Hall, London, second impression, 1925

O'Neill, Norm, *Ins & Outs*, Pelham Books, London, 1964

Parkin, Cecil, *Parkin on Cricket*, Hodder & Stoughton, London, 1923

Peel, Mark, *England Expects: A Biography of Ken Barrington*, The Kingswood Press, London, 1992

Philpott, Peter, *A Spinner's Yarn*, ABC, Sydney, 1990

Piesse, Ken, *All Out for One and Other Cricket Anecdotes*, Viking Books, Melbourne, 2003

Piesse, Ken, *Cricket's Colosseum: 125 Years of Test Cricket at the Melbourne Cricket Ground*, Hardie Grant, Melbourne, 2003

Piesse, Ken, *Cricket's Greatest Scandals: Match-fixing, Corrupt Captains, Selection Scams and More*, Viking Books, Melbourne, 2000

Piesse, Ken, *Down at the Junction, There's a Cricket Ground*, St Kilda Cricket Club, 2005

Piesse, Ken (ed.), *Magic Moments: Glory Days in Australian Cricket 1902–2002*, Emap Australia, Sydney, 2002

Piesse, Ken & Jim Main, *Duel for Glory: English Cricket Tours to Australia from 1862*, Wedneil Publications, Melbourne, 1982

Pilger, Sam & Rob Wightman (eds), *Match of My Life: The Ashes*, Gary Allen Pty Ltd, Sydney, 2006

Pollard, Jack (ed.), *Six and Out*, Penguin, Melbourne, 1990 edition

Pullin (Old Ebor), W., *Alfred Shaw, Cricketer: His Career and Reminiscences*, Cassell and Company, London, 1902

Rayvern-Allen, David, *Sir Aubrey: A Biography of C. Aubrey Smith, England Cricketer, West End Actor, Hollywood Filmstar*, Elm Tree Books, 1982

Ringwood, John, *Ray Lindwall: Cricket Legend*, Kangaroo Press, Sydney, 1995

Roberts, E.L., *England versus Australia 1877–1934*, E.F. Hudson Ltd, Birmingham, 1934

Rosenwater, Irving, *Sir Donald Bradman: A Biography*, B.T. Batsford Ltd, London, 1978

Scoble, Christopher, *Colin Blythe: Lament for a Legend*, SportsBooks Ltd, Cheltenham, 2005

Sheppard, David, *Parson's Pitch*, Hodder & Stoughton, London, 1964

Simpson, Bobby, *Captain's Story*, Stanley Paul, London, 1966

Smith, Ross, *Test Match Sixes*, self-published, Launceston, 1998

Smith, Terry, *Bedside Book of Cricket Centuries*, Angus & Robertson, Sydney, 1991

Stackpole, Keith, *Not Just for Openers*, Stockwell Press, Melbourne, 1974

Steel, A.G. & The Hon. R.H. Lyttelton, *The Badminton Library of Sports and Pastimes: Cricket*, Longmans, Green & Co., London, 1888

Stewart, Alec, *Playing for Keeps*, BBC Books, London, 2003

Strudwick, Herbert, *Twenty-five Years Behind the Stumps*, Hutchinson & Co., London, 1926

Swanton, E.W., *Gubby Allen: Man of Cricket*, Hutchinson/Stanley Paul, London, 1985

Tate, Maurice, *My Cricket Reminiscences*, Stanley Paul & Co., London, 1934

Taylor, Bob & David Gower, *Anyone for Cricket*, Pelham Books, London, 1979

Tinkler, Basil Ashton, *A Somerset Hero Who Beat the Aussies: The Life and Times of J. C. 'Farmer' White*, The Parrs Wood Press, Manchester, 2000

Titmus, Fred, *My Life in Cricket*, John Blake Publishing, London, 2005

Trueman, Fred, *As It Was: The Memoirs of Fred*, Pan Macmillan Ltd, London, 2004

Tyson, Frank, *A Typhoon Called Tyson*, William Heinemann Ltd, London, 1961

Tyson, Frank, *In the Eye of the Typhoon*, The Parrs Wood Press, Manchester, 2004

Wallish, E.A. 'Ned', *The Great Laurie Nash*, Ryan Publishing, Melbourne, 1998

Warner, P.F. 'Plum', *How We Recovered the Ashes*, Chapman & Hall, London, 1904

Warner, P.F. 'Plum', *Long Innings: The Autobiography of Sir Pelham Warner*, George G. Harrap and Co., London, 1951

Waugh, Steve, *Out Of My Comfort Zone*, Penguin Group (Australia), Melbourne, 2005

Webster, Ray, *First-class Cricket in Australia, Vol. 1 1850–51 to 1941–42*, edited by Alan Miller, self-published, Melbourne, 1991

Wellings, E.M., *Dexter v Benaud: MCC Tour, Australia 1962–3*, Bailey Bros & Swinfen, London, 1963

Whimpress, Bernard & Nigel Hart, *Adelaide Oval Test Cricket 1884–1984*, Wakefield Press & the South Australian Cricket Association, Adelaide, 1984

White, Wilfrid S., *Sydney Barnes*, E.F. Hudson Ltd, Birmingham, 1937

Whitington, R.S., *The Quiet Australian: The Lindsay Hassett Story*, William Heinemann Ltd, Melbourne, 1969

Whitington, R.S. & George Hele, *Bodyline Umpire: An Eyewitness Account of a Dramatic Era in Test Cricket*, Rigby Ltd, Adelaide, 1974

Wild, Roland, *The Biography of Colonel His Highness Shri Sir Ranjitsinhji*, Rich & Cowan, London, 1934

Williams, Charles, *Bradman*, Little, Brown & Company, London, 1996

Wynne-Thomas, Peter, *'Give me Arthur': A Biography of Arthur Shrewsbury*, Arthur Barker Ltd, London, 1985

Wynne-Thomas, Peter, *Nottinghamshire Cricketers 1821–1914*, self-published, Nottingham, 1971

Yallop, Graham, *Lambs to the Slaughter*, Outback Press, Melbourne, 1979

Annuals

James Lillywhite's Cricketers' Annual
Wisden Cricketers' Almanack
Scores & Biographies

Newspaper Articles

Hill, Clem, 'Great Leaders' Tactics On and Off the Field', *The Melbourne Sporting Globe*, March 1933, Feature No. 3

Unpublished manuscripts

Sowden, Norm, *Sydney Grade Cricketer Index, from 1893–94 to date*, 1987

Magazines

The Cricketer (Aust)
Playfair Cricket Monthly

DVDs

Bodyline: A Great Australian Story, Kennedy-Miller, 1984

Notes

Unacknowledged quoted material has been taken from interviews by Ken Piesse

ACKNOWLEDGEMENTS

The author would like to thank Ken Williams for his never-before-published decade-by-decade statistics, ongoing support and encyclopaedic memory of all things cricket. He'd also like to thank Jack Atley, Patrick Eager, David Frith, John O'Sullivan, Roger Page, David Studham, Ray Webster, all at Penguin Australia, and his family, particularly Susan.

INDEX OF NAMES

MORE CRICKET BOOKS FROM SPORTSBOOKS

●●●

George Lohmann: Pioneer Professional
Keith Booth

Winner of the 2008 Cricket Society Book of the Year. George Lohmann had a better average and strike rate than any other bowler in Test cricket. Tragically his life was cut short at the age of 36 due to pulmonary tuberculosis. In an ultimately unsuccessful search for a cure he spent the last part of his tragically short life in South Africa where he played a major role in the development of the game and the coaching of its rising stars. Keith Booth, the Surrey scorer, is meticulous in his research of a man who packed an enormous amount into a tragically short life. Perhaps we should be referring to Sir Ian Botham as the 'new' George Lohmann!

"...Keith Booth's biography of the dashing nineteenth-century cricketer George Lohmann is a fascinating appraisal of an era and a type of player long gone." *The Observer*

"Keith Booth has unturned every original source to reveal everything there is to know about one of England's greatest bowlers, the short -lived George Lohmann." Christopher Martin-Jenkins, *The Times*

"...from then on the book is first class, with Booth (or his wife, who does most of the research for her husband) having seemingly read everything of relevance pertaining to Lohmann." *Cricketweb*

ISBN 9781899807 50 5

PRICE £18.99

Colin Blythe: lament for a legend
Christopher Scoble

Colin Blythe was the most famous England cricketer to be killed in the First World War and a man whose career suffered at international level through ill-health, believed to be epilepsy, although he still took 100 wickets at an average of 18.63. He had a truly remarkable career with Kent, taking 2,503 wickets at 16.81. His 17 for 48 (10 for 30 and 7 for 18) against Northamptonshire in a day on June 1, 1907 is still the best bowling analysis in the County Championship. Christopher Scoble's beautifully written account of Blythe's short life evokes the era of Edwardian cricket, a supposed Golden Age when the sun always shined, although many of his best days were on rain-affected wickets!

"Historians with a tragedian's bent will... swoon over Christopher Scoble's poignant, near perfect biography." Frank Keating *The Guardian*

"Scoble's meticulous research and sound reasoning are at the backbone of this admirable book. You can almost smell the grass and hear the sound of ball on bat as he goes about explaining the forgotten genius of an unheralded giant." *The Sunday Times*, Book of the week

ISBN 1899807 31 4

Price £16.99

Local Heroes
John Shawcroft

Local Heroes, short-listed for the Cricket Society's Book of the Year 2007, tells the tale of the Derbyshire team which won cricket's County Championship in 1936, the only time the club has finished first. What was remarkable was that most of its members were drawn from the Derbyshire coalfields from an era when myth had it that you shouted down a pit for a fast bowler and up one would come. John Shawcroft interviewed all the team at one time or another and has written a book which found universal favour with the critics.

"This is a very good cricket book... enthralling narrative... Several fine illustrations complete a really fine book which is much more than the story of a season... recommended". *Association of Cricket Statisticians*

"Some certanties remain in life, among them the knowledge that a book on Derbyshire cricket by John Shawcroft will be researched thoroughly and written with clarity... this is a first-class book." *Derby Evening Telegraph*

"... splendidly produced book with major historic interest to the followers of Rose and Crown history." *Cricket Memorabilia Society*

"This is a work of passion, humanity and deep scholarship which does not merely deal with events on the cricket field, but roots the 1936 triumph in the Derbyshire mining communities and the economic circumstances of the time." Peter Oborne, *Wisden*

"... this is one of the best books of a very good year for cricket writing and in many ways could almost be used as a guide on how to write a cricket book. ... quite simply one of the finest cricket books that I have read and I commend anyone in doubt to purchase it." John Symons, *Cricket Society*

ISBN 1899807 35 7

Price £14.99

Encyclopedia of World Cricket
Roy Morgan

Roy Morgan has compiled a truly comprehensive book about cricket. In the past, books like this have concentrated on the Test-playing nations but this looks at the game all over the world, including non-Test-playing countries and the women's game. It details all the international and domestic competitions and is a must for every cricket fan's bookshelf.

"In his excellent guide to life beyond the Test world, Roy Morgan looks to correct the imbalance. In a world where the ghosted and often bland biography prevails, ... (it) is necessary, informative, well researched and interesting ... This is an excellent, reasonably priced encyclopaedia of world cricket and adds considerably to the profile and understanding of the game." *Cricinfo*.

"I reckon there will have to be a new edition within the next five years, but in the meantime this excellent book records a game that is expanding for the first time in some 70 years." Simon Sweetman, *Association of Cricket Statisticians*

"...the sheer volume of information [Roy Morgan] must have sorted through to write this book is phenomenal. ... this book is a must for all cricket lovers around the world to place on their bookshelves. ... it is certainly a nine and a half [out of ten]." *www.cricketeurope4.net*

ISBN 9781899807 51 2

PRICE £17.99

Lala Amarnath: Life and Times
Rajender Amarnath

Amarnath was the first Indian to score a century when in his first Test match, against England, with the score at 21 for 2, he chose to counter-attack rather than stonewall. He reached his 100 in just 117 minutes, but never made a Test century again. A strong-willed and plain-spoken man, he was sent back from England during India's 1936 tour before the Tests started accused of "indiscipline". In this book his son Rajender, in a lovingly crafted account of his father's eventful life, tells what really happened.

"This is a well-told tale... it all adds to the exotic personality of someone for whom cricket was his life. A great read." David Llewellyn, *The Independent*

ISBN 9781899807 55 0

Price £16.99

Test Cricket Grounds: The complete guide to the world's Test cricket grounds
John Woods

For dedicated England fans who plan to watch their country play overseas. Author John Woods visited all ten Test playing nations to research each ground, establishing how to get there by air, rail and bus, where to stay, where to eat, where to drink. Plus outlines of the history of the city and the ground. The result is 480 pages, packed with information and photographs, in a paperback book you can still slip into your pocket.

"...a welcome addition to any cricket fan's shelves... Comprehensive and entertaining." Paul Daffey. *Melbourne Age*

"Book is absolutely infused with the Barmy spirit as a result... the Barmy Army has its own backpacking bible. Perfect for anyone anticipating their first trip abroad with England." *Wisden Cricketer*

ISBN 1899807 20 9

Price £12.99